California Special Education Programs

A Composite of Laws*

Education Code - Part 30, Other Related Laws, and California Code of Regulations - Title 5

Prepared by the
Special Education Division
California Department of Education

*Revised to Cover Laws Enacted During 1994

Publishing Information

This document was prepared by Paul D. Hinkle, Special Education Consultant, Special Education Division, California Department of Education, and was published by the Department, 721 Capitol Mall, Sacramento, California (mailing address: P.O. Box 944272, Sacramento, CA 94244-2720). Any questions regarding the document should be addressed to the Special Education Division.

Distributed under the provisions of the
Library Distribution Act and
Government Code Section 11096

1995

ISBN 0-8011-1198-6

Ordering Information

A limited number of copies of this publication are available at no charge from the Bureau of Publications, Sales Unit, California Department of Education, P.O. Box 271, Sacramento, CA 95812-0271. A list of other publications available from the Department can be found at the back of this publication. In addition, the 1995 *Educational Resources Catalog* describing publications, videos, and other instructional media available from the Department can be obtained without charge by writing to the address given above or by calling the Sales Unit at (916) 445-1260.

FOREWORD

EDUCATION CODE - PART 30

CALIFORNIA CODE OF REGULATIONS - TITLE 5

SPECIAL EDUCATION PROGRAMS

This seventeenth edition of <u>California Special Education Programs -Composite of Laws</u> covers Part 30 (commencing with Section 56000) of the Education Code relative to special education programs, and includes Chapters 3 (commencing with Section 3000) and 5.1 (commencing with Section 4600) of Division 1 of Title 5 of the California Code of Regulations relative to special education for children and youth with disabilities and uniform complaint procedures.

This composite also includes Part 32 (commencing with Section 59000) of the Education Code covering the statutes governing the State Special Schools and Centers, and Chapter 1 (commencing with Section 60000) of Division 9 of Title 2 of the California Code of Regulations which are the "emergency" joint regulations which have been in effect since January 1, 1986, to cover interagency responsibilities for providing services to children with disabilities (Assembly Bill 3632, Chapter 1747, Statutes of 1984). The composite also contains selected provisions of the Education Code, Health and Safety Code, Government Code, and Welfare and Institutions Code having a direct impact on special education and related services for individuals with exceptional needs.

Part 30 of the Education Code was rewritten in 1980, primarily by Senate Bill 1870 (Rodda), (Chapter 797), which became law on July 28, 1980. This legislation repealed all former special education categorical programs and Master Plan for Special Education program Education Code sections that were in effect on January 1, 1980; and restructured and added code sections implementing the Master Plan for Special Education statewide. Since the passage of SB 1870, 95 legislative measures have modified California's special education statutes.

The California Code of Regulations, Title 5, governing special education were originally adopted and became effective in March of 1981 to implement the Master Plan. Substantive amendments were adopted by the State Board of Education on December 11, 1987, and became operative on April 20, 1988. The most recent amendments to the regulations, relative to behavioral interventions for special education students, became effective on May 20, 1993.

During 1994, 12 legislative bills were chaptered into law amending, adding or repealing education sections under Part 30 of the Education Code.

The measures are:

Senate Bill 732 (Bergeson)	-	Chapter 936 - Statutes of 1994 Effective Date: September 28, 1994
Senate Bill 1347 (Russell)	-	Chapter 333 - Statutes of 1994 Effective Date: January 1, 1995
Assembly Bill 1250 (Campbell)	-	Chapter 921 - Statutes of 1994 Effective Date: January 1, 1995
Assembly Bill 1836 (Eastin)	-	Chapter 1126 - Statutes of 1994 Effective Date: September 30, 1994
Assembly Bill 2445 (Conroy)	-	Chapter 998 - Statutes of 1994 Effective Date: January 1, 1995
Assembly Bill 2587 (Eastin)	-	Chapter 922 - Statutes of 1994 Effective Date: January 1, 1995
Assembly Bill 2798 (Bronshvag)	-	Chapter 513 - Statutes of 1994 Effective Date: January 1, 1995
Assembly Bill 2971 (O'Connell)	-	Chapter 1172 - Statutes of 1994 Effective Date: January 1, 1995
Assembly Bill 3235 (Solis)	-	Chapter 1288 - Statutes of 1994 Effective Date: January 1, 1995
Assembly Bill 3562 (Eastin)	-	Chapter 840 - Statutes of 1994 Effective Date: January 1, 1995
Assembly Bill 3601 (Committee on Judiciary)	-	Chapter 146 - Statutes of 1994 Effective Date: January 1, 1995
Assembly Bill 3793 (Eastin)	-	Chapter 661 - Statutes of 1994 Effective Date: January 1, 1995

Senate Bill 732 (Bergeson), an urgency measure, made numerous amendments to the Community Redevelopment Law Reform Act of 1993, and amended Education Code Section 56712 to include a new property tax "deduct" requirement for a county superintendent to compute as part of the special education funding formula. The provision applies to property taxes for educational purposes in redevelopment project areas under Section 33607.5 of the Health and Safety Code.

Senate Bill 1347 (Russell) amended Education Code Section 56728.9 to extend the repeal date from January 1, 1996, to January 1, 1998, on the special education entitlement for single district special education local plan areas (SELPAs) which are severely impacted by pupils who reside in licensed children's institutions (LCIs). The provision specified that a SELPA that received an increased funding entitlement in the 1994-95 fiscal year would continue to receive that funding in a subsequent fiscal year only if it continues to meet the qualifications for funding and an appropriation is made for those purposes in the annual Budget Act. The measure also specified that a SELPA that did not receive that entitlement in the 1994-95 fiscal year and subsequently qualifies for funding under this section would not receive the entitlement unless an additional appropriation is made for those purposes in the Budget Act.

Assembly Bill 1250 (Campbell) amended various provisions of the Education Code pertaining to special education programs provided by nonpublic, nonsectarian schools and agencies. Education Code Section 56602, regarding program evaluation of data on individuals and settings, was amended to include nonpublic agencies and includes pupils referred to and placed in the various program settings by state and local noneducational public agencies, in accordance with criteria established by the State Board of Education and consistent with federal reporting requirements. Education Code Section 56711 was amended to include nonpublic agencies as part of the county superintendent computation for apportionments. Education Code Section 56728.7, relative to the pilot program for returning nonpublic school pupils to public schools, was amended to extend the program through the 1996-97 fiscal year and reduced the number of pilots from 11 to 10 and the number of participants statewide from 220 to 200. It also extended the date to January 1, 1998, for the Superintendent of Public Instruction to report the results of the evaluations of the pilot programs to the Legislature, and extended the operative date of this section to January 1, 1999.

Education Code Section 56732 was amended to add services provided by nonpublic agencies to the costs to be deducted when submitting the adjusted operating costs in the special education funding formula. Education Code Section 56741, regarding state required information on individual program placement costs for nonpublic schools and agencies, was amended to require the annual report to include full-day nonpublic agency and partial-day nonpublic agency services, rather than placements. Education Code Section 56743 was amended to prohibit the Superintendent of Public Instruction from apportioning additional funds to local educational agencies on behalf of placements and services in nonpublic schools and agencies and provided for the prohibition notwithstanding the apportionment of 70 percent of the cost or the apportionment to each district and county superintendent of difference between the costs of contracts with nonpublic schools to provide special education instruction, related services, or both, to pupils in certain placements and the state and federal income received by the district or county superintendent for providing the programs.

Education Code Section 56775, relative to excess cost for nonpublic school placements of pupils in licensed children's institutions, foster family homes, residential medical facilities, and other similar facilities, was amended to make it consistent with Education Code Section 56740, with respect to the costs of the contract that are not to be included.

A noncodified section included a legislative declaration that Sections 3061 to 3067, inclusive, of Title 5 of the California Code of Regulations, concerning nonpublic, nonsectarian schools and agencies, are void and without effect on or after January 1, 1995.

Assembly Bill 1836 (Eastin), an urgency measure, amended Education Code Section 56000.5, concerning pupils with low incidence disabilities, by adding a number of legislative findings and declarations about deafness, including that deafness involves the most basic of human needs--the ability to communicate with other human beings. Education Code Section 56001, which covers legislative intent about individuals with exceptional needs being offered special assistance programs that provide maximum interaction with the general school population in a manner that is appropriate to the needs of both, was amended to read that this provision take into consideration, for hard-of-hearing and deaf children, the individual's needs for a sufficient number of age and language mode peers and for special education teachers who are proficient in the individual's primary language mode. Education Code Section 56026.2 was added to define "language mode" to mean the method of communication used by hard-of-hearing and deaf children that may include the use of sign language to send or receive messages or the use of spoken language, with or without visual signs or cues.

Education Code Section 56345, pertaining to the content of the individualized education program, was amended to add subdivisions (e), (f) and (g) declaring the intent of the Legislature that for hard-of-hearing or deaf pupils the program include a determination of the specific communication needs of the pupil, and make a placement determination that is consistent with those needs, specified federal law, regulations and policy interpretation, and specified legislative findings, in accordance with prescribed considerations. Two noncodified sections specify legislative intent that state law complies with requirements of the Individuals with Disabilities Education Act; and that the provisions amending the Education Code be implemented only to the extent that funds are specifically appropriated for those purposes in the annual Budget Act.

Assembly Bill 2445 (Conroy) added a new Article 3.5 (commencing with Section 56350) to Chapter 4 of Part 30 of the Education Code, entitled Individualized Education Program for Visually Impaired Pupils. Education Code Section 56350 defines the following: a "functionally blind pupil," a "pupil with low vision," a "visually impaired pupil," and "Braille." Education Code Section 56351 requires that local educational agencies provide opportunities for braille instruction for pupils who, due to a prognosis of visual deterioration, may be expected to have a need for braille as a reading medium. Education Code Section 56352 requires that a functional vision assessment be used as one criterion in determining the appropriate reading medium or media for the pupil; requires that an assessment of braille skills for functionally blind pupils who have the ability to read in accordance with guidelines for the visually impaired; requires that braille instruction be provided by a teacher credentialed to teach visually impaired pupils; requires the determination, by the pupil's individualized education program team, of the most appropriate medium or media, including braille for visually impaired pupils in accordance with guidelines for the visually impaired; and requires that each visually impaired pupil shall be provided with the opportunity to receive an assessment to determine the appropriate reading medium or media, including braille instruction, if appropriate to that pupil. Noncodified language contains legislative findings and declarations related to the needs of visually impaired pupils to receive instruction in reading or writing braille. Noncodified language also says it is the intent of the Legislature in enacting this act not to exceed any requirements mandated by federal law or its implementing regulations.

Assembly Bill 2587 (Eastin), a measure repealing or amending numerous obsolete provisions from the Education Code, repealed Education Code Sections 56441.12 and 56444, relative to the special education preschool program; Education Code Section 56522, relative to a study of behavioral intervention practices; and Education Code Section 56880, relative to evaluating funding procedures under Chapter 9 of Part 30 which has never been implemented. Education Code Section 56446 was amended to eliminate an obsolete requirement for a preschool funding report; and Education Code Section 56830 was amended to delete outdated legislative intent language for the expenditure of special education budget augmentations for 1986-87 and 1987-88.

Assembly Bill 2798 (Bronshvag) amended Education Code Section 56221 to require local special education transportation policies to include procedures to ensure compatibility between mobile seating devices, when used, and the securement systems required by federal standards and to ensure that schoolbus drivers are trained in the proper installation of mobile seating devices in the securement systems. A noncodified section said the Legislature recognizes that disabled pupils are entitled to safe and secure transportation and that it is legislative intent that schoolbuses be properly equipped with restraining devices to safely transport pupils who are confined to wheelchairs, and that no school district deny transportation to any pupil due to the incompatibility of a wheelchair and bus securement systems.

Assembly Bill 2971 (O'Connell), a measure making technical amendments to various provisions of the Education Code, repealed and added Education Code Sections 56365, 56366, 56366.2, and 56740 relative to special education programs for nonpublic, nonsectarian schools and agencies. AB 2971 was double joined with AB 1250 (Campbell) and AB 3793 (Eastin) and was chaptered after those two measures. As a result, amendments originally in AB 1250 and AB 3793 covering Education Code Sections 56365, 56366, 56366.2 and 56740 became law under AB 2971.

Education Code Section 56365 was amended to delete the requirement that local educational agencies obtain a waiver from the State Board of Education prior to making a special education out-of-state placement and substituted language requiring the pupil's individualized education program team to submit a report with specified information to the Superintendent of Public Instruction within 15 days of the placement decision. This section was further amended to require a nonpublic school or agency that is located outside of this state to be eligible for certification only if a pupil is enrolled in a program operated by that school or agency pursuant to the recommendation of an individualized education program team in California, and if that pupil's parents or guardians reside in California. Education Code Section 56366 was amended to change the contract references to "master" contracts; and concerning the certification of a nonpublic, nonsectarian school or agency, the section was amended to state that the certification shall result in the school's or agency's receiving approval to educate pupils under the special education laws for a period of no longer than four years from the date of the approval. Education Code Section 56366.2 was amended to eliminate EC Section 56366.1 from the list of provisions that may be waived in the certification application process; and was further amended to include the Americans with Disabilities Act to the list of federal acts and regulations with which the local educational agencies must comply. Education Code Section 56740 was amended to include within the costs not to be reported to the state, the costs for services provided by public school employees, and other services not specified by a pupil's individualized education program or funded by the state on a caseload basis.

Assembly Bill 3235 (Solis), amended a number of provisions in the Education Code to bring California into compliance with federal laws, regulations and interpretations, and to make other technical modifications. Education Code Sections 49060 and 49070 were amended to extend parental access to the pupil records provisions of the code to public agencies that provide educationally related services to pupils with disabilities, and to permit a parent to challenge the content of any pupil record, by adding two additional instances where the parent can seek to correct or remove information recorded in the written records concerning his or her child. Education Code Section 56100 was amended to permit the State Board of Education to approve local special education plans for up to four years, instead of three years. A corresponding amendment was made to Education Code Section 56429 to allow the Superintendent of Public Instruction to approve a local plan for early education services for not more than four years.

Education Code Section 56346 was amended to require the components of the individualized education program of a disabled student for which the parent has withheld consent shall be the basis for a due process hearing. This section allows a prehearing mediation conference to be held as an alternative to holding a due process hearing. It also provides that during the pendency of a due process hearing, the local educational agency may reconsider the proposed individualized education program, or choose to meet informally with the parent, or hold a mediation conference.

Education Code Section 56363.1 was added to specify that a local educational agency is not required to purchase medical equipment for an individual pupil; however, the school district, special education local plan area, or county office is responsible for providing other specialized equipment for use at a school that is needed to implement the individualized education program. The section specifies that "medical equipment" does not include an assistive technology device defined by the federal Individuals with Disabilities Education Act

Education Code Section 56505 was amended to allow the due process hearing officer, not the Superintendent of Public Instruction, to grant an extension of the hearing. Technical amendments were also made to Education Code Sections 56426.7, 56426.8, 56426.9, 56440, 56441.11, and 56822.

Education Code Section 44265.5, relative to professional preparation and credential authorization in the area of low incidence disabilities, was also amended. Education Code Section 52800 of the School-Based Program Coordination Act was amended to allow team teaching for special day classes, except special day classes for pupils with low incidence disabilities, to include pupils who have not been identified as individuals with exceptional needs.

Assembly Bill 3562 (Eastin), a measure deleting certain reports, certifications, or submittals to be made by the California Department of Education and other state and local agencies, amended Education Code Section 56462 to eliminate the requirement for the Superintendent of Public Instruction to annually report to the Legislature on the implementation and effectiveness of transition services. Modifications were also made to Education Code Section 33595 regarding the state reporting responsibilities of the Advisory Commission on Special Education.

Assembly Bill 3601 (Committee on Judiciary), a maintenance of the codes measure, made technical amendments to Education Code Sections 56034 and 56155.5 regarding the special education definitions of "nonpublic, nonsectarian school" and "licensed children's institution."

Assembly Bill 3793 (Eastin) amended Education Code Section 56366.1 to extend the application filing period for nonpublic, nonsectarian schools and agencies for an additional 30 days, and further amended the section to require the Superintendent of Public Instruction to conduct an onsite review of the facility and program of a nonpublic school or agency within four years of the certification effective date, unless the superintendent conditionally certifies the school or agency or unless a formal complaint has been received which results in annual onsite reviews. Education Code Section 56366.3 was amended, relative to contracting for special education and related services, to exempt school employees who were involuntarily forced to leave the school district, special education local plan area, or county office from working for a nonpublic school or agency within 365 days of their employment with that local educational agency. Education Code Section 56366.7 was amended to require the state superintendent to not certify, or shall decertify, any nonpublic, nonsectarian school or agency that has not complied with submitting a list of uniform tuition fees for providing special education or designated instruction and services to individuals with exceptional needs who are served through contracts with local educational agencies by June 30, 1996. This section becomes inoperative on June 30, 1999, and as of January 1, 2000, is repealed unless modified by a later statute.

Although not amending Part 30 of the Education Code, the following measures were also passed by the Legislature and approved by the Governor:

Assembly Bill 1892 (Polanco), (Chapter 1128, Statutes of 1994), added Government Code Section 7572.55 placing stricter requirements on out-of-state placements of seriously emotionally disturbed children. It specifies that a residential placement for a child with a disability who is seriously emotionally disturbed may be made out-of-state only after in-state alternatives have been considered and are found not to meet the child's needs and only when the requirements of Section 7572.5, and subdivision (e) of Education Code Section 56365 have been met. The provision further requires the local educational agency to document the alternatives to out-of-state residential placement that were considered and the reasons why they were rejected; specifies that out-of-state placements can only be made in a privately operated school certified by the California Department of Education; and requires a plan to be developed for using less restrictive alternatives and in-state alternatives as soon as they become available, unless it is in the best educational interest of the child to remain in the out-of-state school. The measure also amended Section 362.2 of the Welfare and Institutions Code expressing the intent of the Legislature that if a placement out-of-home is necessary pursuant to an individualized education program, that this placement be as near the child's home as possible, unless it is not in the best interest of the child to be placed out-of-state, the court shall read into the record that in-state alternatives have been explored and that they cannot meet the needs of the child, and the court shall state on the record the reasons for the out-of-state placement.

Assembly Bill 3816 (O'Connell), (Chapter 1287, Statutes of 1994), added Education Code Section 48915.6, stating that the restrictions and special procedures provided in Education Code Section 48915.5 for the expulsion of a pupil with exceptional needs because of the pupil's possession of a firearm, knife, explosive, or other dangerous object of no reasonable use for the pupil, at school or at a school activity off school grounds, shall apply only if mandated under federal law, including Section 1415 of Title 20 of the United States Code.

Senate Bill 2120 (Committee on Budget and Fiscal Review), (Chapter 139, Statutes of 1994), the Budget Act of 1994-95, provided a total General Fund appropriation for special education programs in the amount of $1,607,960,000. Budget Item 6110-161-001, Schedule (a), provided the General Fund base appropriation of $1,541,548,479 and full statutory funding for growth at $66,411,521 for special education programs. Of the growth funding, $53.447 million was earmarked to fund growth units for ages 3-21 programs, and the sparsity growth units for ages 3-21. Infant program growth totalled $759,000. The Budget Act also provided $15.851 million to fund the 1993-94 special education deficiency funding. The Budget Act also contained $246,436,000 in federal funds for special education programs, of which $175,839,000 was earmarked for local entitlements and $18,338,000 was earmarked for local entitlements for the preschool program. The total 1994-95 special education funding from all state, federal and local sources was expected to be $2,587,844,000. This represents a 2.46 percent increase over 1993-94.

Budget Act control language included provisional language placing a cap on funding for nonpublic, nonsectarian schools and agencies. While last year's cap was statewide, requiring any overage to be taken from all local educational agencies with nonpublic school and agency costs on a pro rata basis, the Budget Act of 1994-95 cap specified that each local educational agency be individually responsible for the amount, if any, by which it exceeds the cap. Another provision of the cap language contained controversial language that would require decertification of nonpublic schools or agencies that increased rates deemed not justified by a school district or county office of education. A preliminary injunction was filed in the Los Angeles Superior Court on August 4, 1994, by attorneys representing the California Association of Private Specialized Education and Services and Mardan Center of Educational Therapy enjoining and restraining the California Department of Education and the State Board of Education from enforcing the decertification provision of the Budget Act control language. A permanent injunction enjoining all subdivisions of Provision 14 of Budget Item 6110-161-001, regarding the funding cap for nonpublic, nonsectarian schools and agencies, was subsequently filed in the Los Angeles Superior Court in December.

Supplemental Report language on the 1994 Budget Bill adopted in Assembly Concurrent Resolution 151, (Vasconcellos), (Res. Chapter 118, Statutes of 1994), provided legislative intent that the Superintendent of Public Instruction, the Director of Finance, and the Legislative Analyst, or a designee of each of these persons, shall develop a new funding mechanism for special education programs and services on or before May 31, 1995. (See Page E-6)

Assembly Joint Resolution 87 (Baca, et al.), (Res. Chapter 73, Statutes of 1994), resolved by the Assembly and Senate of the State of California, jointly, that the Legislature memorialize the President and Congress of the United States to provide the full 40 percent federal share of funding for special education programs by the year 2000, so that California and other states participating in these critical programs will not have to take funding from other vital state and local programs to fund underfunded federal mandates. (See Page E-5)

TABLE OF CONTENTS

EDUCATION CODE - PART 30 - SPECIAL EDUCATION PROGRAMS

PART 30. SPECIAL EDUCATION PROGRAMS

CHAPTER 1. GENERAL PROVISIONS

Article 1. Intent

- LEGISLATIVE INTENT

56000. The Legislature finds and declares that all individuals with exceptional needs have a right to participate in free appropriate public education and that special educational instruction and services for these persons are needed in order to ensure them of the right to an appropriate educational opportunity to meet their unique needs.

- Free Appropriate
  Public Education

It is the intent of the Legislature to unify and improve special education programs in California under the flexible program design of the Master Plan for Special Education. It is the further intent of the Legislature to assure that all individuals with exceptional needs are provided their rights to appropriate programs and services which are designed to meet their unique needs under the Individuals with Disabilities Education Act (20 U.S.C. Sec. 1400 et seq.).

- Unify and Improve Programs

- Assure Rights to Appro-
  priate Programs and
  Services

It is the further intent of the Legislature that nothing in this part shall be construed to abrogate any right provided individuals with exceptional needs and their parents or guardians under the Individuals with Disabilities Education Act (20 U.S.C. Sec. 1400 et seq.). It is also the intent of the Legislature that nothing in this part shall be construed to set a higher standard of educating individuals with exceptional needs than that established by Congress under the Individuals with Disabilities Education Act (20 U.S.C. Sec. 1400 et seq.).

- Standard of Educating

It is the further intent of the Legislature that the Master Plan for Special Education provide an educational opportunity for individuals with exceptional needs that is equal to or better than that provided prior to the implementation of programs under this part, including, but not limited to, those provided to individuals previously served in a development center for handicapped pupils. It is the intent of the Legislature that the restructuring of special education programs as set forth in the Master Plan for Special Education be implemented in accordance with provisions of this part by all school districts and county offices during a two-year transitional period commencing with fiscal year 1980-81, with full implementation to be completed by June 30, 1982.

- Provide Educational
  Opportunity

- Full Implementation by
  June 30, 1982

56000.5. (a) The Legislature finds and declares that:

(1) Pupils with low-incidence disabilities, as a group, make up less than 1 percent of the total statewide enrollment for

- Low-Incidence Disabilities*

*(Section 56000.5 Amended in 1994)

kindergarten through grade 12.

(2) Pupils with low-incidence disabilities require highly specialized services, equipment, and materials.

(b) The Legislature further finds and declares that:

(1) Deafness involves the most basic of human needs--the ability to communicate with other human beings. Many hard-of-hearing and deaf children use an appropriate communication mode, sign language, which may be their primary language, while others express and receive language orally and aurally, with or without visual signs or cues. Still others, typically young hard-of-hearing and deaf children, lack any significant language skills. It is essential for the well-being and growth of hard-of-hearing and deaf children that educational programs recognize the unique nature of deafness and ensure that all hard-of-hearing and deaf children have appropriate, ongoing, and fully accessible educational opportunities.   – Deafness

(2) It is essential that hard-of-hearing and deaf children, like all children, have an education in which their unique communication mode is respected, utilized, and developed to an appropriate level of proficiency.   – Unique Communication Mode

(3) It is essential that hard-of-hearing and deaf children have an education in which special education teachers, psychologists, speech therapists, assessors, administrators, and other special education personnel understand the unique nature of deafness and are specifically trained to work with hard-of-hearing and deaf pupils. It is essential that hard-of-hearing and deaf children have an education in which their special education teachers are proficient in the primary language mode of those children.   – Trained Personnel

(4) It is essential that hard-of-hearing and deaf children, like all children, have an education with a sufficient number of language mode peers with whom they can communicate directly and who are of the same, or approximately the same, age and ability level.   – Language Mode Peers

(5) It is essential that hard-of-hearing and deaf children have an education in which their parents and, where appropriate, hard-of-hearing and deaf people are involved in determining the extent, content, and purpose of programs.   – Parental Involvement

(6) Hard-of-hearing and deaf children would benefit from an education in which they are exposed to hard-of-hearing and deaf role models.   – Role Models

(7) It is essential that hard-of-hearing and deaf children, like all children, have programs in which they have direct and appropriate access to all components of the educational process, including, but not limited to, recess, lunch, and extracurricular social and athletic activities.   – Access to Educational Process

(8) It is essential that hard-of-hearing and deaf children, like all children, have programs in which their unique vocational needs are provided for, including appropriate research, curricula, programs, staff, and outreach.

— Vocational Needs

(9) Each hard-of-hearing and deaf child should have a determination of the least restrictive educational environment that takes into consideration these legislative findings and declarations.

— Least Restrictive Environment

(10) Given their unique communication needs, hard-of-hearing and deaf children would benefit from the development and implementation of regional programs for children with low-incidence disabilities.

— Regional Programs

56001. It is the intent of the Legislature that special education programs provide all of the following:

(a) Each individual with exceptional needs is assured an education appropriate to his or her needs in publicly supported programs through completion of his or her prescribed course of study or until the time that he or she has met proficiency standards prescribed pursuant to Sections 51215 and 51216.

— Assured an Education*
   Appropriate to Needs

(b) By June 30, 1991, early educational opportunities shall be available to all children between the ages of three and five years, inclusive, who require special education and services.

— Between Ages of 3 and 5

(c) Early educational opportunities shall be made available to children younger than three years of age pursuant to Chapter 4.4 (commencing with Section 56425), appropriate sections of this part, and the California Early Intervention Service Act, Title 14 (commencing with Section 95000) of the Government Code.

— Ages Birth to 3

(d) Any child younger than three years, potentially eligible for special education, shall be afforded the protections provided pursuant to the California Early Intervention Services Act, Title 14 (commencing with Section 95000) of the Government Code and Section 1480 of Title 20 of the United States Code and implementing regulations.

— Protections for Children
   Younger Than 3

(e) Each individual with exceptional needs shall have his or her educational goals, objectives, and special education and related services specified in a written individualized education program.

— Written IEP

(f) Education programs are provided under an approved local plan for special education that sets forth the elements of the programs in accordance with this part. This plan for special education shall be developed cooperatively with input from the community advisory committee and appropriate representation from special and regular teachers and administrators selected by the groups they represent to ensure effective participation and communication.

— Local Plan Development

*(Section 56001 Amended in 1994)

(g) Individuals with exceptional needs are offered special assistance programs that promote maximum interaction with the general school population in a manner that is appropriate to the needs of both, taking into consideration, for hard-of-hearing or deaf children, the individual's needs for a sufficient number of age and language mode peers and for special education teachers who are proficient in the individual's primary language mode. — Maximum Interaction

(h) Pupils be transferred out of special education programs when special education services are no longer needed. — Transferred Out

(i) The unnecessary use of labels is avoided in providing special education and related services for individuals with exceptional needs. — Avoid Unnecessary Use of Labels

(j) Procedures and materials for assessment and placement of individuals with exceptional needs shall be selected and administered so as not to be racially, culturally, or sexually discriminatory. No single assessment instrument shall be the sole criterion for determining placement of a pupil. The procedures and materials for assessment and placement shall be in the individual's mode of communication. Procedures and materials for use with pupils of limited English proficiency, as defined in subdivision (m) of Section 52163, shall be in the individual's primary language. All assessment materials and procedures shall be selected and administered pursuant to Section 56320. — Assessment Procedures and Materials

(k) Educational programs are coordinated with other public and private agencies, including preschools, child development programs, nonpublic nonsectarian schools, regional occupational centers and programs, and postsecondary and adult programs for individuals with exceptional needs. — Coordination of Educational Programs

(l) Psychological and health services for individuals with exceptional needs shall be available to each schoolsite. — Psychological and Health Services

(m) Continuous evaluation of the effectiveness of these special education programs by the school district, special education local plan area, or county office shall be made to ensure the highest quality educational offerings. — Continuous Program Evaluation

(n) Appropriate qualified staff are employed, consistent with credentialing requirements, to fulfill the responsibilities of the local plan and positive efforts are made to employ qualified handicapped individuals. — Qualified Staff

(o) Regular and special education personnel are adequately prepared to provide educational instruction and services to individuals with exceptional needs. — Prepared Personnel

(p) This section shall remain in effect only until California terminates its participation in special education programs for individuals with exceptional needs between the ages of three and five years, pursuant to Section 56448, and as of that date is repealed. — Repeal Clause

(NOTE: If California ever terminates participation in the Federal Preschool Grant Program, Section 56001 reverts to Section 2.5 of Chapter 1126, Statutes of 1994.)

Article 2. Definitions

56020. As used in this part, the definitions prescribed by this article apply unless the context otherwise requires.

56021. "Board" means the State Board of Education. — Board

56022. "County office" means office of the county superintendent of schools. — County Office

56023. "Day" means a calendar day. — Day

56024. "Department" means the Department of Education. — Department

56025. "District" means school district. — District

56026. "Individuals with exceptional needs" means those persons who satisfy all the following: — Individuals with Exceptional Needs

(a) Identified by an individualized education program team as children with disabilities as that phrase is defined in paragraph (1) of subdivision (a) of Section 1401 of Title 20 of the United States Code. — Identified by IEP Team — Federal Definition

(b) Their impairment, as described by subdivision (a), requires instruction, services, or both which cannot be provided with modification of the regular school program. — Impairment Requires Special Instruction/Services

(c) Come within one of the following age categories: — Age Categories

(1) Younger than three years of age and identified by the district, the special education local plan area, or the county office as requiring intensive special education and services, as defined by the State Board of Education. — Younger Than 3

(2) Between the ages of three to five years, inclusive, and identified by the district, the special education local plan area, or the county office as requiring intensive special education and services, as defined by the State Board of Education; or between the ages of three and five years, inclusive, and identified by the district, special education local plan area, or county office pursuant to Section 56441.11. — Between 3 and 5

(3) Between the ages of five and 18 years, inclusive. — Between 5 and 18

(4) Between the ages of 19 and 21 years, inclusive; enrolled in or eligible for a program under this part or other special education program prior to his or her 19th birthday; and has not yet completed his or her prescribed course of study or who has not met proficiency standards prescribed pursuant to Sections 51215 and 51216. — Between 19 and 21

(A) Any person who becomes 22 years of age during the months of January to June, inclusive, while participating in a program under this part may continue his or her participation in the program for the remainder of the current fiscal year, including any extended school year program for individuals with exceptional needs established pursuant to regulations adopted by the State Board of Education, pursuant to Article 1 (commencing with Section 56100) of Chapter 2. — Twenty-two Years of Age (January to June, Inclusive)

(B) Any person otherwise eligible to participate in a program under this part shall not be allowed to begin a new fiscal year in a program if he or she becomes 22 years of age in July, August, or September of that new fiscal year. However, if a person is in a year-round school program and is completing his or her individualized education program in a term that extends into the new fiscal year, then the person may complete that term.

  — (July to September, Inclusive)

(C) Any person who becomes 22 years of age during the months of October, November, or December while participating in a program under this act shall be terminated from the program on December 31 of the current fiscal year, unless the person would otherwise complete his or her individualized education program at the end of the current fiscal year or unless the person has not had an individual transition plan incorporated into his or her individualized education program and implemented from the age of 20 years, in which case the person shall be terminated from the program at the end of the fiscal year.

  — (October, November or December)

(D) No school district, special education local plan area, or county office of education may develop an individualized education program that extends these eligibility dates, and in no event may a pupil be required or allowed to attend school under the provisions of this part beyond these eligibility dates solely on the basis that the individual has not met his or her goals or objectives.

  — IEP Cannot Extend Eligibility Dates

(d) Meet eligibility criteria set forth in regulations adopted by the board, including, but not limited to, those adopted pursuant to Article 2.5 (commencing with Section 56333) of Chapter 4.

  — Eligibility Criteria

(e) Unless disabled within the meaning of subdivisions (a) to (d), inclusive, pupils whose educational needs are due primarily to unfamiliarity with the English language; temporary physical disabilities; social maladjustment; or environmental, cultural, or economic factors are not individuals with exceptional needs.

  — Not Individuals with Exceptional Needs

(f) This section shall remain in effect only until California terminates its participation in special education programs for individuals with exceptional needs between the ages of three and five years, inclusive, pursuant to Section 56448, and as of that date is repealed.

  — Repeal Clause

(NOTE: If California ever terminates participation in the Federal Preschool Grant Program, Section 56026 reverts to Section 13 of Chapter 1296, Statutes of 1993.)

56026.2. "Language mode" means the method of communication used by hard-of-hearing and deaf children that may include the use of sign language to send or receive messages or the use of spoken language, with or without visual signs or cues.

  — Language Mode*

56026.5. "Low incidence disability" means a severe disabling condition with an expected incidence rate of less than one percent of the total statewide enrollment in kindergarten through grade 12. For purposes of this definition, severe disabling conditions

  — Low Incidence Disability

are hearing impairments, vision impairments, and severe orthopedic impairments, or any combination thereof.

56027. "Local plan" means a plan that meets the requirements of Chapter 3 (commencing with Section 56200) and that is submitted by a school district, special education local plan area, or county office.   — Local Plan

56028. "Parent" includes any person having legal custody of a child. "Parent," in addition, includes any adult pupil for whom no guardian or conservator has been appointed and the person having custody of a minor if neither the parent nor legal guardian can be notified of the educational actions under consideration. "Parent" also includes a parent surrogate. "Parent" does not include the state or any political subdivision of government.   — Parent

56029. "Referral for assessment" means any written request for assessment to identify an individual with exceptional needs made by a parent, teacher, or other service provider.   — Referral for Assessment

56030. "Responsible local agency" means the school district or county office designated in the local plan as the entity whose duties shall include, but are not limited to, receiving and distributing regionalized services funds, providing administrative support, and coordinating the implementation of the plan.   — Responsible Local Agency

56030.5. "Severely disabled" means individuals with exceptional needs who require intensive instruction and training in programs serving pupils with the following profound disabilities: autism, blindness, deafness, severe orthopedic impairments, serious emotional disturbances, severe mental retardation, and those individuals who would have been eligible for enrollment in a development center for handicapped pupils under Chapter 6 (commencing with Section 56800) of this part, as it read on January 1, 1980.   — Severely Disabled

56031. "Special education" means specially designed instruction, at no cost to the parent, to meet the unique needs of individuals with exceptional needs, whose educational needs cannot be met with modification of the regular instruction program, and related services, at no cost to the parent, that may be needed to assist these individuals to benefit from specially designed instruction.   — Special Education

— Specially Designed Instruction

Special education is an integral part of the total public education system and provides education in a manner that promotes maximum interaction between children or youth with disabilities and children or youth who are not disabled, in a manner that is appropriate to the needs of both.   — Integral Part of Public Education

— Maximum Interaction

Special education provides a full continuum of program options to meet the educational and service needs of individuals with exceptional needs in the least restrictive environment.   — Full Continuum of Program Options

Individuals with exceptional needs shall be grouped for   — Grouped for Instructional Purposes and Needs instructional purposes according to their instructional needs.

56032. "Individualized education program" means "individualized family service plan" as described in Section 1477 of Title 20 of the United States Code when individualized education program pertains to individuals with exceptional needs younger than three years of age.

- Individualized Family Service Plan

56033. "Superintendent" means the Superintendent of Public Instruction.

- Superintendent

56034. "Nonpublic, nonsectarian school" means a private, nonsectarian school that enrolls individuals with exceptional needs pursuant to an individualized education program, employs at least one full-time teacher who holds an appropriate credential authorizing special education services, and is certified by the department. It does not include an organization or agency that operates as a public agency or offers public service, including, but not limited to, a state or local agency, an affiliate of a state or local agency, including a private, nonprofit corporation established or operated by a state or local agency, or a public university or college. A nonpublic, nonsectarian school also shall meet standards as prescribed by the superintendent and board.

- Nonpublic, Nonsectarian* School

56035. "Nonpublic, nonsectarian agency" means a private, nonsectarian establishment or individual that provides related services necessary for an individual with exceptional needs to benefit educationally from the pupils' educational program pursuant to an individualized education program and that is certified by the department. It does not include an organization or agency that operates as a public agency or offers public service, including, but not limited to, a state or local agency, an affiliate of a state or local agency, including a private, nonprofit corporation established or operated by a state or local agency, a public university or college, or a public hospital. The nonpublic, nonsectarian agency shall also meet standards as prescribed by the superintendent and board.

- Nonpublic, Nonsectarian Agency

Article 3. General Provisions

- GENERAL PROVISIONS

56040. Every individual with exceptional needs, who is eligible to receive educational instruction, related services, or both under this part shall receive such educational instruction, services, or both, at no cost to his or her parents or, as appropriate, to him or her.

- Free Appropriate Educational Instruction/ Services

56041. Except for those pupils meeting residency requirements for school attendance specified in subdivision (a) of Section 48204, and notwithstanding any other provision of law, if it is determined by the individualized education program team that

- Residency Requirements

*(Section 56034 Amended in 1994)

1-8

special education services are required beyond the pupil's 18th birthday, the district of residence responsible for providing special education and related services to pupils between the ages of 18 to 22 years, inclusive, shall be assigned, as follows:

(a) For nonconserved pupils, the last district of residence in effect prior to the pupil's attaining the age of majority shall become and remain as the responsible local educational agency, as long as and until the parent or parents relocate to a new district of residence. At that time, the new district of residence shall become the responsible local educational agency. — Nonconserved Pupils

(b) For conserved pupils, the district of residence of the conservator shall attach and remain the responsible local educational agency, as long as and until the conservator relocates or a new one is appointed. At that time, the new district of residence shall attach and become the responsible local educational agency. — Conserved Pupils

56042. Notwithstanding any other provision of law, an attorney or advocate for a parent of an individual with exceptional needs shall not recommend placement in a nonpublic, nonsectarian school or agency with which the attorney or advocate is employed or contracted, or otherwise has a conflict of interest or from which the attorney or advocate receives a benefit. — Nonpublic, Nonsectarian School/Agency and Attorney or Advocate Conflict of Interest

Article 3.5. Surrogate Parents
— SURROGATE PARENTS

56050. (a) For the purposes of this article, "surrogate parent" shall be defined as it is defined in Section 300.514 of Title 34 of the Code of Federal Regulations. — Definition

(b) A surrogate parent may represent an individual with exceptional needs in matters relating to identification, assessment, instructional planning and development, educational placement, reviewing and revising the individualized education program, and in other matters relating to the provision of a free appropriate education to the individual. Notwithstanding any other provision of law, this representation shall include the provision of written consent to the individualized education program including nonemergency medical services, mental health treatment services, and occupational or physical therapy services pursuant to Chapter 26.5 (commencing with Section 7570) of Division 7 of Title 1 of the Government Code. The surrogate parent may sign any consent relating to individualized education program purposes. — Representation

(c) A surrogate parent shall be held harmless by the State of California when acting in his or her official capacity except for acts or omissions which are found to have been wanton, reckless, or malicious. — Liability Protection

(d) A surrogate parent shall also be governed by Section 7579.5 of the Government Code.

— Also Governed by Section 7579.5 of Government Code

Article 4. Substitute Teachers

— SUBSTITUTE TEACHERS

56060. A noncredentialed person shall not substitute for any special education certificated position.

— Noncredentialed Substitutes Prohibited

56061. A person holding a valid credential authorizing substitute teaching may serve as substitute for the appropriately credentialed special education teacher as follows:

— Substitute Teacher Qualifications

(a) Except as provided in subdivisions (b) and (c), the employer shall not employ an inappropriately credentialed substitute teacher for a period of more than 20 cumulative school days for each special education teacher absent during each school year.

— Number of Days

(b) Upon application by the district or county office, the superintendent may approve an extension of 20 school days in addition to those authorized by subdivision (a).

— Extension of 20 School Days

(c) Only in extraordinary circumstances may additional number of days be granted beyond the 40 school days provided for by subdivisions (a) and (b). Such additional days shall be granted in writing by the superintendent. The superintendent shall report to the board on all requests granted for an additional number of days pursuant to this subdivision.

— Beyond 40 School Days

56062. The employer shall use the following priorities in placing substitute teachers in special education classrooms:

— Substitute Teacher Priorities

(a) A substitute teacher with the appropriate special education credential or credentials.

(b) A substitute teacher with any other special education credential or credentials.

(c) A substitute teacher with a regular teaching credential.

56063. The employer shall be responsible for seeking, and maintaining lists of, appropriately   credentialed substitute teachers.   The employer shall contact institutions of higher education with approved special education programs for possible recommendations of appropriately credentialed special education personnel.

— Employer Maintains Lists

CHAPTER 2. ADMINISTRATION

Article 1. State Board of Education

56100. The State Board of Education shall do all of the following:

(a) Adopt rules and regulations necessary for the efficient administration of this part.

(b) Adopt criteria and procedures for the review and approval by the board of local plans. Local plans may be approved for up to four years.

(c) Adopt size and scope standards for use by districts, special education local plan areas, and county offices, pursuant to subdivision (a) of Section 56170.

(d) Provide review, upon petition, to any district, special education local plan area, or county office that appeals a decision made by the department which affects its providing services under this part except a decision made pursuant to Chapter 5 (commencing with Section 56500).

(e) Review and approve a program evaluation plan for special education programs provided by this part in accordance with Chapter 6 (commencing with Section 56600). This plan may be approved for up to three years.

(f) Recommend to the Commission on Teacher Credentialing the adoption of standards for the certification of professional personnel for special education programs conducted pursuant to this part.

(g) Adopt regulations to provide specific procedural criteria and guidelines for the identification of pupils as individuals with exceptional needs.

(h) Adopt guidelines of reasonable pupil progress and achievement for individuals with exceptional needs. The guidelines shall be developed to aid teachers and parents in assessing an individual pupil's education program and the appropriateness of the special education services.

(i) In accordance with the requirements of federal law, adopt regulations for all educational programs for individuals with exceptional needs, including programs administered by other state or local agencies.

(j) Adopt uniform rules and regulations relating to parental due process rights in the area of special education.

(k) Adopt rules and regulations regarding the ownership and transfer of materials and equipment, including facilities, related to transfer of programs, reorganization, or restructuring of special education local plan areas.

– STATE BOARD OF EDUCATION

– Adopt Rules/Regulations

– Approve Local Plans*

– Adopt Size and Scope Standards

– Provide Review of Department Decisions

– Review/Approve Program Evaluation Plan

– Recommend Adoption of Professional Standards

– Adopt Specific Procedural Criteria for Indentification

– Adopt Reasonable Pupil Progress/Achievement Guidelines

– Adopt Title 5 Regulations

– Adopt Rules/Regulations on Due Process Rights

– Adopt Rules/Regulations on Ownership and Transfer of Materials and Equipment

*(Section 56100 Amended in 1994)

56101. (a) Any district, special education local plan area, county office, or public education agency, as defined in Section 56500, may request the board to grant a waiver of any provision of this code or regulations adopted pursuant to that provision if the waiver is necessary or beneficial to the content and implementation of the pupil's individualized education program and does not abrogate any right provided individuals with exceptional needs and their parents or guardians under the Individuals with Disabilities Education Act (20 U.S.C. Sec. 1400 et seq.), or to the compliance of a district, special education local plan area, or county office with the Individuals with Disabilities Education Act (20 U.S.C. Sec. 1400 et seq.), Section 504 of, the Rehabilitation Act of 1973 (29 U.S.C. Sec. 794), and federal regulations relating thereto.

- State Board Waivers

(b) The board may grant, in whole or in part, any request pursuant to subdivision (a) when the facts indicate that failure to do so would hinder implementation of the pupil's individualized education program or compliance by a district, special education local plan area, or county office with federal mandates for a free, appropriate education for children or youth with disabilities.

- Whole or Partial Waiver

Article 2. Superintendent of Public Instruction

- SUPERINTENDENT OF PUBLIC INSTRUCTION

56120. The superintendent shall administer the provisions of this part.

- Administer Special Education Law

56121. The superintendent shall grant approval of the organization of the local plans within each county.

- Grant Approval of Local Plan Organization

56122. The superintendent shall establish guidelines for the development of local plans, including a standard format for local plans, and provide assistance in the development of local plans. The purposes of such guidelines and assistance shall be to help districts and county offices benefit from the experience of other local agencies that implement programs under this part, including, but not limited to, reducing paperwork, increasing parental involvement, and providing effective staff development activities. To the extent possible, all forms, reports, and evaluations shall be designed to satisfy simultaneously state and federal requirements.

- Establish Local Plan Development Guidelines

56123. The superintendent shall review and recommend to the board for approval, local plans developed and submitted in accordance with this part.

- Review/Recommend to State Board on Local Plans

56124. The superintendent shall promote innovation and improvement in the field of special education at the public and nonpublic, nonsectarian school, district, county, and state levels.

- Promote Innovation/Improvement in Special Education

56125. The superintendent shall monitor the implementation of local plans by periodically conducting onsite program and fiscal reviews.

- Monitor Local Plan Implementation

56126. The superintendent shall encourage the maximum practicable involvement of parents of children enrolled in special education programs.

56127. The superintendent shall make recommendations in the areas of staff development, curriculum, testing and multicultural assessment, and the development of materials for special education programs.

56128. The superintendent shall prepare for board approval, as necessary, any state plan required by federal law in order that this state may qualify for any federal funds available for education of individuals with exceptional needs.

56129. The superintendent shall maintain the state special schools in accordance with Part 32 (commencing with Section 59000) so that the services of those schools are coordinated with the services of the district, special education local plan area, or the county office.

56130. The superintendent shall develop in accordance with Sections 33401 and 56602, an annual program evaluation plan and report of special education programs authorized under this part for submission to the board.

56131. The superintendent shall apportion funds in accordance with Chapter 7 (commencing with Section 56700) and approved local plans.

56132. The superintendent shall assist districts and county offices in the improvement and evaluation of their programs.

56133. The superintendent shall provide for the mediation conference prescribed by Sections 56502 and 56503 and the state hearing prescribed by Section 56505.

56134. The superintendent shall perform the duties prescribed by Chapter 4.5 (commencing with Section 56452).

56135. (a) The superintendent shall be responsible for assuring provision of, and supervising, education and related services to individuals with exceptional needs as specifically required pursuant to the Individuals with Disabilities Education Act (20 U.S.C. Sec. 1400 et seq.).

(b) Nothing in this part shall be construed to authorize the superintendent to prescribe health care services.

56136. The superintendent shall develop guidelines for each low incidence disability area and provide technical assistance to parents, teachers, and administrators regarding the implementation of the guidelines. The guidelines shall clarify the identification, assessment, planning of, and the provision of, specialized services to pupils with low incidence disabilities. The superintendent shall consider the guidelines when monitoring programs serving pupils with low incidence disabilities pursuant to Section 56825. The adopted guidelines shall be promulgated

- Encourage Maximum Parent Involvement

- Make Recommendations for Special Education Programs

- Prepare State Plan

- Maintain State Special Schools and Coordinate Services

- Develop Annual Program Evaluation Plan

- Apportion Funds

- Assist in Improvement/ Evaluation of Local Programs

- Provide for Mediation Conference

- Promote Career/Vocational Education

- Assure Provision of/ Supervise Education/ Related Services Required by Federal Law

- Excludes Prescription of Health Care Services

- Develop Low Incidence Disability Guidelines

for the purpose of establishing recommended guidelines and shall not operate to impose minimum state requirements.

56137. The superintendent shall develop, update every other year, and disseminate directories of public and private agencies providing services to pupils with low-incidence disabilities. The directories shall be made available as reference directories to parents, teachers, and administrators. The directories shall include, but need not be limited to, the following information:

(a) A description of each agency providing services and program options within each disability area.

(b) The specialized services and program options provided, including infant and preschool programs.

(c) The number of credentialed and certificated staff providing specialized services.

(d) The names, addresses, and telephone numbers of agency administrators or other individuals responsible for the programs.

56138. (a) The superintendent shall conduct a pilot program for the 1993-94, 1994-95, and 1995-96 fiscal years to authorize districts, special education local plan areas, and county offices to establish an alternative dispute resolution process, the purpose of which will be to increase opportunities for parents and public education agencies to reach agreements regarding a free and appropriate public education for individuals with exceptional needs, prior to the initiation of due process hearings pursuant to Section 56502. The pilot program shall include participants from urban, suburban, and rural areas of the state. The pilot program shall not abrogate any right provided to individuals with exceptional needs and their parents or guardians under the federal Individuals with Disabilities Act (20 U.S.C. Sec. 1400 and following).

(b) In developing the request for proposals for the pilot program, the superintendent shall consult with the Advisory Commission on Special Education and with other appropriate groups, parents, and persons involved in the education of individuals with exceptional needs. The pilot program shall include, but not be limited to, the following:

(1) Development of the capability for a district, special education local plan area, or county office, to acquire an ombudsperson who shall receive issues or grievances submitted by parents, individuals, public agencies, or organizations and bring the issues to the attention of the public education agency, provide advice regarding available resources and options, propose a resolution, or propose a systemic change related to the issues.

(2) Development of the capability for a district, special education local plan area, or county office, to acquire a mediator who shall provide a structured process that allows parents,

Marginal notes:
- Develop and Disseminate Directories

- Conduct Pilot Program on Alternative Dispute Resolution Process at Local Level

- Develop Request for Proposals

- Ombudsperson

- Mediator

pupils, and public education agencies a voluntary method to reach a settlement of their differences that results in an agreement which describes the future actions of both parties.

(3) Development of the capability for districts, special education local plan areas, or county offices, to acquire a placement specialist who shall assist the parent, pupil, when appropriate, and public education agency to identify and locate an appropriate educational placement or service and assist throughout the individualized education program process.

- Placement Specialist

(c) The superintendent shall evaluate the effectiveness of the alternative dispute resolution process. The evaluation shall include, but not be limited to, reduction in the number of state due process hearings, cost effectiveness, consumer satisfaction, efficiency, and other issues specific to the alternative dispute resolution process. Following the evaluation, the superintendent shall submit a report of findings and recommendations to the Legislature by December 1, 1996.

- Evaluate Effectiveness

(d) The pilot program shall be funded pursuant to Schedule (d) of Item 6110-161-890 of Section 2.00 of the Budget Act.

- Pilot Program Funding

Article 3. County Offices

- COUNTY OFFICES

56140. County offices shall do all of the following:

(a) Initiate and submit to the superintendent a countywide plan for special education which demonstrates the coordination of all local plans submitted pursuant to Section 56200 and which ensures that all individuals with exceptional needs will have access to appropriate special education programs and related services. However, a county office shall not be required to submit a countywide plan when all the districts within the county elect to submit a single local plan.

- Countywide Plan

(b) Within 45 days, approve or disapprove any proposed local plan submitted by a district or group of districts within the county or counties. Such approval shall be based on the capacity of the district or districts to ensure that special education programs and services are provided to all individuals with exceptional needs.

- Approve/Disapprove Proposed Local Plan

(1) If approved, the county office shall submit the plan with comments and recommendations to the superintendent.

- Submit Approved Local Plan to State Superintendent

(2) If disapproved, the county office shall return the plan with comments and recommendations to the district. This district may immediately appeal to the superintendent to overrule the county office's disapproval. The superintendent shall make a decision on such an appeal within 30 days of receipt of the appeal.

- Return Disapproved Plan to District

(3) A local plan may not be implemented without approval of the plan by the county office or a decision by the superintendent

- Local Plan Implementation Approval

to overrule the disapproval of the county office.

(c) Participate in the state onsite review of the district's implementation of an approved local plan.

- State Onsite Review

(d) Join with districts in the county which elect to submit a plan or plans pursuant to subdivision (c) of Section 56170. Any such plan may include more than one county, and districts located in more than one county. Nothing in this subdivision shall be construed to limit the authority of a county office to enter into other agreements with these districts and other districts to provide services relating to the education of individuals with exceptional needs.

- Join Districts to Submit Plan(s)

Article 4. Juvenile Court Schools

- JUVENILE COURT SCHOOLS

56150. Special education programs authorized by this part shall be provided, pursuant to Section 48645.2, for individuals with exceptional needs who have been adjudicated by the juvenile court for placement in a juvenile hall or juvenile home, day center, ranch, or camp, or for individuals with exceptional needs placed in a county community school pursuant to Section 1981.

- Programs Provided Once Individual Adjudicated

Article 5. Licensed Children's Institutions and Foster Family Homes

- LICENSED CHILDREN'S INSTITUTIONS AND FOSTER FAMILY HOMES

56155. The provisions of this article shall only apply to individuals with exceptional needs placed in a licensed children's institution or foster family home by a court, regional center for the developmentally disabled, or public agency, other than an educational agency.

- Application of Article

56155.5. (a) As used in this article, "licensed children's institution" means a residential facility which is licensed by the state, or other public agency having delegated authority by contract with the state to license, to provide nonmedical care to children, including, but not limited to, individuals with exceptional needs. "Licensed children's institution" includes a group home as defined by subdivision (a) of Section 80001 of Title 22 of the California Code of Regulations. As used in this article and Article 8.5 (commencing with Section 56775), a "licensed children's institution" does not include any of the following:

- LCI Definition*

(1) A juvenile court school, juvenile hall, juvenile home, day center, juvenile ranch, or juvenile camp administered pursuant to Article 2 (sic)(commencing with Section 48645) of Chapter 4 of Part 27.

(2) A county community school program provided pursuant to Section 1981.

*(Section 56155.5 Amended in 1994)

(3) Any special education programs provided pursuant to Section 56150.

(4) Any other public agency.

(b) As used in this article, "foster family home" means a family residence that is licensed by the state, or other public agency having delegated authority by contract with the state to license, to provide 24-hour nonmedical care and supervision for not more than six foster children, including, but not limited to, individuals with exceptional needs. "Foster family home" includes a small family home as defined in paragraph (6) of subdivision (a) of Section 1502 of the Health and Safety Code. — Foster Family Home Definition

56156. (a) Each court, regional center for the developmentally disabled, or public agency that engages in referring children to, or placing children in, licensed children's institutions shall report to the special education administrator of the district, special education local plan area, or county office in which the licensed children's institution is located any referral or admission of a child who is potentially eligible for special education. — Referring/Placing Agencies

(b) At the time of placement in a licensed children's institution or foster family home, each court, regional center for the developmentally disabled, or public agency shall identify all of the following: — Identify Responsible Individual

(1) Whether the courts have specifically limited the rights of the parent or guardian to make educational decisions for a child who is a ward or dependent of the court.

(2) The location of the parents, in the event that the parents retain the right to make educational decisions.

(3) Whether the location of the parents is unknown.

(c) Each person licensed by the state to operate a licensed children's institution, or his or her designee, shall notify the special education administrator of the district, special education local plan area, or county office in which the licensed children's institution is located of any child potentially eligible for special education who resides at the facility. — LCI Operators

(d) The superintendent shall provide each county office of education with a current list of licensed children's institutions in that county at least biannually. The county office shall maintain the most current list of licensed children's institutions located within the county and shall notify each district and special education local plan area within the county of the names of licensed children's institutions located in the geographical area of the county covered by the district and special education local plan area. The county office shall notify the director of each licensed children's institution of the appropriate person to contact regarding individuals with exceptional needs. — Superintendent Shall Provide Current List

56156.5. (a) Each district, special education local plan area, or county office shall be responsible for providing appropriate education to individuals with exceptional needs residing in licensed children's institutions and foster family homes located in the geographical area covered by the local plan.

    — Educational Responsibility

(b) In multidistrict and district and county office local plan areas, local written agreements shall be developed, pursuant to subdivision (f) of Section 56220, to identify the public education entities that will provide the special education services.

    — Local Written Agreements

(c) If there is no local agreement, special education services for individuals with exceptional needs residing in licensed children's institutions shall be the responsibility of the county office in the county in which the institution is located, if the county office is part of the special education local plan area, and special education services for individuals with exceptional needs residing in foster family homes shall be the responsibility of the district in which the foster family home is located. If a county office is not a part of the special education local plan area, special education services for individuals with exceptional needs residing in licensed children's institutions, pursuant to this subdivision, shall be the responsibility of the responsible local agency or other administrative entity of the special education local plan area. This program responsibility shall continue until the time local written agreements are developed pursuant to subdivision (f) of Section 56220.

    — No Local Agreement

    — County Office Responsibility

    — District Responsibility

    — RLA Responsibility

56156.6. If the district in which the licensed children's institution or foster family home is located is also the district of residence of the parent of the individual with exceptional needs, and if the parent retains legal responsibility for the child's education, Section 56775 shall not apply.

    — Residence of Parent

56157. (a) In providing appropriate programs to individuals with exceptional needs residing in licensed children's institutions or foster family homes, the district, special education local plan area, or county office shall first consider services in programs operated by public education agencies for individuals with exceptional needs. If those programs are not appropriate, special education and related services shall be provided by contract with a nonpublic, nonsectarian school.

    — First Consider Public Options

(b) If special education and related services are provided by contract with a nonpublic, nonsectarian school, or with a licensed children's institution under this article, the terms of the contract shall be developed in accordance with the provisions of Section 56366.

    — Contracts

56159. If a district, special education local plan area, or county office does not make the placement decision of an individual with exceptional needs in a licensed children's institution or in a foster

    — Residential Costs/Non-education Services

family home, the court, regional center for the developmentally disabled, or public agency, excluding an education agency, placing the individual in the institution, shall be responsible for the residential costs and the cost of noneducation services of the individual.

56160. (a) The superintendent shall apportion, pursuant to Chapter 7 (commencing with Section 56700), funds directly to each district or county office operating programs under this article.

— Apportionment of Funds

(b) Reimbursements for nonpublic, nonsectarian school or agency placements shall be made pursuant to Sections 56366, 56740, and 56775 to each district or county office that contracts for services under this article.

— Nonpublic School Reimbursements

(c) For purposes of the revenue calculations required pursuant to subdivision (a) of Section 56712, the district in which the licensed children's institution or foster family home is located shall be considered the district of residence.

— Revenue Calculations

56161. Individuals with exceptional needs served under this article shall not be subject to subdivision (a) of Section 56760 and the deficit provisions prescribed by Article 10 (commencing with Section 56790) of Chapter 7. In addition, if available funds are insufficient to fully fund entitlements pursuant to Article 10 (commencing with Section 41850) of Chapter 5 of Part 24, no deficit shall be applied to the portion of the entitlements for services to individuals prescribed in Section 56155. However, those pupils and appropriate instructional personnel units required to provide educational services to those pupils, shall be included in the computations prescribed in Section 56728.5.

— Not Subject to Service Proportions and Deficit Provisions

— Included in April Pupil Count
— Grandfather Clause

56162. Individuals with exceptional needs placed in a licensed children's institution or foster family home by a court, regional center for the developmentally disabled, or public agency, other than an educational agency, prior to the effective date of this article, shall be considered residents of the geographical area of the local plan in which the licensed children's institution or foster family home is located, for special education and related services pursuant to the provisions of this article.

56163. A licensed children's institution which provides nonsectarian educational programs for individuals with exceptional needs shall be certified by the department as prescribed by subdivision (c) of Section 56366.

— Certification

56164. This article shall not apply to programs operating in state hospitals and juvenile court schools.

— Exclusion

56165. This article shall not apply to individuals with exceptional needs placed in a licensed children's institution pursuant to Section 56365.

— Exclusion

56166. The board shall adopt rules and regulations to implement the provisions of this article.

- Rules/Regulations

56166.5. This article shall become operative July 1, 1982.

- Operative Date

Article 5.5. Public Hospitals, Proprietary Hospitals and Other Residential Medical Facilities

- PUBLIC HOSPITALS, PROPRIETARY HOSPITALS

56167. (a) Individuals with exceptional needs who are placed in a public hospital, state licensed children's hospital, psychiatric hospital, proprietary hospital, or a health facility for medical purposes are the educational responsibility of the district, special education local plan area, or county office in which the hospital or facility is located, as determined in local written agreements pursuant to subdivision (e) of Section 56220.

- Educational Responsibility

- Local Written Agreements

(b) For the purposes of this part, "health facility" shall have the definition set forth in Sections 1250, 1250.2, and 1250.3 of the Health and Safety Code.

- Health Facility Definition

56167.5. Nothing in this article shall be construed to mean that the placement of any individual with exceptional needs in a hospital or health facility constitutes a necessary residential placement, as described under Section 300.302 of Title 34 of the Code of Federal Regulations, for which the district, special education local plan area, or county office would be responsible as an educational program option under this part.

- Placement Not Educational Program Option

56168. (a) A public hospital, state licensed children's hospital, psychiatric hospital, proprietary hospital, or a health facility for medical purposes located either within and outside of this state is ineligible for certification as a nonpublic, nonsectarian school pursuant to Section 56034 and Sections 56365 to 56366.5, inclusive, to provide special education to individuals with exceptional needs. Districts, special education local plan areas, or county offices shall have until September 1, 1994, to find an appropriate alternative placement for any children currently served in one of these programs.

- Hospitals Ineligible for Certification as a Nonpublic School

(b) The district, special education local plan area, or county office in which the hospital or health facility is located has the educational responsibility for individuals with exceptional needs who reside in these facilities.

- Educational Responsibility

(c) A hospital or health facility is eligible for certification as a nonpublic, nonsectarian agency pursuant to Section 56035 and Sections 56365 to 56366.5, inclusive, to provide designated instruction and services to individuals with exceptional needs whether the child attends a public or nonpublic school or is enrolled in both a public and nonpublic school program as specified in Section 56361.5.

- Hospitals Eligible for Certification as a Nonpublic Agency

56169. (a) The superintendent shall apportion funds pursuant to Chapter 7 (commencing with Section 56700) to the district or county operating programs under this article. Classes operated pursuant to this article shall not be subject to the deficit provisions prescribed by Article 10 (commencing with Section 56790) of Chapter 7.

- Apportionment of Funds

- Not Subject to Deficit Provisions

(b) Except where the hospital or health facility also operates a nonsectarian, nonpublic school, the revenue limit of the district in which the hospital or health facility is located shall be used for computational purposes.

- Revenue Limit Computation

56169.5. This article shall not apply to programs operating in state hospitals.

- Exclusion

56169.7. If any provision of this article, or the application thereof to any person or circumstances, is held invalid by an appellate court of competent jurisdiction, the remainder of the article, and the application of the provision to other persons or circumstances, shall not be affected thereby.

- Severance Clause

Article 6. School Districts

- SCHOOL DISTRICTS

56170. The governing board of a school district shall elect to do one of the following:

- Local Plan Options

(a) If of sufficient size and scope, under standards adopted by the board, submit to the superintendent a local plan for the education of all individuals with exceptional needs residing in the district in accordance with Section 56200.

- Sufficient Size and Scope

(b) In conjunction with one or more districts, submit to the superintendent a local plan for the education of individuals with exceptional needs residing in those districts in accordance with Section 56200. The plan shall, through joint powers agreements or other contractual agreements, include all the following:

- Multidistricts

(1) Provision of a governance structure and any necessary administrative support to implement the plan.

- Governance Structure

(2) Establishment of a system for determining the responsibility of participating agencies for the education of each individual with exceptional needs residing within the special education local plan area.

- Education Responsibilities

(3) Designation of a responsible local agency or alternative administrative entity to perform such functions as the receipt and distribution of regionalized services funds, provision of administrative support, and coordination of the implementation of the plan. Any participating agency may perform any of the services required by the plan.

- RLA/Administrative Entity

(c) Join with the county office, to submit to the superintendent a plan in accordance with Section 56200 to assure access to special education and services for all individuals with exceptional

- Join with County Office

needs residing in the geographic area served by the plan. The county office shall coordinate the implementation of the plan, unless otherwise specified in the plan. The plan shall include, through contractual agreements, all of the following:

(1) Establishment of a system for determining the responsibility of participating agencies for the education of each individual with exceptional needs residing within the geographical area served by the plan.

— Education Responsibilities

(2) Designation of the county office, of a responsible local agency, or of any other administrative entity to perform such functions as the receipt and distribution of regionalized services funds, provision of administrative support, and coordination of the implementation of the plan. Any participating agency may perform any of these services required by the plan.

— RLA/Administrative Entity

(d) The service area covered by the local plan developed under subdivision (a), (b), or (c) shall be known as the special education local plan area.

— SELPA Definition

(e) Nothing in this section shall be construed to limit the authority of a county office and a school district or group of school districts to enter into contractual agreements for services relating to the education of individuals with exceptional needs, subject to the following:

— Contractual Agreements

(1) Except for instructional personnel service units serving infants, the county office of education or school district that reports a unit for funding shall be the agency that employs the personnel who staff the unit, unless the combined unit rate and support service ratio of the nonemploying agency is equal to or lower than that of the employing agency and both agencies agree that the nonemploying agency will report the unit for funding.

(2) For the 1992-93 fiscal year only, paragraph (1) does not apply to instructional personnel service units that were operated and reported for funding by a nonemploying county office or school district during the 1990-91 fiscal year, if the total number of units operated under contract within the special education local plan area in the 1992|93 fiscal year does not exceed the total number operated under contract in 1990-91.

56171. In developing a local plan under Section 56170, each district shall do all of the following:

— Developing Local Plan

(a) Involve special and regular teachers selected by their peers and parents selected by their peers in an active role.

— Involve Teachers/Parents

(b) Cooperate with the county office and other school districts in the geographic areas in planning its option under Section 56170 and, commencing with fiscal year 1982-83 and each fiscal year thereafter, notify the department, impacted special education local plan areas, and participating county offices of its intent to

— Cooperate in Planning Option

elect an alternative option from those specified in Section 56170, at least one year prior to the proposed effective date of the implementation of the alternative plan.

(c) Cooperate with the county office to assure that the plan is compatible with other local plans in the county and any county plan of a contiguous county.

(d) Join with the county office in countywide planning pursuant to subdivision (a) of Section 56140.

(e) Submit to the county office for review any plan developed under subdivision (a) or (b) of Section 56170.

56172. (a) Each county office and district governing board shall have authority over the programs it directly maintains, consistent with the local plan submitted pursuant to Section 56170. In counties with more than one special education local plan area for which the county office provides services, relevant provisions of contracts between the county office and its employees governing wages, hours, and working conditions shall supersede like provisions contained in a plan submitted under Section 56170.

(b) Any county office or district governing board may provide for the education of individual pupils in special education programs maintained by other districts or counties, and may include within their special education programs pupils who reside in other districts or counties. Section 46600 shall apply to interdistrict attendance agreements for programs conducted pursuant to this part.

Article 7. Community Advisory Committee

56190. Each plan submitted under Section 56170 shall establish a community advisory committee. Such committee shall serve only in an advisory capacity.

56191. The members of the community advisory committee shall be appointed by, and responsible to, the governing board of each participating district or county office, or any combination thereof participating in the local plan. Appointment shall be in accordance with a locally determined selection procedure that is described in the local plan. Where appropriate, this procedure shall provide for selection of representatives of groups specified in Section 56192 by their peers. Such procedure shall provide that terms of appointment are for at least two years and are annually staggered to ensure that no more than one half of the membership serves the first year of the term in any one year.

56192. The community advisory committee shall be composed of parents of individuals with exceptional needs enrolled in public or private schools, parents of other pupils enrolled in school,

– Electing Alternative Option

– Compatible Plan

– Countywide Planning

– Submit Plan for Review

– County Office/District Governing Board Authority Over Programs

– Contracts with Employees

– Pupils Who Reside in Other Districts/Counties

– COMMUNITY ADVISORY COMMITTEE

– Advisory Capacity Only

– CAC Appointments

– CAC Composition

pupils and adults with disabilities, regular education teachers, special education teachers and other school personnel, representatives of other public and private agencies, and persons concerned with the needs of individuals with exceptional needs.

56193. At least the majority of such committee shall be composed of parents of pupils enrolled in schools participating in the local plan, and at least a majority of such parents shall be parents of individuals with exceptional needs.

– Parent Majority

56194. The community advisory committee shall have the authority and fulfill the responsibilities that are defined for it in the local plan. The responsibilities shall include, but need not be limited to, all the following:

– CAC Responsibilities

(a) Advising the policy and administrative entity of the district, special education local plan area, or county office, regarding the development, amendment, and review of the local plan. The entity shall review and consider comments from the community advisory committee.

(b) Recommending annual priorities to be addressed by the plan.

(c) Assisting in parent education and in recruiting parents and other volunteers who may contribute to the implementation of the plan.

(d) Encouraging community involvement in the development and review of the local plan.

(e) Supporting activities on behalf of individuals with exceptional needs.

(f) Assisting in parent awareness of the importance of regular school attendance.

CHAPTER 3. ELEMENTS OF THE LOCAL PLAN

Article 1. State Requirements

56200. Each local plan submitted to the superintendent under this part shall contain all the following:

(a) Compliance assurances, including general compliance with the Individuals with Disabilities Education Act (20 U.S.C. Sec. 1400 et seq.), Section 504 of the Rehabilitation Act of 1973 (29 U.S.C. Sec. 794), and this part.

(b) A description of services to be provided by each district and county office. This description shall demonstrate that all individuals with exceptional needs shall have access to services and instruction appropriate to meet their needs as specified in their individualized education programs.

(c) (1) A description of the governance and administration of the plan.

(2) Multidistrict plans, submitted pursuant to subdivision (b) or (c) of Section 56170, shall specify the responsibilities of each participating county office and district governing board in the policymaking process, the responsibilities of the superintendents of each participating district and county in the implementation of the plan, and the responsibilities of district and county administrators of special education in coordinating the administration of the local plan.

(d) Copies of joint powers agreements or contractual agreements, as appropriate, for districts and counties that elect to enter into those agreements pursuant to subdivision (b) or (c) of Section 56170.

(e) An annual budget plan to allocate instructional personnel service units, support services, and transportation services directly to entities operating those services and to allocate regionalized services funds to the county office, responsible local agency, or other alternative administrative structure. The annual budget plan shall be adopted at a public hearing held by the district, special education local plan area, or county office, as appropriate. Notice of this hearing shall be posted in each school in the local plan area at least 15 days prior to the hearing. The annual budget plan may be revised during the fiscal year, and these revisions may be submitted to the superintendent as amendments to the allocations set forth in the plan. However, the revisions shall, prior to submission to the superintendent, be approved according to the policymaking process, established pursuant to paragraph (2) of subdivision (c).

(f) Verification that the plan has been reviewed by the community advisory committee and that the committee had at

– STATE REQUIREMENTS

– Compliance Assurances

– Description of Services

– Description of Governance Administration

– Policymaking Responsibilities

– Joint Powers/Contractual Agreements

– Annual Budget Plan

– CAC Review of Plan

least 30 days to conduct this review prior to submission of the plan to the superintendent.

    (g) A description of the identification, referral, assessment, instructional planning, implementation, and review in compliance with Chapter 4 (commencing with Section 56300).

- Description of Program Requirements

    (h) A description of the process being utilized to meet the requirements of Section 56303.

- Description of Process Utilized in Considering Regular Education Program

    (i) A description of the process being utilized to meet the requirements of the California Early Intervention Services Act, Title 14 (commencing with Section 95000) of the Government Code.

56201. As a part of the local plan submitted pursuant to Section 56200, each special education local plan area shall describe how specialized equipment and services will be distributed within the local plan area in a manner that minimizes the necessity to serve pupils in isolated sites and maximizes the opportunities to serve pupils in the least restrictive environments.

- Specialized Equipment and Services

Article 1.5. Special Education Local Plan Areas with Small or Sparse Populations

- SELPAS WITH SMALL OR SPARSE POPULATIONS

56210. (a) It is the intent of the Legislature in enacting this article to ensure that individuals with exceptional needs residing in special education local plan areas with small or sparse populations have equitable access to the programs and services they may require. It is further the intent of the Legislature to provide a guaranteed minimum level of authorized instructional personnel service units to special education local plan areas with small or sparse populations and the means through which these special education local plan areas may achieve planned orderly growth and maintenance of services through the local planning process. It is also the intent of the Legislature to relieve special education local plan areas with small or sparse populations from the burdensome dependency upon the annual waiver authority of Section 56728.6, 56728.8, and 56761 so that individuals with exceptional needs residing in those areas may have equitable access to required programs and services.

- Legislative Intents

    (b) It is the further intent of the Legislature in enacting this article that special education local plan areas with small or sparse populations be provided with supplemental funding to facilitate their ability to perform the regionalized service functions listed in Section 56780 and provide the direct instructional support of program specialists in accordance with Section 56368.

- Further Intent

56211. (a) A special education local plan area submitting a local plan, pursuant to subdivision (c) of Section 56170, which includes all of the school districts located in the county

- Request Designation

submitting the plan, except those participating in a countywide special education local plan area located in an adjacent county, and which meets the criteria for special education local plan areas with small or sparse populations set forth in Section 56212, is eligible to request that designation in its local plan application and may request exemption for the three-year period covered by its approved plan from compliance with one or more of the standards, ratios, and criteria specified in subdivision (b). In requesting the designation in its local plan application, the special education local plan area shall include a maintenance of service section, pursuant to Section 56213, in which it may request authorization to operate pursuant to the provisions of this article for the three-year period covered by its approved local plan. Each request shall specify which of the standards, ratios, proportions, and criteria would prevent the provision of a free appropriate public education or would create undue hardship.

(b) An eligible special education local plan area submitting a local plan application pursuant to this section may request exemption from the standards, ratios, and criteria set forth in Sections 56728.6, 56728.8 and 56760 pertaining to the authorization, recapture, retention, and operation of instructional personnel service units.

— Exemption Request

56212. An eligible special education local plan area, which submits a local plan under the provisions of Section 56211, may request designation as a small or sparsely populated special education local plan area in one of the following categories:

— Categories for Designation

(a) A necessary small special education local plan area in which the total enrollment in kindergarten and grades 1 to 12, inclusive, is less than 15,000, and which includes all of the school districts located in the county or counties participating in the local plan.

— Total Enrollment Less Than 15,000

(b) A sparsely populated special education local plan area in which the total enrollment in kindergarten and grades 1 to 12, inclusive, is less than 25,000, in which the combined pupil density ratio is not more than 20 pupils in those grades per square mile, and which includes all of the school districts located in the county submitting the plan except those that are participants in a countywide special education local plan area located in an adjacent county.

— Total Enrollment Less Than 25,000

(c) A special education local plan area with a sparsely populated county in which a special education local plan area includes all of the districts in two or more adjacent counties and in which at least one of the counties would have met the criteria set forth in subdivision (a) or (b) of this section if the districts and the county office of education had elected to submit a single county plan.

— Includes All Districts in Two or More Adjacent Countie

3-3

56213. (a) Each eligible special education local plan area that submits a local plan pursuant to Section 56211 and that elects exemptions from the standards, ratios, proportions, and criteria set forth in Sections 56728.6, 56728.8, and 56760 pertaining to the authorization, recapture, retention, and operation of instructional personnel service units shall, for the duration of its local plan, retain, as minimum annual authorization, the number of authorized instructional personnel service units, and portions thereof, that it reported as operated at the second principal apportionment of the fiscal year immediately preceding the initial year of implementation of the local plan submitted pursuant to this article.

— Retaining IPSUs

(b) In addition to the contents required to be included in the local plan pursuant to Section 56200, a local plan application submitted pursuant to this article shall include a maintenance of service section in which the eligible special education local plan area shall project the type and total number of additional instructional personnel service units, and portions thereof, it will require for each year of the duration of the local plan, the locations in which instructional personnel service units will be utilized, their estimated caseloads, and a description of the services to be provided.

— Maintenance of Service Section in Local Plan

56214. Each small or sparsely populated special education local plan area which anticipates that its service needs will require instructional personnel service units, or portions thereof, in excess of those authorized in its approved local plan may submit, prior to March 1 of any year, an amendment to the maintenance of service section of its local plan in which it may request an increase in its total number of authorized instructional personnel service units beginning in the following year. The amendment shall project the type and total number of additional instructional personnel service units, and portions thereof, the small or sparsely populated special education local plan area will require for each remaining year of the duration of the local plan, the locations in which additional instructional personnel service units will be utilized, their estimated caseloads, and a description of the services to be provided.

— Amendment to Maintenance of Service Section

56214.5. A special education local plan area which ceases meeting the criteria set forth in Sections 56211 and 56212 during any year in which the local plan area is implementing an approved local plan pursuant to this article shall retain the exemptions authorized pursuant to Section 56213 and the then current level of authorized instructional personnel service units for the following year.

— Retaining Exemptions and Authorized IPSUs

56217. Plans and amendments submitted pursuant to this article shall be approved by the State Board of Education prior

— State Board of Education Approval

to the implementation of those plans and amendments.

56218. Instructional personnel service units authorized pursuant to this article shall not increase the statewide total number of instructional personnel service units for the purposes of state apportionments unless an appropriation specifically for an increase in the number of instructional personnel service units is made in the annual Budget Act or other legislation. If an appropriation is made, instructional personnel service units authorized pursuant to this article shall be included in the increased number of units and shall be funded only by the appropriation and no other funds may be apportioned for them.

- IPSUs and State Apportionment

Article 2. Local Requirements

- LOCAL REQUIREMENTS

56220. In addition to the provisions required to be included in the local plan pursuant to Section 56200, each special education local plan area that submits a local plan pursuant to subdivision (b) of Section 56170 and each county office that submits a local plan pursuant to subdivision (c) of Section 56170 shall develop written agreements to be entered into by entities participating in the plan. The agreements need not be submitted to the superintendent. These agreements shall include, but not be limited to, the following:

- Written Agreements

(a) A coordinated identification, referral, and placement system pursuant to Chapter 4 (commencing with Section 56300).

- Coordinated IRP System

(b) Procedural safeguards pursuant to Chapter 5 (commencing with Section 56500).

- Procedural Safeguards

(c) Regionalized services to local programs, including, but not limited to, all the following:

- Regionalized Services

(1) Program specialist service pursuant to Section 56368.

(2) Personnel development, including training for staff, parents, and members of the community advisory committee pursuant to Article 3 (commencing with Section 56240).

(3) Evaluation pursuant to Chapter 6 (commencing with Section 56600).

(4) Data collection and development of management information systems.

(5) Curriculum development.

(6) Provision for ongoing review of programs conducted, and procedures utilized, under the local plan, and a mechanism for correcting any identified problem.

(d) A description of the process for coordinating services with other local public agencies that are funded to serve individuals with exceptional needs.

- Coordination with Local Public Agencies

(e) A description of the process for coordinating and providing services to individuals with exceptional needs placed in public

- Public/Proprietary Hospitals

hospitals, proprietary hospitals, and other residential medical facilities pursuant to Article 5.5 (commencing with Section 56167) of Chapter 2.

 (f) A description of the process for coordinating and providing services to individuals with exceptional needs placed in licensed children's institutions and foster family homes pursuant to Article 5 (commencing with Section 56155) of Chapter 2.

– Licensed Children's Institutions/Foster Family Homes

 (g) A description of the process for coordinating and providing services to individuals with exceptional needs placed in juvenile court schools or county community schools pursuant to Section 56150.

– Juvenile Court Schools/ County Community Schools

 56221. (a) Each entity providing special education under this part shall adopt policies for the programs and services it operates, consistent with agreements adopted pursuant to subdivision (b) or (c) of Section 56170, or Section 56220. The policies need not be submitted to the superintendent.

– Adopt Policies

 (b) The policies shall include, but not be limited to, all of the following:

 (1) Nonpublic, nonsectarian services, including those provided pursuant to Sections 56365 and 56366.

– Nonpublic Services

 (2) Review, at a regular education or special education teacher's request, of the assignment of an individual with exceptional needs to his or her class and a mandatory meeting of the individualized education program team if the review indicates a change in the pupil's placement, instruction, related services, or any combination thereof. The procedures shall indicate which personnel are responsible for the reviews and a timetable for completion of the review.

– Review of Class Assignment at Teacher's Request

 (3) Procedural safeguards pursuant to Chapter 5 (commencing with Section 56500).

– Procedural Safeguards

 (4) Resource specialists pursuant to Section 56362.

– Resource Specialists

 (5) Transportation, where appropriate, which describes how special education transportation is coordinated with regular home-to-school transportation. The policy shall set forth criteria for meeting the transportation needs of special education pupils. The policy shall include procedures to ensure compatibility between mobile seating devices, when used, and the securement systems required by Federal Motor Vehicle Safety Standard No. 222 (49 C.F.R. 571.222) and to ensure that schoolbus drivers are trained in the proper installation of mobile seating devices in the securement systems.

– Transportation*

 (6) Caseloads pursuant to Chapter 4.45 (commencing with Section 56440) of Part 30. The policies, with respect to caseloads, shall not be developed until guidelines or proposed regulations are issued pursuant to Section 56441.7. The guidelines or proposed regulations shall be considered when

– Caseloads

*(Section 56221 Amended in 1994)

developing the caseload policy. A statement of justification shall be attached if the local caseload policy exceeds state guidelines or proposed regulations.

(c) The policies may include, but are not limited to, provisions for involvement of district and county governing board members in any due process hearing procedure activities conducted pursuant to, and consistent with, state and federal law.

- Governing Board Members/
  Due Process Hearing
  Procedures

56222. The plan for special education shall be developed and updated cooperatively by a committee of representatives of special and regular teachers and administrators selected by the groups they represent and with input from the community advisory committee to ensure adequate and effective participation and communication.

Article 3. Staff Development

- STAFF DEVELOPMENT

56240. Staff development programs shall be provided for regular and special education teachers, administrators, certificated and classified employees, volunteers, community advisory committee members and, as appropriate, members of the district and county governing boards. The programs shall be coordinated with other staff development programs in the district, special education local plan area, or county office, including school level staff development programs authorized by state and federal law.

- Participants

56241. Staff development programs shall include, but not be limited to, all the following:

(a) Provision of opportunities for all school personnel, paraprofessionals, and volunteers to participate in ongoing development activities pursuant to a systematic identification of pupil and personnel needs.

- Opportunities

(b) Be designed and implemented by classroom teachers and other participating school personnel, including the school principal. Teachers shall comprise the majority of any group designated to design local staff development programs for instructional personnel to be established pursuant to this part. Positive efforts shall be made to ensure the individuals with exceptional needs and parents of such individuals are involved in the design and implementation of staff development programs.

- Design and Implementation

(c) Allowance for diversity in development activities, including, but not limited to, small groups, self-directed learning, and systematic observation during visits to other classrooms or schools.

- Diversity in Development

(d) Scheduling of time which is set aside for such purpose throughout the school year, including, but not limited to, time when participating school personnel are released from their regular duties.

- Scheduling

(e) Evaluation and modification on a continuing basis by participating school personnel with the aid of outside personnel, as necessary.

– Evaluation/Modification

(f) Inclusion of the school principal and other administrative personnel as active participants in one or more staff development activities implemented pursuant to this chapter.

– Administrators

(g) Provision of a budget for reasonable and necessary expenses, relating to staff development programs.

– Expense Budget

56242. (a) A district, special education local plan area, or county office, shall receive its full average daily attendance apportionment during the regular school year to conduct staff development programs pursuant to this article. Except as provided in subdivision (b), the time shall not exceed two days each year for each participating staff member. However, no district, special education local plan area, or county office shall receive average daily attendance reimbursement under this section if it is reimbursed pursuant to Chapter 1147 of the Statutes of 1972, Chapter 3.1 (commencing with Section 44670) of Part 25, or Chapter 6 (commencing with Section 52000) of Part 28.

– ADA Reimbursement

(b) Whenever a school operates a school-based coordinated program pursuant to Chapter 12 (commencing with Section 52800 of Part 28 and that program includes special education programs and services, staff members teaching in special classes and centers may receive the same number of staff development days as other staff members are receiving at that schoolsite.

– Number of Staff Development Days

56243. It is the intent of the Legislature, pursuant to this article, that each district, special education local plan area, and county office provide regular classroom teachers serving individuals with exceptional needs appropriate training each year relating to the needs of those individuals.

– Regular Classroom Teachers

56244. The superintendent shall, to the extent possible using federal and state funds appropriated for this purpose, provide staff development to child care center staff and family day care providers to improve child care services to individuals with exceptional needs.

– Staff Development to Improve Child Care Services

56245. The Legislature encourages the inclusion, in local in-service training programs for regular education teachers and special education teachers in school districts, special education local plan areas, and county offices of education, of a component on the recognition of, and teaching strategies for, specific learning disabilities, including dyslexia and related disorders.

– In-Service Training Regarding Specific Learning Disabilities Including Dyslexia

CHAPTER 4. IDENTIFICATION AND REFERRAL, ASSESSMENT, INSTRUCTIONAL PLANNING, IMPLEMENTATION, AND REVIEW

Article 1. Identification and Referral

56300. Each district, special education local plan area, or county office shall actively and systematically seek out all individuals with exceptional needs, ages 0 through 21 years, including children not enrolled in public school programs, who reside in the district or are under the jurisdiction of a special education local plan area or a county office.

– Systematically Seek Out

56301. Each district, special education local plan area, or county office shall establish written policies and procedures for a continuous child-find system which addresses the relationships among identification, screening, referral, assessment, planning, implementation, review, and the triennial assessment. The policies and procedures shall include, but need not be limited to, written notification of all parents of their rights under this chapter, and the procedure for initiating a referral for assessment to identify individuals with exceptional needs.

– Continuous Child-Find

56302. Each district, special education local plan area, or county office shall provide for the identification and assessment of an individual's exceptional needs, and the planning of an instructional program to meet the assessed needs. Identification procedures shall include systematic methods of utilizing referrals of pupils from teachers, parents, agencies, appropriate professional persons, and from other members of the public. Identification procedures shall be coordinated with school site procedures for referral of pupils with needs that cannot be met with modification of the regular instructional program.

– Identification Procedures

56303. A pupil shall be referred for special educational instruction and services only after the resources of the regular education program have been considered and, where appropriate, utilized.

– Consider Regular Education Program Resources

Article 2. Assessment

– ASSESSMENT

56320. Before any action is taken with respect to the initial placement of an individual with exceptional needs in special education instruction, an individual assessment of the pupil's educational needs shall be conducted, by qualified persons, in accordance with requirements including, but not limited to, all the following:

– Individual Assessment Conducted by Qualified Persons

(a) Testing and assessment materials and procedures used for the purposes of assessment and placement of individuals with exceptional needs are selected and administered so as not to be racially, culturally, or sexually discriminatory.

— Testing/Assessment Materials

(b) Tests and other assessment materials meet all the following requirements:

(1) Are provided and administered in the pupil's primary language or other mode of communication, unless the assessment plan indicates reasons why such provision and administration are not clearly feasible.

— Provided in Primary Language

(2) Have been validated for the specific purpose for which they are used.

— Validated for Specific Purpose

(3) Are administered by trained personnel in conformance with the instructions provided by the producer of such tests and other assessment materials, except that individually administered tests of intellectual or emotional functioning shall be administered by a psychometrist or credentialed school psychologist where available. It is not the intent of the Legislature to require that new personnel be hired for this purpose.

— Administered by Trained Personnel

(c) Tests and other assessment materials include those tailored to assess specific areas of educational need and not merely those which are designed to provide a single general intelligence quotient.

— Specific Areas

(d) Tests are selected and administered to best ensure that when a test administered to a pupil with impaired sensory, manual, or speaking skills produces test results that accurately reflect the pupil's aptitude, achievement level, or any other factors the test purports to measure and not the pupil's impaired sensory, manual, or speaking skills unless those skills are the factors the test purports to measure.

— Accurate Test Results

(e) No single procedure is used as the sole criterion for determining an appropriate educational program for an individual with exceptional needs.

— No Single Procedure Used

(f) The pupil is assessed in all areas related to the suspected disability including, where appropriate, health and development, vision, including low vision, hearing, motor abilities, language function, general ability, academic performance, self-help, orientation and mobility skills, career and vocational abilities and interests, and social and emotional status. A developmental history is obtained, when appropriate. For pupils with residual vision, a low vision assessment shall be provided in accordance with guidelines established pursuant to Section 56136.

— Assessed in All Areas

— Low Vision Assessment

(g) The assessment of a pupil, including the assessment of a pupil with a suspected low incidence disability, shall be conducted by persons knowledgeable of that disability. Special attention shall be given to the unique educational needs,

— Assessment Conducted by Persons Knowledgeable of Disability

— Unique Educational Needs

including, but not limited to, skills and the need for specialized services, materials, and equipment consistent with guidelines established pursuant to Section 56136.

56320.1. All identification, evaluation, and assessment procedures for individuals with exceptional needs who are younger than three years of age shall be provided pursuant to Chapter 4.4 (commencing with Section 56425) and the California Early Intervention Services Act, Title 14 (commencing with Section 95000) of the Government Code.

– Identification, Evaluation and Assessment Procedures for Infants

56321. (a) Whenever an assessment for the development or revision of the individualized education program is to be conducted, the parent of the pupil shall be given, in writing, a proposed assessment plan within 15 days of the referral for assessment not counting days between the pupil's regular school sessions or terms or days of school vacation in excess of five schooldays from the date of receipt of the referral, unless the parent agrees, in writing, to an extension. However, in any event, the assessment plan shall be developed within 10 days after the commencement of the subsequent regular school year or the pupil's regular school term as determined by each district's school calendar for each pupil for whom a referral has been made 10 days or less prior to the end of the regular school year. In the case of pupil school vacations, the 15-day time shall recommence on the date that the pupil's regular schooldays reconvene. A copy of the notice of parent rights shall be attached to the assessment plan. A written explanation of all the procedural safeguards under the Individuals with Disabilities Education Act (20 U.S.C. Sec. 1400 and following), and the rights and procedures contained in Chapter 5 (commencing with Section 56500), shall be included in the notice of parent rights, including information on the procedures for requesting an informal meeting, prehearing mediation conference, mediation conference, or due process hearing; the timelines for completing each process; whether the process is optional; and the type of representative who may be invited to participate.

– Proposed Assessment Plan

– Notice of Parent Rights

(b) The proposed assessment plan given to parents shall meet all the following requirements:

– Requirements

(1) Be in language easily understood by the general public.

(2) Be provided in the primary language of the parent or other mode of communication used by the parent, unless to do so is clearly not feasible.

(3) Explain the types of assessments to be conducted.

(4) State that no individualized education program will result from the assessment without the consent of the parent.

(c) No assessment shall be conducted unless the written consent of the parent is obtained prior to the assessment except

– Written Consent of Parent

pursuant to subdivision (e) of Section 56506. The parent shall have at least 15 days from the receipt of the proposed assessment plan to arrive at a decision. Assessment may begin immediately upon receipt of the consent.

56321.5. The copy of the notice of parent rights shall include the right to electronically record the proceedings of individualized education program meetings as specified in Section 56341.

56322. The assessment shall be conducted by persons competent to perform the assessment, as determined by the school district, county office, or special education local plan area.

56323. Admission of a pupil to special education instruction shall be made only in accordance with this article, Article 2.5 (commencing with Section 56333) and standards established by the board and upon a recommendation by the individualized education program team.

56324. (a) Any psychological assessment of pupils shall be made in accordance with Section 56320 and shall be conducted by a credentialed school psychologist who is trained and prepared to assess cultural and ethnic factors appropriate to the pupil being assessed.

(b) Any health assessment of pupils shall be made in accordance with Section 56320 and shall be conducted by a credentialed school nurse or physician who is trained and prepared to assess cultural and ethnic factors appropriate to the pupil being assessed.

56325. (a) Whenever a pupil transfers into a school district from a school district not operating programs under the same local plan in which he or she was last enrolled in a special education program, the administrator of a local program under this part shall ensure that the pupil is immediately provided an interim placement for a period not to exceed 30 days. The interim placement must be in conformity with an individualized education program, unless the parent or guardian agrees otherwise. The individualized education program implemented during the interim placement may be either the pupil's existing individualized education program, implemented to the extent possible within existing resources, which may be implemented without complying with subdivision (a) of Section 56321, or a new individualized education program, developed pursuant to Section 56321.

(b) Before the expiration of the 30-day period, the interim placement shall be reviewed by the individualized education program team and a final recommendation shall be made by the team in accordance with the requirements of this chapter. The team may utilize information, records, and reports from the

- Right to Electronically Record IEP Proceedings

- Assessment Conducted by Competent Persons

- Admission to Special Education

- Psychological Assessment

- Health Assessment

- Pupil Transfers

- Interim Placement Not to Exceed 30 Days and Must Be in Conformity with an IEP, as Specified

- IEP Team Review/Final Recommendation

school district or county program from which the pupil transferred.

56326. A pupil may be referred, as appropriate, for further assessment and recommendations to the California Schools for the Deaf or Blind or the Diagnostic Centers.

– Assessment Referral to State Schools

56327. The personnel who assess the pupil shall prepare a written report, or reports, as appropriate, of the results of each assessment. The report shall include, but not be limited to, all the following:

– Written Assessment Report

(a) Whether the pupil may need special education and related services.

(b) The basis for making the determination.

(c) The relevant behavior noted during the observation of the pupil in an appropriate setting.

(d) The relationship of that behavior to the pupil's academic and social functioning.

(e) The educationally relevant health and development, and medical findings, if any.

(f) For pupils with learning disabilities whether there is such a discrepancy between achievement and ability that it cannot be corrected without special education and related services.

(g) A determination concerning the effects of environmental, cultural, or economic disadvantage, where appropriate.

(h) The need for specialized services, materials, and equipment for pupils with low incidence disabilities, consistent with guidelines established pursuant to Section 56136.

56328. Notwithstanding the provisions of this chapter, a district, special education local plan area, or county office may utilize a school site level and a regional level service, as provided for under Section 56336.2 as it read immediately prior to the operative date of this section, to provide the services required by this chapter.

– School Site/Regional Level Assessment Options

56329. The parent of the pupil shall be provided with written notice that he or she may obtain, upon request, a copy of the findings of the assessment or assessments conducted pursuant to Section 56321. This notice may be provided as part of the assessment plan given to parents pursuant to Section 56321. The notice shall include all the following:

– Written Notice Provided to Parent

(a) An individualized education program team conference, including the parent and his or her representatives, shall be scheduled, pursuant to Section 56341, to discuss the assessment, the educational recommendations, and the reasons for these recommendations.

– IEP Team Conference

(b) A parent has the right to obtain, at public expense, an independent educational assessment of the pupil from qualified specialists, as defined by regulations of the board, if the parent

– Independent Educational Assessment

disagrees with an assessment obtained by the public education agency.

However, the public education agency may initiate a due process hearing pursuant to Chapter 5 (commencing with Section 56500) to show that its assessment is appropriate. If the final decision resulting from the due process hearing is that the assessment is appropriate, the parent still has the right for an independent educational assessment, but not at public expense.

— Due Process Hearing on Assessment

If the parent obtains an independent educational assessment at private expense, the results of the assessment shall be considered by the public education agency with respect to the provision of free, appropriate public education to the child, and may be presented as evidence at a due process hearing pursuant to Chapter 5 (commencing with Section 56500) regarding such child.

— Results of Independent Assessment

Article 2.5. Eligibility Criteria for Special Education and Related Services on the Basis of Language and Speech Disorder or Specific Learning Disabilities

— ELIGIBILITY CRITERIA

56333. A pupil shall be assessed as having a language or speech disorder which makes him or her eligible for special education and related services when he or she demonstrates difficulty understanding or using spoken language to such an extent that it adversely affects his or her educational performance and cannot be corrected without special education and related services. In order to be eligible for special education and related services, difficulty in understanding or using spoken language shall be assessed by a language, speech, and hearing specialist who determines that such difficulty results from any of the following disorders:

— Language/Speech Disorder Eligibility Criteria

(a) Articulation disorders, such that the pupil's production of speech significantly interferes with communication and attracts adverse attention.

(b) Abnormal voice, characterized by persistent, defective voice quality, pitch, or loudness. An appropriate medical examination shall be conducted, where appropriate.

(c) Fluency difficulties which result in an abnormal flow of verbal expression to such a degree that these difficulties adversely affect communication between the pupil and listener.

(d) Inappropriate or inadequate acquisition, comprehension, or expression of spoken language such that the pupil's language performance level is found to be significantly below the language performance level of his or her peers.

(e) Hearing loss which results in a language or speech disorder and significantly affects educational performance.

56337. A pupil shall be assessed as having a specific learning disability which makes him or her eligible for special education and related services when it is determined that all of the following exist:

(a) A severe discrepancy exists between the intellectual ability and achievements in one or more of the following academic areas:

(1) Oral expression.

(2) Listening comprehension.

(3) Written expression.

(4) Basic reading skills.

(5) Reading comprehension.

(6) Mathematics calculation.

(7) Mathematics reasoning.

(b) The discrepancy is due to a disorder in one or more of the basic psychological processes and is not the result of environmental, cultural, or economic disadvantages.

(c) The discrepancy cannot be corrected through other regular or categorical services offered within the regular instructional program.

56337.5. (a) A pupil who is assessed as being dyslexic and meets eligibility criteria specified in Section 56337 and subdivision (j) of Section 3030 of Title 5 of the California Code of Regulations for the federal Individuals with Disabilities Education Act (20 U.S.C. Sec. 1400 and following) category of specific learning disabilities is entitled to special education and related services.

(b) If a pupil who exhibits the characteristics of dyslexia or another related reading dysfunction is not found to be eligible for special education and related services pursuant to subdivision (a), the pupil's instructional program shall be provided in the regular education program.

(c) It is the intent of the Legislature that the program guidelines developed pursuant to Section 2 of Chapter 1501 of the Statutes of 1990, for specific learning disabilities, including dyslexia and other related disorders, be available for use by teachers and parents in order for them to have knowledge of the strategies that can be utilized with pupils for the remediation of the various types of specific learning disabilities.

56338. As used in Section 56337, "specific learning disability" includes, but is not limited to, disability within the function of vision which results in visual perceptual or visual motor dysfunction.

Marginal notes:
- Specific Learning Disability Eligibility Criteria
- Assessed as Being Dyslexic
- Regular Education Responsibility
- Program Guidelines
- Visual Perceptual/Visual Motor Dysfunction

Article 2.6. Attention Deficit and Hyperactivity Disorders

56339. (a) A pupil whose educational performance is adversely affected by a suspected or diagnosed attention deficit disorder or attention deficit hyperactivity disorder and demonstrates a need for special education and related services by meeting eligibility criteria specified in subdivision (f) or (i) of Section 3030 of Title 5 of the California Code of Regulations or Section 56337 and subdivision (j) of Section 3030 of Title 5 of the California Code of Regulations for the federal Individuals with Disabilities Education Act (20 U.S.C. Sec. 1400 and following) categories of "other health impairments," "serious emotional disturbance," or "specific learning disabilities," is entitled to special education and related services.

(b) If a pupil with an attention deficit disorder or attention deficit hyperactivity disorder is not found to be eligible for special education and related services pursuant to subdivision (a), the pupil's instructional program shall be provided in the regular education program.

(c) It is the intent of the Legislature that local educational agencies promote coordination between special education and regular education programs to ensure that all pupils, including those with attention deficit disorders or attention deficit hyperactivity disorders, receive appropriate instructional interventions.

(d) It is further the intent of the Legislature that regular education teachers and other personnel be trained to develop an awareness about attention deficit disorders and attention deficit hyperactivity disorders and the manifestations of those disorders, and the adaptations that can be implemented in regular education programs to address the instructional needs of pupils having these disorders.

Article 3. Instructional Planning and Individualized Education Program

56340. Each district, special education local plan area, or county office shall initiate and conduct meetings for the purposes of developing, reviewing, and revising the individualized education program of each individual with exceptional needs.

56340.1. All instructional planning procedures for individuals with exceptional needs who are younger than three years of age shall be provided pursuant to Chapter 4.4 (commencing with Section 56425) and the California Early Intervention Services

Act, Title 14 (commencing with Section 95000) of the Government Code.

56341. (a) Each meeting to develop, review, or revise the individualized education program of an individual with exceptional needs, shall be conducted by an individualized education program team.

    – IEP Team

(b) The individualized education program team shall include all of the following:

    – IEP Team Members

(1) A representative other than the pupil's teacher designated by administration who may be an administrator, program specialist, or other specialist who is knowledgeable of program options appropriate for the pupil and who is qualified to provide, or supervise the provision of, special education.

(2) The pupil's present teacher. If the pupil does not presently have a teacher, this representative shall be the teacher with the most recent and complete knowledge of the pupil who has also observed the pupil's educational performance in an appropriate setting. If no teacher is available, this representative shall be a regular classroom teacher referring the pupil, or a special education teacher qualified to teach a pupil of his or her age.

(3) One or both of the pupil's parents, a representative selected by the parent, or both, pursuant to the Individuals with Disabilities Education Act (20 U.S.C. Sec. 1400 et seq.).

(c) When appropriate, the team shall also include the following persons:

    – Other Team Members

(1) The individual with exceptional needs.

(2) Other individuals, at the discretion of the parent, district, special education local plan area, or county office who possess expertise or knowledge necessary for the development of the individualized education program.

(d) If the team is developing, reviewing, or revising the individualized education program of an individual with exceptional needs who has been assessed for the purpose of that individualized education program, the district, special education local plan area, or county office, shall ensure that a person is present at the meeting who has conducted an assessment of the pupil or who is knowledgeable about the assessment procedures used to assess the pupil and is familiar with the results of the assessment. The person shall be qualified to interpret the results if the results or recommendations, based on the assessment, are significant to the development of the pupil's individualized education program and subsequent placement.

    – Assessment Person Present at Meeting

(e) For pupils with suspected learning disabilities, at least one member of the individualized education program team, other than the pupil's regular teacher, shall be a person who has

    – Observation of Educational Performance

observed the pupil's educational performance in an appropriate setting. If the child is younger than five years or is not enrolled in a school, a team member shall observe the child in an environment appropriate for a child of that age.

(f) The parent shall have the right to present information to the individualized education program team in person or through a representative and the right to participate in meetings relating to eligibility for special education and related services, recommendations, and program planning.

- Right of Parent to Present Information

(g) (1) Notwithstanding Section 632 of the Penal Code, the parent, district, special education local plan area, or county office shall have the right to electronically record the proceedings of individualized education program meetings on an audio tape recorder. The parent, district, special education local plan area, or county office shall notify the members of the individualized education program team of their intent to record a meeting at least 24 hours prior to the meeting. If the district, special education local plan area, or county office initiates the notice of intent to audio tape record a meeting and the parent objects or refuses to attend the meeting because it will be tape recorded, then the meeting shall not be recorded on an audio tape recorder.

- Right to Electronically Audio Tape Record IEP Meetings

(2) The Legislature hereby finds as follows:

(A) Under federal law, audio tape recordings made by a district, special education local plan area, or county office are subject to the federal Family Educational Rights and Privacy Act of 1974 (20 U.S.C. Sec. 1232g).

(B) Parents have the right, pursuant to Sections 99.10 to 99.22, inclusive, of Title 34 of the Code of Federal Regulations, to (i) inspect and review the tape recordings, (ii) request that the tape recordings be amended if the parent believes that they contain information that is inaccurate, misleading, or in violation of the rights of privacy or other rights of the individual with exceptional needs, and (iii) challenge, in a hearing, information that the parent believes is inaccurate, misleading, or in violation of individual's rights of privacy or other rights.

(h) It is the intent of the Legislature that the individualized education program team meetings be nonadversarial and convened solely for the purpose of making educational decisions for the good of the individual with exceptional needs.

- Nonadversarial IEP Meetings

56342. The individualized education program team shall review the assessment results, determine eligibility, determine the content of the individualized education program, consider local transportation policies and criteria developed pursuant to

- IEP Team Responsibilities

paragraph (5) of subdivision (b) of Section 56221, and make program placement recommendations.

Prior to recommending a new placement in a nonpublic, nonsectarian school, the individualized education program team shall submit the proposed recommendation to the local governing board of the district, special education local plan area, or county office for its review and recommendation regarding the cost of such placement.

– Local Governing Board Reviews Nonpublic School Recommendations

The local governing board shall complete its review and make its recommendations, if any, at the next regular meeting of the board. A parent or representative shall have the right to appear before the board and submit written and oral evidence regarding the need for nonpublic school placement for his or her child. Any recommendations of the board shall be considered at an individualized education program team meeting, to be held within five days of the board's review.

– Right of Parent to Appear Before Board

Notwithstanding Section 56344, the time limit for the development of an individualized education program shall be waived for a period not to exceed 15 additional days to permit the local governing board to meet its review and recommendation requirements.

– IEP Development Time Waiver

56343. An individualized education program team shall meet whenever any of the following occurs:

– IEP Team Meetings Required

(a) A pupil has received an initial formal assessment. The team may meet when a pupil receives any subsequent formal assessment.

(b) The pupil demonstrates a lack of anticipated progress.

(c) The parent or teacher requests a meeting to develop, review, or revise the individualized education program.

(d) At least annually, to review the pupil's progress, the individualized education program, and the appropriateness of placement, and to make any necessary revisions. The individualized education program team conducting the annual review shall consist of those persons specified in subdivision (b) of Section 56341. Other individuals may participate in the annual review if they possess expertise or knowledge essential for the review.

56343.5. A meeting of an individualized education program team requested by a parent to review an individualized education program pursuant to subdivision (c) of Section 56343 shall be held within 30 days, not counting days in July and August, from the date of receipt of the parent's written request. If a parent makes an oral request, the school district shall notify the parent of the need for a written request and the procedure for filing a written request.

– Parent Request for IEP Review

56344. An individualized education program required as a result of an assessment of a pupil shall be developed within a total time not to exceed 50 days, not counting days between the pupil's regular school sessions, terms, or days of school vacation in excess of five schooldays, from the date of receipt of the parent's written consent for assessment, unless the parent agrees, in writing, to an extension. However, such an individualized education program shall be developed within 30 days after the commencement of the subsequent regular school year as determined by each district's school calendar for each pupil for whom a referral has been made 20 days or less prior to the end of the regular school year. In the case of pupil school vacations, the 50-day time shall recommence on the date that pupil schooldays reconvene.

56345. (a) The individualized education program is a written statement determined in a meeting of the individualized education program team and shall include, but not be limited to, all of the following:

(1) The present levels of the pupil's educational performance.

(2) The annual goals, including short-term instructional objectives.

(3) The specific special educational instruction and related services required by the pupil.

(4) The extent to which the pupil will be able to participate in regular educational programs.

(5) The projected date for initiation and the anticipated duration of the programs and services included in the individualized education program.

(6) Appropriate objective criteria, evaluation procedures, and schedules for determining, on at least an annual basis, whether the short-term instructional objectives are being achieved.

(b) When appropriate, the individualized education program shall also include, but not be limited to, all of the following:

(1) Prevocational career education for pupils in kindergarten and grades 1 to 6, inclusive, or pupils of comparable chronological age.

(2) Vocational education, career education or work experience education, or any combination thereof, in preparation for remunerative employment, including independent living skill training for pupils in grades 7 to 12, inclusive, or comparable chronological age, who require differential proficiency standards pursuant to Section 51215.

(3) For pupils in grades 7 to 12, inclusive, any alternative means and modes necessary for the pupil to complete the district's prescribed course of study and to meet or exceed

- IEP Development Timeline

- IEP Contents*

- Appropriate Additional
  IEP Content

- Prevocational Career
  Education

- Vocational Education/
  Career Development

- Prescribed Course of
  Study

*(Section 56345 Amended in 1994)

proficiency standards for graduation in accordance with Section 51215.

(4) For individuals whose primary language is other than English, linguistically appropriate goals, objectives, programs and services.

(5) Extended school year services when needed, as determined by the individualized education program team.

(6) Provision for the transition into the regular class program if the pupil is to be transferred from a special class or center, or nonpublic, nonsectarian school into a regular class in a public school for any part of the schoolday, including the following:

(A) A description of activities provided to integrate the pupil into the regular education program. The description shall indicate the nature of each activity, and the time spent on the activity each day or week.

(B) A description of the activities provided to support the transition of pupils from the special education program into the regular education program.

(7) For pupils with low-incidence disabilities, specialized services, materials, and equipment, consistent with guidelines established pursuant to Section 56136.

(c) It is the intent of the Legislature in requiring individualized education programs that the district, special education local plan area, or county office is responsible for providing the services delineated in the individualized education program. However, the Legislature recognizes that some pupils may not meet or exceed the growth projected in the annual goals and objectives of the pupil's individualized education program.

(d) Pursuant to subdivision (d) of Section 51215, a pupil's individualized education program shall also include the determination of the individualized education program team as to whether differential proficiency standards shall be developed for the pupil. If differential proficiency standards are to be developed, the individualized education program shall include these standards.

(e) Consistent with Section 56000.5, it is the intent of the Legislature that, in making a determination of what constitutes an appropriate education to meet the unique needs of a deaf or hard-of-hearing pupil in the least restrictive environment, the individualized education program team shall consider the related services and program options that provide the pupil with an equal opportunity for communication access. The individualized education program team shall specifically discuss the communication needs of the pupil, consistent with the

- Linguistic Goals

- Extended School Year Services

- Transition into Regular Program

- Specialized Services, Materials, and Equipment

- Responsibility for Providing Services

- Differential Proficiency Standards

- Communication Access for Deaf and Hard-of-Hearing Pupils

guidelines adopted pursuant to Section 56136 and Page 49274 of Volume 57 of the Federal Register, including all the following:

(1) The pupil's primary language mode and language, which may include the use of spoken language with or without visual cues, or the use of sign language, or a combination of both.

(2) The availability of a sufficient number of age, cognitive, and language peers of similar abilities which may be met by consolidating services into a local plan areawide program or providing placement pursuant to Section 56361.

(3) Appropriate, direct, and ongoing language access to special education teachers and other specialists who are proficient in the pupil's primary language mode and language consistent with existing law regarding teacher training requirements.

(4) Services necessary to ensure communication-accessible academic instructions, school services, and extracurricular activities consistent with the Vocational Rehabilitation Act of 1973 as set forth in Section 794 of Title 29 of the United States Code and the Americans with Disabilities Act of 1990 as set forth in Section 12000 and following of Title 42 of the United States Code.

(f) No General Fund money made available to school districts or local agencies may be used for any additional responsibilities and services associated with paragraphs (1) and (2) of subdivision (e), including the training of special education teachers and other specialists, even if those additional responsibilities or services are required pursuant to a judicial or state agency determination. Those responsibilities and services shall only be funded by a local educational agency as follows:

— Restrictions on the Use of Funds

(1) The costs of those activities shall be funded from existing programs and funding sources.

(2) Those activities shall be supported by the resources otherwise made available to those programs.

(3) Those activities shall be consistent with the provisions of Sections 56240 to 56243, inclusive.

(g) It is the intent of the Legislature that the communication skills of teachers who work with hard-of-hearing and deaf children be improved, however, nothing in this section shall be construed to remove the local educational agency's discretionary authority in regard to in-service activities.

— Communication Skills of Teachers of Hearing Impaired

56345.1. A statement of needed transition services, pursuant to paragraphs (19) and (20) of subsection (a) of Section 1401 of Title 20 of the United States Code, shall be included in the pupil's individualized education program beginning not later than age 16 years and annually thereafter, or when determined

— Statement of Needed Transition Services

appropriate for the pupil, beginning at age 14 years or younger. In addition, the program shall include, when appropriate, a statement of the interagency responsibilities or linkages, or both, before the pupil leaves the school setting.

56345.5. Except as prescribed in subdivision (b) of Section 56324, nothing in this part shall be construed to authorize districts, special education local plan areas, or county offices to prescribe health care services.

– Health Care Services Exclusion

56346. (a) No pupil shall be required to participate in all or part of any special education program unless the parent is first informed, in writing, of the facts that make participation in the program necessary or desirable, and of the contents of the individualized education program, and after this notice, consents, in writing, to all or part of the individualized education program. If the parent does not consent to all the components of the individualized education program, then those components of the program to which the parent has consented shall be implemented so as not to delay providing instruction and services to the pupil.

– Parent Written Consent* for IEP Contents

(b) If the district, special education local plan area, or county office determines that the part of the proposed special education program to which the parent does not consent is necessary to provide a free and appropriate public education to the pupil, a due process hearing shall be initiated pursuant to Chapter 5 (commencing with Section 56500), unless a prehearing mediation conference is held. During the pendency of the due process hearing, the district, special education local plan area, or county office may reconsider the proposed individualized education program, may choose to meet informally with the parent pursuant to subdivision (b) of Section 56502, or may hold a mediation conference pursuant to Section 56503. As an alternative to holding a due process hearing, the parties may hold a prehearing mediation conference pursuant to Section 56500.3 to resolve any issue or dispute. If a due process hearing is held, the hearing decision shall be the final administrative determination and shall be binding upon the parties. While a prehearing mediation conference or due process hearing is pending, the pupil shall remain in his or her then-current placement unless the parent and the district, special education local plan area, or county office agree otherwise.

– If Parent Does Not Consent

56347. Each district, special education local plan area, or county office shall, prior to the placement of the individual with exceptional needs, ensure that the regular teacher or teachers, the special education teacher or teachers, and other persons who provide special education, related services, or both to the individual with exceptional needs shall be knowledgeable of the

– Be Knowledgeable of Content

*(Section 56346 Amended in 1994)

content of the individualized education program. A copy of each individualized education program shall be maintained at each school site where the pupil is enrolled. Service providers from other agencies who provide instruction or a related service to the individual off the school site shall be provided a copy of the individualized education program. All individualized education programs shall be maintained in accordance with state and federal pupil record confidentiality laws.

Article 3.5. Individualized Education Program for Visually Impaired Pupils

- IEP FOR VISUALLY*
  IMPAIRED PUPILS

56350. Unless the context otherwise requires, the definitions set forth in this section shall govern the construction of this article.

- Definitions

(a) A "functionally blind pupil" means a pupil who relies basically on senses other than vision as major channels for learning.

- Functionally Blind Pupil

(b) A "pupil with low vision" means a pupil who uses vision as a channel for learning, but who may also benefit from instruction in braille.

- Pupil with Low Vision

(c) A "visually impaired pupil" means a pupil who is functionally blind or a pupil with low vision.

- Visually Impaired Pupil

(d) "Braille" means the system of reading and writing through touch commonly known as "Standard English Braille, American Edition."

- Braille

56351. School districts, special education local plan areas, or county offices of education shall provide opportunities for braille instruction for pupils who, due to a prognosis of visual deterioration, may be expected to have a need for braille as a reading medium.

- Provide Opportunities for Braille Instruction

56352. (a) A functional vision assessment conducted pursuant to Section 56320 shall be used as one criterion in determining the appropriate reading medium or media for the pupil.

- Functional Vision Assessment

(b) An assessment of braille skills shall be required for functionally blind pupils who have the ability to read in accordance with guidelines established pursuant to Section 56136.

- Assessment of Braille Skills

(c) Braille instruction shall be provided by a teacher credentialed to teach pupils who are visually impaired.

- Braille Instruction

(d) The determination, by a pupil's individualized education program team, of the most appropriate medium or media, including braille, for visually impaired pupils shall be in accordance with guidelines established pursuant to Section 56136.

- Determining Appropriate Medium or Media

*(Article 3.5 Added in 1994)

(e) Each visually impaired pupil shall be provided with the opportunity to receive an assessment to determine the appropriate reading medium or media, including braille instruction, if appropriate, for that pupil.

- Opportunity for Assessment

Article 4. Implementation

- IMPLEMENTATION

56360. Each district, special education local plan area, or county office shall ensure that a continuum of program options is available to meet the needs of individuals with exceptional needs for special education and related services.

- Ensure Continuum of Program Options

56361. The continuum of program options shall include all of the following:

- List of Program Options

(a) A resource specialist program pursuant to Section 56362.

(b) Designated instruction and services pursuant to Section 56363.

(c) Special classes and centers pursuant to Section 56364.

(d) Nonpublic, nonsectarian school services pursuant to Section 56365.

(e) State special schools pursuant to Section 56367.

(f) Instruction in settings other than classrooms where specially designed instruction may occur.

56361.2. All special education and related services for any individual with exceptional needs who is younger than three years of age shall be provided pursuant to Chapter 4.4 (commencing with Section 56425).

- Infant Programs

56361.5. (a) In addition to the continuum of program options listed in Section 56361, a district, special education local plan area, or county office may contract with a hospital to provide designated instruction and services, as defined in subdivision (b) of Section 56363, required by the individual with exceptional needs, as specified in the individualized education program. However, a district, special education local plan area, or county office of education may not contract with a sectarian hospital for instructional services. A district, special education local plan area, or county office shall contract with a hospital for designated instruction and services required by the individual with exceptional needs only when no appropriate public education program is available.

- Contracting with Hospitals for DIS

- Sectarian Limitations

- No Public Program Available

For the purposes of this section "hospital" means a health care facility licensed by the State Department of Health Services.

- Definition of Hospital

(b) Contracts with hospitals pursuant to subdivision (a) shall be subject to the procedures prescribed in Sections 56365, 56366, and 56366.5.

- Contract Procedures

56362. (a) The resource specialist program shall provide, but not be limited to, all of the following:

- Resource Specialist Duties

(1) Provision for a resource specialist or specialists who shall provide instruction and services for those pupils whose needs have been identified in an individualized education program developed by the individualized education program team and who are assigned to regular classroom teachers for a majority of a schoolday.

(2) Provision of information and assistance to individuals with exceptional needs and their parents.

(3) Provision of consultation, resource information, and material regarding individuals with exceptional needs to their parents and to regular staff members.

(4) Coordination of special education services with the regular school programs for each individual with exceptional needs enrolled in the resource specialist program.

(5) Monitoring of pupil progress on a regular basis, participation in the review and revision of individualized education programs, as appropriate, and referral of pupils who do not demonstrate appropriate progress to the individualized education program team.

(6) Emphasis at the secondary school level on academic achievement, career and vocational development, and preparation for adult life.

(b) The resource specialist program shall be under the direction of a resource specialist who is a credentialed special education teacher, or who has a clinical services credential with a special class authorization, who has had three or more years of teaching experience, including both regular and special education teaching experience, as defined by rules and regulations of the Commission on Teacher Credentialing and who has demonstrated the competencies for a resource specialist, as established by the Commission on Teacher Credentialing. — Resource Specialist Qualifications

(c) Caseloads for resource specialists shall be stated in the local policies developed pursuant to Section 56221 and in accordance with regulations established by the board. No resource specialist shall have a caseload which exceeds 28 pupils. — Caseloads

(d) Resource specialists shall not simultaneously be assigned to serve as resource specialists and to teach regular classes. — Shall Not Teach Regular Classes

(e) Resource specialists shall not enroll a pupil for a majority of a schoolday without prior approval by the superintendent. — Prior Approval for Majority of School Day

(f) At least eighty percent of the resource specialists within a local plan shall be provided with an instructional aide. — Eighty Percent Mandate

56362.1. For the purposes of Section 56362, "caseload" shall include, but not be limited to, all pupils for whom the resource — Caseload Definition specialist performs any of the services described in subdivision (a) of Section 56362.

56362.5. By July 1982, the Commission on Teacher Credentialing shall adopt rules and regulations for a resource specialist certificate of competence. The certificate shall provide all the following:

(a) Definition of the competencies required of a resource specialist.

(b) Provision for a system of direct application to the commission for a certificate of competence for each teacher who holds a valid special education credential, other than an emergency credential, and who satisfies any one of the following criteria:

(1) Provided instruction and services as specified in subdivision (a) of Section 80070.1 of Title 5 of the California Administrative Code as it read immediately prior to July 28, 1980, for two years prior to September 1, 1981.

(2) Provided instruction and services as specified in subdivision (b) of Section 80070.2 of Title 5 of the California Administrative Code as it read immediately prior to July 28, 1980, for two years prior to June 30, 1983.

(c) Provision for the issuance, for up to three years, of a preliminary nonrenewable certificate of competence for the resource specialist, and adoption of the standards for the issuance and continuing validity of such a certificate.

(d) Establishment of a system for verification of competencies through both of the following:

(1) Commission on Teacher Credentialing approved institution of higher education resource specialist certificate program.

(2) Commission on Teacher Credentialing approved competency assessment panels for resource specialist certification.

(e) Cooperation with the department in implementing these provisions.

Notwithstanding any other provision of law, any person who held a preliminary resource specialist certificate of competence on January 28, 1982, and who met the requirements for a clear resource specialist certificate of competence as specified in paragraph (1) of subdivision (b) may be issued a clear resource specialist certificate of competence upon submission of a completed application, but without any additional fee.

56362.7. (a) The Legislature recognizes the need for specially trained professionals to assess and serve pupils of limited-English proficiency. This is particularly true of pupils with exceptional needs or pupils with suspected handicaps.

- Certificate of Competence Provisions

- Definition of the Competencies

- Direct Application

- Preliminary Nonrenewable Certificate

- System of Verification

- Cooperation with Department of Education

- Issuance of Certificate Without Additional Fee

(b) The commission shall develop a bilingual-crosscultural certificate of assessment competence for those professionals who may participate in assessments for placements in special education programs. The certificate shall be issued to holders of appropriate credentials, certificates, or authorizations who demonstrate, by written and oral examination, all of the following:

(1) That the person is competent in both the oral and written skills of a language other than English.

(2) That the person has both the knowledge and understanding of the cultural and historical heritage of the limited-English-proficient individuals to be served.

(3) That the person has the ability to perform the assessment functions the candidate is certified or authorized to perform in English and in a language other than English.

(4) That the person has knowledge of the use of instruments and other assessment techniques appropriate to evaluate limited-English-proficient individuals with exceptional needs and ability to develop appropriate data, instructional strategies, individual educational plans, and evaluations.

(c) Certificates of bilingual-crosscultural competence for special education professionals who implement individual education plans requiring bilingual services shall be granted by the commission pursuant to Section 44253.7.

(d) It is not the intent of the Legislature in enacting this section that possession of any certificate established by this section be a state-mandated requirement for employment or continued employment. It is the intent that this is a matter for local educational agencies to determine.

56363. (a) Designated instruction and services as specified in the individualized education program shall be available when the instruction and services are necessary for the pupil to benefit educationally from his or her instructional program. The instruction and services shall be provided by the regular class teacher, the special class teacher, or the resource specialist if the teacher or specialist is competent to provide such instruction and services and if the provision of such instruction and services by the teacher or specialist is feasible. If not, the appropriate designated instruction and services specialist shall provide such instruction and services. Designated instruction and services shall meet standards adopted by the board.

(b) These services may include, but are not limited to, the following:

(1) Language and speech development and remediation.

(2) Audiological services.

(3) Orientation and mobility instruction.

- Bilingual-Crosscultural Certificate of Assessment Competence

- Written and Oral Exam

- Certificates for Implementers

- Not State-Mandated for Employment

- Designated Instruction and Services (DIS)

- Providers

- DIS Services

(4) Instruction in the home or hospital.

(5) Adapted physical education.

(6) Physical and occupational therapy.

(7) Vision services.

(8) Specialized driver training instruction.

(9) Counseling and guidance.

(10) Psychological services other than assessment and development of the individualized education program.

(11) Parent counseling and training.

(12) Health and nursing services.

(13) Social worker services.

(14) Specially designed vocational education and career development.

(15) Recreation services.

(16) Specialized services for low-incidence disabilities, such as readers, transcribers, and vision and hearing services.

56363.1. A district, special education local plan area, or county office is not required to purchase medical equipment for an individual pupil. However, the school district, special education local plan area, or county office is responsible for providing other specialized equipment for use at school that is needed to implement the individualized education program. For purposes of this section, "medical equipment" does not include an assistive technology device, as defined in paragraph (25) of subsection (a) of Section 1401 of Title 20 of the United States Code.

– Medical Equipment*

56363.3. The average caseload for language, speech, and hearing specialists in districts, county offices, or special education local plan areas shall not exceed 55 cases, unless the local comprehensive plan specifies a higher average caseload and the reasons for the greater average caseload.

– Caseload for Language, Speech, and Hearing Specialists

56363.5. School districts, county offices of education, and special education local plan areas may seek, either directly or through the pupil's parents, reimbursement from insurance companies to cover the costs of related services to the extent permitted by federal law or regulation.

– Reimbursement from Insurance Companies

56364. Special classes and centers that enroll pupils with similar and more intensive educational needs shall be available. The classes and centers shall enroll the pupils when the nature or severity of the disability precludes their participation in the regular school program for a majority of a schoolday. Special classes and centers and other removal of individuals with exceptional needs from the regular education environment shall occur only when education in regular classes with the use of supplementary aids and services cannot be achieved

– Special Classes and Centers

*(Section 56363.1 Added in 1994)

satisfactorily due to the nature or severity of the exceptional need.

In providing or arranging for the provision of activities, each public agency shall ensure that each individual with exceptional needs participates in those activities with nondisabled pupils to the maximum extent appropriate to the needs of the individual with exceptional needs, including nonacademic and extracurricular services and activities. Special classes and centers shall meet standards adopted by the board.

— Participate with Non-disabled Pupils

56364.1. Notwithstanding the provisions of Section 56364, pupils with low incidence disabilities may receive all or a portion of their instruction in the regular classroom and may also be enrolled in special classes taught by appropriately credentialed teachers who serve these pupils at one or more school sites. The instruction shall be provided in a manner which is consistent with the guidelines adopted pursuant to Section 56136 and in accordance with the individualized education program.

— Special Classes for Pupils with Low-Incidence Disabilities

56364.5. The Commission on Teacher Credentialing shall establish standards for the issuance of credentials or permits for persons employed in special centers pursuant to Section 56364.

— Credentials/Permits for Special Centers' Personnel

56365. (a) Nonpublic, nonsectarian school services, including services by nonpublic, nonsectarian agencies shall be available. These services shall be provided pursuant to Section 56366 under contract with the district, special education local plan area, or county office to provide the appropriate special educational facilities, special education, or designated instruction and services required by the individual with exceptional needs when no appropriate public education program is available.

— Nonpublic, Nonsectarian* Schools/Agencies

— No Public Program Available

(b) Pupils enrolled in nonpublic, nonsectarian schools and agencies under this section shall be deemed to be enrolled in public schools for all purposes of Chapter 4 (commencing with Section 41600) of Part 24 and Section 42238. The district, special education local plan area, or county office shall be eligible to receive allowances under Chapter 7 (commencing with Section 56700) for services that are provided to individuals with exceptional needs pursuant to the contract.

— Deemed Enrolled in Public Schools

— Funding Eligibility

(c) If the state participates in the federal program of assistance for state-operated or state-supported programs for children with disabilities (P.L. 89-313, Sec. 6), pupils enrolled in nonpublic, nonsectarian schools shall be deemed to be enrolled in state-supported institutions for all purposes of that program and shall be eligible to receive allowances under Chapter 7 (commencing with Section 56700) for supplemental services provided to individuals with exceptional needs pursuant

— P.L. 89-313 Funding

*(Section 56365 Repealed/ Added in 1994)

to a contract with a district, special education local plan area, or county office of education. In order to participate in the federal program, the state must find that participation will not result in any additional expenditures from the General Fund.

(d) The district, special education local plan area, or county office shall pay to the nonpublic, nonsectarian school or agency the full amount of the tuition for individuals with exceptional needs that are enrolled in programs provided by the nonpublic, nonsectarian school pursuant to the contract.

— Full Amount of Tuition

(e) Before contracting with a nonpublic, nonsectarian school or agency outside of this state, the district, special education local plan area, or county office shall document its efforts to utilize public schools or to locate an appropriate nonpublic, nonsectarian school or agency program, or both, within the state.

— Before Contracting Outside of California

(f) If a district, special education local plan area, or county office places a pupil with a nonpublic, nonsectarian school or agency outside of this state, the pupil's individualized education program team shall submit a report to the superintendent within 15 days of the placement decision. The report shall include information about the special education and related services provided by the out-of-state program placement and the costs of the special education and related services provided, as specified in subdivisions (a) and (b) of Section 56741, and shall indicate the efforts of the local educational agency to locate an appropriate public school or nonpublic, nonsectarian school or agency, or a combination thereof, within the state. The superintendent shall submit a report to the State Board of Education on all placements made outside of this state.

— Reporting Out-of-State Placements

(g) If a school district, special education local plan area, or county office of education decides to place a pupil with a nonpublic, nonsectarian school or agency outside of this state, that local education agency shall indicate the anticipated date for the return of the pupil to a public or nonpublic, nonsectarian school or agency placement, or a combination thereof, located in the state and shall document efforts during the previous placement year to return the pupil.

— Indicate Anticipated Date for Return of the Pupil

(h) In addition to meeting the requirements of Section 56366.1, a nonpublic, nonsectarian school or agency that operates a program outside of this state shall be certified or licensed by that state to provide, respectively, special education and related services and designated instruction and related services to pupils under the Individuals with Disabilities Education Act (20 U.S.C. Sec. 1400 et seq.).

— Out-of-State School/Agency Shall be Certified or Licensed

(i) A nonpublic, nonsectarian school or agency that is located outside of this state is eligible for certification pursuant

— Requirements for Certification Out-of-State

to Section 56366.1 only if a pupil is enrolled in a program operated by that school or agency pursuant to the recommendation of an individualized education program team in California, and if that pupil's parents or guardians reside in California.

56365.5. Before state funds can be used for new public and nonpublic school special education placements of individuals with exceptional needs, the superintendent shall review the appropriateness of the placement if the cost of the placement exceeds twenty thousand dollars ($20,000).

- State Superintendent's Review of Placements Exceeding $20,000

The district, special education local plan area, or county office shall submit documentation to the superintendent of all efforts made to locate an appropriate alternative placement within the state and outside of the state.

- Documentation

The superintendent or his or her designee shall review the educational placement decision to determine if every effort was made by the district, special education local plan area, or county office to utilize an appropriate public or nonpublic, nonsectarian school costing less than twenty thousand dollars ($20,000).

- Review Placement Decision

The superintendent shall notify the district, special education local plan area, or county office of his or her findings within 10 days.

- Notification of Findings

The twenty thousand-dollars ($20,000) threshold shall be cumulatively increased by the annual percentage increase specified by Section 56723, or by the in-lieu percentage specified in the Budget Act.

- Annual Percentage Increase

Within five days following receipt of the superintendent's findings indicating availability of alternative placements, an individualized education program team meeting shall be convened to consider those findings.

- IEP Team Considers Findings

If the superintendent fails to make findings within 10 days, the original placement decision of the individualized education program team shall be final.

- Failure to Make Findings

56366. It is the intent of the Legislature that the role of the nonpublic, nonsectarian school or agency shall be maintained and continued as an alternative special education service available to districts, special education local plan areas, county offices, and parents.

- Role of Nonpublic School/* Agency

(a) The master contract for nonpublic, nonsectarian school or agency services shall be developed in accordance with the following provisions:

- Master Contract Provisions

(1) The master contract shall specify the general administrative and financial agreements between the nonpublic, nonsectarian school or agency and the district, special education local plan area, or county office to provide the special education

- Administrative/Financial Agreements

*(Section 56366 Repealed/ Added in 1994)

4-24

and designated instruction and services, as well as transportation specified in the pupil's individualized education program on forms provided by the superintendent in January of each year for the following fiscal year. The administrative provisions of the contract also shall include procedures for recordkeeping and documentation, and the maintenance of school records by the contracting district, special education local plan area, or county office to ensure that appropriate high school graduation credit is received by the pupil. The contract may allow for partial or full-time attendance at the nonpublic, nonsectarian school.

(2) The master contract shall include an individual services agreement on forms provided by the superintendent in January of each year for the following fiscal year for each pupil placed by a district, special education local plan area, or county office that will be negotiated for the length of time for which nonpublic, nonsectarian school or agency special education and designated instruction and services are specified in the pupil's individualized education program.

— Individual Services Agreement

Changes in educational instruction, services, or placement provided under contract may only be made on the basis of revisions to the pupil's individualized education program.

At any time during the term of the contract or individual services agreement, the parent; nonpublic, nonsectarian school or agency; or district, special education local plan area, or county office may request a review of the pupil's individualized education program by the individualized education program team. Changes in the administrative or financial agreements of the master contract that do not alter the individual services agreement that outlines each pupil's educational instruction, services, or placement may be made at any time during the term of the contract as mutually agreed by the nonpublic, nonsectarian school or agency and the district, special education local plan area, or county office.

(3) The master contract or individual services agreement may be terminated for cause. The cause shall not be the availability of a public class initiated during the period of the contract unless the parent agrees to the transfer of the pupil to a public school program. To terminate the contract either party shall give 20 days' notice.

— May Terminate for Cause

(4) The nonpublic, nonsectarian school or agency shall provide all services specified in the individualized education program, unless the nonpublic, nonsectarian school or agency and the district, special education local plan area, or county office agree otherwise in the contract.

— Provide Specified Services

(5) Related services provided pursuant to a nonpublic, nonsectarian agency master contract shall only be provided during the period of the child's regular or extended school year program, or both, unless otherwise specified by the pupil's individualized education program.

— Related Services

(6) The nonpublic, nonsectarian school or agency shall report attendance of pupils receiving special education and designated instruction and services as defined by Section 46307 for purposes of submitting a warrant for tuition to each contracting district, special education local plan area, or county office on forms developed by the superintendent.

— Report Attendance of Pupils

(b) The master contract or individual services agreement shall not include special education transportation provided through the use of services or equipment owned, leased, or contracted by a district, special education local plan area, or county office for pupils enrolled in the nonpublic, nonsectarian school or agency unless provided directly or subcontracted by that nonpublic, nonsectarian school or agency.

— Transportation Restrictions

The superintendent shall withhold 20 percent of the amount apportioned to a school district or county office for costs related to the provision of nonpublic, nonsectarian school or agency placements if the superintendent finds that the local education agency is in noncompliance with this subdivision. This amount shall be withheld from the apportionments in the fiscal year following the superintendent's finding of noncompliance. The superintendent shall take other appropriate actions to prevent noncompliant practices from occurring and report to the Legislature on those actions.

— Penalty for Noncompliance

(c) (1) If the pupil is enrolled in the nonpublic, nonsectarian school or agency with the approval of the district, special education local plan area, or county office prior to agreement to a contract or individual services agreement, the district, special education local plan area, or county office shall issue a warrant, upon submission of an attendance report and claim, for an amount equal to the number of creditable days of attendance at the per diem rate agreed upon prior to the enrollment of the pupil. This provision shall be allowed for 90 days during which time the contract shall be consummated.

— Issuance of Warrant

(2) If after 60 days the master contract or individual services agreement has not been finalized as prescribed in paragraph (1) of subdivision (a), either party may appeal to the county superintendent of schools, if the county superintendent is not participating in the local plan involved in the nonpublic, nonsectarian school or agency contract, or the superintendent, if the county superintendent is participating in the local plan involved in the contract, to negotiate the contract. Within 30

— Appeal

days of receipt of this appeal, the county superintendent or the superintendent, or his or her designee, shall mediate the formulation of a contract which shall be binding upon both parties.

– Mediate Formulation of
  Contract

(d) (1) No master contract for special education and related services provided by a nonpublic, nonsectarian school or agency shall be authorized under this part unless the school or agency has been certified as meeting those standards relating to the required special education and specified related services and facilities for individuals with exceptional needs. The certification shall result in the school's or agency's receiving approval to educate pupils under this part for a period no longer than four years from the date of the approval. The procedures, methods, and areas of certification, including information required for purposes of the application specified in subdivision (a) of Section 56366.1, shall be established by rules and regulations issued by the board that shall include, but not be limited to, procedures for conducting onsite reviews of the nonpublic, nonsectarian school or agency program and include provisions specific to the provision of special education and related services to individuals with exceptional needs from birth to preschool. In addition to those standards adopted by the board, the school or agency shall meet all applicable standards relating to fire, health, sanitation, and building safety.

– Certification Standards

(e) The school or agency shall be charged a reasonable fee for certification. The superintendent may adjust the fee annually commensurate with the statewide average percentage inflation adjustment computed for revenue limits of unified school districts with greater than 1,500 units of average daily attendance if the percentage increase is reflected in the district revenue limit for inflation purposes. For purposes of this section, the base fee shall be the following:

– Certification Fees

(A) 1-5 pupils -- $150.
(B) 6-10 pupils -- $250.
(C) 11-24 pupils -- $500.
(D) 25-75 pupils -- $750.
(E) 76 pupils and over -- $1,000.

The school or agency shall pay this fee when it applies for certification and when it updates its application for annual review by the superintendent. The superintendent shall use these fees to conduct onsite reviews, which may include field experts. No fee shall be refunded if the application is withdrawn or is denied by the superintendent.

(f) (1) Notwithstanding any other provision of law, only those nonpublic, nonsectarian schools and agencies that provide special education and designated instruction and services

– Staff Qualifications

utilizing staff who hold, or are receiving training under the supervision of staff who hold, a current valid California credential or license in the service rendered shall be eligible to receive certification. Only those nonpublic, nonsectarian schools or agencies located outside of California that employ staff who hold a current valid credential or license to render special education and related services as required by that state be eligible to be certified.

(2) Nothing in this subdivision restricts student teachers, interns, or other staff who are enrolled in training programs that lead to a license or credential that authorize the holder to render services to special education pupils and who are under the direct supervision of a staff member who holds a current valid California credential, license, or certificate of registration document.

– Student Teachers

(3) A nonpublic, nonsectarian school or agency that employs only persons who hold a valid California credential authorizing substitute teaching pursuant to Section 56060 shall not be certified. At least one full-time person with a current valid California credential, license, or certificate of registration in the area of service to be rendered, or a current valid credential, license, or certificate of registration for appropriate special education and related services rendered that is required in another state, shall be required for purposes of certification under subdivision (d).

– Restrictions on Staffing

(4) A nonpublic, nonsectarian school or agency that employs persons holding a valid emergency credential shall document efforts of recruiting appropriately credentialed, licensed, or registered personnel for the special education and related services rendered as a condition of renewing certification.

– Document Efforts

56366.1. (a) A nonpublic, nonsectarian school or agency that seeks certification shall file an application with the superintendent on forms provided by the department and include the following information on the application:

– Application for Certifi-*
cation

(1) A description of the special education and designated instruction and services provided to individuals with exceptional needs if the application is for nonpublic, nonsectarian school certification.

(2) A description of the designated instruction and services provided to individuals with exceptional needs if the application is for nonpublic, nonsectarian agency certification.

(3) A list of appropriately qualified staff, a description of the credential, license, or registration that qualifies each staff member to render special education or designated instruction and services, and copies of their credentials, licenses, or certificates of registration with the appropriate state or national

*(Section 56366.1 Amended in 1994)

4-28

organization that has established standards for the service rendered.

(4) An annual operating budget.

(5) Affidavits and assurances necessary to comply with all applicable federal, state, and local laws and regulations which include criminal record summaries required of all nonpublic school or agency personnel having contact with minor children under Section 44237.

(b) Unless the board grants a waiver pursuant to Section 56101, a nonpublic, nonsectarian school or agency shall file an application for certification between January 1 and March 31, except as provided in paragraph (4) of subdivision (j).

— Period for Filing
  Application for Certification

(c) If the applicant operates a facility or program on more than one site, each site shall be certified.

— Each Site Shall Be
  Certified

(d) If the applicant is part of a larger program or facility on the same site, the superintendent shall consider the effect of the total program on the applicant. A copy of the policies and standards for the nonpublic, nonsectarian school or agency and the larger program shall be available to the superintendent.

— Effect of Total Program

(e) Prior to certification, the superintendent shall conduct an onsite review of the facility and program for which the applicant seeks certification. The superintendent may be assisted by representatives of the special education local plan area in which the applicant is located and a nonpublic, nonsectarian school or agency representative who does not have a conflict of interest with the applicant. The superintendent shall conduct an additional onsite review of the facility and program within four years of the certification effective date, unless the superintendent conditionally certifies the school or agency or unless the superintendent receives a formal complaint against the school or agency. In the latter two cases, the superintendent shall conduct an onsite review at least annually.

— Onsite Review

(f) The superintendent shall make a determination on an application within 120 days of receipt of the application and shall certify, conditionally certify, or deny certification to the applicant. If the superintendent fails to take one of these actions within 120 days, the applicant is automatically granted conditional certification for a period terminating on August 31, of the current school year. If certification is denied, the superintendent shall provide reasons for the denial. The superintendent may certify the school or agency for a period of not longer than four years.

— Action on Application
  Within 120 Days of
  Receipt

(g) Certification becomes effective on the date the nonpublic, nonsectarian school or agency meets all the application requirements and is approved by the superintendent. Certification may be retroactive if the school or agency met all

— Effective Date of
  Certification

the requirements of this section on the date the retroactive certification is effective. Certification expires on August 31 of the terminating year.

(h) The superintendent shall annually review the certification of each nonpublic, nonsectarian school and agency. For this purpose, a certified school or agency shall annually update its application between August 1 and October 31, unless the board grants a waiver pursuant to Section 56101. The superintendent may conduct an onsite review as part of the annual review.

– Annual Review of Certification

(i) The superintendent may monitor a nonpublic, nonsectarian school or agency onsite at any time without prior notice when there is substantial reason to believe that there is an immediate danger to the health, safety, or welfare of a child. The superintendent shall document the concern and submit it to the nonpublic, nonsectarian school or agency at the time of the onsite monitoring. The superintendent shall require a written response to any noncompliance or deficiency found.

– Monitor Nonpublic School/Agency Onsite at Any Time Without Notice

(j) (1) Notwithstanding any other provision of law, the superintendent may not certify a nonpublic, nonsectarian school or agency to do any of the following, unless the nonpublic, nonsectarian school or agency notifies the county superintendent of schools and the special education local plan area in which the proposed new or expanded nonpublic, nonsectarian school or agency is located of its intent to seek certification:

– Certification Exceptions and Notice to Initiate or Expand Services

(A) Initiate or expand services to pupils currently educated, or pupils who were educated in the immediate prior fiscal year, in a juvenile court program or community school pursuant to Section 56150.

(B) Operate any other nonspecial education program, including independent study or adult school, or both.

(C) Operate a special education program previously provided by a district, special education local plan area, or county office, pursuant to Sections 56362 to 56364, inclusive.

(2) The notification shall occur no later than the December 1 prior to the new fiscal year in which the proposed or expanding school or agency intends to initiate services. The notice shall include the following:

(A) The specific date upon which the proposed nonpublic, nonsectarian school or agency is to be established.

(B) The location of the proposed program or facility.

(C) The number of pupils proposed for services, the number of pupils currently served in the juvenile court, community school, or other nonspecial education program, the current school services including special education and related services provided for these pupils, and the specific program of special education and related services to be provided under the proposed program.

(D) The reason for the proposed change in services.

(3) In addition to the requirements in subdivisions (a) through (e), inclusive, the superintendent shall require and consider the following in determining whether to certify a nonpublic, nonsectarian school or agency as described in this subdivision:

(A) A complete statement of the information required as part of the notice under paragraph (1).

(B) Documentation of the steps taken in preparation for the conversion to a nonpublic, nonsectarian school or agency, including information related to changes in the population to be served and the services to be provided pursuant to each pupil's individualized education program.

(4) Unless the board grants a waiver pursuant to Section 56101, a new or expanded nonpublic, nonsectarian school or agency shall file an application for certification between April 1 and June 30 of each year prior to the fiscal year. Before certifying the school or agency, the superintendent shall determine that certification of the new or expanding school or agency program is necessary for the provision of a free appropriate special education program to the affected pupils in the least restrictive environment.

(5) Notwithstanding any other provision of law, the certification becomes effective no earlier than July 1, if the school or agency provided the notification required pursuant to paragraph (1).

56366.2. (a) A district, special education local plan area, county office, nonpublic, nonsectarian school, or nonpublic, nonsectarian agency may petition the superintendent to waive one or more of the requirements under Sections 56365, 56366, 56366.3, 56366.6, and 56366.7. The petition shall state the reasons for the waiver request, and shall include the following:

– Petition to Waive*
  Requirements

(1) Sufficient documentation to demonstrate that the waiver is necessary to the content and implementation of a specific pupil's individualized education program and the pupil's current placement.

(2) The period of time that the waiver will be effective during any one school year.

(3) Documentation and assurance that the waiver does not abrogate any right provided individuals with exceptional needs and their parents or guardians under state or federal law, and does not hinder the compliance of a district, special education local plan area, or county office with the Individual(s) with Disabilities Education Act (20 U.S.C. Sec. 1400 and

*(Section 56366.2 Repealed/
  Added in 1994)

following), Section 504 of the Rehabilitation Act of 1973 (29 U.S.C. Sec. 794), the Americans with Disabilities Act of 1990 (42 U.S.C. 12101 and following), and federal regulations relating thereto.

(b) No waiver shall be granted for reimbursement of those costs prohibited under Section 56740 or 56775 or certification pursuant to Section 56366.1 unless approved by the board pursuant to Section 56101.

(c) In submitting the annual report on waivers granted under Section 56101 and this section to the State Board of Education, the superintendent shall specify information related to the provision of special education and related services to individuals with exceptional needs through contracts with nonpublic, nonsectarian schools and agencies located in the state, nonpublic, nonsectarian school and agency placements in facilities located out of state, and the specific section waived pursuant to this section.

56366.3. (a) No contract for special education and related services provided by a nonpublic, nonsectarian school or agency shall be reimbursed by the state pursuant to Sections 56740 and 56775 if the contract covers special education and related services, administration, or supervision by an individual who was an employee of a contracting district, special education local plan area, or county office within the last 365 days, unless the contract contains an addendum establishing that the individual was involuntarily terminated or laid off as part of necessary staff reductions from the district, special education local plan area, or county office.

(b) This section does not apply to any person who is able to provide designated instruction and services during the extended school year because he or she is otherwise employed for up to 10 months of the school year by the district, special education local plan area, or county office.

56366.4. (a) The superintendent may revoke or suspend the certification of a nonpublic, nonsectarian school or agency for any of the following reasons:

(1) Violation of any applicable state or federal rule or regulation, or aiding, abetting, or permitting the violation of any applicable state or federal rule or regulation.

(2) Falsification or intentional misrepresentation of any element of the application, pupil records, or program presented for certification purposes.

(3) Conduct in the operation or maintenance of the nonpublic, nonsectarian school or agency that is harmful to the health, welfare, or safety of an individual with exceptional needs.

*(Section 56366.3 Amended in 1994)

(4) Failure to comply with any provision in the contract with the local education entity.

(5) Failure to notify the department in writing of any of the following within 60 days of the occurrence:

(A) Changes in credentialed, licensed, or registered staff who render special education and related services, ownership, management, or control of the nonpublic, nonsectarian school or agency.

(B) Major modification or relocation of facilities.

(C) Significant modification of the nonpublic, nonsectarian school or agency program.

(6) Failure to implement recommendations and compliance requirements following an onsite review of the school or agency.

(7) Failure to provide appropriate services, supplies, equipment, or facilities for a pupil as required in his or her individualized education program.

(8) Failure to notify the superintendent in writing within 10 days of the revocation or suspension of any license or permit including, but not limited to, any residential care license, business license, or other required license or permit.

(9) Failure to implement a pupil's individualized education program.

(10) Failure to notify the superintendent in writing within 10 days of the death of a pupil or any other individual of unnatural causes within the school or agency, including the circumstances surrounding the death and any appropriate preventative measures being taken or recommended.

(b) The superintendent shall notify contracting local education agencies and the special education local plan area in which the nonpublic, nonsectarian school or agency is located of the determination to suspend or revoke state certification.

— Notification to Suspend or Revoke State Certification

56366.5. (a) Upon receipt of a request from a nonpublic, nonsectarian school for payment for services provided under a contract entered into pursuant to Sections 56365 and 56366, the district, special education local plan area, or county office shall either (1) send a warrant for the amount requested within 45 days, or (2) notify the nonpublic, nonsectarian school within 10 working days of any reason why the requested payment shall not be paid.

— Payment for Services

(b) If the district, special education local plan area, or county office fails to comply with subdivision (a), the nonpublic, nonsectarian school may require the district, special education local plan area, or county office to pay an additional amount of 1-1/2 percent of the unpaid balance per month until full payment is made. The district, special education local plan

— Penalty for Late Payment

area, or county office may not claim reimbursement from the state for such additional amount pursuant to any provision of law, including any provision contained in Chapter 3 (commencing with Section 2201) of Part 4 of Division 1 of the Revenue and Taxation Code.

56366.6. (a) Within 20 working days following the nonpublic, nonsectarian school's or agency's receipt of the notice of denial, revocation, or suspension of certification, the nonpublic, nonsectarian school or agency may file a written petition to request a review of the decision by the superintendent. The petition may include written arguments or a request to present an oral argument.

(b) Within 30 working days after the receipt of the written petition, the superintendent or a designee shall review a written, reasoned decision that shall be the final administrative decision. The designee of the superintendent shall be impartial, unbiased, and shall not have participated in the department decision to deny, revoke, or suspend the nonpublic, nonsectarian school or agency certification.

(c) Any public education agency that contracts with a certified nonpublic, nonsectarian school or agency may request the superintendent to review the status of the nonpublic school or agency. The request shall be in writing and a copy sent to the nonpublic school or agency.

56366.7. (a) As a condition of certification, a nonpublic, nonsectarian school or agency shall submit, on forms developed by the superintendent in consultation with statewide organizations representing providers of special education and designated instruction and services, a list of uniform tuition fees for providing special education and designated instruction and services to individuals with exceptional needs who are served through contracts with local education agencies. The superintendent shall not certify, or shall decertify, any nonpublic, nonsectarian school or agency that has not complied with this section by June 30, 1996. The superintendent shall ensure that tuition fee information is uniformly collected from nonpublic, nonsectarian schools and agencies that seek certification each year.

(b) This section shall become inoperative on June 30, 1999, and as of January 1, 2000, is repealed, unless a later enacted statute, that becomes effective on or before January 1, 2000, deletes or extends the dates on which it becomes inoperative and is repealed.

56367. (a) Placements in state special schools pursuant to Sections 59020, 59120, and 59220 shall be made only as a result of recommendations from the individualized education

*(Section 56366.7 Amended in 1994)

program team, upon a finding that no appropriate placement is available in the local plan area.

(b) Notwithstanding the provisions of subdivision (a), referrals for further assessment and recommendations to the California Schools for the Deaf and Blind or the Diagnostic Centers, pursuant to Section 56326, shall not constitute placements in state special schools.

— Referrals for Further Assessment

56368. (a) A program specialist is a specialist who holds a valid special education credential, clinical services credential, health services credential, or a school psychologist authorization and has advanced training and related experience in the education of individuals with exceptional needs and a specialized in-depth knowledge in preschool disabilities, career vocational development, or one or more areas of major disabling conditions.

— Program Specialist Qualifications

(b) A program specialist may do all the following:

— Program Specialist Activities

(1) Observe, consult with, and assist resource specialists, designated instruction and services instructors, and special class teachers.

(2) Plan programs, coordinate curricular resources, and evaluate effectiveness of programs for individuals with exceptional needs.

(3) Participate in each school's staff development, program development, and innovation of special methods and approaches.

(4) Provide coordination, consultation and program development primarily in one specialized area or areas of his or her expertise.

(5) Be responsible for assuring that pupils have full educational opportunity regardless of the district of residence.

(c) For purposes of Section 41403, a program specialist shall be considered a pupil services employee, as defined in subdivision (c) of Section 41401.

— Considered as Pupil Services Employee

56369. A district, special education local plan area, or county office, may contract with another public agency to provide special education or related services to an individual with exceptional needs.

— Contracting with Another Public Agency

56370. In addition to the requirements in Section 56828, a transfer of special education programs from a school district to the county superintendent of schools or to other school districts, or from the county superintendent of schools to school districts, shall not be approved by the Superintendent of Public Instruction if the transfer would result in diminishing the level of services or the opportunity of the affected pupils to interact with the general school population, as required in the individualized education programs of the affected pupils.

— Transfer of Special Education Programs

Article 5. Review

56380. (a) The district, special education local plan area, or county office shall maintain procedures for conducting, on at least an annual basis, reviews of all individualized education programs. The procedures shall provide for the review of the pupil's progress and the appropriateness of placement, and the making of any necessary revisions.

– At Least Annual Basis

(b) The district, special education local plan area, or county office shall notify, in writing, parents of their right to request a review by the individualized education program team. The notice may be part of the individualized education program.

– Parent Notification

(c) Each individualized education program review shall be conducted in accordance with the notice and scheduling requirements for the initial assessment.

– Conducting IEP Review

56381. A reassessment of the pupil, based upon procedures specified in Article 2 (commencing with Section 56320) shall be conducted at least every three years or more frequently, if conditions warrant, or if the pupil's parent or teacher requests a new assessment and a new individualized education program to be developed.

– Reassessment

If the reassessment so indicates, a new individualized education program shall be developed.

56382. All review and reassessment procedures for individuals with exceptional needs who are younger than three years of age shall be provided pursuant to Chapter 4.4 (commencing with Section 56425) and the California Early Intervention Services Act, Title 14 (commencing with Section 95000) of the Government Code.

– Review and Reassessment Procedures for Infants

CHAPTER 4.3. DEMONSTRATION PROGRAMS

56400. Any special education local plan area may submit an application to the State Department of Education to operate a demonstration program for individuals with exceptional needs. Demonstration programs shall demonstrate creative methods of improving instruction, motivation, and achievement of individuals with exceptional needs by bringing together available resources, including, but not limited to, local districts, special education local plan areas, county offices, the State Department of Education, public agencies and private agencies. The total financial requirement of the demonstration program may not exceed the state entitlement which would otherwise be available.

    – Application

The State Department of Education shall develop criteria for demonstration programs. The criteria shall be reviewed by the Advisory Commission on Special Education and approved by the State Board of Education. The special education local plan area shall include the criteria in its demonstration program application.

    – Criteria

The goal of demonstration programs is to enhance instructional programs for individuals with exceptional needs. The program shall be under the direction of a qualified special education teacher, and the application to the state shall be reviewed by the special education local plan area community advisory committee and the bargaining unit for the certificated employees of the school district or county office that will conduct the demonstration program, and approved by the local board prior to submission. The State Department of Education may approve the initial application for a two-year period, and may renew the approval only if the department's evaluation of the demonstration program shows that there is evidence that the objectives of the program, as stated in the application are being achieved.

    – Enhance Instructional
      Programs

CHAPTER 4.4. EARLY EDUCATION FOR* INDIVIDUALS WITH EXCEPTIONAL NEEDS

56425. As a condition of receiving state aid pursuant to this part, each district, special education local plan area, or county office that operated early education programs for individuals with exceptional needs younger than three years of age, as defined in Section 56026, and that received state or federal aid for special education for those programs in the 1980-81 fiscal year, shall continue to operate early education programs in the 1981-82 fiscal year and each fiscal year thereafter.

— Infant Program Mandate

If a district or county office offered those programs in the 1980-81 fiscal year but in a subsequent year transfers the programs to another district or county office in the special education local plan area, the district or county shall be exempt from the provisions of this section in any year when the programs are offered by the district or county office to which they were transferred.

— Program Transfer

A district, special education local plan area, or county office that is required to offer a program pursuant to this section shall be eligible for funding pursuant to Chapter 7 (commencing with Section 56700) of Part 30.

— Funding

56425.5. The Legislature hereby finds and declares that early education programs for infants identified as individuals with exceptional needs, which provide educational services with active parent involvement, can significantly reduce the potential impact of many disabling conditions, and positively influence later development when the child reaches schoolage.

— Legislative Findings, Declarations, and Intent

Early education programs funded pursuant to Sections 56427, 56428, and 56728.8 shall provide a continuum of program options provided by a transdisciplinary team to meet the multiple and varied needs of infants and their families. Recognizing the parent as the infant's primary teacher, it is the Legislature's intent that early education programs shall include opportunities for the family to receive home visits and to participate in family involvement activities pursuant to Sections 56426.1 and 56426.4. It is the intent of the Legislature that, as an infant grows older, program emphasis would shift from home-based services to a combination of home-based and group services.

It is further the intent of the Legislature that services rendered by state and local agencies serving infants with exceptional needs and their families be coordinated and maximized.

56426. An early education program shall include services specially designed to meet the unique needs of infants, from birth to three years of age, and their families. The primary purpose of an early education program is to enhance

— Purpose and Focus

*(See Early Intervention Services Act Beginning on Page H-12)

development of the infant. To meet this purpose, the program shall focus upon the infant and his or her family, and shall include home visits, group services, and family involvement activities. Early education programs funded pursuant to Sections 56427, 56428, and 56728.8 shall include, as program options, home-based services pursuant to Section 56426.1, and home-based and group services pursuant to Section 56426.2 and shall be provided in accordance with the Individuals with Disabilities Education Act (20 U.S.C. 1471 to 1485), and the California Early Intervention Services Act, Title 14 (commencing with Section 95000) of the Government Code.

– Program Options

56426.1. (a) Home-based early education services funded pursuant to Sections 56427, 56428, and 56728.8 shall include, but not be limited to, all of the following:

– Home-Based Services

(1) Observing the infant's behavior and development in his or her natural environment.

(2) Presenting activities that are developmentally appropriate for the infant and are specially designed, based on the infant's exceptional needs, to enhance the infant's development. Those activities shall be developed to conform with the infant's individualized family service plan and to ensure that they do not conflict with his or her medical needs.

(3) Modeling and demonstrating developmentally appropriate activities for the infant to the parents, siblings, and other caregivers, as designated by the parent.

(4) Interacting with the family members and other caregivers, as designated by the parent, to enhance and reinforce their development of skills necessary to promote the infant's development.

(5) Discussing parental concerns related to the infant and the family, and supporting parents in coping with their infant's needs.

(6) Assisting parents to solve problems, to seek other services in their community, and to coordinate the services provided by various agencies.

(b) The frequency of home-based services shall be once or twice a week, depending on the needs of the infant and the family.

56426.2. (a) Early education services funded pursuant to Sections 56427, 56428, and 56728.8 shall be provided through both home visits and group settings with other infants, with or without the parent. Home-based and group services shall include, but not be limited to, all of the following:

– Home Visits and Group Services

(1) All services identified in subdivision (a) of Section 56426.1.

(2) Group and individual activities that are developmentally appropriate and specially designed, based on the infant's

exceptional needs, to enhance the infant's development. Those activities shall be developed to conform with the infant's individualized family service plan and to ensure that they do not conflict with his or her medical needs.

(3) Opportunities for infants to socialize and participate in play and exploration activities.

(4) Transdisciplinary services by therapists, psychologists, and other specialists as appropriate.

(5) Access to various developmentally appropriate equipment and specialized materials.

(6) Opportunities for family involvement activities, including parent education and parent support groups.

(b) Services provided in a center under this chapter shall not include child care or respite care.

(c) The frequency of group services shall not exceed three hours a day for up to, and including, three days a week, and shall be determined on the basis of the needs of the infant and the family.

(d) The frequency of home visits provided in conjunction with group services shall range from one to eight visits per month, depending on the needs of the infant and the family.

(e) Group services shall be provided on a ratio of no more than four infants to one adult.

(f) Parent participation in group services shall be encouraged.

56426.25. The maximum service levels set forth in Sections 56426.1 and 56426.2 apply only for purposes of the allocation of funds for early education programs pursuant to Sections 56427, 56428, and 56728.8, and may be exceeded by a district, special education local plan area, or county office, in accordance with the infants' individualized family service plan, provided that no change in the level of entitlement to state funding under this part thereby results.

— Maximum Service Levels

56426.3. In addition to home-based or home-based and group early education services, related services as defined in Section 300.13 of Title 34 of the Code of Federal Regulations, as that section read on April 1, 1986, shall be available to infants and their families. Related services may be provided in the home or at the center according to needs of the infant and the family.

— Related Services

56426.4. (a) Family involvement activities funded pursuant to Sections 56427, 56428, and 56728.8 shall support family members in meeting the practical and emotional issues and needs of raising their infant. These activities may include, but are not limited to, the following:

— Family Involvement Activities

(1) Educational programs that present information or demonstrate techniques to assist the family to promote their infant's development.

(2) Parent education and training to assist families in understanding, planning for, and meeting the unique needs of their infant.

(3) Parent support groups to share similar experiences and possible solutions.

(4) Instruction in making toys and other materials appropriate to their infant's exceptional needs and development.

(b) The frequency of family involvement activities shall be at least once a month.

(c) Participation by families in family involvement activities shall be voluntary.

56426.5. If the transdisciplinary team determines home-based and group early education services to be appropriate, but the parent chooses not to receive home-based services, group services shall be made available to the infant. Similarly, the choice not to participate in family involvement activities shall not limit the availability to the infant and his or her family of home-based services or home-based and group services as determined appropriate by the individualized education program team.

— Parental Choice

56426.6. (a) Early education services shall be provided by the district, special education local plan area, or county office through a transdisciplinary team consisting of a group of professionals from various disciplines, agencies, and parents who shall share their expertise and services to provide appropriate services for infants and their families. Each team member shall be responsible for providing and coordinating early education services for one or more infants and their families, and shall serve as a consultant to other team members and as a provider of appropriate related services to other infants in the program.

— Services Provided Through Transdisciplinary Team

(b) Credentialed personnel with expertise in vision or hearing impairments shall be made available by the district, special education local plan area, or county office to early education programs serving infants identified in accordance with subdivision (a), (b), or (d) of Section 3030 of Title 5 of the California Code of Regulations, and shall be the primary providers of services under those programs whenever possible.

— Provision of Services for Vision and Hearing Impairments

(c) Transdisciplinary teams may include, but need not be limited to, qualified persons from the following disciplines:

— Composition of Transdisciplinary Teams

(1) Early childhood special education.

(2) Speech and language therapy.

(3) Nursing, with a skill level not less than that of a registered nurse.

(4) Social work, psychology, or mental health.

(5) Occupational therapy.

(6) Physical therapy.

(7) Audiology.

(8) Parent to parent support.

(d) Any person who is authorized by the district, special education local plan area, or county office to provide early education or related services to infants shall have appropriate experience in normal and atypical infant development and an understanding of the unique needs of families of infants with exceptional needs, or, absent that experience and understanding, shall undergo a comprehensive training plan for that purpose, which plan shall be developed and implemented as part of the staff development component of the local plan for early education services.

– OT/PT Consultation Services

56426.7. Medically necessary occupational therapy and physical therapy shall be provided to the infant when warranted by medical diagnosis and contained in the individualized family service plan, as specified under Chapter 26.5 (commencing with Section 7570) of Division 7 of Title 1 of the Government Code.

– Medically Necessary* OT/PT

56426.8. (a) Early education and related services shall be based on the needs of the infant and the family as determined by the individualized family service plan team, and shall be specified in the individualized family service plan, including the frequency and duration of each type of service. Any early education or related service may be provided only upon written parental consent.

– Education and Services Based on Needs of Infant/Family

(b) The individualized family service plan for any infant shall be developed in consultation with the infant's physician in order to ensure that the services specified in the plan do not conflict with the infant's medical needs.

– Infant's Physician

56426.9. Any infant who becomes three years of age while participating in an early education program under this chapter may continue in the program until June 30 of the current program year, if determined appropriate by the individualized family service plan team. No later than June 30 of that year, an individualized family service plan team shall meet to review the infant's progress, determine eligibility for preschool special education services, and develop the individualized family service plan accordingly. That individualized family service plan team meeting shall be conducted by the local educational agency responsible for the provision of preschool special education services. Representatives of the early education program shall be invited to that meeting.

– Services Beyond Age Three

56427. (a) Not less than two million three hundred twenty-four thousand dollars ($2,324,000) of the federal discretionary funds appropriated to the State Department of Education under the Individuals with Disabilities Education Act (20 U.S.C. Sec. 1400 et seq.) in any fiscal year shall be expended for early education programs for infants with

– Discretionary Funds for Infant Program

*(Sections 56426.7, 56426.8 and 56426.9 Amended in 1994)

exceptional needs and their families, until the department determines, and the Legislature concurs, that the funds are no longer needed for that purpose.

(b) Programs ineligible to receive funding pursuant to Section 56425 or 56728.8 may receive funding pursuant to subdivision (a).

56428. For the 1985-86 fiscal year, and each fiscal year thereafter, any instructional personnel service unit that was used in the prior fiscal year to provide services to children younger than three years of age shall continue to be used for that purpose. If a special education local plan area becomes ineligible for all or any portion of those instructional personnel service units operated and fundable in the prior fiscal year, the Superintendent of Public Instruction shall allocate those units to another local plan area for the purpose of providing services to children younger than three years of age.

– Maintenance of Infant Services

56429. In order to assure the maximum utilization and coordination of local early education services, eligibility for the receipt of funds pursuant to Section 56425, 56427, 56428, or 56728.8 is conditioned upon the approval by the Superintendent of Public Instruction of a local plan for early education services, which approval shall apply for not less than one, nor more than four, years. The local plan shall identify existing public and private early education services, and shall include an interagency plan for the delivery of early education services in accordance with the California Early Intervention Services Act, Title 14 (commencing with Section 95000) of the Government Code.

– Local Plan for Early* Education Services

56430. (a) Early education services may be provided by any of the following methods:

(1) Directly by a local educational agency.

(2) Through an interagency agreement between a local educational agency and another public agency.

(3) Through a contract with another public agency pursuant to Section 56369.

(4) Through a contract with a certified nonpublic, nonsectarian school, or nonpublic, nonsectarian agency pursuant to Section 56366.

(5) Through a contract with a nonsectarian hospital in accordance with Section 56361.5.

– Methods of Providing Services

(b) Contracts or agreements with agencies identified in subdivision (a) for early education services are strongly encouraged when early education services are currently provided by another agency, and when found to be cost-effective means of providing the services. The placement of individual infants under any such contract shall not require

– Contracts or Agreements

*(Section 56429 Amended in 1994)

specific approval by the governing board of the district or the county office.

(c) Early education services provided under this chapter shall be funded pursuant to Sections 56427, 56428, and 56728.8. Early education programs shall not be funded pursuant to any of Sections 56740 to 56743, inclusive.

— Funding

56431. The superintendent shall develop procedures and criteria to enable a district, special education local plan area, or county office to contract with private nonprofit preschools or child development centers to provide special education and related services to infant and preschool age individuals with exceptional needs. The criteria shall include minimum standards that the private, nonprofit preschool or center shall be required to meet.

— Criteria for Private Preschool Contracting

CHAPTER 4.45. SPECIAL EDUCATION PROGRAMS FOR INDIVIDUALS WITH EXCEPTIONAL NEEDS BETWEEN THE AGES OF THREE AND FIVE YEARS, INCLUSIVE

56440. (a) Each special education local plan area shall submit a plan to the superintendent by September 1, 1987, for providing special education and services to individuals with exceptional needs, as defined by the State Board of Education, who are between the ages of three and five years, inclusive, who do not require intensive special education and services under Title II of the Education of the Handicapped Act Amendments of 1986, Public Law 99-457 (20 U.S.C. Secs. 1411, 1412, 1413, and 1419).

    — Local Plan*

(b) The superintendent shall provide for a five-year phase-in of the individuals with exceptional needs qualifying for special education and services under Public Law 99-457, who do not require intensive special education and services, through an application process to be developed by the superintendent.

    — Five-Year Phase-In

(c) All individuals with exceptional needs between the ages of three and five years, inclusive, identified in subdivision (a) shall be served by the districts and county offices within each special education local plan area by June 30, 1992, to the extent required under federal law and pursuant to the local plan and application approved by the superintendent.

    — Serve All by June 30, 1992

(d) Individuals with exceptional needs between the ages of three and five years, inclusive, who are identified by the district, special education local plan area, or county office as requiring special education and services, as defined by the State Board of Education, shall be eligible for special education and services pursuant to this part and shall not be subject to any phase-in plan.

    — Eligibility

(e) In special education local plan areas where individuals with exceptional needs between the ages of three and five, inclusive, who do not require intensive special education and services, are expected to have an increased demand on school facilities as a result of projected growth, pursuant to this chapter, the special education local plan area director shall submit a written report on the impacted local educational agencies to the State Allocation Board by December 1, 1987. The State Allocation Board shall assess the situation and explore ways of resolving the school facilities impaction situation.

    — School Facilities Impaction

(f) The superintendent shall provide technical assistance to local educational agencies in order to help identify suitable alternative instructional settings to alleviate the school facilities impact situation. Alternative instructional settings may include,

    — Alternative Instructional Settings

*(Section 56440 Amended in 1994)

but are not limited to, state preschool programs, or the child's home. Nothing in this chapter shall cause the displacement of children currently enrolled in these settings.

(g) Special education facilities operated by local educational agencies serving children under this chapter and Chapter 4.4 (commencing with Section 56425) shall meet all applicable standards relating to fire, health, sanitation, and building safety, but are not subject to Chapter 3.4 (commencing with Section 1596.80), Chapter 3.5 (commencing with Section 1596.90), and Chapter 3.6 (commencing with Section 1597.30) of Division 2 of the Health and Safety Code. — Special Education Facilities

(h) This chapter applies to all individuals with exceptional needs between the ages of three and five years, inclusive. — Application of Chapter

56441. The Legislature hereby finds and declares that early education programs for individuals with exceptional needs between the ages of three and five years, inclusive, that provide special education and related services within the typical environment appropriate for young children, and include active parent involvement, may do the following: — Legislative Findings and Declarations

(a) Significantly reduce the potential impact of any disabling conditions.

(b) Produce substantial gains in physical development, cognitive development, language and speech development, psychosocial development, and self-help skills development.

(c) Help prevent the development of secondary disabling conditions.

(d) Reduce family stresses.

(e) Reduce societal dependency and institutionalization.

(f) Reduce the need for special class placement in special education programs once the children reach schoolage.

(g) Save substantial costs to society and our schools.

56441.1. (a) Services rendered by state and local agencies serving preschool children with exceptional needs and their families shall be provided in coordination with other state and local agencies. Educational agencies offering similar educational services shall coordinate and not duplicate these services. The Superintendent of Public Instruction shall identify similar services by other state and local agencies. Any child identified as currently being served and qualified as an individual with exceptional needs as defined in Section 56026, and who meets the eligibility criteria of Section 56441.11 shall be counted as an individual under the funding cap prescribed by Section 56447. — Services Provided in Coordination with Other Agencies

(b) As the preschool child approaches the age to enter an elementary school environment, the child's preparation shall be geared toward a readiness for kindergarten and later school success. — Readiness for Kindergarten and Later School Success

56441.2. An early education program for individuals with exceptional needs between the ages of three and five, inclusive, shall include specially designed services to meet the unique needs of preschool children and their families. To meet this purpose, the program focus is on the young child and his or her family and shall include both individual and small group services which shall be available in a variety of typical age-appropriate environments for young children, including the home, and shall include opportunities for active parent involvement.

56441.3. (a) Early education services for preschool children may be provided to individuals or small groups and shall include:

(1) Observing and monitoring the child's behavior and development in his or her environment.

(2) Presenting activities that are developmentally appropriate for the preschool child and are specially designed, based on the child's exceptional needs, to enhance the child's development. Those activities shall be developed to conform with the child's individualized education program and shall be developed so that they do not conflict with his or her medical needs.

(3) Interacting and consulting with the family members, regular preschool teachers, and other service providers, as needed, to demonstrate developmentally appropriate activities necessary to implement the child's individualized education program in the appropriate setting pursuant to Section 56441.4 and necessary to reinforce the expansion of his or her skills in order to promote the child's educational development. These interactions and consultations may include family involvement activities.

(4) Assisting parents to seek and coordinate other services in their community that may be provided to their child by various agencies.

(5) Providing opportunities for young children to participate in play and exploration activities, to develop self-esteem, and to develop preacademic skills.

(6) Providing access to various developmentally appropriate equipment and specialized materials.

(7) Providing related services as defined in Section 300.13 of Title 34 of the Code of Federal Regulations, that include parent counseling and training to help parents understand the special needs of their children and their children's development, as that section read on May 1, 1987.

(b) The duration of group services shall not exceed four hours per day unless determined otherwise by the individualized education program team.

56441.4. Appropriate settings for these services include any of the following:

(a) The regular public or private nonsectarian preschool program.

(b) The child development center or family day care home.

(c) The child's regular environment, that may include the home.

(d) A special site where preschool programs for both children with disabilities and children who are not disabled are located close to each other and have an opportunity to share resources and programming.

(e) A special education preschool program with children who are not disabled attending and participating for all or part of the program.

(f) A public school setting which provides an age-appropriate environment, materials, and services, as defined by the superintendent.

56441.5. Appropriate instructional adult-to-child ratios for group services shall be dependent on the needs of the child. However, because of the unique needs of individuals with exceptional needs between the ages of three and five years, inclusive, who require special education and related services, the number of children per instructional adult shall be less than ratios set forth in subsection (b) of Section 18204 of Title 5 of the California Code of Regulations, as it read on May 1, 1987, for young children in a regular preschool program. Group services provided to individuals with exceptional needs between the ages of three and five years, inclusive, identified as severely disabled pursuant to Section 56030.5 shall not exceed an instructional adult-to-child ratio of one to five.

56441.6. Early education services for preschool children shall be provided through a transdisciplinary team approach of professionals as described in Section 56426.6. Responsibilities of early education program staff shall include consultation with regular preschool program providers, consultation with other specialists, assessment services, and direct services.

56441.7. (a) The maximum caseload for a speech and language specialist providing services exclusively to individuals with exceptional needs, between the ages of three and five years, inclusive, as defined in Section 56441.11 or 56026, shall not exceed a count of 40.

(b) The superintendent shall issue caseload guidelines or proposed regulations to local educational agencies for individuals with exceptional needs between the ages of three and five years, inclusive, by January 1, 1988.

56441.8. Early education services for preschoolers may be provided by any of the following methods:

- Appropriate Settings

- Instructional Adult-to-Child Ratios

- Transdisciplinary Team Approach

- Maximum Caseload for Speech and Language Specialist

- Caseload Guidelines/ Proposed Regulations

- Methods of Providing Early Education Services

(a) Directly by a local educational agency.

(b) Through an interagency agreement between a local educational agency and another public agency.

(c) Through a contract with another public agency pursuant to Section 56369.

(d) Through a contract with a certified nonpublic, nonsectarian school; or nonpublic, nonsectarian agency pursuant to Section 56366.

(e) Through a contract with a nonsectarian hospital in accordance with Section 56361.5.

56441.9. Contracts or agreements with agencies identified in Section 56441.8 are strongly encouraged when these services are currently provided by another agency, and when found to be a cost-effective means of providing the services. The placement of an individual preschool child under any of these contracts shall not require specific approval by the governing board of the school district or the county superintendent of schools.

– Contracts/Agreements

56441.10. Early education services provided under this chapter for preschoolers identified as individuals with exceptional needs pursuant to subdivisions (a) to (e), inclusive, of Section 56441.11 shall not be funded pursuant to any of Sections 56740 to 56743, inclusive, unless a waiver of this section is approved by the superintendent.

– Nonpublic, Nonsectarian School Funding Waiver

56441.11. (a) Notwithstanding any other provision of law or regulation, the special education eligibility criteria in subdivision (b) shall apply to preschool children, between the ages of three and five years.

– Eligibility Requirements* for Preschool Children

(b) A preschool child, between the ages of three and five years, qualifies as a child who needs early childhood special education services if the child meets the following criteria:

(1) Is identified as having one of the following disabling conditions, as defined in Section 300.7 of Title 34 of the Code of Federal Regulations, or an established medical disability, as defined in subdivision (d):

– Disabling Conditions

(A) Autism.

(B) Deaf-blindness.

(C) Deafness.

(D) Hearing impairment.

(E) Mental retardation.

(F) Multiple disabilities.

(G) Orthopedic impairment.

(H) Other health impairment.

(I) Serious emotional disturbance.

(J) Specific learning disability.

(K) Speech or language impairment in one or more of voice, fluency, language and articulation.

*(Section 56441.11 Amended in 1994)

(L) Traumatic brain injury.

(M) Visual impairment.

(N) Established medical disability.

(2) Needs specially designed instruction or services as defined in Sections 56441.2 and 56441.3.

— Needs Specially Designed Instruction or Services

(3) Has needs that cannot be met with modification of a regular environment in the home or school, or both, without ongoing monitoring or support as determined by an individualized education program team pursuant to Section 56431.

— Needs Cannot Be Met with Modification of Regular Environment

(4) Meets eligibility criteria specified in Section 3030 of Title 5 of the California Code of Regulations.

— Meets Specified Eligibility Criteria

(c) A child is not eligible for special education and services if the child does not otherwise meet the eligibility criteria and his or her educational needs are due primarily to:

— Not Individual with Exceptional Needs

(A) Unfamiliarity with the English language.

(B) Temporary physical disabilities.

(C) Social maladjustment.

(D) Environmental, cultural, or economic factors.

(d) For purposes of this section, "established medical disability" is defined as a disabling medical condition or congenital syndrome that the individualized education program team determines has a high predictability of requiring special education and services.

— Definition of Established Medical Disability

(e) When standardized tests are considered invalid for children between the ages of three and five years, alternative means, for example, scales, instruments, observations, and interviews shall be used as specified in the assessment plan.

— Alternative Means to Standardized Tests

(f) In order to implement the eligibility criteria in subdivision (b), the superintendent shall:

— Implementing the Eligibility Criteria

(1) Provide for training in developmentally appropriate practices, alternative assessment and placement options.

(2) Provide a research-based review for developmentally appropriate application criteria for young children.

(3) Provide program monitoring for appropriate use of the eligibility criteria.

(g) If legislation is enacted mandating early intervention services to infants and toddlers with disabilities pursuant to the Individuals with Disabilities Education Act (20 U.S.C. Sec. 1400 et seq.), the superintendent shall reconsider the eligibility criteria for preschool children, between the ages of three and five years, and recommend appropriate changes to the Legislature.

— Reconsider Eligibility Criteria

56441.13. The superintendent shall provide training and technical assistance for the implementation of early education programs for preschool children with exceptional needs, and shall develop:

— Training and Technical Assistance

(a) Methods and models for modifications to the regular program prior to referral.

(b) Guidelines for program providers.

(c) Curriculum and content for programs.

(d) Personnel standards for program providers.

(e) A plan to meet the unique needs of preschool children who require special education services and who are limited-English proficient and of diverse cultural backgrounds.

56441.14. Criteria and options for meeting the special education transportation needs of individuals with exceptional needs between the ages of three and five, inclusive, shall be included in the local transportation policy required pursuant to paragraph (5) of subdivision (b) of Section 56221.

56442. The superintendent shall ensure that state preschool programs and programs for individuals with exceptional needs between the ages of three and five years, inclusive, provided pursuant to this part, are coordinated at the state and local levels.

56443. (a) The State Department of Education shall amend its interagency agreement with the Administration for Children, Youth, and Families, Region IX, Head Start, United States Department of Health and Human Services, to permit a district, special education local plan area, or county office to contract with a Head Start program for special education and services for individuals with exceptional needs between the ages of three and five years pursuant to this part.

(b) Apportionments allocated to Head Start programs for special education and services to individuals with exceptional needs between the ages of three and five years shall supplement and not supplant funds for which the Head Start programs are eligible, or are already receiving, from other funding sources.

56445. (a) Prior to transitioning an individual with exceptional needs from a preschool program to kindergarten, or first grade as the case may be, an appropriate reassessment of the individual shall be conducted pursuant to Article 2 (commencing with Section 56320) of Chapter 4 to determine if the individual is still in need of special education and services.

(b) It is the intent of the Legislature that gains made in the special education program for individuals who received special education and services, in accordance with this chapter, are not lost by too rapid a removal of individualized programs and supports for these individuals.

(c) As part of the transitioning process, a means of monitoring continued success of the child shall be identified by the individualized education program team for those children of kindergarten or first grade equivalency who are determined to be eligible for less intensive special education programs.

(d) As part of the exit process from special education, the present performance levels and learning style shall be noted by the individualized education program team. This information shall be made available to the assigned regular education teacher upon the child's enrollment in kindergarten or first grade as the case may be.

56446. (a) The superintendent shall develop a funding formula for the distribution of federal funds under Title II of the Education of the Handicapped Act Amendments of 1986, Public Law 99-457 (20 U.S.C. Secs. 1411, 1412, 1413, and 1419) to local providers. The funding formula shall be developed in consultation with the Legislative Analyst and the Director of Finance. The funding formula shall include a provision to address planning and development, program startup costs, including assessments and equipment, staff development, rental or leasing of facilities, and transportation. Any carry over funds shall be reported to the superintendent. The federal incentive funds for this program received for individuals with exceptional needs between the ages of three and five years, inclusive, who are not identified as having intensive needs, shall not be included for purposes of subdivision (a) of Section 56712, including additional funds received for these children under the Individuals with Disabilities Education Act (20 U.S.C. Sec. 1400 et seq.) These individuals shall not be included in the enrollment counts or computations prescribed by Section 56728.6.

(b) Public special education funding shall not be used to purchase regular preschool services or to purchase any instructional service other than special education and services permitted by this chapter.

56447. (a) The superintendent shall adopt rules and regulations to ensure that apportionments, inclusive of federal funds, for all individuals with exceptional needs between the ages of three and five years, inclusive, shall be paid to the extent permitted by federal law for no more than 3 percent of the statewide population of all children between the ages of three and five years, inclusive, as determined in the demographics prepared by the Department of Finance in the 1990-91 fiscal year.

(b) Individuals with exceptional needs served under this chapter shall not be subject to subdivision (a) of Section 56760. However, individuals with intensive needs and appropriate instructional personnel service units required to provide educational services to individuals with exceptional needs shall be included in the computations prescribed in Section 56728.6.

56447.1. (a) Nothing in this chapter shall be construed to limit the responsibility of noneducational public agencies in the

- Exit Process from
  Special Education

- Funding Formula*

- Prohibition on Purchasing
  Regular Preschool Services

- Three Percent Service
  Level for Apportionments

- Exclusion from 10 Percent
  Funding Ratio

- Funding Responsibilities
  of Other Public Agencies

*(Section 56446 Amended in 1994

State of California from providing or paying for some or all of the costs of a free appropriate public education for individuals with exceptional needs between the ages of three and five years, inclusive.

(b) Nothing in this chapter shall be construed to permit a noneducational public agency to reduce medical and other assistance available or to alter eligibility under Titles V and XIX of the Social Security Act (Subchapter V (commencing with Section 701) and Subchapter XIX (commencing with Section 1396) of Chapter 7 of Title 42 of the United States Code) with respect to the provision of a free appropriate public education for individuals with exceptional needs between the ages of three and five years, inclusive, within the State of California.

56448. (a) If the amount of funding provided by the federal government pursuant to Sections 1411 and 1419 of Title 20 of the United States Code for the 1990-91 fiscal year, or any fiscal year thereafter, is not sufficient to fund the full costs of the programs and services required pursuant to this chapter, which are defined as the costs of the program in the prior fiscal year as adjusted for caseload growth and by the Implicit Price Deflator for State and Local Government Purchase of Goods and Services for the United States, as published by the United States Department of Commerce for the 12-month period ending in the third quarter of the prior fiscal year, for pupils identified pursuant to subdivision (g) of Section 56440, except for those pupils identified pursuant to paragraph (2) of subdivision (c) of Section 56026, as it read on January 8, 1987, and that lack of federal funding would require any contribution from the General Fund or any contribution from a local educational agency in order to fund those costs, California shall terminate its participation in that program.

– Termination Provisions

(b) The voluntary contribution by a local educational agency of funding for any of the programs or services required pursuant to this chapter shall not constitute grounds for terminating California's participation in that federal program.

– Voluntary Contribution

(c) If the Superintendent of Public Instruction determines that the conditions set forth in subdivision (a) have occurred, the superintendent, not later than December 1, shall notify the Legislature and the Secretary of State that those conditions have occurred, and the termination of the program shall occur on July 1 after the current fiscal year has elapsed or six months from the notice of the superintendent to the Legislature and the Secretary of State, whichever is later, and shall be carried out in an orderly manner with timely notification of parents and certificated personnel, as prescribed by statute.

– Responsibility of Superintendent of Public Instruction

(d) During the period prior to termination of the program, as set forth in subdivision (c), all funds provided from federal or state sources for the program set forth in this chapter shall be apportioned on a prorated basis to all eligible local educational agencies operating those programs.

56449. This chapter shall remain in effect only until California terminates its participation in special education programs for individuals with exceptional needs between the ages of three and five year, pursuant to Section 56448, and as of that date is repealed.

— Automatic Repeal Provision

CHAPTER 4.5. CAREER AND VOCATIONAL EDUCATION PROGRAMS, TRANSITION SERVICES, AND PROJECT WORKABILITY

Article 1. Career and Vocational Education Programs

56452. The superintendent shall ensure that the state annually secures all federal funds available for career and vocational education of individuals with exceptional needs.

56453. The superintendent and the Department of Rehabilitation shall enter into an interagency agreement to ensure that the state annually secures all federal funds available under the Rehabilitation Act of 1973, as amended, and that coordination in applying for, distributing, and using funds available under the Vocational Education Act, as amended, the Rehabilitation Act of 1973, as amended, and the Education For All Handicapped Children Act of 1975, (P.L. 94-142), as amended, including, but not limited to, application for, and use thereof, be provided.

56454. In order to provide districts, special education local plan areas, and county offices with maximum flexibility to secure and utilize all federal funds available to enable those entities to meet the career and vocational needs of individuals with exceptional needs more effectively and efficiently, and to provide maximum federal funding to those agencies for the provision of that education, the superintendent shall do all the following:

(a) Provide necessary technical assistance to districts, special education local plan areas, and county offices.

(b) Establish procedures for these entities to obtain available federal funds.

(c) Apply for necessary waivers of federal statutes and regulations including, but not limited to, those governing federal career and vocational education programs.

56456. It is the intent of the Legislature that districts, special education local plan areas, and county offices may use any state or local special education funds for approved vocational programs, services, and activities to satisfy the excess cost matching requirements for receipt of federal vocational education funds for individuals with exceptional needs.

Article 2. Transition Services

56460. The Legislature finds and declares all of the following:

(a) That while the passage of the Education for All Handicapped Children Act of 1975 (Public Law 94-142) and the California Master Plan for Special Education have resulted in improved educational services for individuals with exceptional needs; this has not translated into paid employment opportunities or maximum integration into our heterogeneous communities for individuals with exceptional needs.

(b) That there is no formalized process that bridges the gap between the security and structure of school and the complexity of service options and resources available for individuals with exceptional needs in the adult community.

(c) That there is insufficient coordination between educators, adult service providers, potential employers, and families and students in order to effectively plan and implement a successful transition for students to the adult world of paid employment and social independence.

(d) That because of insufficient vocational training throughout the middle and secondary school years, and effective interagency coordination and involvement of potential employers in a planning process, the majority of options available for individuals with exceptional needs in the adult community are programs that support dependence rather than independence.

(e) The goal of transition services is planned movement from secondary education to adult life that provides opportunities which maximize economic and social independence in the least restrictive environment for individuals with exceptional needs. Planning for transition from school to postsecondary environments should begin in the school system well before the student leaves the system.

56461. The superintendent shall establish the capacity to provide transition services for a broad range of individuals with exceptional needs such as employment and academic training, strategic planning, interagency coordination, and parent training.

– Covers a Broad Range of Individuals

56462. The transition services shall include, but not be limited to, the following:

– Components of Transition* Services

(a) In-service training programs, resource materials, and handbooks that identify the following:

(1) The definition of "transition," including the major components of an effective school-based transition program.

(2) Relevant laws and regulations.

(3) The roles of other agencies in the transition process including, but not limited to, the scope of their services, eligibility criteria, and funding.

(4) The components of effective transition planning.

*(Section 56462 Amended in 1994)

(5) The role of families in the individualized transition process.

(6) Resources and model programs currently available in this state.

(b) Development of the role and responsibilities of special education in the transition process, including the following:

- Role of Special Education in Transition Process

(1) The provision of work skills training, including those skills that are necessary in order to exhibit competence on the job.

(2) The provision of multiple employment options and facilitating job or career choice by providing a variety of vocational experiences.

(3) The collection and analysis of data on what happens to pupils once they leave the school system and enter the adult world.

(4) The coordination of the transition planning process, including development of necessary interagency agreements and procedures at both state and local levels.

(5) The provision of instructional learning strategies that will assist pupils who find learning difficult in acquiring skills that will enable them to obtain diplomas, promote a positive attitude toward secondary and postsecondary education and training, and make a successful transition to postsecondary life.

(c) The development and implementation of systematic and longitudinal vocational education curriculum including the following:

- Systematic and Longitudinal Vocational Education Curriculum

(1) Instructional strategies that will prepare pupils with severe disabilities to make a successful transition to supported employment and the community.

(2) The introduction of vocational and career education curriculum in the elementary grades for those pupils who can benefit from it.

(d) Materials, resource manuals, and in-service training programs to support the active participation of families in the planning and implementation of transition-related goals and activities.

- Support Active Participation of Families

(e) The development of resources and in-service training that will support the implementation of individualized transition planning for all pupils with exceptional needs.

- Resources and In-Service Training

(f) The development of a network of model demonstration sites that illustrate a wide variety of transition models and implementation strategies.

- Demonstration Sites

(g) Coordination with other specialized programs that serve students who face barriers to successful transition.

- Coordination with Other Programs

(h) A research, evaluation, and dissemination program that will support the major programmatic aspects of transition services. Through a variety of competitive grants, bids,

- Research, Evaluation, and Dissemination

contracts, and other awards specific content areas will be developed in cooperation with a variety of field-based agencies, including local education agencies, special education local plan areas, county offices, institutions of higher education, and in-service training agencies.

56463. Transition services shall be funded pursuant to the Budget Act.

Article 3. Project Workability

56470. The Legislature finds and declares all of the following:

(a) That an essential component of transition services developed and supported by the State Department of Education is project workability.

(b) That the workability program provides instruction and experiences that reinforce core curriculum concepts and skills leading to gainful employment.

(c) That since project workability was established by the State Department of Education in 1981, substantial numbers of individuals with exceptional needs have obtained full- or part-time employment.

(d) That project workability is a true partnership established at the state level through nonfinancial interagency agreements between the State Department of Education, the Department of Employment Development, and the Department of Rehabilitation, and has elevated awareness in the private sector of the employment potential of individuals with exceptional needs, and focuses its efforts in developing careers for these youth, and preventing needless economic and social dependency on state and community agencies and resources.

(e) That local education agencies in California establish linkage between agencies, eliminate duplication of effort, and develop precedent-setting employment training practices which should be preserved and advanced to better assure future productive employable citizens.

56471. (a) The program shall be administered by the State Department of Education.

(b) The department shall establish an advisory committee. This committee will include representatives from local workability projects to ensure ongoing communications.

(c) The superintendent shall develop criteria for awarding grants, funding, and evaluating workability projects.

(d) Workability project applications shall include, but are not limited to, the following elements: (1) recruitment, (2) assessment, (3) counseling, (4) preemployment skills training, (5) vocational training, (6) student wages for try-out employment, (7) placement in unsubsidized employment, (8) other assistance with transition to a quality adult life, and (9) utilization of an interdisciplinary advisory committee to enhance project goals.

56472. The population served by workability projects may include secondary students with disabilities, adults with disabilities and other individuals who experience barriers to successful completion of school. — Population Served

56473. Project workability shall be funded pursuant to Item 6100-161-001 and Item 6100-161-890 of the Budget Act. — Funded Pursuant to Budget Act

56474. The superintendent shall continue to seek additional state and federal funding for project workability. — Seek Additional Funding

CHAPTER 4.7. INTERAGENCY AGREEMENTS

56475. (a) The superintendent and the directors of the State Department of Health Services, the State Department of Mental Health, the State Department of Developmental Services, the State Department of Social Services, the Department of Rehabilitation, the Department of the Youth Authority, and the Employment Development Department shall develop written interagency agreements or adopt joint regulations that include fiscal responsibilities for the provision of special education and related services to individuals with exceptional needs in the State of California.

    – Written Agreements

    – Fiscal Responsibilities

(b) The superintendent shall develop interagency agreements with other state and local public agencies, as deemed necessary by the superintendent, to carry out the provisions of state and federal law.

    – Other Agreements

(c) (1) Each interagency agreement shall be submitted by the superintendent to each legislative fiscal committee, education committee, and policy committee, responsible for legislation relating to those individuals with exceptional needs that will be affected by the agreement if it is effective.

    – Submit to Legislature

(2) An interagency agreement shall not be effective sooner than 30 days after it has been submitted to each of the legislative committees specified in paragraph (1).

    – Effective Date of Agreements

CHAPTER 5. PROCEDURAL SAFEGUARDS

56500. As used in this chapter, "public education agency" means a district, special education local plan area, or county office, depending on the category of local plan elected by the governing board of a school district pursuant to Section 56170, or any other public agency providing special education or related services.

– Public Education Agency Definition

56500.1. (a) All procedural safeguards under the Individuals with Disabilities Education Act (20 U.S.C. Sec. 1400 and following) shall be established and maintained by each noneducational and educational agency that provides education, related services, or both, to children who are individuals with exceptional needs.

– Federal Procedural Safeguards

56500.2. An expeditious and effective process shall be implemented for the resolution of complaints regarding any alleged violations of the Individuals with Disabilities Education Act (20 U.S.C. Sec. 1400 and following).

– Resolution of Complaints

56500.3. (a) It is the intent of the Legislature that parties to special education disputes be encouraged to seek resolution through mediation prior to filing a request for a due process hearing. It is also the intent of the Legislature that these voluntary prehearing request mediation conferences be an informal process conducted in a nonadversarial atmosphere to resolve issues relating to the identification, assessment, or educational placement of the child, or the provision of a free, appropriate public education to the child, to the satisfaction of both parties. Therefore, attorneys or other independent contractors used to provide legal advocacy services shall not attend or otherwise participate in the prehearing request mediation conferences.

– Prehearing Mediation Conference

– Mediation Conference to Be Nonadversarial

(b) Nothing in this part shall preclude the parent or the public education agency from being accompanied and advised by nonattorney representatives in the mediation conferences and consulting with an attorney prior to or following a mediation conference. For purposes of this section, "attorney" means an active, practicing member of the State Bar of California or another independent contractor used to provide legal advocacy services, but does not mean a parent of the pupil who is also an attorney.

– Nonattorney Representatives

– Definition of Attorney

(c) Requesting or participating in a mediation conference is not a prerequisite to requesting a due process hearing.

– Not a Prerequisite

(d) All requests for a mediation conference shall be filed with the superintendent. The party initiating a mediation conference by filing a written request with the superintendent shall provide the other party to the mediation with a copy of the request at the same time the request is filed with the

– Requests for Mediation Conference

superintendent. The mediation conference shall be conducted by a person knowledgeable in the process of reconciling differences in a nonadversarial manner and under contract with the department pursuant to Section 56504.5. The mediator shall be knowledgeable in the laws and regulations governing special education.

— Mediator

(e) The prehearing mediation conference shall be scheduled within 15 days of receipt by the superintendent of the request for mediation. The mediation conference shall be completed within 30 days after receipt of the request for mediation unless both parties to the prehearing mediation conference agree to extend the time for completing the mediation.

— Scheduled Within 15 Days

(f) Based upon the mediation conference, the district superintendent, the county superintendent, or the director of the public education agency, or his or her designee, may resolve the issue or issues. However, this resolution shall not conflict with state or federal law and shall be to the satisfaction of both parties. A copy of the written resolution shall be mailed to each party within 10 days following the mediation conference.

— Resolution of Issues

(g) If the mediation conference fails to resolve the issues to the satisfaction of all parties, the party who requested the mediation conference has the option of filing for a state-level hearing pursuant to Section 56505. The mediator may assist the parties in specifying any unresolved issues to be included in the hearing request.

— Failure to Resolve Issues

(h) Any mediation conference held pursuant to this section shall be held at a time and place reasonably convenient to the parent and pupil.

— Time and Place

(i) The mediation conference shall be conducted in accordance with regulations adopted by the board.

— State Board of Education Regulations

(j) Notwithstanding any procedure set forth in this chapter, a public education agency and a parent may, if the party initiating the mediation conference so chooses, meet informally to resolve any issue or issues to the satisfaction of both parties prior to the mediation conference.

— Meeting Informally to Resolve Issues

(k) The procedures and rights contained in this section shall be included in the notice of parent rights attached to the pupil's assessment plan pursuant to Section 56321.

— Notice of Parent Rights

56501. (a) The due process hearing procedures prescribed by this chapter extend to the parent, as defined in Section 56028, a pupil who has been emancipated, and a pupil who is a ward or dependent of the court or for whom no parent can be identified or located when the hearing officer determines that either the local educational agency has failed to appoint a surrogate parent as required by Section 7579.5 of the Government Code or the surrogate parent appointed by the local educational agency does not meet the criteria set forth in

— Due Process Hearing Procedures

subdivision (e) of Section 7579.5 of the Government Code, and the public education agency involved in any decisions regarding a pupil. The appointment of a surrogate parent after a hearing has been requested by the pupil shall not be cause for dismissal of the hearing request. The parent and the public education agency involved may initiate the due process hearing procedures prescribed by this chapter under any of the following circumstances:

– Due Process Hearing
    Circumstances

(1) There is a proposal to initiate or change the identification, assessment, or educational placement of the child or the provision of a free, appropriate public education to the child.

(2) There is a refusal to initiate or change the identification, assessment, or educational placement of the child or the provision of a free, appropriate public education to the child.

(3) The parent refuses to consent to an assessment of the child.

(b) The due process hearing rights prescribed by this chapter include, but are not limited to, all the following:

– Hearing Rights

(1) The right to a mediation conference pursuant to Section 56500.3.

(2) The right to request a mediation conference at any point during the hearing process. A mediation conference shall be scheduled if both parties to the hearing agree to mediate and are willing to extend the 45-day limit for issuing a hearing decision for a period equal to the length of the mediation process. This limitation on the period of extension is not applicable if the parties agree to take the hearing off calendar. Notwithstanding subdivision (a) of Section 56500.3, attorneys and advocates are permitted to participate in mediation conferences scheduled after the filing of a request for due process hearing.

(3) The right to examine pupil records pursuant to Section 56504. This provision shall not be construed to abrogate the rights prescribed by Chapter 6.5 (commencing with Section 49060) of Part 27.

(4) The right to a fair and impartial administrative hearing at the state level, before a person knowledgeable in the laws governing special education and administrative hearings, under contract with the department, pursuant to Section 56505.

(c) In addition to the rights prescribed by subdivision (b), the parent has the following rights:

– Additional Parent Rights

(1) The right to have the pupil who is the subject of the state hearing present at the hearing.

(2) The right to open the state hearing to the public.

56502. (a) All requests for a due process hearing shall be filed with the superintendent. The party initiating a due process hearing by filing a written request with the superintendent shall

– Written Request for·
    Hearing

provide the other party to the hearing with a copy of the request at the same time as the request is filed with the superintendent. The superintendent shall take steps to ensure that within 45 days after receipt of the written hearing request the hearing is immediately commenced and completed, including, any mediation requested at any point during the hearing process pursuant to paragraph (2) of subdivision (b) of Section 56501, and a final administrative decision is rendered, unless a continuance has been granted pursuant to Section 56505.

– Forty-five Days to Complete Hearing

(b) Notwithstanding any procedure set forth in this chapter, a public education agency and a parent may, if the party initiating the hearing so chooses, meet informally to resolve any issue or issues relating to the identification, assessment, or education and placement of the child, or the provision of a free, appropriate public education to the child, to the satisfaction of both parties prior to the hearing. The informal meeting shall be conducted by the district superintendent, county superintendent, or director of the public education agency or his or her designee. Any designee appointed pursuant to this subdivision shall have the authority to resolve the issue or issues.

– Informal Meeting to Resolve Issues

(c) Upon receipt by the superintendent of a written request by the parent or public education agency, the superintendent or his or her designee or designees shall immediately notify, in writing, all parties of the request for the hearing and the scheduled date for the hearing. The notice shall advise all parties of all their rights relating to procedural safeguards. The superintendent or his or her designee shall provide both parties with a list of persons and organizations within the geographical area that can provide free or reduced cost representation or other assistance in preparing for the due process hearing. This list shall include a brief description of the requirement to qualify for the services. The superintendent or his or her designee shall have complete discretion in determining which individuals or groups shall be included on the list.

– Notification of All Parties

– Free or Reduced Cost Representation

56503. Nothing in this chapter shall preclude the parties to a hearing from agreeing to use a mediation conference or resolving their dispute in an informal, nonadversarial manner, even though a request for a state level hearing has been filed or even if the hearing has commenced.

– Mediation Conference to Be Nonadversarial

56504. The parent shall have the right and opportunity to examine all school records of the child and to receive copies pursuant to this section and to Section 49065 within five days after such request is made by the parent, either orally or in writing. A public educational agency may charge no more than the actual cost of reproducing such records, but if this cost

– Parent Right to Examine School Records/Receive Copies

effectively prevents the parent from exercising the right to receive such copy or copies the copy or copies shall be reproduced at no cost.

56504.5. The department shall contract with a single, nonprofit organization or entity to conduct mediation conferences and due process hearings that does the following:

– Contract for Mediators and Hearing Officers

(a) Employs persons knowledgeable in administrative hearings and laws and regulations governing special education.

(b) Does not have a conflict of interest under state and federal laws and regulations governing special education and related services in conducting mediation conferences and due process hearings.

(c) Is not in the business of providing, or supervising, special education, related services, or care to children and youth.

56505. (a) The state hearing shall be conducted in accordance with regulations adopted by the board.

– State Hearing*

(b) The hearing shall be held at a time and place reasonably convenient to the parent and the pupil.

– Time and Place

(c) The hearing shall be conducted by a person knowledgeable in the laws governing special education and administrative hearings pursuant to Section 56504.5. The hearing officer shall encourage the parties to a hearing to consider the option of mediation as an alternative to a hearing.

– Conducted by Knowledgeable Person

(d) During the pendency of the hearing proceedings, including the actual state level hearing, the pupil shall remain in his or her present placement unless the public agency and the parent agree otherwise.

– Pupil Placement During Hearing

(e) Any party to the hearing held pursuant to this section shall be afforded the following rights consistent with state and federal statutes and regulations.

– Additional Hearing Rights

(1) The right to be accompanied and advised by counsel and by individuals with special knowledge or training relating to the problems of children and youth with disabilities.

(2) The right to present evidence, written arguments, and oral arguments.

(3) The right to confront, cross-examine, and compel the attendance of witnesses.

(4) The right to a written or electronic verbatim record of the hearing.

(5) The right to written findings of fact and decisions. The findings and decisions shall be made available to the public consistent with the requirements of subsection (c) of Section 1417 of Title 20 of the United States Code and shall also be transmitted to the Advisory Commission on Special Education pursuant to subsection (d) of Section 1415 of Title 20 of the United States Code.

*(Section 56505 Amended in 1994)

(6) The right to be informed by the other parties to the hearing, at least 10 days prior to the hearing, as to what those parties believe are the issues to be decided at the hearing and their proposed resolution of those issues. Upon the request of a parent who is not represented by an attorney, the agency responsible for conducting hearings shall provide a mediator to assist the parent in identifying the issues and the proposed resolution of the issues.

(7) The right to prohibit the introduction of any evidence at the hearing that has not been disclosed to the party at least five days before the hearing.

(f) The hearing conducted pursuant to this section shall be completed and a written, reasoned decision mailed to all parties to the hearing within 45 days from the receipt by the superintendent of the request for a hearing. Either party to the hearing may request the hearing officer to grant an extension. The extension shall be granted upon a showing of good cause. Any extension shall extend the time for rendering a final administrative decision for a period only equal to the length of the extension.

    — Written Decision Within 45 Days

    — Extension

(g) The hearing conducted pursuant to this section shall be the final administrative determination and binding on all parties.

    — Final Administrative Determination

(h) In decisions relating to the placement of individuals with exceptional needs, the person conducting the state hearing shall consider cost, in addition to all other factors that are considered.

    — Hearing Officer Considers Cost

(i) Nothing in this chapter shall preclude a party from exercising the right to appeal the decision to a court of competent jurisdiction. An appeal shall be made within 90 days of receipt of the hearing decision. During the pendency of any administrative or judicial proceeding conducted pursuant to Chapter 5 (commencing with Section 56500), unless the public education agency and the parents of the child agree otherwise, the child involved in the hearing shall remain in his or her present educational placement.

    — Right to Appeal to Court

56505.1. The hearing officer may do any of the following during the hearing:

    — Hearing Officer Rights

(a) Question a witness on the record prior to any of the parties doing so.

    — Question Witness

(b) With the consent of both parties to the hearing, request that conflicting experts discuss an issue or issues with each other while on the record.

    — Request Conflicting Experts Discuss Issues

(c) Visit the proposed placement site or sites when the physical attributes of the site or sites are at issue.

    — Visit Proposed Placement Sites

(d) Call a witness to testify at the hearing if all parties to the hearing consent to the witness giving testimony or the hearing

    — Call a Witness

is continued for at least five days after the witness is identified and before the witness testifies.

(e) Order that an impartial assessment of the pupil be conducted for purposes of the hearing and continue the hearing until the assessment has been completed. The cost of any assessment ordered under this subdivision shall be included in the contract between the department and the organization or entity conducting the hearing.

– Order an Impartial Assessment

(f) In decisions relating to the provision of related services by other public agencies, the hearing officer may call as witnesses independent medical specialists qualified to present evidence in the area of the pupil's medical disability. The cost for any witness called to testify under this subdivision shall be included in the contract between the department and the organization or entity conducting the hearing.

– Call as Witnesses Independent Medical Specialists

56505.2. (a) A hearing officer may not render a decision that results in the placement of an individual with exceptional needs in a nonpublic, nonsectarian school, or that results in a service for an individual with exceptional needs provided by a nonpublic agency, if the school or agency has not been certified pursuant to Section 56366.1.

– Nonpublic School/Agency Placement/Service Restriction

(b) A hearing officer shall consider Sections 56365, 56365.5, 56366, and 56366.1 during a due process hearing concerning an issue of placement of an individual with exceptional needs in a nonpublic, nonsectarian school, or services for an individual with exceptional needs provided by a nonpublic, nonsectarian agency.

56506. In addition to the due process hearing rights enumerated in subdivision (b) of 56501, the following due process rights extend to the pupil and the parent:

– Additional Due Process Rights

(a) Written notice to the parent of his or her rights in language easily understood by the general public and in the primary language of the parent or other mode of communication used by the parent, unless to do so is clearly not feasible. The written notice of rights shall include, but not be limited to, those prescribed by Section 56341.

(b) The right to initiate a referral of a child for special education services pursuant to Section 56303.

(c) The right to obtain an independent educational assessment pursuant to subdivision (b) of Section 56329.

(d) The right to participate in the development of the individualized education program and to be informed of the availability under state and federal law of free appropriate public education and of all available alternative programs, both public and nonpublic.

(e) Written parental consent pursuant to Section 56321 shall be obtained before any assessment of the pupil is conducted unless the public education agency prevails in a due process hearing relating to such assessment.

(f) Written parental consent pursuant to Section 56321 shall be obtained before the pupil is placed in a special education program.

56507. (a) If either party to a due process hearing intends to be represented by an attorney in the state hearing, notice of that intent shall be given to the other party at least 10 days prior to the hearing. The failure to provide that notice shall constitute good cause for a continuance.

— Use of Attorneys

(b) An award of reasonable attorneys' fees to the prevailing parent, guardian, or pupil, as the case may be, may only be made either with the agreement of the parties following the conclusion of the administrative hearing process or by a court of competent jurisdiction pursuant to paragraph (4) of subsection (e) of Section 1415 of Title 20 of the United States Code.

— Award of Attorneys' Fees

(c) Public education agencies shall not use federal funds distributed under Part B of the Individuals with Disabilities Education Act (20 U.S.C. Sec. 1400 and following), or other federal special education funds, for the agency's own legal counsel or other advocacy costs, that may include, but are not limited to, a private attorney or employee of an attorney, legal paraprofessional, or other paid advocate, related to a due process hearing or the appeal of a hearing decision to the courts. Nor shall the funds be used to reimburse parents who prevail and are awarded attorneys' fees, pursuant to subdivision (b), as part of the judgment. Nothing in this subdivision shall preclude public agencies from using these funds for attorney services related to the establishment of policy and programs, or responsibilities, under Part B of the Individuals with Disabilities Education Act (20 U.S.C. Sec. 1400 and following) and the program administration of these programs. This subdivision does not apply to attorneys and others hired under contract to conduct administrative hearings pursuant to subdivision (a) of Section 56505.

— Use of Federal Funds

(d) The hearing decision shall indicate the extent to which each party has prevailed on each issue heard and decided, including issues involving other public agencies named as parties to the hearing.

— Extent Each Party
  Prevailed

56508. It is the intent of the Legislature that the department develop training materials that can be used locally by parents, public education agencies, and others and conduct workshops on alternative resolutions for resolving differences in a nonadversarial atmosphere with the mutual goal of providing a free and appropriate public education for children and youth with disabilities.

— Training Materials for
  Alternative Resolutions
  for Resolving Differences

CHAPTER 5.5. BEHAVIORAL INTERVENTIONS

56520. (a) The Legislature finds and declares all of the following:

– Legislative Findings and Declarations

(1) That the state has continually sought to provide an appropriate and meaningful educational program in a safe and healthy environment for all children regardless of possible physical, mental, or emotionally disabling conditions.

(2) That teachers of children with special needs require training and guidance that provides positive ways for working successfully with children who have difficulties conforming to acceptable behavioral patterns in order to provide an environment in which learning can occur.

(3) That procedures for the elimination of maladaptive behaviors shall not include those deemed unacceptable under Section 49001 of or those that cause pain or trauma.

(b) It is the intent of the Legislature:

– Legislative Intent

(1) That when behavioral interventions are used, they be used in consideration of the pupil's physical freedom and social interaction, be administered in a manner that respects human dignity and personal privacy, and that ensure a pupil's right to placement in the least restrictive educational environment.

(2) That behavioral management plans be developed and used, to the extent possible, in a consistent manner when the pupil is also the responsibility of another agency for residential care or related services.

(3) That a statewide study be conducted of the use of behavioral interventions with California individuals with exceptional needs receiving special education and related services.

(4) That training programs be developed and implemented in institutions of higher education that train teachers and that in-service training programs be made available as necessary in school districts and county offices of education to assure that adequately trained staff are available to work effectively with the behavioral intervention needs of individuals with exceptional needs.

56521. (a) This chapter applies to any individual with exceptional needs who is in a public school program, including a state school for the disabled pursuant to Part 32 (commencing with Section 59000), or who is placed in a nonpublic school program pursuant to Sections 56365 to 56366.5, inclusive.

– Application of Chapter

(b) The Superintendent of Public Instruction shall monitor and supervise the implementation of this chapter.

– Monitor and Supervise Implementation

56523. (a) On or before September 1, 1992, the Superintendent of Public Instruction shall develop and the State Board of Education shall adopt regulations governing the use of

– Regulations

behavioral interventions with individuals with exceptional needs receiving special education and related services.

(b) The regulations shall do all of the following: – Scope of Regulations

(1) Specify the types of positive behavioral interventions which may be utilized and specify that interventions which cause pain or trauma are prohibited.

(2) Require that, if appropriate, the pupil's individual education plan includes a description of the positive behavioral interventions to be utilized which accomplishes the following:

(A) Assesses the appropriateness of positive interventions.

(B) Assures the pupil's physical freedom, social interaction, and individual choices.

(C) Respects the pupil's human dignity and personal privacy.

(D) Assures the pupil's placement in the least restrictive environment.

(E) Includes the method of measuring the effectiveness and the interventions.

(F) Includes a timeline for the regular and frequent review of the pupil's progress.

(3) Specify standards governing the application of restrictive behavioral interventions in the case of emergencies. These emergencies must pose a clear and present danger of serious physical harm to the pupil or others. These standards shall include:

(A) The definition of an emergency.

(B) The types of behavioral interventions that may be utilized in an emergency.

(C) The duration of the intervention which shall not be longer than is necessary to contain the dangerous behavior.

(D) A process and timeline for the convening of an individual education plan meeting to evaluate the application of the emergency intervention and adjust the pupil's individual education plan in a manner designed to reduce or eliminate the negative behavior through positive programming.

(E) A process for reporting annually to the State Department of Education and the Advisory Commission on Special Education the number of emergency interventions applied under this chapter.

56524. The superintendent shall explore with representatives of institutions of higher education and the Commission on Teacher Credentialing, the current training requirements for teachers to ensure that sufficient training is available in appropriate behavioral interventions for people entering the field of education. – Explore Current Training Requirements

CHAPTER 6. EVALUATION, AUDITS, AND INFORMATION

56600. It is the intent of the Legislature to provide for ongoing comprehensive evaluation of special education programs authorized by this part. The Legislature finds and declares that the evaluation of these programs shall be designed to provide the Legislature, the State Board of Education, the State Department of Education, and program administrators at special education local plan area, county, district, and school levels with the information necessary to refine and improve programs, policies, regulations, guidelines, and procedures on a continuing basis, and to assess the overall merits of these efforts.

– Legislative Intent on Program Evaluation

56600.5. (a) The superintendent shall submit to the board, not later than July 1, 1989, an evaluation plan for special education. This plan shall outline a procedure to identify statewide evaluation priorities in special education and strategies to involve the special education local plan areas for their cooperation in conducting the studies.

– Evaluation Plan

(b) The plan developed pursuant to subdivision (a) shall be developed in consultation with the Advisory Commission on Special Education and with other groups or individuals the superintendent deems appropriate.

– Plan Development

(c) The plan developed pursuant to subdivision (a) shall include, but not be limited to, all of the following:

– Plan Components

(1) The identification of outcomes and goals against which programs can be judged.

(2) Questions requiring further research and how they are addressed in the evaluation plan.

(3) Research that has been conducted in these questions to date, including a brief summary of findings.

(4) Potential evaluation methodologies.

(5) The scope and probable duration of the evaluations.

(6) Organizations that could conduct these evaluations.

(7) Funding requirements for the evaluations.

(8) The potential policy implications of the proposed studies.

(d) The evaluation plan developed pursuant to subdivision (a) shall also include provisions for both of the following:

– Eligibility Criteria and Exit Criteria

(1) Analyzing the existing eligibility criteria for special education programs and services.

(2) The appropriateness of establishing specific, exit criteria for special education programs, and strengthening the exit process.

56601. (a) Each special education local plan area shall submit to the superintendent at least annually information, in a form and

– Submit Annual Information

manner prescribed by the superintendent and developed in consultation with the special education local plan areas, in order for the superintendent to carry out the evaluation responsibilities pursuant to Section 56602. This information shall include other statistical data, program information, and fiscal information that the superintendent may require. The superintendent shall use this information to answer questions from the Legislature and other state and federal agencies on program, policy, and fiscal issues of statewide interest.

(b) In order to assist the state in evaluating the effectiveness of special education programs, including transition and work experience programs, the superintendent is authorized to collect and utilize social security numbers of individuals with exceptional needs as pupil identification numbers beginning in the 1993-94 fiscal year and phased in over a two-year period. In a situation where a social security number is not available, the superintendent shall assign another student identification number for purposes of evaluating special education programs and related services. The superintendent shall not disclose personally identifiable, individual pupil records to any person, institution, agency, or organization except as authorized by Section 1232g of Title 20 of the United States Code and Part 99 of Title 34 of the Code of Federal Regulations.

– Utilize Social Security Numbers

56602. In accordance with a program evaluation plan adopted pursuant to subdivision (e) of Section 56100, the superintendent shall submit to the board, the Legislature, and the Governor, an annual evaluation of the special education programs implemented under this part. This evaluation shall do all of the following:

– Annual Special Education* Evaluation

(a) Utilize existing information sources including fiscal records, enrollment data, and other descriptive data, and program reviews to gather ongoing information regarding implementation of programs authorized by this chapter.

– Existing Information Sources

(b) Utilize existing information sources including fiscal records, enrollment data, and other descriptive data, and program reviews to gather ongoing information regarding implementation of programs authorized by this chapter.

– Special Evaluation Studies

(1) Pupil performance. The State Department of Education shall assist special education local plan areas in the development of models of pupil performance in order to determine the success or failure of special education programs and services. As appropriate, special education pupils and parents of special education pupils shall be involved in the development of these models.

(2) Placement of pupils in least restrictive environments.

(3) Degree to which services identified in individualized education programs are provided.

*(Section 56602 Amended in 1994)

(4) Parent, pupil, teacher, program specialist, resource specialist, and administrator attitudes toward services and processes provided.

(5) Program costs, including, but not limited to:

(A) Expenditures for instructional personnel services, support services, special transportation services, and regionalized services.

(B) Capital outlay costs at the district and school levels, and for special education local plan areas, county offices, state special schools, and nonpublic, nonsectarian schools.

(C) Funding sources at the district, special education local plan area, county office, state special school, nonpublic, nonsectarian school, and agency levels, including funding provided by state and local noneducational public agencies.

(c) Identify the numbers of individuals with exceptional needs, their racial and ethnic data, their classification by designated instructional services, resource specialist, special day class or center, nonpublic, nonsectarian schools, and agencies, including pupils referred to and placed in those programs by state and local noneducational public agencies, in accordance with criteria established by the board and consistent with federal reporting requirements. — Data on Individuals/ Settings

(d) The State Department of Education shall, as part of the department's regular data collection process for special education programs, collect data on the types of agencies that provide designated instruction and services or related services that are contracted for by special education local plan areas or programs for the disabled operated by the state pursuant to Public Law 89-313, in order to determine the number of special education pupils who are enrolled in nonpublic, nonsectarian special education schools or who are receiving nonpublic, nonsectarian agency services. — Data on Types of Agencies That Provide DIS

56603. The Department of Education shall, as part of the annual evaluation, report the information necessary to refine and improve statewide policies, regulations, guidelines, and procedures developed pursuant to this part. — Report Information

56604. (a) The superintendent shall coordinate the design of evaluations to prevent duplication and to minimize data collection and reporting requirements at the school and district levels. — Coordinate Design of Evaluations

(b) The Department of Education shall utilize sampling procedures whenever feasible. — Utilize Sampling Procedures

56605. The superintendent shall periodically sponsor or conduct workshops and seminars for the education of local education agency personnel assigned to, and responsible for, the evaluation of local special education programs. — Workshops and Seminars

56606. The superintendent shall provide for onsite program and fiscal reviews of the implementation of plans approved under this part. In performing the reviews and audits, the superintendent may utilize the services of persons outside of the department chosen for their knowledge of special education programs. Each district, special education local plan area, or county office shall be reviewed at least once during the period of approval of its local plan.

– Onsite Program/Fiscal Reviews

CHAPTER 7. FUNDING OF SPECIAL EDUCATION PROGRAMS

Article 1. State Aid Apportionments

56700. In fiscal year 1980-81 and in each fiscal year thereafter all apportionments to districts, special education local plan areas, and county offices for special education programs and services shall be computed pursuant to this chapter.

56701. The superintendent shall apportion funds for instructional personnel services, support services, and transportation services from Section A of the State School Fund directly to districts and county offices in accordance with the annual budget plan submitted pursuant to subdivision (e) of Section 56200, unless the plan specifies an alternative recipient.

56702. The superintendent shall apportion funds for regionalized services from Section A of the State School Fund to the administrative entity specified in the local plan to receive and distribute such funds. Upon receipt, each entity shall distribute the funds in accordance with the allocation plan adopted pursuant to subdivision (e) of Section 56200.

Article 2. Computation of State Aid

56710. The county superintendent shall compute, pursuant to this article, apportionments for state aid for special education programs and services for each district or county office operating special education programs and services.

56711. The county superintendent shall compute for each district and county office the sum of all the following:

(a) Instructional personnel services amount pursuant to Article 3 (commencing with Section 56720).

(b) Support services amount pursuant to Article 4 (commencing with Section 56730).

(c) Amount for pupils in nonpublic, nonsectarian schools and agencies pursuant to Article 5 (commencing with Section 56740).

(d) Amount for instructional time entitlement for special day classes under Sections 46200.5 and 46201.5.

56712. From the sum computed pursuant to Section 56711, the county superintendent shall subtract all the following:

(a) Applicable special education federal funds received by each district or county office.

(b) For the 1981-82 fiscal year only, an amount equal to the difference, if positive, between the sum of state aid received pursuant to this chapter, local general fund contribution, federal funds, and district revenue limits for special day classes and

*(Sections 56711 and 56712 Amended in 1994)

centers, and county taxes for special education for the prior fiscal year, and the amount actually spent on special education programs and services pursuant to this part, for the prior fiscal year.

(c) The property taxes allocated to special education programs pursuant to Section 2572.

— Property Taxes

(d) The district revenue limit amounts for pupils in special day classes and centers in each district or county office.

— District Revenue Limit for SDC Classes/Center

(e) The local general fund contribution for special education computed pursuant to Article 6 (commencing with Section 56750).

— Local General Fund Contribution

(f) Any amounts allocated to school districts for special education programs pursuant to subdivision (b) of Section 56713.

— Amounts Allocated Pursuant to 56713(b)

(g) The amount received pursuant to subparagraph (D) of paragraph (3) of subdivision (a) of Section 33607.5 of the Health and Safety Code that is considered property taxes pursuant to that section.

— Community Redevelopment Project Property Taxes

56713. (a) The amount computed pursuant to Section 56712 shall be apportioned as state aid. Commencing with the 1980-81 fiscal year and each fiscal year thereafter, state aid shall be apportioned as part of the apportionments prescribed by Sections 41330, 41332, and 41335.

— State Aid Apportioned as Prescribed

(b) Commencing in the 1982-83 fiscal year and for each fiscal year thereafter if, for any county office, the remainder computed pursuant to Section 56712 is a negative amount, no state aid shall be distributed to that county office for purposes of Section 56711. In addition, the county superintendent shall allocate an amount equal to that negative amount to school districts in that county on the basis of the district's average unduplicated pupil counts for the fall and spring semesters for the then current fiscal year.

— Reallocation of Excess Revenues

56714. The superintendent shall adopt rules and regulations for the implementation of this chapter.

— Superintendent's Rules/ Regulations

Article 3. Instructional Personnel Services

— INSTRUCTIONAL PERSONNEL SERVICES

56720. The county superintendent shall compute, pursuant to this article, instructional personnel services amounts for each district and county office operating special education programs and services.

— County Superintendent Computes IPS Amounts

56721. Each district or county office shall submit to the county superintendent its 1979-80 average salaries and benefits paid for providing special education services, based on the regular school year, for the following instructional personnel:

— Average Salaries/Benefits Paid for Instructional Personnel

(a) Special class teachers.

(b) Resource specialists; or for entities that did not operate under the master plan during fiscal year 1979-80, learning disability group teachers; or for entities that operated partially under the master plan during fiscal year 1979-80, resource specialists, and learning disability group teachers.

(c) Certificated specialists providing designated instruction and services.

(d) (1) Special education instructional aides for special classes and centers, and resource specialists. — Instructional Aides

(2) Average salaries and benefits for such aides for the purpose of this section only shall be the greater of the district's or county office's:

(A) Average salary and benefits for a full-time equivalent special education instructional aide based on the average number of hours actually worked per instructional aide per day.

(B) Average annual salaries and benefits for six hours of special education instructional aide time.

56722. For each district or county office, the county superintendent shall compute an instructional personnel cost unit rate based on the 1979-80 costs submitted pursuant to Section 56721 for each of the following instructional personnel services: — Compute Unit Rate Based on 1979-80 Costs for Instructional Personnel Services

(a) Special classes and centers with one special class teacher, using the amount computed pursuant to subdivision (a) of Section 56721.

(b) Special classes and centers for the severely disabled, as defined in Section 56030.5, with one special class teacher and one instructional aide, using the amounts computed pursuant to subdivisions (a) and (d) of Section 56721.

(c) Special classes and centers for the severely disabled, as defined in Section 56030.5, with one special class teacher and two instructional aides, using the amounts computed pursuant to subdivisions (a) and (d) of Section 56721.

(d) Resource specialist programs with one resource specialist only, using the amount computed pursuant to subdivision (b) of Section 56721.

(e) Resource specialist programs with one resource specialist and one instructional aide, using the amounts computed pursuant to subdivision (b) of Section 56721 and 85 percent of the amount computed to subdivision (d) of Section 56721.

(f) Certificated specialists providing designated instruction and services, using the amount computed pursuant to subdivision (c) of Section 56721. For the purpose of this subdivision, aides providing designated instruction and services may be funded in lieu of a certificated specialist.

(g) Special classes and centers for other than the severely disabled with one special class teacher and one instructional aide using the amount computed pursuant to subdivision (a) and 85 percent of the amount computed pursuant to subdivision (d) of

Section 56721.

(h) Special classes and centers for other than the severely disabled with one special class teacher and two instructional aides using the amount computed pursuant to subdivision (a) and 85 percent of the amount computed pursuant to subdivision (d) of Section 56721.

56723. For fiscal year 1980-81 the county superintendent shall multiply the unit rates computed pursuant to Section 56722 by 1.09. For fiscal year 1981-82, the unit rates shall be increased by 5 percent. For fiscal year 1983-84, the unit rates shall be increased by 8 percent. Commencing with fiscal year 1984-85 and each fiscal year thereafter, the unit rates shall be increased by the statewide average percentage inflation adjustment computed for revenue limits of school districts. — Inflation Factor

56724. In the event a district or county office claims special education allowances for an instructional personnel service it did not offer in 1979-80 and for which an instructional personnel cost unit rate was not computed, such district or county office shall use the statewide average unit rate for the then current fiscal year for that instructional personnel service. — Statewide Average Unit Rate

56725. For each of the instructional personnel services specified in Section 56722 for which funds have been budgeted pursuant to subdivision (e) of Section 56200, the county superintendent shall multiply the units of instructional personnel service computed pursuant to Section 56760 by the appropriate unit rate for the district or county office for the then current fiscal year. — County Superintendent Multiplies Units

56726. For each district and county office that operates an extended year program, that is required by statute, the following amount shall be computed: — Extended Year Computation

(a) For special classes, excluding those funded under subdivision (b): — Special Classes/Non-severely Disabled

(1) Divide the number of days taught in extended session for special classes, not to exceed 30, by the number of days in the regular school year.

(2) Multiply the quotient computed pursuant to paragraph (1) by the unit rate computed pursuant to subdivision (g) of Section 56722, as adjusted pursuant to Section 56723, and multiply the product by 0.6.

(3) Divide the enrollment in special classes as of the second week of extended session by 11; round up to the nearest whole number; and multiply by the product computed pursuant to paragraph (2).

(b) For special centers or classes for severely disabled pupils, as defined in Section 56030.5: — Special Centers or Classes/Severely Disabled

(1) Divide the number of days taught in extended session for special classes or centers, not to exceed 55, by the number of days in the regular school year.

(2) Multiply the quotient computed pursuant to paragraph (1) by the unit rate computed pursuant to subdivision (c) of Section 56722, as adjusted pursuant to Section 56723.

(3) Divide the enrollment in special classes or centers as of the second week of extended session by 7; round up to the nearest whole number; and multiply by the product computed pursuant to paragraph (2).

(c) For designated instruction and services for pupils in special — DIS in Special Classes
classes during extended session:

(1) Divide the number of classes computed pursuant to paragraph (3) of subdivision (a) by 3 and multiply that amount by the product computed by multiplying the quotient computed pursuant to paragraph (1) of subdivision (a) by the unit rate computed pursuant to subdivision (f) of Section 56722, as adjusted pursuant to Section 56723.

(2) Divide the number of classes computed pursuant to paragraph (3) of subdivision (b) by 3 and multiply that amount by the product computed by multiplying the quotient computed pursuant to paragraph (1) of subdivision (b) by the unit rate computed pursuant to subdivision (f) of Section 56722, as adjusted pursuant to Section 56723.

(3) Multiply the amount computed pursuant to paragraph (1) by 0.6.

56727. The county superintendent shall compute the sum of — County Superintendent Computes Sum
the amounts computed pursuant to Sections 56725 and 56726.

56728. Notwithstanding subdivision (d) of Section 56760, state — State Aid Shall Not Exceed Units Actually in Operation
aid for instructional personnel service units operated during the regular school year and during extended year programs shall not exceed the number of units actually in operation for the then current fiscal year. Districts and county offices shall be entitled to the full unit rates computed pursuant to subdivisions (b), (c), (e), (g), and (h) of Section 56722 in regular year and extended year programs only if the appropriate number of instructional aides are actually used.

For the purposes of computing funding for aides other than — Full-time Equivalent Aide
those in classes for the severely disabled, a full-time equivalent aide shall be equivalent to 1.00 times a full-time equivalent aide entitlement for those aides in the 1980-81 fiscal year.

56728.5. As a condition of receiving state aid pursuant to this — April Unduplicated Pupil Count
chapter, a district or county office of education shall report in April of each year, on forms provided for this purpose by the Superintendent of Public Instruction, the count of the number of pupils receiving special education services provided by the

district or county office in the spring semester. The report shall individually report the unduplicated count in special day classes, resource specialist programs, and designated instructional services, and shall distinguish between pupils residing in licensed children's institutions, foster family homes, residential medical facilities, other similar facilities, and all other pupils.

The Superintendent of Public Instruction shall collect, as necessary, data from school districts, county offices of education, and other public and private agencies having information on licensed children's institutions, foster family homes, residential medical facilities, and other similar facilities.

– Data Collection

56728.6. (a)   Notwithstanding subdivision (d) of Section 56760, in the 1985-86 fiscal year and each fiscal year thereafter, a special education local plan area shall be eligible for state funding of those instructional personnel service units operated and fundable for services to children three years of age or older at the second principal apportionment of the prior fiscal year, so long as the pupil count divided by the number of instructional personnel service units is equal to or greater than the following:

– Loading of Instructional
    Units for Growth

(1)   For special classes and centers -- 9, based on the unduplicated pupil count.

(2)   For resource specialist programs -- 21, based on the unduplicated pupil count.

(3)   For designated instruction and services -- 20, based on the unduplicated pupil count, or 39, based on the duplicated pupil count.

(b)   Notwithstanding subdivision (d) of Section 56760, in the 1984-85 fiscal year and each fiscal year thereafter, a special education local plan area shall be eligible for state funding of instructional personnel service units for services to children three years of age or older in excess of the number of instructional personnel service units operated and fundable at the second principal apportionment of the prior fiscal year only with the authorization of the Superintendent of Public Instruction.

– Authorization for
    Additional Units

(1)   The superintendent shall not authorize additional units for a special education local plan area if, for that special education local plan area, the percentage of pupils in kindergarten and grades 1 to 12, inclusive, enrolled in special education programs, excluding pupils less than three years of age, would exceed 10 percent.

(2)   The superintendent shall not authorize additional units for a special education local plan area if, for that special education local plan area, the ratio of pupils in kindergarten and grades 1 to 12, inclusive, receiving a specific instructional service, excluding pupils less than three years of age, would exceed the following:

(A) For special classes and centers - 0.028 percent.

(B) For resource specialist programs - 0.040 percent.

(C) For designated instruction services - 0.042 percent.

(3) The superintendent may authorize additional units for a special education local plan area only if the area's pupil-instructional personnel unit ratios, based on the unduplicated pupil count, meet or exceed the ratios specified in paragraphs (1), (2), and (3) of subdivision (a).

(c) The Superintendent of Public Instruction shall base the authorization of funding for special education local plan areas pursuant to this section, including the reallocation of instructional personnel service units, upon criteria which shall include, but not be limited to, all of the following:

– Growth Criteria

(1) Changes in the total number of pupils enrolled in kindergarten and grades 1 to 12, inclusive.

(2) High- and low-average caseloads per instructional personnel service unit for each instructional setting.

(3) Lower than average and higher than average percentages of pupils in kindergarten and grades 1 to 12, inclusive, who are currently enrolled in special education programs.

(d) Notwithstanding Sections 56211 and 56212, a special education local plan area may apply for, and the superintendent may grant, a waiver of any of the standards and criteria specified in this section if compliance would prevent the provision of a free, appropriate public education or would create undue hardship. In granting the waivers, the superintendent shall consider the following:

– Superintendent's Waivers of Standards and Criteria

(1) Applications from special education local plan areas for waivers for a period not to exceed three years to specifically maintain or increase the level of special education service requirements of individuals with exceptional needs residing in sparsely populated districts or attending isolated schools designated in the application.

– Waivers Not to Exceed Three Years

(A) Sparsely populated districts are school districts that meet one of the following conditions:

– Sparsely Populated Districts

(i) A school district or combination of contiguous school districts in which the total enrollment is less than 600 pupils, kindergarten and grades 1 to 12, inclusive, and in which one or more of the school facilities is an isolated school

(ii) A school district or combination of contiguous school districts in which the total pupil density ratio is less than 15 pupils, kindergarten and grades 1 to 12, inclusive, per square mile and in which one or more of the school facilities is an isolated school.

(B) Isolated schools are schools with enrollments of less than 600 pupils, kindergarten and grades 1 to 12, inclusive, that meet

– Isolated Schools

one or more of the following conditions:

(i) The school is located more than 45 minutes average driving time over commonly used and well-traveled roads from the nearest school, including schools in adjacent special education local plan areas, with an enrollment greater than 600 pupils, kindergarten and grades 1 to 12, inclusive.

(ii) The school is separated, by roads that are impassable for extended periods of time due to inclement weather, from the nearest school, including schools in adjacent special education local plan areas, with an enrollment greater than 600 pupils, kindergarten and grades 1 to 12, inclusive.

(iii) The school is of a size and location that, when its enrollment is combined with the enrollments of the two largest schools within an average driving time of not more than 30 minutes over commonly used and well-traveled roads, including schools in adjacent special education local plan areas, the combined enrollment is less than 600 pupils, kindergarten and grades 1 to 12, inclusive.

(iv) The school is the one of normal attendance for a severely disabled individual, as defined in Section 56030.5, or an individual with low-incidence disability, as defined in Section 56026.5, who otherwise would be required to be transported more than 75 minutes average one-way driving time over commonly used and well-traveled roads, to the nearest appropriate program.

(2) The location of licensed children's institutions, foster family homes, residential medical facilities, and other similar facilities within the boundaries of a local plan if 3 percent or more of the local plan's unduplicated pupil count resides in those facilities.

(e) For the purpose of this section, a special education local – Waiver of Standards
plan area may apply for, and the superintendent may grant, a waiver of the standards specified in paragraph (2) of subdivision (b) if the waiver is programmatically justified.

(f) By authorizing units pursuant to this section, the – Restrictions on Author-
superintendent shall not increase the statewide total number of   izing Growth Units
instructional personnel   service units for purposes of state apportionments unless an appropriation specifically for growth in the number of instructional personnel service units is made in the annual Budget Act or other legislation. If that growth appropriation is made, units authorized by the superintendent pursuant to this subdivision that result in an increase in the statewide total number of instructional personnel service units are subject to the following restrictions:

(1) The units shall be funded only by this appropriation and no other funds may be apportioned for the units.

(2) All units shall be fully funded pursuant to Chapter 7 (commencing with Section 56700) of Part 30.

(g) This section shall become operative July 1, 1985.

(h) The superintendent shall monitor the use of instructional personnel service units retained or authorized by the granting of waivers pursuant to subdivision (d) to assure that the instructional personnel service units are used in a manner wholly consistent with the basis for the waiver request.

56728.7. (a) The Superintendent of Public Instruction may conduct a pilot program for the 1992-93, 1993-94, and 1994-95, 1995-96, and 1996-97 fiscal years to enable and encourage school districts and county offices of education, either individually or through special education local plan areas, to establish programs in public schools for individuals with exceptional needs who are currently placed in nonpublic, nonsectarian schools and to develop plans for the return of these pupils to an appropriate public school program, with a view of determining whether these new programs can provide an effective mainstreaming education program in a less restrictive environment that is appropriate to each pupil's needs for services as specified in his or her written individualized education program. Services provided pursuant to this section to each pupil by an individualized education program, including, but not limited to, psychotherapy, mental health, residential, or other services provided under provisions of Chapter 26.5 (commencing with Section 7570) of Division 7 of Title 1 of the Government Code, shall be continued unless otherwise agreed to by a review of the pupil's expanded individualized education program team. The superintendent shall select, for this purpose, no more than 10 school districts or county offices of education that are willing to participate in the pilot project, through an application process to be developed by the superintendent during the 1991-92 fiscal year in accordance with subdivision (c). A maximum of 200 pupils shall participate in the statewide pilot program at any given time. Of the 200 pupils, not more than 50 pupils shall be from any one school district, and no more than 15 pupils from any one school district shall be funded pursuant to Article 8.5 (commencing with Section 56775).

(b) In addition, the Superintendent of Public Instruction shall conduct a pilot program in San Mateo County and in the Contra Costa County special education local plan area for the 1993-94, 1994-95, 1995-96, and 1996-97 fiscal years to encourage and enable the San Mateo County Office of Education and the Contra Costa County special education local plan area to identify pupils who currently are placed into a nonpublic school program by San Mateo County school districts or Contra Costa County school

- Operative Date

- Superintendent Shall Monitor Use of Units

- Pilot Program for*
  Returning Pupils from
  Nonpublic Schools to an
  Appropriate Public School
  Placement

- No More than 10 School
  Districts or County Offices
  of Education

- No More than 200 Pupils
  Participating in the
  Statewide Pilot Progam

- Specified Pilot Programs

*(Section 56728.7 Amended in 1994)

districts, respectively, but are able to be returned to an appropriate public school program, and to identify seriously emotionally disturbed pupils who currently are in a public school program who are imminently at risk of placement in a nonpublic school program or another more restrictive setting. The purpose of each pilot program is to establish new public school programs that maintain an effective mainstreaming education program that is appropriate to each pupil's needs for the services specified in a pupil's individualized education program, and thereby avoid placing those pupils in a nonpublic school setting.

Services provided to a pupil pursuant to this section according to the pupils' individualized education program, including, but not limited to, psychotherapy, mental health, residential, or other services provided under the provisions of Chapter 26.5 (commencing with Section 7570) of Division 7 of Title 1 of the Government Code, shall be continued unless otherwise agreed to by a review of the pupil's expanded individualized education program team.

(c) The superintendent shall ensure that the local application to participate in a pilot program pursuant to subdivision (a) describes the program and fiscal resources that it will use in implementing the pilot program, including, but not limited to, the establishment of the Local Pilot Program Advisory Committee and its implementing policies for the pilot program. The superintendent shall make every effort to ensure that the racial, ethnic, and socioeconomic composition of the Local Pilot Program Advisory Committee reflects the current racial, ethnic, and socioeconomic composition of the exceptional pupil population in the school districts in which the pilot programs are established.

– Local Application

In its preparation of the application for participation in the pilot program, the local education agency shall consult with the special education local plan area in which it is a member and describe the impact the pilot program would have on other programs and resources available within the special education local plan area.

In addition, the superintendent shall ensure that there is a sampling of multiple sizes of school districts and county offices of education, including special education local plan areas whose special education plan serves an average daily attendance of 30,000 or more. The sampling shall also include all of the following:

(1) Local education agencies in urban and rural settings.

(2) Local education agencies serving large populations of individuals with exceptional needs from low-income and ethnic and linguistic minority families.

(3) Local education agencies impacted by a large number of

individuals with exceptional needs who are served by nonpublic, nonsectarian schools and agencies.

(4) Local education agencies impacted by a large number of individuals with exceptional needs who reside in a foster family home, licensed children's institution, hospital, or other similar medical facility and who are served by nonpublic, nonsectarian schools or agencies.

(d) Consistent with Section 56366 and other provisions of law, it is the intent of the Legislature that programs developed pursuant to this section shall ensure the participation of, and coordination with, local contracted nonpublic, nonsectarian schools through the establishment of a Local Pilot Program Advisory Committee in order to develop, monitor, and evaluate policies to ensure that pupils' placements are changed when adequate progress is made and readiness for placement in a less restrictive environment located in a public school is achieved.

    – Local Pilot Program Advisory Committee

(1) The Local Pilot Program Advisory Committee shall be comprised of representatives of local public and contracted nonpublic school programs, parents, and other local public agencies providing services pursuant to Chapter 26.5 (commencing with Section 7570) of Division 7 of Title 1 of the Government Code. Representatives of each Local Pilot Program Advisory Committee shall include two representatives of local contracted nonpublic schools designated by the California Association of Private Specialized Education and Services without regard to membership, one of whom shall be a representative of a licensed children's institution when it is determined that pupils in a licensed children's institution in a nonpublic school program placement may be considered for placement in a mainstreaming educational program, a representative of the special education local plan area administrative unit, a teacher representative of a local public school participating in the pilot, a parent representative of the local community advisory committee, pursuant to the Individuals with Disabilities Education Act (20 U.S.C. Sec. 1400 and following), a representative of a parent advocate, a representative of the local mental health advisory board, and a representative of each local public agency providing services to exceptional pupils within the special education local plan area under Chapter 26.5 (commencing with Section 7570) of Division 7 of Title 1 of the Government Code.

    – Composition of Advisory Committee

(2) Notwithstanding any other provision of law, the Local Pilot Program Advisory Committee shall advise on the development, monitoring, and evaluation of policies and procedures that are necessary to implement the pilot program. The advisement shall include, but not necessarily be limited to, the following subjects:

    – Duties of the Advisory Committee

(A) Pupil behaviors.

(B) Pupil achievement and classroom performance reports.

(C) Curriculum and class size.

(D) Adequate support services.

(E) Personnel qualifications.

(3) The Local Pilot Program Advisory Committee shall also advise on development procedures and criteria for evaluating the effectiveness of the pilot program pursuant to paragraph (1) of subdivision (h) and shall annually submit a written evaluation of the pilot program to the Superintendent of Public Instruction. The Superintendent of Public Instruction shall evaluate selected pilot programs, based on the report of each advisory committee of how goals for an effective mainstream education program have been met in accordance with pupils' individualized education programs.

– Local Evaluation of Pilot Programs

(e) (1) Notwithstanding any other provision of law, in the 1992-93, 1993-94, 1994-95, 1995-96, and 1996-97 fiscal years for pilot programs operated pursuant to subdivision (a), and in the 1993-94, 1994-95, 1995-96, and 1996-97 fiscal years for the pilot programs operated pursuant to subdivision (b), the Superintendent of Public Instruction shall apportion to each of the school districts or county offices of education selected pursuant to subdivision (a), and to the San Mateo County office of Education and Contra Costa County special education local plan area in addition to any funds to which that district or county office is entitled under this chapter, an apportionment for each pupil who is returned by that district or county office from a nonpublic school program pursuant to this section. The apportionment shall be equal to the average amount apportioned to the special education local plan area in which that district or county office is located for pupils under Sections 56740 and 56775 in the 1991-92 fiscal year for pilot programs operated pursuant to subdivision (a), and the average amount apportioned to the San Mateo County special education local plan area and the Contra Costa County special education local plan area, respectively, under those sections in the 1992-93 fiscal year for the pilot programs operated pursuant to subdivision (b), excluding the costs of room and board as identified by Section 56741. The costs resulting to that district or county office from the placement of any pupil in a public program operated by the district or county office pursuant to this section, including any residual nonpublic school costs for pupils transitioning into the public program, shall be funded from this apportionment. No school district or county office of education shall be entitled to receive any funding under Section 56740 or 56775 in any fiscal year based on the enrollment of any pupil for which that district or

– Apportionment of Funds

county office receives funding in that fiscal year under this subdivision.

(2) The apportionment authorized under paragraph (1) may only be provided for pupils who were enrolled in a nonpublic, nonsectarian school in the fiscal year prior to the new year in which the pupil is returned to public school placement. Each pupil's placement shall be changed, in accordance with this part, to a public school special education program as described under this section no later than June 30, 1996, for pupils in a pilot program operated pursuant to subdivision (a) or subdivision (b). — Apportionment Condition

(3) A school district or county office of education is not entitled to receive both a nonpublic school entitlement under Section 56740 or 56775, and a pilot program apportionment as authorized by paragraph (1) in any fiscal year for pupils' participation in the statewide pilot project. — Entitlement Restriction

(4) If a participating pupil leaves the pilot program due to age or achievement, a change of district of residence, or if it is subsequently determined by an individual education program team that a pupil's programmatic needs cannot be successfully met in the mainstream education program, another pupil may replace that pupil if the new pupil qualifies under paragraph (2). If a pupil leaves the pilot program during any fiscal year for any of the above reasons, and the pupil cannot be replaced by another pupil who qualifies under paragraph (2), the school district or county office shall provide an adjusted full-time equivalent number of pupils who actually participated in the statewide pilot program for each fiscal year to the Superintendent of Public Instruction by no later than November 30 following each fiscal year of the pilot project. The adjusted full-time equivalent number of pupils shall be used to compute an appropriate reduction in the preceding fiscal year's annualized pilot program apportionment authorized under paragraph (1) before the adjustments, if any, as specified in paragraph (7) are performed. — Replacing Pupils in the Pilot Program

(5) If a nonpublic school program is resumed for a pupil due to an unsuccessful transition to a mainstream education program, the district or county office may resume the reporting of nonpublic school costs under Sections 56740 and 56775 if the Superintendent of Public Instruction has been notified as specified in paragraph (4). — Reporting of Nonpublic School Costs for Pupil No Longer in Pilot Progam

(6) For a pilot program operated pursuant to subdivision (a), the apportionment authorized under this section shall include the costs of one certificated person who shall serve as a mainstream education liaison. The workload of a mainstream education liaison shall not exceed a full-time equivalent per pupil caseload of 20. — Mainstream Education Liaison

(7) The apportionment authorized under paragraph (1) shall be — Apportionment Shall Be Used Solely for Providing Special Education Programs

7--13

used solely for purposes of providing special education programs. Any excess apportionment remaining from the costs of operating pilot programs pursuant to this section shall be adjusted from the subsequent year's apportionment which the district or county office of education may be eligible to receive. The amount of excess pilot program apportionment shall be reported to the Superintendent of Public Instruction by not later than November 30 following each fiscal year of the pilot project.

(f) Notwithstanding any other provision of law, pilot project pupils shall not be included in the calculation of the number of instructional personnel services units to which a school district or county office is entitled, in the calculation of pupil service ratio as provided in Section 56760, or in the enrollment used to compute extended year entitlements pursuant to Section 56726.

— Pilot Program Shall Not Be Considered in IPSU Calculation

(g) This section shall not be construed to authorize any increase in state apportionments for special education to which a participating school district or county office of education is entitled under this chapter.

— No Increase in State Apportionments for Special Education

(h) The Superintendent of Public Instruction shall evaluate the pilot program or programs operated pursuant to criteria developed in consultation with the participating school districts or county offices of education and a statewide representative of contracted nonpublic, nonsectarian schools. The evaluation shall include, but not necessarily be limited to, descriptive information and supporting data provided by the Local Pilot Program Advisory Committee and others as appropriate in determining whether the program operated by each participating district or county office accomplished each of the following objectives:

— State Evaluation of Pilot Programs

(A) Provided pupils who were formerly placed in nonpublic, nonsectarian schools with an appropriate and effective mainstreaming education program which is consistent with each pupil's needs as specified in his or her individualized education program and located in a less restrictive environment in a public school.

(B) Served those pupils in age-appropriate, less restrictive environments, including interaction or receiving instruction with their nonhandicapped peers.

(C) Provided pupils who were identified as being imminently at risk of nonpublic school placement with an appropriate and effective mainstreaming education program that is consistent with each pupil's needs, as specified in his or her individualized education program.

(D) Provided programs and services located in a public school to those pupils at a cost to the public that was no greater than that incurred in the nonpublic, nonsectarian school setting, from which pupils are returned and those identified as being at risk of placement under subparagraph (C), including the public program costs for instruction, designated instruction and services, direct support services, indirect support services, and the costs of services provided by local public agencies under Chapter 26.5 (commencing with Section 7570) of Division 7 of Title 1 of the Government Code. It is the intent of the Legislature that the comparison of the costs for services provided by public and nonpublic school programs be based on uniform program cost accounting procedures prescribed by the Superintendent of Public Instruction pursuant to Section 56730.5.

(i) The superintendent shall report the results of the evaluation to the Legislature no later than July 1, 1998.

             – Evaluation Results Report to Legislature

(j) This section shall remain in effect only until January 1, 1999, and as of that date is repealed.

             – Automatic Repeal Provision

56728.8. (a) Notwithstanding subdivision (d) of Section 56760, for the 1985-86 fiscal year and each fiscal year thereafter, a special education local plan area shall be eligible for state funding of those instructional personnel service units operated and fundable for services to individuals with exceptional needs younger than three years of age at the second principal apportionment of the prior fiscal year, so long as the pupil count of these pupils divided by the number of instructional personnel service units is not less than the following:

             – Loading of Instructional Units for Growth for Infant Programs

(1) For special classes and centers - 12, based on the unduplicated pupil count.

(2) For resource specialist programs - 24, based on the unduplicated pupil count.

(3) For designated instruction and services -12, based on the unduplicated pupil count, or 39, based on the duplicated pupil count.

(b) Notwithstanding subdivision (d) of Section 56760, in the 1985-86 fiscal year and each fiscal year thereafter, a special education local plan area shall be eligible for state funding of instructional personnel service units for services to individuals with exceptional needs younger than three years of age in excess of the number of instructional personnel service units operated and fundable at the second principal apportionment of the prior fiscal year only with the authorization of the Superintendent of Public Instruction.

             – Authorization for Additional Units

(c) The Superintendent of Public Instruction shall base the authorization of funding for special education local plan areas pursuant to this section, including the reallocation of instructional personnel service units, upon criteria that shall include, but not be limited to, the following:

             – Growth Criteria

(1) Changes in the total number of pupils younger than three years of age enrolled in special education programs.

(2) High- and low-average caseloads per instructional personnel service unit for each instructional setting.

(d) Notwithstanding subdivision (e) of Section 56760, infant programs in special classes and centers funded pursuant to this item shall be supported by two aides, unless otherwise required by the Superintendent of Public Instruction.

— Two Aides for Special Classes/Centers

(e) Infant services in resource specialist programs funded pursuant to this item shall be supported by one aide.

— One Aide for Resource Specialist Program

— Minimums

(f) In determining the number of instructional personnel service units for which a special education local plan area may qualify, a minimum of six infants shall constitute eligibility for the initial unit. However, programs operating pursuant to Section 56425 shall be allowed a minimum of one initial unit for the 1985-86 fiscal year. When units are allocated pursuant to this subdivision, the Superintendent of Public Instruction shall allocate only the least expensive unit appropriate.

(g) Beginning with the 1986-87 fiscal year, those programs operating pursuant to Section 56425 with fewer than six infants shall receive a partial unit, as determined by the Superintendent of Public Instruction.

— Partial Unit

(h) Notwithstanding Sections 56211 and 56212, a special education local plan area may apply for, and the superintendent may grant, a waiver of any of the standards and criteria specified in this section if compliance would prevent the provision of a free, appropriate public education or would create undue hardship. In granting the waivers, the superintendent shall give priority to the following factors:

— Superintendent's Waivers of Standards and Criteria

(1) Applications from special education local plan areas for waivers for a period not to exceed three years to specifically maintain or increase the level of special education services necessary to address the special education service requirements of individuals with exceptional needs residing in sparsely populated districts or attending isolated schools designated in the application.

— Waivers Not to Exceed Three Years

(A) Sparsely populated districts are school districts that meet one of the following conditions:

— Sparsely Populated Districts

(i) A school district or combination of contiguous school districts in which the total enrollment is less than 600 pupils, kindergarten and grades 1 to 12, inclusive, and in which one or more of the school facilities is an isolated school.

(ii) A school district or combination of contiguous school districts in which the total pupil density ratio is less than 15 pupils, kindergarten and grades 1 to 12, inclusive, per square mile and in which one or more of the school facilities is an isolated school.

(B) Isolated schools are schools with enrollments of less than

— Isolated Schools

600 pupils, kindergarten and grades 1 to 12, inclusive, that meet one or more of the following conditions:

(i) The school is located more than 45 minutes average driving time over commonly used and well-traveled roads from the nearest school, including schools in adjacent special education local plan areas, with an enrollment greater than 600 pupils, kindergarten and grades 1 to 12, inclusive.

(ii) The school is separated, by roads that are impassable for extended periods of time due to inclement weather, from the nearest school, including schools in adjacent special education local plan areas, with an enrollment greater than 600 pupils, kindergarten and grades 1 to 12, inclusive.

(iii) The school is of a size and location that, when its enrollment is combined with the enrollments of the two largest schools within an average driving time of not more than 30 minutes over commonly used and well-traveled roads, including schools in adjacent special education local plan areas, the combined enrollment is less than 600 pupils, kindergarten and grades 1 to 12, inclusive.

(iv) The school is the one of normal attendance for a severely disabled individual, as defined in Section 56030.5, or an individual with a low-incidence disability, as defined in Section 56026.5, who otherwise would be required to be transported more than 75 minutes, average one-way driving time over commonly used and well-traveled roads, to the nearest appropriate program.

(2) The location of licensed children's institutions, foster family homes, residential medical facilities, or similar facilities within the boundaries of a local plan if 3 percent or more of the local plan's unduplicated pupil count resides in those facilities.

(i) By authorizing units pursuant to this section, the superintendent shall not increase the statewide total number of instructional personnel service units for purposes of state apportionments unless an appropriation specifically for growth in the number of instructional personnel service units is made in the annual Budget Act or other legislation. The allocation for implementation in fiscal year 1990-91 shall not exceed the amount of five hundred thousand dollars ($500,000) provided by subdivision (a) of Provision 6 of Item 6110-161-001 of Section 2.00 of the Budget Act of 1990. If that growth appropriation is made, units authorized by the superintendent pursuant to this section are subject to the following restrictions:

— IPSU Restrictions

(1) The units shall be funded only by that growth appropriation and no other funds may be apportioned for the units.

(2) All units shall be fully funded pursuant to Chapter 7

(commencing with Section 56700) of Part 30.

(j) The superintendent shall monitor the use of instructional personnel service units retained or authorized by the granting of waivers pursuant to subdivision (h) to assure that the instructional personnel service units are used in a manner wholly consistent with the basis for the waiver request.

— Superintendent Shall Monitor Use of Units

56728.9. (a) Notwithstanding any other provision of this article, any special education local plan area that is a single district and that is severely impacted by pupils who reside in licensed children's institutions, as defined in Section 56155.5, shall be entitled to a support services amount calculated pursuant to Section 56734, except that the quotient computed pursuant to Section 56733 shall be multiplied by 150 percent for classes in which a majority of the pupils enrolled reside in licensed children's institutions, if the special education local plan area meets all of the requirements of this section.

— Single District, LCI* Severely Impacted SELPA, Support Service

(b) A special education local plan area is severely impacted, for purposes of this section, if all of the following requirements are satisfied:

— Determination of Severely Impacted

(1) Pupils who reside in licensed children's institutions represent more than 15 percent of the special education enrollment of the special education local plan area.

(2) Special education enrollment of pupils who reside in licensed children's institutions has increased by more than 50 percent since 1985.

(3) The special education local plan area does not enroll more than 10 percent of its pupils who do not reside in licensed children's institutions in special education programs.

(c) Any special education local plan area that is severely impacted pursuant to subdivision (b) may make the calculation adjustments provided by subdivision (a) only for those classes in which a majority of the pupils enrolled during the 1989-90 school year resided in licensed children's institutions.

— Calculation Adjustments

(d) The calculation provided by this section is a base year calculation, based on the enrollment in classes in the 1989-90 school year, creating a limit on funding adjustments provided by this section. Special education local plan areas shall not be required to maintain the 1989-90 level of eligible classes in order to be eligible for the calculation in future years. Special education local plan areas are encouraged to place pupils who reside in licensed children's institutions in the educational environment that best meets the pupil's needs in keeping with the least restrictive environment requirements of the Individuals with Disabilities Education Act (20 U.S.C. Sec. 1400 et seq.) and the Master Plan for Special Education.

— Base Year Calculation

(e) A special education local plan area may claim an amount

— Restriction on Allocation of Funds

*(Section 56728.9 Amended in 1994)

of funding in a fiscal year that is not greater than the amount claimed pursuant to this section in the prior fiscal year. The amount claimed may be increased only if a specific appropriation is made for that purpose in that fiscal year. A special education local plan area that received funding for purposes of this section in the 1994-95 fiscal year shall continue to receive that funding in a subsequent fiscal year only if it continues to meet the qualifications of this section and an appropriation is made for those purposes in the annual Budget Act. A special education local plan area that did not receive funding for purposes of this section in the 1994-95 fiscal year that subsequently qualifies for that funding, shall not receive that funding unless an additional appropriation is made for those purposes in the annual Budget Act.

(f) This section shall remain in effect only until January 1, 1998, and as of that date is repealed, unless Assembly Bill 3757 or Senate Bill 1640 of the 1993-94 Regular Session is enacted and becomes operative on or before January 1, 1996, in which case this section shall remain in effect only until January 1, 1996, and as of that date is repealed. — Automatic Repeal Provision

Article 4. Support Services
— SUPPORT SERVICES

56730. The county superintendent shall compute, pursuant to this article, a support services amount for each district and county office operating special education programs and services pursuant to this article. — County Superintendent Computes Support Services Amount

56730.5. (a) For the 1985-86 fiscal year, the Superintendent of Public Instruction shall adopt and disseminate to all local education agencies, program cost accounting procedures that meet all of the following conditions: — Program Cost Accounting Procedures

(1) The procedures shall require all local education agencies to use the same methods of allocating direct support costs to specific programs.

(2) The methodology used to allocate direct support costs shall be readily supported by documentation or be the result of standards prescribed by the cost accounting procedures.

(3) For each category of support costs, a single allocation method shall be employed unless documentation as prescribed by the accounting procedures specified by the Superintendent of Public Instruction is available.

(b) Local education agencies shall be required to use the cost accounting procedures provided for under this section during the 1985-86 fiscal year, and to report their 1985-86 fiscal year costs to the State Department of Education using these procedures on forms prescribed by the Superintendent of Public Instruction.

56730.6. Within one year of the issuance of accounting standards and criteria pursuant to Section 56730.5, the Legislative Analyst and the Department of Finance shall review and comment upon the results of a study of comparable public and nonpublic school costs for services provided to individuals with exceptional needs to be conducted by the California Association of Private Special Education Schools.

– Study of Comparable Public/Nonpublic School Costs

56730.7. (a) Notwithstanding Section 42100, the department shall not require the filing of a program cost accounting report more frequently than once every two fiscal years for those school districts with less than 2,500 pupils in average daily attendance if the department obtains an exemption from the United States Department of Education of specified reporting requirements for those districts. If approval is secured, then in the fiscal year in which the report is not filed, the approved indirect cost rate calculated in the previous year for those districts shall be used instead of the current calculation.

– Cost Accounting Report

(b) The department shall streamline the annual program cost accounting report for school districts not later than the 1993-94 fiscal year reporting period. Areas to be reexamined for elimination or revision should include, but not be limited to, the methods for allocating direct support costs and the manner in which school districts compile the report. The streamlined version of the annual program cost accounting report shall be developed with the intent of reducing the burden of paperwork on school districts while at the same time providing the Legislature and other interested parties with uniform and consistent program cost information regarding school districts.

– Streamlined Version

56731. Each district and county office shall submit to the county superintendent the sum of salaries and benefits paid to instructional personnel, excluding substitute teachers, specified in Section 56721 for providing special education services, based on the regular school year, plus the sum of salaries and benefits paid to instructional personnel specified in Section 56721 for providing special education services for extended year programs during fiscal year 1979-80, plus the increase in salary and benefit costs for instructional aides associated with the unit rates computed pursuant to Article 3 (commencing with Section 56720) of this part.

– Submit Sum of Salaries and Benefits

56732. Each district and county office shall submit to the county superintendent the adjusted operating costs for special education in fiscal year 1979-80. Adjusted operating costs shall be computed by reducing the total cost for special education reported by the district or county superintendent for fiscal year 1979-80 less the costs of special transportation, services provided by nonpublic, nonsectarian schools and agencies, tuition paid to

– Submit Adjusted Operating* Costs

*(Section 56732 Amended in 1994)

7-20

other school districts or county offices for special education programs and services during the 1979-80 fiscal year but not paid during the 1980-81 fiscal year, pregnant minors programs, programs to provide instruction in the home or hospital for pupils with temporary physical disabilities, and, if appropriate, regionalized services, as enumerated in subdivision (c) of Section 56220.

The amount included in the total cost of special education for indirect support costs shall not exceed 4 percent of the sum of direct costs plus direct support costs.

- Indirect Support Costs 4 Percent Cap

56733. The county superintendent shall compute a support services quotient as follows:

- County Superintendent Computes Support Services Ratio

(a) Subtract the sum computed pursuant to Section 56731 from the sum computed pursuant to Section 56732.

(b) Divide the amount computed pursuant to subdivision (a) by the sum computed pursuant to Section 56731.

56734. The support services amounts to each district and county office for the 1980-81 fiscal year shall be the amount computed pursuant to Section 56727 multiplied by the quotient computed pursuant to Section 56733, except as otherwise provided in Section 56728.9.

- 1980-81 Support Services Computation

56735. (a) The superintendent shall recommend for audit to the Controller districts or county offices whose 1979-80 fiscal year support services quotient exceeded 125 percent of the state average support services quotient, computed pursuant to subdivision (b), for comparably sized districts.

- Controller Audit of Support Services

(b) The superintendent shall compute average support services quotients for the 1979-80 fiscal year for the following groups of districts. As used in this section, "average daily attendance" is the district's regular average daily attendance.

(1) Elementary districts of 100 or less units of average daily attendance.

(2) Elementary districts with more than 100 and less than 901 units of average daily attendance.

(3) High school districts with less than 301 units of average daily attendance.

(4) Unified districts with less than 1,501 units of average daily attendance.

(5) Elementary districts with greater than 900 units of average daily attendance.

(6) High school districts with more than 300 units of average daily attendance.

(7) Unified districts with greater than 1,500 units of average daily attendance.

(c) For purposes of this section, county offices shall be treated as districts within the meaning of paragraph (7) of subdivision (b).

(d) In addition to the audits specified in subdivision (a), the Controller may select a representative cross-section of districts to audit.

(e) The Controller may review the criteria for identifying special education costs to be issued pursuant to Section 56730.5, and make recommendations in their audit report.

56736. It is the intent of the Legislature that the adjusted operating costs for special education as computed pursuant to Section 56732 exclude all costs associated with the services enumerated in subdivision (c) of Section 56220 regardless of whether the district or county office operated under the Master Plan for Special Education during the 1979-80 fiscal year and regardless of whether the district or county office received special funding for these services. The Superintendent of Public Instruction shall:

    – Adjusted Operating Costs Exclude Regionalized Services Costs

(a) Identify the costs associated with the services enumerated in subdivision (c) of Section 56220 for all districts and county offices during the 1979-80 fiscal year.

    – Identify Regionalized Services Costs

(b) Recompute the support services quotients for districts and county offices, excluding the costs identified in subdivision (a) from the computation, not to exceed ninety-three dollars ($93) per unduplicated pupil count.

    – Recompute Support Services Ratio, Minus Regionalized Services Costs, Not to Exceed $93 Per Pupil

56737. For the 1981-82 fiscal year and for each fiscal year thereafter, the Superintendent of Public Instruction shall do the following:

(a) Compute the statewide unweighted average of the support services quotients computed pursuant to Section 56736, for the 1980-81 fiscal year.

    – Support Services Ratio Squeeze

(b) Compute a support services quotient for each district and county office claiming reimbursement pursuant to this chapter for the then current fiscal year for instructional personnel services units, other than for the severely disabled, as defined in Section 56030.5, in the following manner:

    – Nonseverely Disabled Support Services Ratio

(1) If the support services quotient for the prior fiscal year is greater than 1.5 times the average quotient computed pursuant to subdivision (a), then the quotient for the current fiscal year shall be 1.5 times the average quotient computed pursuant to subdivision (a).

    – Greater Than 150 Percent Statewide Average

(2) If the support services quotient for the prior fiscal year is less than or equal to 1.5 times the average quotient computed pursuant to subdivision (a) but greater than the average quotient computed pursuant to subdivision (a), then the quotient for the then current fiscal year shall be the greater of (A) or (B):

    – Equal to or Below 150 Percent Statewide Average

(A) The average computed pursuant to subdivision (a).

(B) The support services quotient for the prior fiscal year minus 0.1.

(3) If the support services quotient for the prior fiscal year is less than or equal to the average quotient computed pursuant to subdivision (a), then the quotient for the then current fiscal year shall be equal to the quotient for the prior fiscal year.

Less Than or Equal to Statewide Average

(4) If a district or county office did not operate special education programs and services in the fiscal year, its support services quotient for the then current fiscal year shall be the lesser of (A) or (B).

Average Ratio

(A) The average quotient computed pursuant to subdivision (a).

(B) The statewide unweighted average for the appropriate class district or county office identified in Section 56735.

(c) The support services quotient for special day class instructional personnel services units for the severely disabled, as defined in Section 56030.5, shall be the quotient for the prior fiscal year, except that that quotient shall not exceed 1.5 times the average quotient computed pursuant to subdivision (a).

Severely Disabled Support Services Ratio Shall Not Exceed 150 Percent of Statewide Average

(d) No district or county office which had a nonseverely disabled support services ratio of 1.5 times the average in the 1981-82 fiscal year shall have that average reduced below 1.15 times the average in subsequent years.

Nonseverely Disabled Support Services Ratio Reduced to 115 Percent of Statewide Average

(e) Compute a total support services amount for each district and county office equal to the sum of (1) and (2):

Compute Total Support Services Amount

(1) Multiply the support services quotient for the current fiscal year computed pursuant to subdivision (b) or (c) by the instructional amounts for the appropriate types of programs, computed pursuant to Section 56725.

Instructional Amounts

(2) Multiply the support services quotient for the current fiscal year computed pursuant to subdivision (b) by the extended year amount computed pursuant to Section 56726. Support services amounts for extended year programs for other than the severely disabled, as defined in Section 56030.5, shall be divided by 2.

Extended Year Nonseverely Disabled Support

Services Amounts Reduced by 50 Percent

56738. Notwithstanding Section 56737, the support services amounts for all instructional personnel services units added between the end of the first principal apportionment period and the end of the second principal apportionment period during a single fiscal year shall be one-half of the amounts computed for those units pursuant to Section 56737.

Fifty Percent Limitation for Support Services

56739. (a) When allocating funds received for special education pursuant to this article, it is the intent of the Legislature that, to the extent funding is available, school districts and county offices shall give first priority to expenditures to provide specialized books, materials, and equipment which are necessary and appropriate for the individualized education programs of pupils with low-incidence disabilities, up to a maximum of five hundred dollars ($500) per pupil with low-

Legislative Intent for Expenditure of Funds for Specialized Books, Materials, and Equipment

incidence disability. Nothing in this subdivision shall be construed to prohibit pooling the prioritized funds to purchase equipment to be shared by several pupils.

(b) Equipment purchased pursuant to this section shall include, but not necessarily be limited to, nonprescriptive equipment, sensory aids, and other equipment and materials as appropriate.

Article 5. Nonpublic, Nonsectarian School Services

– NONPUBLIC, NONSECTARIAN SCHOOL SERVICES

56740. (a) The superintendent shall apportion to each district and county office 70 percent of the cost of tuition in excess of the revenue limit and applicable federal funds for pupils enrolled in nonpublic, nonsectarian schools and agencies pursuant to Sections 56365 and 56366.

– Seventy Percent* Excess Cost

(b) The superintendent also may apportion to each nonpublic, nonsectarian school providing special education and designated instruction and services to individuals with exceptional needs an amount for pupils counted under the federal program of assistance for state-operated or state-supported programs for children with disabilities (P.L. 89-313, Sec. 6).

– P.L. 89-313 Funding

(c) The cost of master contracts with nonpublic, nonsectarian schools and agencies that a district or county office of education reports under this section shall not include any of the following costs that a district, county office, or special education local plan area may incur:

– Limitations on Cost of Master Contracts

(1) Administrative or indirect costs for the local education agency.

(2) Direct support costs for the local education agency.

(3) Transportation costs provided either directly, or through a nonpublic, nonsectarian school or agency contract for use of services or equipment owned, leased, or contracted, by a district, special education local plan area, or county office for any pupils enrolled in nonpublic, nonsectarian schools or agencies, unless provided directly or subcontracted by that nonpublic, nonsectarian school or agency pursuant to subdivisions (a) and (b) of Section 56366.

(4) Costs for services routinely provided by the district, special education local plan area, or county office including the following, unless the board grants a waiver under Section 56101:

(A) School psychologist services other than those described in Sections 56324 and 56363 and included in a master contract and individual services agreement under subdivision (a) of Section 56366.

(B) School nurse services other than those described in Sections 49423.5, 56324, and 56363 and included in a master contract and individual services agreement under subdivision (a)

*(Section 56740 Repealed/Added in 1994)

of Section 56366.

(C) Language, speech, and hearing services other than those included in a master contract and individual services agreement under subdivision (a) of Section 56366.

(D) Modified, specialized, or adapted physical education services other than those included in a master contract and individual services agreement under subdivision (a) of Section 56366.

(E) Other services not specified by a pupil's individualized education program or funded by the state on a caseload basis.

(5) Costs for nonspecial education programs or settings, including those provided for individuals with exceptional needs between the ages of birth and five years, inclusive, pursuant to Sections 56431 and 56441.8.

(6) Costs for nonpublic, nonsectarian school or agency placements outside of the state unless the board has granted a waiver pursuant to subdivisions (e) and (f) of Section 56365.

(7) Costs for related nonpublic, nonsectarian school pupil assessments by a school psychologist or school nurse pursuant to Sections 56320 and 56324.

(8) Costs for services that the nonpublic, nonsectarian school or agency is not certified to provide.

(9) Costs for services provided by personnel who do not meet the requirements specified in subdivision (e) of Section 56366.

(10) Costs for services provided by public school employees.

(d) A nonpublic, nonsectarian school or agency shall not claim and is not entitled to receive reimbursement for attendance unless the site where the pupil is receiving special education or designated instruction and services is certified.

— No Reimbursement for Attendance Unless Site Is Certified

56741. As a condition to receiving an apportionment pursuant to Sections 56740 and 56775, together with other financial reports required by the superintendent for purposes of apportioning funds, a district or county office shall submit an annual report to the superintendent in April of each year pursuant to Section 56728.5, on forms provided by the superintendent for that purpose, which shall include all of the following information:

— Nonpublic School Program* Placement Costs Data

(a) The individual contracted program placement costs of providing special education, transportation, residential, and designated instruction and services to individuals with exceptional needs placed in nonpublic, nonsectarian schools and agencies pursuant to Sections 56365 and 56366.

(b) The individual program placement costs specified in subdivision (a) shall be listed according to the placement categories of individuals with exceptional needs, including, but not limited to, all of the following categories:

(1) Full-day nonpublic, nonsectarian school placement.

*(Section 56741 Amended in 1994)

(2) Partial-day nonpublic, nonsectarian school placement.

(3) Residential nonpublic, nonsectarian school and agency placement within the state.

(4) Residential nonpublic, nonsectarian school and agency placement outside the state.

(5) Full-day nonpublic, nonsectarian agency services.

(6) Partial-day nonpublic, nonsectarian agency services.

56742. Every district or county office of education which receives state funding pursuant to Section 56740 shall, as a condition of that apportionment, report to the Superintendent of Public Instruction on forms provided for that purpose, when the total cost of a placement of an individual with exceptional needs in a nonpublic, nonsectarian school exceeds by more than 100 percent the average cost, both instructional and support, including transportation and designated instructional services, of serving a pupil in a special day class in the district or county office. If the district or county office does not operate special day classes, then the figure used shall be the average special day class cost, both instructional and support, in the region.

- Reporting Cost Exceeding More Than 100 Percent the Average Cost

The report shall include:

(a) The name of the nonpublic, nonsectarian school in which the individual with exceptional needs is placed.

(b) A brief description of the services provided to that individual.

(c) The total costs of the placement for that individual.

56743. Notwithstanding Section 56740 and 56775, the Superintendent of Public Instruction shall not apportion additional funds to districts or county offices on behalf of placements and services in nonpublic, nonsectarian schools and agencies reported by districts and county offices pursuant to Section 56742 if the increase claimed from one year to the next exceeds the percentage increase specified by Section 56723, or an in-lieu percentage specified by the Budget Act, unless the superintendent makes a specific and individual funding that a greater increase is warranted.

- Nonpublic School Cost* Increases Exceeding Inflation Factor

Article 6. Local General Fund Contribution

- LOCAL GENERAL FUND CONTRIBUTION

56750. The county superintendent shall compute, pursuant to this article, a local general fund contribution for special education for each district operating special education programs and services.

- Computation by County Superintendent

56751. The county superintendent shall compute an adjusted local general fund contribution amount for each district by subtracting the amount computed pursuant to subdivision (a) from the amount computed pursuant to subdivision (b).

- Method of Computation

*(Section 56743 Amended in 1994)

(a) The sum of the district's state aid apportionments for special education, applicable federal funds, revenue limits for pupils in special classes and centers, and tuition earned by the district from operating special education programs for other districts and county offices, exclusive of such revenue earned for providing special transportation, contracting for nonpublic, nonsectarian school services, and earned on account of pregnant minors programs and programs to provide instruction in the home or hospital for pupils with temporary physical disabilities for the 1979-80 fiscal year.

(b) The district's total reported cost of operating special education programs and services exclusive of the costs of providing special transportation, contracting for nonpublic, nonsectarian school services, and providing pregnant minors programs and instruction in the home or hospital for pupils with temporary physical disabilities for the 1979-80 fiscal year.

The amount included in total cost of special education for indirect support costs shall not exceed 4 percent of the sum of direct costs plus direct support costs. — Indirect Support Costs Limitation

56752. The amount computed pursuant to Section 56751 shall be divided by such district's second principal apportionment regular average daily attendance in the 1979-80 fiscal year. — ADA Adjustments for Fiscal Year 1979-80

56753. The amount computed pursuant to Section 56752 shall be multiplied by the second principal apportionment regular average daily attendance of such district for the then current fiscal year. — ADA Adjustment for Current Fiscal Year

56754. The local general fund contribution for each district shall be the lesser of the amounts computed pursuant to Section 56751 or Section 56753. — Local General Fund Contribution

Article 7. Service Proportions

— SERVICE PROPORTIONS

56760. The annual budget plan, required by subdivision (e) of Section 56200, shall comply with the following proportions, unless a waiver is granted by the superintendent pursuant to Section 56761: — Annual Budget Plan Compliance

(a) The district, special education local plan area, or county office, shall estimate the pupils to be served in the subsequent fiscal year by instructional personnel service. The estimate shall be computed as the ratio of pupils to be served by instructional personnel service to the enrollment of pupils in kindergarten and grades 1 to 12, inclusive, of the districts and county offices participating in the plan.

(1) The ratio of pupils funded by the state by instructional personnel service during the regular school year, including pupils for whom education and services are provided for by contract — Funded Ratio Not to Exceed 10 Percent

with nonpublic, nonsectarian schools, to the enrollment in kindergarten and grades 1 to 12, inclusive, shall not exceed 0.10.

(2) The ratio of pupils funded by the state by instructional personnel service to the enrollment in kindergarten and grades 1 to 12, inclusive, receiving a specific instructional service shall not exceed the following:

   — Specific Instructional Service Ratio Caps

(A) For special classes and centers, 0.028.

(B) For resource specialist programs, 0.040.

(C) For designated instruction services, 0.042.

(b) The district, special education local plan area, or county office shall divide the amounts in paragraphs (1), (2), and (3) by the appropriate ratios computed pursuant to paragraph (2) of subdivision (a).

   — Divide Amounts by Appropriate Computed Ratios

(1) For special classes and centers, 10 pupils.

(2) For resource specialist programs, 24 pupils.

(3) For designated instruction and services, 24 pupils.

(c) The district, special education local plan area, or county office shall divide the sum of the estimated enrollments on October 1 of the subsequent fiscal year in kindergarten and grades 1 to 12, inclusive, of each district and county office participating in the plan by each of the amounts computed pursuant to paragraphs (1), (2), and (3) of subdivision (b).

   — Divide Sum of Estimated Enrollments

(d) The amounts computed pursuant to subdivision (c) shall be the authorized instructional personnel service units the state will fund for the district, special education local plan area, or county office in the then current year. The allocation of these instructional personnel service units shall be described in the annual budget plan.

   — Authorized IPSUs State Will Fund

(e) The number of units of instructional services funded pursuant to this article for a local plan shall not exceed for special classes and centers, an average of one teacher and 1.05 aide per special class or center actually operated.

   — Special Class/Center Average: 1 Teacher to 1.05 Aide

56761. (a) A district, special education local plan area, or county office may request, and the superintendent may waive, any of the proportions specified in Section 56760. The waiver shall be granted only if compliance would both prevent the provision of a free, appropriate public education and would create undue hardship, as follows:

   — State Superintendent's Waivers of Service Proportions

(1) For special classes and centers: proximity of the district, special education local plan area, or county office to state hospitals, licensed children's institutions, foster care facilities, or other facility may increase the expected numbers of individuals with exceptional needs requiring placement in special classes and centers.

   — Special Classes/Center

(2) For resource specialist programs and designated instruction and services: the district, special education local plan area, or

   — Resource Specialist Program/DIS

county office has implemented the eligibility criteria adopted by the board, and failure to grant the waiver may result in eligible pupils receiving inappropriate services.

(3) For the proportions specified in subdivision (b) of Section 56760: low pupil density in sparsely populated areas creates problems of distance and inaccessibility for the district, special education local plan area, or county office.

 — Proportions

(b) A school district, special education local plan area, or county office may request the superintendent to waive one or more of the maximum unit proportions set forth in Section 56760. The request shall be granted only if it demonstrates that the increased cost of exceeding the standard in one instructional setting is offset by savings in another instructional setting.

 — Request to Waive Maximum Unit Proportions

56762. The superintendent shall adopt rules and regulations to ensure that apportionments made pursuant to this chapter shall be paid on account of no more than 10 percent of the statewide enrollment in kindergarten and grades 1 to 12, inclusive, for the then current fiscal year.

 — Superintendent's Rules/ Regulations – 10 Percent Statewide Enrollment

Article 8. Low Incidence Funding

 — LOW INCIDENCE FUNDING

56771. (a) Commencing with the 1985-86 fiscal year, and for each fiscal year thereafter, funds to support specialized books, materials, and equipment as required under the individualized education program for each pupil with low incidence disabilities, as defined in Section 56026.5, shall be determined by dividing the total number of pupils with low incidence disabilities in the state, as reported on December 1 of the prior fiscal year, into the annual appropriation provided for this purpose in the Budget Act.

 — Funding Formula

(b) The per-pupil entitlement determined pursuant to subdivision (a) shall be multiplied by the number of pupils with low incidence disabilities in each special education local plan area to determine the total funds available for each local plan.

 — Per-Pupil Entitlement Multiplied

(c) The superintendent shall apportion the amount determined pursuant to subdivision (b) to the responsible local agency in the special education local plan area for purposes of purchasing and coordinating the use of specialized books, materials, and equipment.

 — Apportion Funds to Responsible Local Agency

(d) As a condition of receiving these funds, the responsible local agency shall ensure that the appropriate books, materials, and equipment are purchased, that the use of equipment is coordinated as necessary, and that the books, materials, and equipment are reassigned to local educational agencies within the special education local plan area once the agency that originally received the books, materials, and equipment no longer needs them.

 — Funding Condition

(e) It is the intent of the Legislature that special education local plan areas share unused specialized books, materials, and equipment with neighboring special education local plan areas.

– Share Unused Books, Materials, and Equipment

Article 8.5. Licensed Children's Institutions

– LICENSED CHILDREN'S INSTITUTIONS

56775. (a) For the 1980-81 fiscal year and each fiscal year thereafter, the superintendent shall apportion to each district and county superintendent providing programs pursuant to Article 5 (commencing with Section 56155) of Chapter 2 an amount equal to the difference, if any, between (1) the costs of master contracts with nonpublic, nonsectarian schools and agencies to provide special education instruction, designated instruction and services, or both, to pupils in licensed children's institutions, foster family homes, residential medical facilities, and other similar facilities funded under this chapter, and (2) the state and federal income received by the district or county superintendent for providing these programs. The sum of the excess cost, plus any state or federal income for these programs, shall not exceed the cost of master contracts with nonpublic, nonsectarian schools and agencies to provide special education and designated instruction and services for these pupils, as determined by the superintendent.

– Excess Cost for Nonpublic* School Placements

(b) The cost of contracts with nonpublic, nonsectarian schools and agencies that a district or county office of education reports under this section shall not include any of the following costs that a district, county office, or special education local plan area may incur:

– Costs Prohibited in Contracts

(1) Administrative or indirect costs for the local education agency.

(2) Direct support costs for the local education agency.

(3) Transportation costs provided either directly, or through a nonpublic, nonsectarian school or agency master contract or individual services agreement for use of services or equipment owned, leased, or contracted, by a district, special education local plan area, or county office for any pupils enrolled in nonpublic, nonsectarian school or agencies, unless provided directly or subcontracted by that nonpublic, nonsectarian school or agency pursuant to subdivisions (a) and (b) of Section 56366.

(4) Costs for services routinely provided by the district or county office including the following, unless the board grants a waiver under 56101:

(A) School psychologist services other than those described in Sections 56324 and 56363 and included in a master contract and individual services agreement under subdivision (a) of Section 56366.

*(Section 56775 Amended in 1994)

(B) School nurse services other than those described in Sections 49423.5, 56324, and 56363 and included in a master contract and individual services agreement under subdivision (a) of Section 56366.

(C) Language, speech, and hearing services other than those included in a master contract and individual services agreement under subdivision (a) of Section 56366.

(D) Modified, specialized, or adapted physical education services other than those included in a master contract and individual services agreement under subdivision (a) Section 56366.

(E) Other services not specified by a pupil's individualized education program or funded by the state on a caseload basis.

(5) Costs for nonspecial education programs or settings, including those provided for individuals with exceptional needs between the ages of birth and five years, inclusive, pursuant to Sections 56431 and 56441.8.

(6) Costs for nonpublic, nonsectarian school or agency placements outside of the state unless the board has granted a waiver pursuant to subdivisions (e) and (f) of Section 56365.

(7) Costs for related nonpublic, nonsectarian school pupil assessments by a school psychologist or school nurse pursuant to Sections 56320 and 56324.

(8) Costs for services that the nonpublic, nonsectarian school or agency is not certified to provide.

(9) Costs for services provided by personnel who do not meet the requirements specified in subdivision (e) of Section 56366.

(10) Costs for services provided by public school employees.

(d) A nonpublic, nonsectarian school or agency shall not claim and is not entitled to receive reimbursement for attendance unless the site where the pupil is receiving special education or designated instruction and services is certified.

– No Reimbursement for Attendance Unless Site Is Certified

56775.5. The Superintendent of Public Instruction may reimburse each district and county office of education providing programs pursuant to Article 5 (commencing with Section 56155 of Chapter 2 for assessment and identification costs for pupils in licensed children's institutions, foster family homes, residential medical facilities, and other similar facilities who are placed in state-certified nonpublic, nonsectarian schools.

– Reimbursement for Assessment – Identification Costs – Nonpublic School Placements

Actual costs under this section shall not include either administrative or indirect costs, or any proration of support costs.

The total amount reimbursed statewide under this section shall not exceed the amount appropriated for these purposes in any fiscal year. If the superintendent determines that this amount is insufficient to reimburse all claims, the superintendent shall prorate the deficiency among all districts or county offices submitting claims.

56776. (a) The superintendent shall establish and maintain an emergency fund for the purpose of providing relief to special education local plan areas when a licensed children's institution, foster family home, residential medical facility, or other similar facility serving individuals with exceptional needs opens or expands in a special education local plan area during the course of the school year which impacts the special education local plan area, or when a pupil is placed in a facility for which no public or state-certified nonpublic program exists within the special education local plan area in which the pupil's individualized education program can be implemented during the course of the school year and impacts the educational program.

                     — Emergency Fund

(b) The special education local plan area in which the impaction occurs shall be responsible for submitting a written request to the superintendent for emergency instructional personnel units. The written request shall, at a minimum, contain all of the following:

                      — Written Request Requirements

(1) Specific information on the new or expanded licensed children's institution, foster family home, residential medical facility, or other similar facility described in subdivision (a), including information on the new unserved or underserved pupils residing in the facility, or specific information relating to the new unserved or underserved pupils residing in those facilities.

(2) The identification of the steps undertaken demonstrating that no public special education program exists with the special education local plan area capable of programmatically meeting the needs of identified pupils.

(3) A plan from the special education local plan area describing the services to be provided.

(4) A description of the number of emergency instructional personnel service units requested and their specific uses.

(c) The superintendent shall approve, modify, or disapprove the written request for emergency instructional personnel service units within 30 days of the receipt of the written request and shall notify the special education local plan area administrator, in writing, of the final decision.

                    — Superintendent Shall Act Within 30 Days

(d) It is the intent of the Legislature that appropriations necessary to fund these emergency instructional personnel service units shall be included in the Budget Act for each fiscal year.

                    — Legislative Intent

56777. In the 1986-87 fiscal year and each fiscal year thereafter, the superintendent shall determine the need in that fiscal year for the purposes for which funding was provided in the prior fiscal year pursuant to Section 56776.

                    — Permanent Funding Priority

If the need still exists in the current fiscal year, the permanent funding of the need shall be the first priority in the allocation of the instructional personnel service units from any appropriation for growth in instructional personnel service units, or from instructional personnel service units that were released by another special education local plan area pursuant to subdivision (a) of Section 56728.6. In the event that permanent funding for these units is not available in the current year, the units shall receive first priority for funding pursuant to Section 56776.

Article 9. Program Specialists and Regionalized Services

— PROGRAM SPECIALISTS AND REGIONALIZED SERVICES

56780. (a) Funds for regionalized services shall be apportioned to the administrative agency of special education local plan areas. As a condition of receiving funds for regionalized services, the administrative agency shall assure that all functions listed below are performed in accordance with the governance structure of the special education local plan area.

— Regionalized Services Funds

(1) Coordination of the special education local plan area.

(2) Coordinated system of identification and assessment.

(3) Coordinated system of procedural safeguards.

(4) Coordinated system of personnel development.

(5) Coordinated system of curriculum development.

(6) Coordinated system of internal program review.

(7) Coordinated system of data collection and management.

(8) Coordinated system of evaluation of the effectiveness of the local plan.

(9) Coordination of interagency agreements.

(10) Coordination of services to medical facilities.

(11) Coordination of services to licensed children's institutions and foster homes.

(12) Preparation of special education local plan area reports.

(13) Incidental expenses of the community advisory committee.

(14) Coordination of transportation.

(15) Coordination of career and vocational education.

(16) Assurance of full educational opportunity.

(b) Direct instructional support may be provided by program specialists in accordance with Section 56368.

— Direct Instructional Support

56781. (a) Commencing with the 1982-83 fiscal year and each fiscal year thereafter, the superintendent shall multiply the average of the unduplicated pupil counts for the fall and spring semesters of the then current fiscal year, not to exceed 10 percent of the enrollment in kindergarten and grades 1 to 12, inclusive, in the local plan, by forty-four dollars ($44), as adjusted pursuant to Section 56782.

— Formula for 1982-83 and Thereafter

— $44 per Unduplicated Count

(b) Funds received pursuant to this section shall be expended only for the following purposes:

— Optional Use of Funds

(1) Program specialists.

(2) Regionalized services as defined pursuant to subdivision (c) of Section 56220.

(3) Instructional personnel services units in excess of those funded pursuant to Article 2 (commencing with Section 56710) of Chapter 7. Units funded pursuant to this section shall not be considered part of the base number of units funded or operated for any district, county office, or local plan area for the purposes of the growth tests specified in Section 56728.6.

56782. For the 1981-82 fiscal year, and for each fiscal year thereafter, the superintendent shall apportion funds for regionalized services, other than program specialists, as enumerated in subdivision (c) of Section 56220 by multiplying the average of the total unduplicated counts for the fall and spring semesters of the then current fiscal year in the local plan, not to exceed 10 percent of the enrollment in kindergarten and grades 1 to 12, inclusive, in the local plan, by twenty-five dollars ($25).

    – Regionalized Services Apportionment

    – $25 per Unduplicated Count

56783. For fiscal year 1983-84, the amounts per unduplicated pupil provided pursuant to Sections 56781 and 56782 shall be increased by 8 percent. Commencing with the 1984-85 fiscal year and in each fiscal year thereafter, the amounts per unduplicated pupil provided pursuant to Sections 56781 and 56782 shall be increased annually by the statewide average percentage inflation adjustment computed for revenue limits of school districts.

    – Annual Inflation Adjustment for Program Specialists and Regionalized Services

Article 10. Deficit Funding

    – DEFICIT FUNDING

56790. If available funds are insufficient to permit full apportionments, the deficit shall be applied pursuant to this chapter.

    – Insufficient Funds

56791. If state funds are insufficient to fully fund programs, the deficit shall be applied equally to all apportionments to all districts and county offices.

    – Deficits Applied Equally to All Apportionments

56792. If programs operated in accordance with a locally approved budget plan submitted pursuant to subdivision (e) of Section 56200 are in excess of those that are funded pursuant to Article 2 (commencing with Section 56710), Article 8 (commencing with Section 56770), and Article 9 (commencing with Section 56780), available funds shall be allocated by the superintendent on a pro-rata basis against all claims for funds by districts and county offices operating under that local plan, unless the plan specifies an alternative allocation mechanism.

    – Local Plan Available Funds Allocated on Pro-Rata Basis

Article 12. General Provisions

56820. Any facilities constructed or leased after July 1, 1981, for individuals with exceptional needs shall be designed and, if possible, located to achieve maximum possible interaction between individuals with exceptional needs and other pupils.

– Design and Location of Facilities

56821. The department shall include in its budget sufficient funds to make apportionments under this part and an amount sufficient for the administration by the department of the provisions of this part.

– Funds for Apportionments/ Administration

56822. Sound recordings, large print, braille, and other specialized technology, media, or materials purchased, instructional materials transcribed from regular print into special media, and special supplies and equipment purchased for individuals with exceptional needs for which state or federal funds were allowed are property of the state and shall be available for use by individuals with exceptional needs throughout the state as the board shall provide.

– Special Instructional* Materials

56823. Apportionments under this part shall be made by the superintendent as early as practicable in the fiscal year. Upon order of the superintendent, the State Controller shall draw warrants upon the money appropriated, in favor of the eligible districts or counties in the amounts ordered.

– Apportionments Made as Early as Practicable

56824. Each district, special education local plan area, and county office participating in special education programs pursuant to this part shall maintain a fiscal effort with respect to each pupil participating in special education programs that is no less than the fiscal effort of the district or county office per elementary, intermediate, or secondary pupil not participating in a special education program. The department shall annually review individual district and county office expenditures to assure the comparability of local support. This review shall be based on rules and regulations adopted by the board which take into account growth in district enrollment and increases in district costs.

– Comparability of Local Support/Fiscal Effort

56825. The department shall continuously monitor and review all special education programs approved under this part to assure that all funds appropriated to districts, special education local plan areas, and county offices under this part are expended for the purposes intended.

– Monitor and Review by State Department of Education

56826. Funds apportioned to districts, special education local plan areas, and county offices pursuant to this chapter shall be expended exclusively for programs operated under this part.

– Funds Expended Exclusively for Special Education Programs

56827. The Superintendent of Public Instruction shall review the information and calculations submitted by districts and county offices in support of all apportionment computations described in

– State Superintendent's Review of Information/ Calculations

*(Section 56822 Amended in 1994)

this chapter. The review shall be conducted on the data submitted during the initial year of apportionment and for first succeeding fiscal year only. Adjustments to any year's apportionment shall be received by the superintendent from the district or county office prior to the end of the first fiscal year following the fiscal year to be adjusted. The superintendent shall consider and adjust only the information and computational factors originally established during an eligible fiscal year, if the superintendent's review determines that they are correct.

 — Adjustments

56828. (a) No educational programs already in operation in school districts pursuant to Part 30 (commencing with Section 56000) shall be transferred to the county superintendent of schools, or to other school districts, or from the county superintendent of schools to school districts, without the approval of the Superintendent of Public Instruction.

 — Transfer of Programs

(b) The Superintendent of Public Instruction shall not approve a program transfer unless all of the following conditions have been met:

 — Conditions for Approving Program Transfer

(1) A detailed plan has been developed that addresses, at a minimum, the following considerations:

(A) Pupil needs.

(B) Availability of the full continuum of services to affected pupils.

(C) Functional continuation of the current individualized education plans of all affected pupils.

(D) Provision of services in the least restrictive environment from which the affected pupils can benefit.

(E) Maintenance of all appropriate support services.

(F) Adherence to all state laws and regulations and special education local plan area policies.

(G) Representation of parents and staff in the planning process.

(2) The date on which the program transfer will take effect is no earlier than the first day of the second fiscal year beginning after the date on which the sending or receiving agency informed the other agency, in writing, of its intent to transfer the program, except that units being operated in 1992-93 by a local education agency, other than the one that is claiming them for state funding under contract arrangements, may be transferred immediately.

(3) The sending agency, the receiving agency, and the governing body of the special education local plan area of which the agencies are members, agree to the transfer. If only two of the three entities agree to the transfer, they may appeal to the superintendent to approve the transfer without the agreement of the third.

(c) If the transfer is approved, the Superintendent of Public Instruction shall ensure that the transfer does not result in an

 — Transfer Does Not Result in an Increase or Decrease in Cost to State

increase or decrease in cost to the state by recalculating the appropriate support service ratio and instructional personnel service unit rates of the receiving school district or county superintendent of schools as follows: determining a weighted average of the sending and receiving agencies' support service ratios and instructional personnel service unit rates that were applied to the units transferred and the units in operation at the receiving agency for the second principal apportionment immediately preceding the initial year of the program transfer. The recalculated ratio and unit rates thereafter shall become the support service ratio and instructional personnel service unit rates of the school district or county superintendent of schools operating the transferred program.

(d) If, as a result of a program transfer, no special education programs will be operated by a school district that has a local general fund contribution calculated pursuant to Article 6 (commencing with Section 56750) of this chapter, the Superintendent of Public Instruction shall adjust permanently the school district's base revenue limit by an amount equal to the local general fund contribution. — Adjust Base Revenue Limit

56829. For the 1981-82 fiscal year and each fiscal year thereafter, if the total amount of state aid for special education claimed by districts and county offices pursuant to this chapter is less than the amount appropriated for those claims, the balance may be used by the Superintendent of Public Instruction to reimburse districts and county offices of education whose expenditures for special education programs and services in the current year exceed the sum of current year revenues from all sources, including state and federal aid for special education district revenue limits for special day classes and centers, county taxes for special education, and an amount equal to the 1979-80 local general fund contribution. — Appropriations Greater Than Claims — Use of Balance

The sum of the reimbursement received by districts and county offices pursuant to this section plus the total current year revenues received, including state and federal aid for special education, district revenue limits for special day classes and centers, county taxes for special education, and an amount equal to the 1979-80 local general fund contribution, shall not exceed the actual expenditures of the district or county office for special education programs and services. — Reimbursement Shall Not Exceed Actual Expenditures

56830. The Legislature hereby finds and declares that, since the 1980-81 fiscal year, there have been significant annual deficiencies in special education funding that have created fiscal hardships for many school districts and county offices of education and adversely impacted the quality of services to many individuals with exceptional needs, in abrogation of the objectives — Annual Deficiencies*

*(Section 56830 Amended in 1994)

set forth in Section 56000.

56831. (a) The Legislature hereby finds and declares that adjudicated individuals with exceptional needs in juvenile court schools, pursuant to Section 56150, require instructional programs in special education for up to 246 schooldays, depending on the number of schooldays court schools operate in that county, each fiscal year in order to comply with Section 104.33 of Title 34 of the Code of Federal Regulations, which is enforced in juvenile court schools by the federal Office for Civil Rights.

(b) The superintendent shall develop a funding formula, in consultation with the Legislative Analyst and the Director of Finance, for the distribution of increased federal funds under Part B of the federal Individuals with Disabilities Education Act (20 U.S.C. Sec. 1400 and following), in an amount not to exceed three million dollars ($3,000,000), to augment instructional units for the special education programs in juvenile court schools, beginning in fiscal year 1993, to cover the required number of days of instruction. The funding formula augmentation shall be developed and operational by July 1, 1993. Any adjustment to the funding level for the purposes of this section shall be made through the Budget Act.

– Adjudicated Individuals
   in Juvenile Court Schools

– Increased Funding

CHAPTER 7.5. EMOTIONALLY DISTURBED CHILDREN PILOT PROJECT

56840. (a) A school district or county office of education may provide educational and supportive services under this chapter to pupils eligible under subdivision (b).

— Educational and Supportive Services

(b) For the purposes of this chapter and subject to Section 56845.1, "eligible pupil" means a child specified as eligible under this part who meets the following criteria:

— Definition of "Eligible Pupil"

(1) The child is eligible for special education services under the Individuals with Disabilities Education Act (Public Law 101-476).

(2) The child has been determined to be seriously emotionally disturbed, as defined in Section 300.5 of Title 34 of the Code of Federal Regulations.

(3) The child has, as a result of his or her emotional disturbance, been placed in the Program for Children and Youth at Napa State Hospital, has successfully met his or her treatment goals, is not at risk of requiring restraint, and is being discharged from the Program for Children and Youth.

(4) The child is eligible for out-of-home care upon discharge from the Program for Children and Youth, in accordance with one or both of the following:

(A) The child is eligible for services under Chapter 26.5 (commencing with Section 7570) of Division 7 of Title 1 of the Government Code.

(B) The child is otherwise eligible for Aid to Families with Dependent Children-Foster Care benefits in accordance with Article 5 (commencing with Section 11400) of Chapter 2 of Part 3 of, and Chapter 6 (commencing with Section 18350) of Part 6 of, Division 9 of the Welfare and Institutions Code.

(5) The child has been determined by an interagency review team, as defined in Section 56840.1, to be eligible for participation in this pilot project.

A determination of eligibility for services under this chapter shall be made in accordance with Section 56840.1.

(c) For the purposes of this chapter, unless the context requires otherwise, "county" means the county of the child's parents' residence, or the county otherwise responsible for the child's residential placement and case management.

— Definition of "County"

56840.1. (a) A child's eligibility for services under this pilot project shall be determined by a meeting of the child's interagency review team, which shall include, but not be limited to, the following persons:

— Interagency Review Team

(1) The child's natural parents, guardian, conservator, or surrogate parent.

(2) The county's case manager.

(3) A representative of the county's mental health program.

(4) Representatives of social service agencies, as appropriate.

(5) Representatives from the special education local planning agency of the parents' residence, or the responsible school district.

(6) The state hospital social worker and other members of the hospital treatment team familiar with the child.

(7) The child's current teacher.

(b) The interagency review team meeting shall be held as soon as discharge appears imminent, and may occur concurrently with a regularly scheduled quarterly conference meeting at which a child's hospital treatment goals are reviewed. If necessary to ensure full participation, team members may participate through telephone conference.

– Meeting of Interagency Review Team

(c) Factors determining a child's eligibility for participation in the pilot project shall include all of the following:

– Factors for Determining Child's Eligibility

(1) Determination by the child's interagency review team as follows:

(A) The child, upon discharge from the Program for Children and Youth at Napa State Hospital, may be appropriately placed in intensive foster care and public school as the least restrictive residential and educational environments, under the conditions of the pilot project.

(B) The child would otherwise be placed upon discharge in a group home of a minimum rate classification level of 10, and in a nonpublic, nonsectarian school.

(2) Availability of a foster family agency within the county of the parents' residence or a nearby county that can provide the services required by this chapter.

(3) The agreement of the local education agency to provide educational services under the conditions of the pilot project.

(d) Pursuant to the recommendations of the interagency review team, the responsible county case manager shall work with the Napa County Office of Education as sponsoring agency to contract with a participating foster family agency to secure a foster family home in keeping with the pilot project requirements described in Sections 18362, 18363, and 18365 of the Welfare and Institutions Code.

– Contract to Secure a Foster Family Home

56841. (a) Following a child's interagency review team meeting at which postdischarge residential placement and pilot project eligibility is determined, but prior to the pupil's discharge from the Program for Children and Youth at Napa State Hospital, a joint meeting of the pupil's individualized education program team and his or her interagency review team, shall be held. The joint team shall identify the pupil's educational and transitional

– Joint Meeting

7.5-2

needs and his or her support services requirements, which may include, but need not be limited to, those stated in Sections 56345, 56345.1, and 56363.

(b) The joint team may also determine the need for an instructional assistant skilled in nonconfrontational behavior management, to provide escort, tutorial, and classroom support, as needed.

— Determine Need for an Instructional Assistant

(c) The individualized education program team shall attempt to place the child in a classroom setting where the teacher is skilled in nonconfrontational behavior management, where there exists a clear, consistent, positive classroom behavior management system, good communication with, and support from, site administration and faculty, and access to mainstreaming opportunities and vocational training or work experience as appropriate.

— Placement in Classroom Setting

(d) The interagency review team shall collaborate with and advise the individualized education program planning team on the development, monitoring, implementation, and evaluation of the child's educational program. The advisement may include, but need not be limited to, the following subjects:

— Collaboration on Child's Educational Program

(1) Management of pupil behaviors.

(2) Pupil achievement and classroom performance.

(3) Curriculum and optimal teaching methods for addressing the pupil's individual learning strengths and needs.

(4) Appropriate support services.

(5) Transitional and vocational services.

56842. The individualized education program planning team shall include, but not be limited to, all of the following:

— IEP Team Members

(a) The pupil's current teacher.

(b) An administrator from the pupil's current educational placement.

(c) An administrative representative from the responsible and the receiving special education local plan areas or school districts.

(d) The pupil's parents, guardian, conservator, or surrogate parent.

(e) The pupil's foster parents and the pupil's foster family agency social work case manager.

(f) The county case manager or mental health representative.

56843. If necessary to ensure full participation in the planning meetings, members of the teams described in Sections 56840.1 and 56842 may participate through telephone conference. The individualized education program team meeting may be held in conjunction with the individual case plan meeting held pursuant to Section 11404 of the Welfare and Institutions Code, at which other interagency review team members shall be in attendance or

— Participation of IEP Team Members

participating by telephone.

56844. (a) The individualized education program team shall determine all of the following for pilot project eligible pupils:

(1) Individualized education program goals, objectives, and services pursuant to Section 56841.

(2) Supplemental services required to support the pupil in the public school setting.

(3) An indication of which of these services would need to be provided in addition to the service options currently available in the receiving local education agency, and the estimated costs of these additional services.

(b) The receiving local education agency shall submit to the Napa County Office of Education a copy of the pupil's individualized education program, with indication of services to be provided, additional services to be purchased, and the estimated costs of those services, as approved by the individualized education program team and the interagency review team.

(c) The Napa County Office of Education shall apportion funds to cover these additional costs on a claims basis, pursuant to Section 56845.1.

56845.1. (a) For the purposes of this pilot project, the Superintendent of Public Instruction shall apportion to the Napa County Office of Education a sum of one hundred thirty-five thousand dollars ($135,000) per year from Item 6100-161-001 of the annual Budget Act, for apportioning to local education agencies for the purchase of supplemental special educational services for pupils participating in this pilot project, pursuant to Section 56844.

(b) The annual apportionment provided to a district for a child participating in this pilot project shall not exceed fifteen thousand dollars ($15,000).

(c) The Napa County Office of Education shall be responsible for allocating funds apportioned pursuant to subdivision (a) to participating local education agencies for the purchase of those supplemental services required by the pupil's individualized education program that are not currently available within the local education agency, for fiscal accounting, for evaluating the pilot project, and for reporting to the Superintendent of Public Instruction and the Legislature.

56845.2. The local education agency serving the participating pupil shall be responsible for reporting to the Napa County Office of Education information required for the purpose of evaluating the effectiveness of the pupil's program plan and this pilot project, which shall include, but not be limited to, both of the following:

- Duties of IEP Team

- Receiving Local Education Agency

- Napa County Office of Education Shall Apportion Funds

- Apportion $135,000 to the Napa County Office of Education

- Amount Per Child

- Allocating Funds to Participating Local Education Agencies

- Reporting Information

(a) Services delivered and costs of supplemental services purchased.

(b) Any and all information pertaining to the evaluation required by Section 18367 of the Welfare and Institutions Code.

56845.5. (a) If participation of a pupil terminates due to a change in the district of residence, the sending district or county office of education shall convene, with the receiving district or county office, a joint team planning meeting, in accordance with Sections 56841 to 56843, inclusive. If the receiving district or county office elects to participate in the pilot project provided for under this chapter, the district or county office shall notify the Napa County Office of Education of its decision, and may apply for an apportionment pursuant to Section 56844.

    — Termination of Partici-
       pation of a Pupil

(b) If a pupil's participation under this chapter terminates due to age or achievement, or if it is subsequently determined by his or her individual education program team that the pupil's programmatic needs cannot be successfully met in a public school education program, the district or county office shall notify the Napa County Office of Education of the termination, and the Napa County Office of Education shall make the appropriate reduction in the apportionment to the district or county office.

(c) If a nonpublic, nonsectarian school program placement is made for a pupil participating under this chapter due to an unsuccessful transition to a public school education program, the district or county office may begin the reporting of nonpublic school costs under Sections 56740 and 56775.

56848. (a) To determine the cost and treatment effectiveness of the pilot project operated under this chapter, the Napa County Office of Education as sponsoring agency shall conduct an evaluation of the pilot project pursuant to Section 18367 of the Welfare and Institutions Code.

    — Evaluation of the Pilot
       Project

(b) The superintendent shall report the results of the evaluation to the Legislature no later than January 1, 1997.

56848.5. County participation in the pilot project established under this chapter shall be at the option of the county.

    — County Participation

56849. This chapter shall become inoperative on September 30, 1996, and, as of January 1, 1997, is repealed, unless a later enacted statute, that becomes effective on or before January 1, 1997, deletes or extends the dates on which it becomes inoperative and is repealed.

    — Automatic Repeal Provision

[For related provisions to this pilot project not found in this document, see Chapter 6.3 (commencing with Section 18360) of Part 6 of Division 9 of the Welfare and Institutions Code, relative to intensive foster care programs for emotionally disturbed children.]

CHAPTER 8. SPECIAL EDUCATION PROGRAMS FOR INDIVIDUALS WITH EXCEPTIONAL NEEDS RESIDING IN STATE HOSPITALS

56850. The purpose of the Legislature, in enacting this chapter, is to recognize that individuals with exceptional needs of mandated schoolage, residing in California's state hospitals for the developmentally disabled and mentally disordered, are entitled to, under the Individuals with Disabilities Education Act (20 U.S.C. Sec. 1400 et seq.), and the Rehabilitation Act of 1973 (29 U.S.C. Sec. 701 et seq.), the same access to educational programs as is provided for individuals with exceptional needs residing in our communities.

— Legislative Intent

— Equal Access to Educational Services

It is the intent of the Legislature to ensure that services shall be provided in the community near the individual state hospitals to the maximum extent appropriate, and in the least restrictive environment.

— Ensure Services in Community

It is the further intent of the Legislature to ensure equal access to the educational process and to a full continuum of educational services for all individuals, regardless of their physical residence.

— Full Continuum of Educational Services

It is the further intent of the Legislature that educational services designated for state hospital residents not eligible for services mandated by the Individuals with Disabilities Education Act (20 U.S.C. Sec. 1400 et seq.) shall not be reduced or limited in any manner as a result of the enactment of this chapter.

— No Reduction in Services for Others

It is the further intent of the Legislature that any cooperative agreements to provide educational services for state hospitals shall seek to maximize federal financial participation in funding these services.

— Maximize Federal Funding

56851. (a) In developing the individualized educational program for an individual residing in a state hospital who is eligible for services under the Individuals with Disabilities Education Act (20 U.S.C. Sec. 1400 et seq.), a state hospital shall include on its interdisciplinary team a representative of the district, or special education local plan area, or county office in which the state hospital is located, and the individual's state hospital teacher, depending on whether the state hospital is otherwise working with the district, special education local plan area, or county office for the provision of special education programs and related services to individuals with exceptional needs residing in state hospitals. However, if a district or special education local plan area that is required by this section to provide a representative from the district or special education local plan area does not do so, the county office shall provide a representative.

— Representative on Hospital's Interdisciplinary Team

(b) The state hospital shall reimburse the district, special

— State Hospital Reimburses

education local plan area, or the county office, as the case may be, for the costs, including salary, of providing the representative.

(c) Once the individual is enrolled in the community program, the educational agency providing special education shall be responsible for reviewing and revising the individualized education program with the participation of a representative of the state hospital and the parent. The agency responsible for the individualized education program shall be responsible for all individual protections, including notification and due process.

— Reviewing and Revising IEP

56852. In developing the individualized educational program and providing all special education programs and related services to individuals with exceptional needs residing in the state hospitals, the state hospitals shall comply with the requirements of the Individuals with Disabilities Education Act (20 U.S.C. Sec. 1400 et seq.), the Rehabilitation Act of 1973 (29 U.S.C. Sec. 701 et seq.), and special education provisions of this part and implementing regulations. Special education and related services shall be provided to each individual residing in a state hospital pursuant to the individualized education program for that individual.

— State Hospital Shall Comply with Federal/ State Laws and Regulations

56852.5. The State Department of Education, within its existing program review process, shall specifically review the appropriateness of pupil placement for educational services as designated in the pupil's individualized education program and the criteria used in determining such placement.

— Department of Education Reviews Appropriateness

56853. Nothing contained in this chapter shall affect the continued authority of the State Departments of Developmental Services and Mental Health over educational programs for individuals not eligible for services under the Individuals with Disabilities Education Act (20 U.S.C. Sec. 1400 et seq.) nor shall it affect the overall responsibility of the state hospitals for the care, treatment, and safety of individuals with exceptional needs under their control. The state hospitals shall continue to render appropriate and necessary developmental services, health related services, psychiatric services, and related services assigned to the state hospitals in the local written agreements, as part of their responsibilities for the care and treatment of state hospital residents.

— Department of Developmental Services/Mental Health Authority/ Responsibility

— State Hospital Services

Health related services shall include services provided by physicians, psychiatrists, psychologists, audiologists, registered nurses, social workers, physical therapists, occupational therapists, psychiatric technicians, and developmental specialists, and shall be the responsibility of the state hospital if the individual with exceptional needs requires these services while in the community program.

— Health-Related Services

56854. (a) The Superintendent of Public Instruction and the Directors of the State Departments of Developmental Services and Mental Health shall develop written interagency agreements to carry out the purposes of this chapter.

(b) For each county in which a state hospital is located, the county superintendent of schools, with the approval of the county board of education and the administrator of the state hospital, shall develop a local written agreement to carry out the purposes of this chapter. Such agreements shall be reviewed and updated annually and may be modified at any time with the concurrence of both parties to the agreements.

56855. For each county in which a state hospital is located the county superintendent of schools shall ensure that appropriate special education and related services are available in the community for which the state hospitals can contract. Such contract shall provide for any eligible individual with exceptional needs residing in the state hospitals whose individualized education program specifies that educational services for that individual should be most appropriately provided, in whole or in part, in a program other than on the hospital grounds. The county board of education shall approve any programs operated by the county superintendent pursuant to this chapter.

56856. In order to provide appropriate special education and related services to an individual residing in a state hospital, the State Departments of Developmental Services and Mental Health shall contract with a county superintendent of schools, nonpublic, nonsectarian school, or other agency to provide all or part of the services that the individual's individualized education program indicates should be provided in a program other than on state hospital grounds. A contract between a state hospital and a nonpublic, nonsectarian school shall only be entered into when no appropriate public education program is available.

56857. Nothing in this chapter shall preclude the State Departments of Developmental Services and Mental Health from contracting with a local public education agency, a nonpublic, nonsectarian school, or another agency to provide special education and related services on the state hospital grounds for those pupils whose individualized education programs do not indicate that such education and services should be provided in a program other than on state hospital grounds. These contracts shall not involve funds appropriated for purposes of community-based special education.

56857.5. (a) Commencing with the 1982-83 fiscal year, community school agencies providing school programs on state hospital grounds shall begin the orderly transfer of all state hospital pupils whose individualized education programs indicate that a community school program is appropriate, to schools located in the community.

(b) Commencing with the 1983-84 fiscal year, all pupils covered by subdivision (a) shall be served in community schools other than on state hospital grounds, and the contracting provisions of this chapter shall apply only to pupils in community school programs other than on state hospital grounds.

- Contracting Provisions

(c) Waivers to subdivisions (a) and (b) may be granted only when approved by both the State Superintendent of Public Instruction and the Director of the State Department of Developmental Services.

- Waiver Provision

56858. (a) The State Department of Developmental Services shall, commencing August 1, 1985, and on the first day of each month thereafter, upon submission of an invoice by the county superintendent of schools, pay to the county superintendent of schools 8 percent of the amount projected to cover the cost of hospital pupils education in community school programs.

- Contract Payments

(b) The amount projected to cover the cost of hospital pupils educated in community school programs shall be determined according to procedures agreed by the State Department of Developmental Services and the State Department of Education.

(c) Upon completion of the fiscal year, the county superintendent of schools shall calculate the actual cost of hospital pupils educated in community schools according to procedures in subdivision (b) approved by the State Department of Developmental Services and the State Department of Education.

(d) If the calculated actual cost of educating these pupils is more or less than the total amount the county superintendent of schools has received for the fiscal year pursuant to subdivision (a), the following year's distribution shall be adjusted accordingly.

(e) The county superintendent of schools shall distribute funds to participating districts on a pro rata basis.

56858.5. (a) Any contract prescribed by this chapter shall become effective unless disapproved by the State Department of Finance or State Department of General Services within 20 working days of receipt of the contract. Each department shall have 10 working days to consider the contract.

- Contract Review by Departments of Finance and General Services

(b) Contracts shall be submitted to the State Department of Developmental Services for approval before May 15.

- Contract Submittal

(c) No payments shall be processed in advance of contract approval, and no educational services shall be provided in the community school programs in advance of contract approval.

- Conditions for Payment

56858.7. (a) Nothing in this chapter shall prohibit the inclusion of in-kind services or the assignment of state hospital

- In-Kind Services

personnel in a contract for services pursuant to this chapter.

(b) Ten percent of the contract costs shall be attributed to in-kind services. In-kind services above 10 percent of the contract costs shall be mutually agreed upon by both parties to the contract. Any disagreement over in-kind services above 10 percent shall not be cause for delaying approval of the contract.

(c) A 60 day prior written notice shall be given by the state hospital to the county superintendent of schools for the initiation or removal of in-kind state hospital classified personnel.

56859. All certificated state hospital employees hired to provide educational services to individuals of mandated school age after September 29, 1980, shall possess an appropriate California credential in special education. Current certificated state hospital employees who do not possess appropriate California credentials in special education shall be given a period of not more than five years from September 29, 1980, to obtain such appropriate credentials. Certificated state hospital employees who do not possess appropriate California credentials in special education at the end of the five-year period shall be reassigned to provide educational services to individuals residing in state hospitals who are not eligible for services under the Individuals with Disabilities Education Act (20 U.S.C. Sec. 1400 et seq.).

56860. Special transportation shall be the responsibility of the state hospital.

56862. It is not the intent of this chapter to displace educational and related services personnel already employed by the state hospitals under the administration of the State Department of Developmental Services or the State Department of Mental Health, or to reduce their salaries or other employee benefits.

The State Department of Developmental Services and the State Department of Mental Health shall complete an annual review of the impact that implementation of this act will have in reducing the need for positions in state hospitals due to time spent by residents in community education programs and shall submit a report on its findings to the Department of Finance for approval.

56863. The state hospitals, as part of the notification to parents of pupils of their rights pursuant to the Individuals with Disabilities Education Act (20 U.S.C. Sec. 1400 et seq.), the Rehabilitation Act of 1973 (29 U.S.C. Sec. 701 et seq.), and this part and implementing regulations, shall notify parents of the right that their child can be considered for education programs other than on state hospital grounds.

For the purposes of this section, the term "parent of pupil" shall mean a parent, a legal guardian, a conservator, a person

---

- Ten Percent of Contract Costs

- Initiation or Removal of In-Kind Personnel

- Employees Shall Possess Appropriate Credential

- Transportation Responsibility

- Impact on State Hospital Personnel

- Notification to "Parent of Pupil"

acting as a parent of a child, or a surrogate parent appointed pursuant to Public Law 94-142.

Information and records concerning state hospital patients in the possession of the Superintendent of Public Instruction shall be treated as confidential under Section 5328 of the Welfare and Institutions Code and the Federal Privacy Act of 1974, Public Law 93-579.

— Confidentiality of Records

56864. Individuals with exceptional needs served under this chapter shall not be subject to the service proportions prescribed by Article 7 (commencing with Section 56760) of Chapter 7, or the growth tests prescribed by Section 56728.6.

— Not Subject to Service Proportions

56865. Funds appropriated by Section 11 of Chapter 1191 of the Statutes of 1980 may be used for remodeling classrooms located in a community school, in addition to the purposes of Chapter 25 (commencing with Section 17785) of Part 10, in order to serve state hospital pupils whose individualized education programs require a community school program.

— Remodeling Classrooms

CHAPTER 9. JOINT FUNDING FOR EDUCATION OF HANDICAPPED CHILDREN ACT OF 1980

56875. (a) The Legislature hereby finds and declares that numerous federal and state programs make funds available for the provision of education and related services to individuals with exceptional needs. The Legislature further finds and declares that the state has not maximized the use of available federal funds for provision of such services to these children. The Legislature further recognizes the need to simplify procedures for securing all available funds for services to individuals with exceptional needs and for utilizing federal financial resources to the greatest possible extent.

    – Legislative Findings, Declarations, and Intent

(b) It is the intent of the Legislature to provide local educational agencies with maximum flexibility to secure and utilize all available state and federal funds so as to enable such agencies to meet the needs of individuals with exceptional needs more effectively and efficiently. Furthermore, it is the intent of the Legislature to provide maximum federal funding to local educational agencies for the provision of education and related services to individuals with exceptional needs.

56876. On or before April 1, 1981, the Department of Education, the State Department of Health Services, the State Department of Mental Health, the State Department of Developmental Services, the State Department of Social Services, the Department of Rehabilitation, the Employment Development Department, the Department of the Youth Authority, and the State Council on Developmental Disabilities shall, in conformance with procedures established by the Office of Planning and Research, submit a plan to both the Senate Finance Committee and the Assembly Ways and Means Committee that shall include a timetable for implementation of this chapter, including, but not limited to the following:

    – Timetable for Implementation of Chapter

(a) A list of provisions of state regulations and laws for which waivers may be granted in order that local educational agencies may maximize available federal funds to provide education and related services to individuals with exceptional needs without decreasing funds available to other state and local agencies.

(b) A list of provisions of federal law, federal regulations, or both, for which it is recommended that the state seek waiver.

(c) A list of specific related services which shall be provided by the respective departments and their political subdivisions to carry out the mandate of the Individuals with Disabilities Education Act (20 U.S.C. Sec. 1400 et seq.) and its implementing regulations.

56877. (a) Implementation of the funding procedures

    – Implementation of Funding

established pursuant to this chapter shall commence on July 1, 1981.

(b) The State Department of Education shall, in order to implement the provisions of this chapter, do all of the following:

(1) Provide necessary technical assistance to local educational agencies.

(2) Establish procedures for such agencies to obtain available federal funds.

(3) Apply for necessary waivers of federal statutes and regulations governing federal education programs that provide education and related services to individuals with exceptional needs.

(c) The State Board of Education shall grant necessary waivers of applicable state laws and administrative regulations relating to special education programs to participating local educational agencies.

56878. If necessary to simplify procedures for securing all available funds for services to individuals with exceptional needs and for utilizing federal financial resources to the greatest possible extent, the Health and Welfare Agency, at the request of the State Department of Health Services, the State Department of Mental Health, the State Department of Developmental Services, the State Department of Social Services, the Department of Rehabilitation, or the Employment Development Department; and the Youth and Adult Corrections Agency, at the request of the Department of the Youth Authority, may grant waivers of state laws and regulations for which they have administrative responsibility. Waivers granted pursuant to this section may be only for those laws and regulations identified in the plan submitted to the Legislature pursuant to Section 56876, and only when necessary to implement this part.

– Waivers of State Laws/ Regulations

56879. Based upon the plan submitted pursuant to Section 56876, the State Department of Health Services, the State Department of Mental Health, the State Department of Developmental Services, the State Department of Social Services, the Department of Rehabilitation, the Employment Development Department, and the Department of the Youth Authority shall, in order to implement the provisions of this chapter, do the following:

– Duties of State Agencies

(1) Grant necessary waivers of applicable state laws and administrative regulations under their respective jurisdictions to local educational agencies and other agencies, and issue such other administrative regulations as are necessary.

(2) Apply for necessary waivers of federal statutes and regulations governing federal programs which provide services to individuals with exceptional needs and which are under their

respective jurisdictions.

56881. (a) The Office of Planning and Research shall establish procedures for development and review of state agency plans for funds available under all federal programs which may provide services to individuals with exceptional needs and which are within the jurisdictions of the Department of Education, the State Department of Health Services, the State Department of Mental Health, the State Department of Developmental Services, the State Department of Social Services, the Department of Rehabilitation, the Employment Development Department, the Department of the Youth Authority, and the State Council on Developmental Disabilities. Results of the review shall be transmitted to the state agency preparing the plan and to the responsible cabinet level agency to make a determination if the plan shall be changed. Such planning procedures and review shall assure coordination between state agencies and shall assure that applicable plans enable local education agencies to secure maximum available federal funding, without decreasing funds available to other state and local agencies, under each of the following federal programs:

(1) Education for All Handicapped Children as provided under P.L. 91-230, Education of the Handicapped Act, Title VI, Part B, as amended by P.L. 93-380 and by P.L. 94-142.

(2) Medical Assistance (Medicaid), as provided under the Social Security Act of 1935, Title XIX, as amended.

(3) Early and Periodic Screening, Diagnosis and Treatment as provided under P.L. 74-271, Social Security Act of 1935, Title XIX as amended, Section 1905 (a)(4)(B).

(4) Developmental Disabilities Services as provided under P.L. 91-517, the Developmental Disabilities Services and Construction Act of 1970, as amended by P.L. 94-103 and the Developmental Disabilities Assistance and Bill of Rights Act, as amended by P.L. 95-602, Amendments to the Rehabilitation Act of 1973.

(5) Social Services as provided under P.L. 74-271, Social Security Act of 1935, Title XX, as amended by P.L. 93-647, P.L. 94-401, P.L. 94-566, and P.L. 95-171.

(6) Crippled Children's Services as provided under P.L. 74-271, Social Security Act of 1935, Title V, Section 504, as amended.

(7) Vocational Training and Counseling Services as provided under P.L. 94-482, Vocational Educational Act; P.L. 93-112, as amended by P.L. 93-516, the Rehabilitation Act of 1973; and P.L. 93-203, the Comprehensive Employment and Training Act, as amended.

– Governor's Office of Planning and Research Responsible for Development and Review of State Agency Plans for Funds Available Under Federal Programs

(8) Maternal and Child Health Services, as provided under P.L. 74-271, Social Security Act of 1935, Title V, Section 503, as amended.

(9) Supplementary Security Income, Disabled Children's Program, as provided under P.L. 74-271, Social Security Act of 1935, Title XVI, Section 1615(b) as amended by P.L. 94-566.

(b) In addition to the programs enumerated in subdivision (a), any other programs under which the following services may be provided to individuals with exceptional needs shall be subject to the review procedure specified in subdivision (a) as conducted by the Office of Planning and Research.

(1) Screening and identification.

(2) Assessment and diagnosis.

(3) Health related services, including, but not limited to, speech pathology and audiological services, physical therapy, occupational therapy, and vision services and therapy.

(4) Psychological counseling.

(5) Mental health services.

(6) Vocational related services.

(7) Social services.

(8) Transportation services.

(9) Other services necessary to assist individuals with exceptional needs in benefiting from their education.

56882. On or before May 1, 1981, the State Board of Education shall, after consultation with the Office of Planning and Research and all state agencies listed in Section 56876, issue regulations for implementation of the provisions of this chapter, to be used by local educational agencies, in implementing the provisions of this chapter. Such regulations shall identify all other administrative regulations relating to education and related services which shall be waived for local educational agencies. Such regulations shall include, but not be limited to regulations relating to application, accounting, and reporting procedures for programs which may provide education and related services for individuals with exceptional needs.

— State Board of Education Issues Regulations for Local Educational Agencies

56883. (a) On or before July 1, 1981, the Department of Education shall, after consultation with the Office of Planning and Research and the agencies listed in Section 56876, and based upon the plan required in Section 56876, issue guidelines to local educational agencies, for implementation of the provisions of this chapter.

— Department of Education Issues Guidelines to Local Educational Agencies

(b) Such guidelines shall include, but not be limited to, the following:

(1) Identification of sources of funds available under all state and federal programs which may provide education and related services to individuals with exceptional needs and for which local

educational agencies and other applicable agencies are eligible.

(2) Identification of all statutes and regulations applicable to programs for individuals with exceptional needs under the jurisdictions of the Department of Education, the State Department of Health Services, the State Department of Mental Health, the State Department of Developmental Services, the State Department of Social Services, the Department of Rehabilitation, the Employment Development Department, and the Department of the Youth Authority, which may be waived pursuant to subdivisions (b), (c), and (d) of Section 56877.

56884. To assist in implementation of the provisions of this chapter, the Department of Education and state agencies listed in Section 56876 shall, by April 1, 1981, after consultation with representatives of their respective local administering agencies, negotiate and enter into interagency agreements to help promote coordination of services for individuals with exceptional needs. The interagency agreements shall include, but not be limited to, the definition of each agency's roles and responsibilities for serving individuals with exceptional needs.

– State Interagency Agreements

– Definition of Each Agency's Roles and Responsibilities

56885. The Department of Finance shall, after consultation with appropriate state agencies, ascertain the amounts of funds, if any, that should be transferred between state agencies in order to achieve the purposes of the bill and shall notify the Joint Legislative Budget Committee, the Senate Education Committee, and the Assembly Education Committee of those amounts pursuant to the Budget Act.

– Amounts of Funds to Be Transferred Between State Agencies

Any savings that may occur to any program due to maximized use of federal funds or services to individuals with exceptional needs as provided in this article shall be utilized to defer projected increased costs to meet full mandates of the Individuals with Disabilities Education Act (20 U.S.C. Sec. 1400 et seq.).

CALIFORNIA CODE OF REGULATIONS - TITLE 5
DIVISION 1
CHAPTER 3. HANDICAPPED CHILDREN

SUBCHAPTER 1. SPECIAL EDUCATION

Article 1. General Provisions

Article 2. Administration

Article 3. Identification, Referral, and Assessment

Article 3.1. Individuals with Exceptional Needs

*(See Chapter 4.5 of Part 30 of the Education Code)

Article 4. Instructional Planning and Individualized Education Program

Article 5. Implementation (Program Components)

Article 6. Nonpublic, Nonsectarian School and
Agency Services

Article 7. Procedural Safeguards

CHAPTER 5.1. UNIFORM COMPLAINT PROCEDURES
SUBCHAPTER 1. COMPLAINT PROCEDURES

Article 1. Definitions

Article 2. Purpose and Scope

Article 3. Local Agency Compliance

Article 4. Local Complaint Procedures

CALIFORNIA CODE OF REGULATIONS - TITLE 5
DIVISION 1
CHAPTER 3. HANDICAPPED CHILDREN

SUBCHAPTER 1. SPECIAL EDUCATION

Article 1. General Provisions

3000. (a) This chapter applies to those special education programs which are administered under a local plan as defined in Section 56027 and Part 30 of the Education Code. Provisions of this chapter shall be construed as supplemental to, and in the context of, Federal laws and regulations relating to individuals with exceptional needs in effect on January 1, 1981, and state laws and regulations relating to individuals with exceptional needs. The intent of this chapter is to assure conformity with the Education for All Handicapped Children Act, Public Law 94-142 (20 USC 1401, et seq.) and Section 504 of the Rehabilitation Act of 1973, Public Law 93-112 (29 USC 794), and their implementing regulations including Title 34, Code of Federal Regulations, Sections 300.1 et seq.; Sections 104.1 et seq.; and Sections 76.1 et seq..

— Scope

(b) A school district, special education local plan area, or county office shall use federal, state, local, and private sources of support which are available to provide services as specified in an individualized education program.

(c) Nothing in this chapter relieves any other agency from an otherwise valid obligation to provide or pay for services for individuals with exceptional needs. Clarification and specificity of responsibilities shall be included in but not limited to interagency agreements.

[Authority cited: Section 56100(a), (i), and (j), Education Code]
[Reference: Sections 56000-56001, Education Code; and 34 CFR 300.301]

3001. In addition to those found in Education Code Sections 56020-56033, Public Law 94-142 as amended (20 USC 1401 et seq.), and Title 34, Code of Federal Regulations, Part 300 and 301, the following definitions are provided:

— Definitions

(a) "Applicant" means an individual, firm, partnership, association, or corporation who has made application for certification as a nonpublic, nonsectarian school, or agency.

— Applicant

(b) "Appropriate education," as in 'free, appropriate, public education,' is an educational program and related service(s) as

— Appropriate Education

determined on an individual basis which meets the unique needs of each individual with exceptional needs. Such an educational program and related service(s) shall be based on goals and objectives as specified in an individualized education program (IEP) and determined through the process of assessment and IEP planning in compliance with state and federal laws and regulations. Such an educational program shall provide the equal opportunity for each individual with exceptional needs to achieve his or her full potential, commensurate with the opportunity provided to other individuals.

(c) "Behavioral emergency" is the demonstration of a serious behavior problem: (1) which has not previously been observed and for which a behavioral intervention plan has not been developed; or (2) for which a previously designed behavioral intervention is not effective. Approved behavioral emergency procedures must be outlined in the special education local planning area (SELPA) local plan.

– Behavioral Emergency

(d) "Behavioral intervention" means the systematic implementation of procedures that result in lasting positive changes in the individual's behavior. "Behavioral interventions" are designed to provide the individual with greater access to a variety of community settings, social contacts and public events; and ensure the individual's right to placement in the least restrictive educational environment as outlined in the individual's IEP. "Behavioral interventions" do not include procedures which cause pain or trauma. "Behavioral interventions" respect the individual's human dignity and personal privacy. Such interventions shall assure the individual's physical freedom, social interaction, and individual choice.

– Behavioral Intervention

(e) "Behavioral intervention case manager" means a designated certificated school/district/county staff member(s) or other qualified personnel pursuant to subsection (x) contracted by the school district or county office who has been trained in behavior analysis with an emphasis on positive behavioral interventions. The "behavioral intervention case manager" is not intended to be a new staffing requirement and does not create any new credentialing or degree requirements. The duties of the "behavioral intervention case manager" may be performed by any existing staff member trained in behavior analysis with an emphasis on positive behavioral interventions, including, but not limited to, a teacher, resource specialist, school psychologist, or program specialist.

– Behavioral Intervention Case Manager

(f) The "behavioral intervention plan" is a written document which is developed when the individual exhibits a serious behavior problem that significantly interferes with the implementation of the goals and objectives of the individual's

– Behavioral Intervention Plan

IEP. The "behavioral intervention plan shall become part of the IEP. The plan shall describe the frequency of the consultation to be provided by the behavioral intervention case manager to the staff members and parents who are responsible for implementing the plan. The plan shall include the following:

(1) a summary of relevant and determinative information gathered from a functional analysis assessment;

(2) an objective and measurable description of the targeted maladaptive behavior(s) and replacement positive behavior(s);

(3) the individual's goals and objectives specific to the behavioral intervention plan;

(4) a detailed description of the behavioral interventions to be used and the circumstances for their use;

(5) specific schedules for recording the frequency of the use of the interventions and the frequency of the targeted and replacement behaviors; including specific criteria for discontinuing the use of the intervention for lack of effectiveness or replacing it with an identified and specified alternative;

(6) criteria by which the procedure will be faded or phased-out, or less intense/frequent restrictive behavioral intervention schedules or techniques will be used;

(7) the extent to which the behavioral interventions will be used in the home, residential facility, work site or other settings; and

(8) specific dates for periodic review by the IEP team of the efficacy of the program.

(g) "Certification" means authorization by the Superintendent for a nonpublic school or nonpublic agency to service individuals with exceptional needs under a contract pursuant to the provisions of Education Code Section 56366(c).

– Certification

(h) "Contract" means the legal document which binds the public education agency and the nonpublic school or nonpublic agency.

– Contract

(i) "Contracting education agency," as used in this chapter, means school district, special education local plan area, or county office.

– Contracting Education Agency

(j) "Credential" means a valid credential in special education or individual personnel services issued by the California State Commission on Teacher Credentialing.

– Credential

(k) "Dual enrollment" means the concurrent attendance of the individual in a public education agency and a nonpublic school and/or a nonpublic agency.

– Dual Enrollment

(l) "Feasible" as used in Education Code Section 56363(a) means the individualized education program team:

– Feasible

(1) has determined the regular class teacher, special class teacher, and/or resource specialist possesses the necessary

competencies and credentials/certificates to provide the designated instruction and service specified in the individualized education program, and

(2) has considered the time and activities required to prepare for and provide the designated instruction and service by the regular class teacher, special class teacher, and/or resource specialist.

(m) "Instructional day" shall be the same period of time as constitutes the regular school day for that chronological peer group unless otherwise specified in the individualized education program.

- Instructional Day

(n) "Intensive special education and services" means instruction and services, without which the individual would be unable to develop the skills necessary to achieve educational goals appropriate to his or her developmental and cognitive level or potential. Such instruction and services may be provided in any of the program options as stated in Education Code Section 56361.

- Intensive Special Education and Services

(o) "License" means a valid license issued by the Board of Medical Quality Assurance, Board of Consumer Affairs, Board of Behavioral Sciences Examiners, or other state licensing office authorized to grant licenses which may be applicable to providing services for individuals with exceptional needs. If a license is not available through an appropriate state licensing agency, a certificate of registration with the appropriate professional organization at the national and/or state level which has standards established for the certificate is equivalent to a license.

- License

(p) "Linguistically appropriate goals, objectives, and programs" means:

- Linguistically Appropriate Goals, Objectives, and Programs

(1) (A) Those activities which lead to the development of English language proficiency through the use of the primary language of the individual with exceptional needs; and

(B) Those instructional systems either at the elementary or secondary level which meet the language development needs of the limited English proficient individual by building on the individual's existing language skills in order to develop English proficiency.

(2) For individuals whose primary language is other than English, nothing in this section shall preclude the individual learning program, as defined by Section 52163 of the Education Code, from being included in the individual's IEP.

(3) For individuals whose primary language is other than English, and whose potential for learning a second language, as determined by the individualized education program team, is severely limited, nothing in this section shall preclude the individualized education program team from determining that

instruction may be provided in the individual's primary language, provided that the IEP team periodically, but not less than annually, reconsiders the individual's ability to receive instruction in the English language.

(q) "Local governing board," for purposes of Section 3080, means either district or county board of education, depending on which agency, district, governing board, or county is alleged to be in violation of a law or regulation.

– Local Governing Board

(r) "Nonpublic agency" means any private, nonsectarian establishment or individual providing related services necessary for an individual with exceptional needs to benefit educationally from the individual's educational program.

– Nonpublic Agency

(s) "Nonpublic school" means any private, nonsectarian school enrolling individuals with exceptional needs, and employing at least one full-time teacher holding an appropriate credential authorizing special education services, and certified by the California Department of Education. The nonpublic school shall meet those standards as prescribed in Section 3062 herein.

– Nonpublic School

(t) "Nonsectarian" status means a nonpublic school or agency that is not owned, operated, controlled by, or formally affiliated with a religious group or sect, whatever might be the actual character of the education program or the primary purpose of the facility.

– Nonsectarian Status

(u) "Prescribed course of study," as used in Education Code Section 56026(c)(4), means the course of study that is established by the local board of education pursuant to Education Code Section 51000 et seq.

– Prescribed Course of Study

(v) "Primary language" means the language other than English, or other mode of communication, the person first learned, or the language which is spoken in the person's home. In the case of an individual identified as an individual of limited English proficiency pursuant to Education Code Sections 52164 and 52164.1, limited English proficiency shall be defined pursuant to Education Code Section 52163(m).

– Primary Language

(w) "Program" means:

"Program," when referring to an individual with exceptional needs, means the individualized education program.

"Program," when referring to an educational agency, means that system of procedures and resources established by a district, special education local plan area, or county office to provide special education.

– Program

(x) "Qualified" means that a person has met federal and state certification, licensing, registration, or other comparable requirements which apply to the area in which he or she is providing special education or related services, or, in the absence of such requirements, the state-education-agency-approved or

– Qualified

recognized requirements, and adheres to the standards of professional practice established in federal and state law or regulation, including the standards contained in the California Business and Professions Code. Nothing in this definition shall be construed as restricting the activities in services of a graduate needing direct hours leading to licensure, or of a student teacher or intern leading to a graduate degree at an accredited or approved college or university, as authorized by state laws or regulations.

(y) "Serious behavior problems" are defined as the individual's behaviors which are self-injurious, assaultive, or causing property damage which could lead to suspension or expulsion pursuant to Education Code Section 48900(f) and other severe behavior problems that are pervasive and are maladaptive that require a systematic and frequent application of behavioral interventions.

– Serious Behavior Problems

(z) "Specialized physical health care services" are those health services prescribed by the individual's licensed physician and surgeon requiring medically related training for the individual who performs the services and which are necessary during the school day to enable the individual to attend school.

– Specialized Health Care Services

(aa) "Temporary physical disability" means a disability incurred while an individual was in a regular education class and which at the termination of the temporary physical disability, the individual can, without special intervention, reasonably be expected to return to his or her regular education class.

– Temporary Physical Disability

[NOTE: Authority cited: Sections 56100(a), (i) and (j) and 56523(a), Education Code. Reference: Sections 49423.5, 56026, 56320, 56520, and 56523, Education Code; and 34 CFR 300.4 and 300.12.]

Article 2. Administration

– ADMINISTRATION

3010. Educational programs and services administered by other public agencies which provide educational programs and services to individuals with exceptional needs shall adhere to the provisions of federal and state laws and regulations relating to individuals with exceptional needs.

– Other Public Agencies

[Authority cited: Education Code Section 56100(a) and (i); 20 USC 1414(c)(2)(B); and 34 CFR 300.600] [Reference: Sections 56000, 56100(i), and 56500, Education Code; and 34 CFR 300.2, 300.11, 300.60]

Article 3. Identification, Referral, and Assessment

3021. (a) All referrals for special education and related services shall initiate the assessment process and shall be documented. When a verbal referral is made, staff of the school district, special education local plan area, or county office shall offer assistance to the individual in making a request in writing, and shall assist the individual if the individual requests such assistance.

(b) All school staff referrals shall be written and include:

(1) A brief reason for the referral.

(2) Documentation of the resources of the regular education program that have been considered, modified, and when appropriate, the results of intervention. This documentation shall not delay the time lines for completing the assessment plan or assessment.

[Authority cited: Section 56100(a), (i), and (j), Education Code]
[Reference: Sections 56300-56303, Education Code; 34 CFR 300.128, 300.220]

3021.1. (a) When a pupil has been medically diagnosed as having a chronic illness or acute health problem, the pupil may be referred to the school district or county office for an assessment to determine the need for special education.

(b) The following information shall be reviewed by the individualized education program team:

(1) The type of chronic illness;

(2) The possible medical side effects and complications of treatment that could affect school functioning;

(3) The educational and social implications of the disease and treatment to include but not limited to the likelihood of fatigue, absences, changes in physical appearance, amputations, or problems with fine and gross motor control, and

(4) Special considerations necessitated by outbreaks of infectious diseases, if applicable.

(c) The individualized education program team shall designate the school's liaison with the pupil's primary health provider.

[Authority cited: Section 56100(a), (i), and (j), Education Code]
[Reference: Sections 56300-56303, Education Code; 34 CFR 300.128, 300.220]

3022. In addition to the assessment plan requirements of Education Code Section 56321, the proposed written assessment plan shall include a description of any recent assessment conducted, including any available independent assessments and any assessment information the parent requests to be considered, and information indicating the pupil's primary language and the pupil's language proficiency in the primary language as determined by Education Code Section 52164.1.

[Authority cited: Section 56100(a), (i), (j), Education Code; and 20 USC 1414(c)(2)(B)] [Reference: Sections 56321, 56329, Education Code; and 34 CFR 300.500-502, and 300.515-541]

3023. (a) In addition to provisions of Section 56320 of the Education Code, assessments shall be administered by qualified personnel who are competent in both the oral or sign language skills and written skills of the individual's primary language or mode of communication and have a knowledge and understanding of the cultural and ethnic background of the pupil. If it clearly is not feasible to do so, an interpreter must be used, and the assessment report shall document this condition and note that the validity may have been affected.

- Assessment
- Administered by Qualified Personnel

(b) The normal process of second-language acquisition, as well as manifestations of dialect and sociolinguistic variance shall not be diagnosed as a handicapping condition.

- Exceptions

[Authority cited: Section 56100(a), (i), and (j), Education Code] [Reference: Sections 56001, 56320, 56324, and 56327, Education Code; and 34 CFR 300.530, 300.532 and 300.543]

3024. In addition to the requirements specified in Education Code Section 56325 and all applicable sections in this chapter, the following shall apply:

- Transfer

(a) Transfer of Records. Upon receipt of a request from an educational agency where an individual with exceptional needs has enrolled, a former educational agency shall send the pupil's special education records, or a copy thereof, within five working days.

- Records

(b) Transition from Elementary School District to High School District. When a pupil is to enroll in a high school district from an elementary district, the elementary district shall invite the high school district to the individualized education program team meeting prior to the last scheduled review. If the authorized high school personnel participate with the elementary district personnel in the individualized education program team meeting, the individualized education program shall specify the appropriate high school placement.

- Transition from Elementary School District to High School District

If the authorized representative of the high school district has not participated in the individualized education program development prior to transfer from the elementary program, the elementary school district shall notify the high school district of those individuals with exceptional needs who require special education and related services. For each pupil listed who enrolls in the high school district, the administrator shall make an interim placement in accordance with Education Code 56325 or shall immediately convene an individualized education program team meeting.

[Authority cited: Sections 49068 and 56100(a), Education Code]
[Reference: Section 49068 and 56325, Education Code]

3025. (a) Prior to referring a pupil for further assessment to California Schools for the Deaf or Blind or the Diagnostic Schools, districts, special education local plan areas, counties, or other agencies providing education services, shall first conduct assessments at the local level within the capabilities of that agency. Results of local assessments shall be provided to parent(s) and shall state the reasons for referral to the State School. Results of local assessments shall accompany the referral request.

    (b) The Schools for the Deaf and Blind and the Diagnostic Schools shall conduct assessments pursuant to the provisions of Education Code Section 56320 et seq..

    (c) A representative of the district, special education local plan area, or county individualized education program team shall participate in the staffing meeting and shall receive the final report and recommendations. Conference calls are acceptable forms of participation, provided that written reports and recommendations have been received by the representative prior to the meeting.

- Assessment Option:
  Referral to State Schools
  for Further Assessment

- Local Assessments

- Pursuant to EC 56320

- Local Participation

[Authority cited: Section 56100(a), Education Code] [Reference: Section 56326, Education Code]

3027. All pupils being assessed for initial and three-year review for special education services shall have had a hearing and vision screening, unless parental permission was denied.

- Hearing and Vision Screening

[Authority cited: Section 56100(a), Education Code]
[Reference: Sections 56320, 56321 and 56327, Education Code; and 34 CFR 300.532]

3028. All pupils continuing to fail a threshold hearing test shall be assessed by a licensed or credentialed audiologist and such assessment shall be a part of the assessment plan.

– Audiological Assessment

[Authority cited: Section 56100(a), Education Code] [Reference: Sections 56320 and 56327, Education Code; and 34 CFR 300.532]

3029. (a) School districts, county offices, and special education local plan areas shall ensure that credentialed school psychologists are available to perform individually administered tests of intellectual or emotional functioning pursuant to Section 56320(b)(3) of the Education Code.

– Contracting for Individually Administered Tests of Psychological Functioning Due to Unavailability of School Psychologists

(b) Due to the temporary unavailability of a credentialed school psychologist, a school district or county office may contract with qualified personnel to perform individually administered tests of intellectual or emotional functioning including necessary reports pursuant to Section 56327 of the Education Code.

(c) The district or county office shall seek appropriately credentialed school psychologists for employment. These efforts, which include but are not limited to contacting institutions of higher education having approved school psychology programs and utilizing established personnel recruitment practices, shall be documented and available for review.

(d) The only persons qualified to provide assessment services under this section shall be educational psychologists licensed by the Board of Behavioral Science Examiners.

[Authority cited: Sections 56100(a), 56320(f), Education Code] [Reference: Sections 56320(b)(3), and 56327, Education Code]

Article 3.1. Individuals with Exceptional Needs

– INDIVIDUALS WITH EXCEPTIONAL NEEDS

3030. A pupil shall qualify as an individual with exceptional needs, pursuant to Section 56026 of the Education Code, if the results of the assessment as required by Section 56320 demonstrate that the degree of the pupil's impairment as described in Section 3030 (a through j) requires special education in one or more of the program options authorized by Section 56361 of the Education Code. The decision as to whether or not the assessment results demonstrate that the degree of the pupil's impairment requires special education shall be made by the individualized education program team, including assessment personnel in accordance with Section 56341(d) of the Education Code. The individualized education program team shall take into

– Eligibility Criteria

account all the relevant material which is available on the pupil. No single score or product of scores shall be used as the sole criterion for the decision of the individualized education program team as to the pupil's eligibility for special education. The specific processes and procedures for implementation of these criteria shall be developed by each special education local plan area and be included in the local plan pursuant to Section 56220(a) of the Education Code.

(a) A pupil has a hearing impairment, whether permanent or fluctuating, which impairs the processing of linguistic information through hearing, even with amplification, and which adversely affects educational performance. Processing linguistic information includes speech and language reception and speech and language discrimination. — Hearing Impairment

(b) A pupil has concomitant hearing and visual impairments, the combination of which causes severe communication, developmental, and educational problems. — Hearing and Visual Impairment

(c) A pupil has a language or speech disorder as defined in Section 56333 of the Education Code, and it is determined that the pupil's disorder meets one or more of the following criteria: — Language or Speech Disorder

(1) Articulation disorder.

(A) The pupil displays reduced intelligibility or an inability to use the speech mechanism which significantly interferes with communication and attracts adverse attention. Significant interference in communication occurs when the pupil's production of single or multiple speech sounds on a developmental scale of articulation competency is below that expected for his or her chronological age or developmental level, and which adversely affects educational performance.

(B) A pupil does not meet the criteria for an articulation disorder if the sole assessed disability is an abnormal swallowing pattern.

(2) Abnormal Voice. A pupil has an abnormal voice which is characterized by persistent, defective voice quality, pitch, or loudness.

(3) Fluency Disorders. A pupil has a fluency disorder when the flow of verbal expression including rate and rhythm adversely affects communication between the pupil and listener.

(4) Language Disorder. The pupil has an expressive or receptive language disorder when he or she meets one of the following criteria:

(A) The pupil scores at least 1.5 standard deviations below the mean, or below the 7th percentile, for his or her chronological age or developmental level on two or more standardized tests in one or more of the following areas of language development: morphology, syntax, semantics, or pragmatics. When standardized tests are considered to be invalid for the specific pupil, the expected language performance level shall be determined by alternative means as specified on the assessment plan, or

(B) The pupil scores at least 1.5 standard deviations below the mean or the score is below the 7th percentile for his or her chronological age or developmental level on one or more standardized tests in one of the areas listed in subsection (A) and displays inappropriate or inadequate usage of expressive or receptive language as measured by a representative spontaneous or elicited language sample of a minimum of fifty utterances. The language sample must be recorded or transcribed and analyzed, and the results included in the assessment report. If the pupil is unable to produce this sample, the language, speech, and hearing specialist shall document why a fifty utterance sample was not obtainable and the contexts in which attempts were made to elicit the sample. When standardized tests are considered to be invalid for the specific pupil, the expected language performance level shall be determined by alternative means as specified in the assessment plan.

(d) A pupil has a visual impairment which, even with correction, adversely affects a pupil's educational performance.

– Visual Impairment

(e) A pupil has a severe orthopedic impairment which adversely affects the pupil's educational performance. Such orthopedic impairments include impairments caused by congenital anomaly, impairments caused by disease, and impairments from other causes.

– Severe Orthopedic Impairment

(f) A pupil has limited strength, vitality or alertness, due to chronic or acute health problems, including but not limited to a heart condition, cancer, leukemia, rheumatic fever, chronic kidney disease, cystic fibrosis, severe asthma, epilepsy, lead poisoning, diabetes, tuberculosis and other communicable infectious diseases, and hematological disorders such as sickle cell anemia and hemophilia which adversely affects a pupil's educational performance. In accordance with Section 56026(e) of the Education Code, such physical disabilities shall not be temporary in nature as defined by Section 3001(v). *

– Other Health Impairments

(g) A pupil exhibits any combination of the following autistic-like behaviors, to include but not limited to:

– Autistic-Like Behaviors

(1) An inability to use oral language for appropriate communication.

(2) A history of extreme withdrawal or relating to people inappropriately and continued impairment in social interaction from infancy through early childhood.

(3) An obsession to maintain sameness.

(4) Extreme preoccupation with objects or inappropriate use

*(NOTE: This should reference Section 3001(aa) not 3001(v).

of objects or both.

(5) Extreme resistance to controls.

(6) Displays peculiar motoric mannerisms and motility patterns.

(7) Self-stimulating, ritualistic behavior.

(h) A pupil has significantly below average general intellectual functioning existing concurrently with deficits in adaptive behavior and manifested during the developmental period, which adversely affect a pupil's educational performance. — Mental Retardation

(i) Because of a serious emotional disturbance, a pupil exhibits one or more of the following characteristics over a long period of time and to a marked degree, which adversely affect educational performance: — Serious Emotional Disturbance

(1) An inability to learn which cannot be explained by intellectual, sensory, or health factors.

(2) An inability to build or maintain satisfactory interpersonal relationships with peers and teachers.

(3) Inappropriate types of behavior or feelings under normal circumstances exhibited in several situations.

(4) A general pervasive mood of unhappiness or depression.

(5) A tendency to develop physical symptoms or fears associated with personal or school problems.

(j) A pupil has a disorder in one or more of the basic psychological processes involved in understanding or in using language, spoken or written, which may manifest itself in an impaired ability to listen, think, speak, read, write, spell, or do mathematical calculations, and has a severe discrepancy between intellectual ability and achievement in one or more of the academic areas specified in Section 56337(a) of the Education Code. For the purpose of Section 3030(j): — Specific Learning Disabilities

(1) Basic psychological processes include attention, visual processing, auditory processing, sensory-motor skills, cognitive abilities including association, conceptualization and expression.

(2) Intellectual ability includes both acquired learning and learning potential and shall be determined by a systematic assessment of intellectual functioning.

(3) The level of achievement includes the pupil's level of competence in materials and subject matter explicitly taught in school and shall be measured by standardized achievement tests.

(4) The decision as to whether or not a severe discrepancy exists shall be made by the individualized education program team, including assessment personnel in accordance with Section 56341(d), which takes into account all relevant material which is available on the pupil. No single score or product of scores, test or procedure shall be used as the sole criterion for the decisions of the individualized education program team as to the pupil's

eligibility for special education. In determining the existence of a severe discrepancy, the individualized education program team shall use the following procedures:

(A) When standardized tests are considered to be valid for a specific pupil, a severe discrepancy is demonstrated by: first, converting into common standard scores, using a mean of 100 and standard deviation of 15, the achievement test score and the ability test score to be compared; second, computing the difference between these common standard scores; and third, comparing this computed difference to the standard criterion which is the product of 1.5 multiplied by the standard deviation of the distribution of computed differences of students taking these achievement and ability tests. A computed difference which equals or exceeds this standard criterion, adjusted by one standard error of measurement, the adjustment not to exceed 4 common standard score points, indicates a severe discrepancy when such discrepancy is corroborated by other assessment data which may include other tests, scales, instruments, observations and work samples, as appropriate.

(B) When standardized tests are considered to be invalid for a specific pupil, the discrepancy shall be measured by alternative means as specified on the assessment plan.

(C) If the standardized tests do not reveal a severe discrepancy as defined in subparagraphs (A) or (B) above, the individualized education program team may find that a severe discrepancy does exist, provided that the team documents in a written report that the severe discrepancy between ability and achievement exists as a result of a disorder in one or more basic psychological processes. The report shall include a statement of the area, the degree, and the basis and method used in determining the discrepancy. The report shall contain information considered by the team which shall include, but not be limited to:

1. Data obtained from standardized assessment instruments;
2. Information provided by the parent;
3. Information provided by the pupil's present teacher;
4. Evidence of the pupil's performance in the regular and/or special education classroom obtained from observations, work samples, and group test scores;
5. Consideration of the pupil's age, particularly for young children; and
6. Any additional relevant information.

(5) The discrepancy shall not be primarily the result of limited school experience or poor school attendance.

[Authority cited: Statutes of 1981, Chapter 1094, Section 25(a); and Section 56100(a), (g), (i), Education Code] [Reference: 20

USC 1401(a)(15) and 1412(5); 34 CFR 300.5(b)(7) and (9), 300.532(a) (2), (d) and (e), 300.533, 300.540, 300.541-43; and Sections 56026, 56320, 56333, and 56337, Education Code]

3031. (a) A child, age birth to four years and nine months, shall qualify as an individual with exceptional needs pursuant to Education Code Section 56026(c)(1) and (2) if the Individualized Education Program Team determines that the child meets the following criteria:

(1) Is identified as an individual with exceptional needs pursuant to Section 3030, and

(2) Is identified as requiring intensive special education and services by meeting one of the following:

(A) The child is functioning at or below 50% of his or her chronological age level in any one of the following skill areas:

1. gross or fine motor development;
2. receptive or expressive language development;
3. social or emotional development;
4. cognitive development; and
5. visual development.

(B) The child is functioning between 51% and 75% of his or her chronological age level in any two of the skill areas identified in Section 3031(2)(A).

(C) The child has a disabling medical condition or congenital syndrome which the Individualized Education Program Team determines has a high predictability of requiring intensive special education and services.

(b) Programs for individuals with exceptional needs younger than three years of age are permissive in accordance with Section 56001(c) of the Education Code except for those programs mandated pursuant to Section 56425 of the Education Code.

[Authority cited: Statutes of 1981, Chapter 1094, Section 25(a); and Section 56100(a), (g), (i), Education Code] [Reference: 20 USC 1401(a)(15); 34 CFR 300.5; Statutes of 1981, Chapter 1094, Section 25 (a); and Sections 56026, 56030.5, 56333 and 56337, Education Code]

Article 4. Instructional Planning and Individualized Education Program

3040. (a) Upon completion of the individualized education program, that individualized education program shall be implemented as soon as possible following the individualized education program team meeting.

(b) A copy of the individualized education program shall be

- Additional Eligibility*
  Criteria for Individuals
  with Exceptional Needs -
  Age Birth to Four Years
  and Nine Months

*
(NOTE: The eligibility criteria
in subdivision (a) for children
ages 3 to 5, inclusive has been
superseded by Education Code
Section 56441.11. Subdivision
(b), pertaining to infants/
toddlers has been superseded
by Title 14 (commencing with
Section 95000 of the Government Code.)

- INSTRUCTIONAL PLANNING
  AND IEP

- Individualized Education
  Program Implementation

provided to the parents at no cost, and a copy of the individualized education program shall be provided in the primary language at the request of the parent.

(c) The individualized education program shall show a direct relationship between the present levels of performance, the goals and objectives, and the specific educational services to be provided.

[Authority cited: Section 56100(a), (i), and (j), Education Code] [Reference: Section 56341, Education Code; 34 CFR 300.342-300.345]

3042. (a) Specific educational placement means that unique combination of facilities, personnel, location or equipment necessary to provide instructional services to an individual with exceptional needs, as specified in the individualized education program, in any one or a combination of public, private, home and hospital, or residential settings.

– Placement

(b) The individualized education program team shall document its rationale for placement in other than the pupil's school and classroom in which the pupil would otherwise attend if the pupil were not handicapped. The documentation shall indicate why the pupil's handicap prevents his or her needs from being met in a less restrictive environment even with the use of supplementary aids and services.

[Authority cited: Section 56100(a), Education Code] [Reference: Sections 56001(g), 56031, 56341 and 56343, Education Code]

3043. Extended school year services shall be provided for each individual with exceptional needs who has unique needs and requires special education and related services in excess of the regular academic year. Such individuals shall have handicaps which are likely to continue indefinitely or for a prolonged period, and interruption of the pupil's educational programming may cause regression, when coupled with limited recoupment capacity, rendering it impossible or unlikely that the pupil will attain the level of self-sufficiency and independence that would otherwise be expected in view of his or her handicapping condition. The lack of clear evidence of such factors may not be used to deny an individual an extended school year program if the individualized education program team determines the need for such a program and includes extended school year in the individualized education program pursuant to subsection (f).

– Extended School Year Services

(a) Extended year special education and related services shall be provided by a school district, special education local plan

– Provided During Regular Academic Year

area, or county office offering programs during the regular academic year.

(b) Individuals with exceptional needs who may require an extended school year are those who:

– Individuals Who May Require Extended Year

(1) Are placed in special classes or centers; or

(2) Are individuals with exceptional needs whose individualized education programs specify an extended year program as determined by the individualized education program team.

(c) The term "extended year" as used in this section means the period of time between the close of one academic year and the beginning of the succeeding academic year. The term "academic year" as used in this section means that portion of the school year during which the regular day school is maintained, which period must include not less than the number of days required to entitle the district, special education services region, or county office to apportionments of state funds.

– Definition of Extended Year

(d) An extended year program shall be provided for a minimum of 20 instructional days, including holidays. For reimbursement purposes:

– Minimum Instructional Days

(1) A maximum of 55 instructional days excluding holidays, shall be allowed for individuals in special classes or centers for the severely handicapped; and

(2) A maximum of 30 instructional days excluding holidays, shall be allowed for all other eligible pupils needing extended year.

(e) A local governing board may increase the number of instructional days during the extended year period, but shall not claim revenue for average daily attendance generated beyond the maximum instructional days allowed in subsection (d)(1) and (2).

– Increase in Instructional Days

(f) An extended year program, when needed, as determined by the individualized education program team, shall be included in the pupil's individualized education program.

– Included in IEP

(g) In order to qualify for average daily attendance revenue for extended year pupils, all of the following conditions must be met:

– Conditions to Qualify for ADA

(1) Extended year special education shall be the same length of time as the school day for pupils of the same age level attending summer school in the district in which the extended year program is provided, but not less than the minimum school day for that age unless otherwise specified in the individualized education program to meet a pupil's unique needs.

(2) The special education and related services offered during the extended year period are comparable in standards, scope and quality to the special education program offered during the regular academic year.

(h) If during the regular academic year an individual's

– Integration in the Regular Education Program

individualized education program specifies integration in the regular classroom, a public education agency is not required to meet that component of the individualized education program if no regular summer school programs are being offered by that agency.

(i)   This section shall not apply to schools which are operating a continuous school program pursuant to Chapter 5 (commencing with Section 37600) of Part 22, Division 3, Title 2, of the Education Code.

- Continuous School
  Program

[Authority cited: Section 56100(a) and (j), Education Code] [Reference: Sections 37600, 41976.5 and 56345, Education Code; and 34 CFR 300.346]

Article 5. Implementation (Program Components)

- IMPLEMENTATION
  (PROGRAM COMPONENTS)

3051. (a) General Provisions.

(1) Designated instruction and services may be provided to individuals or to small groups in a specialized area of educational need, and throughout the full continuum of educational settings.

- Standards for Designated
  Instruction and Services
  (DIS)

(2) Designated Instruction and Services, when needed as determined by the individualized education program team, shall be specified in the individualized education program, including frequency and duration of services.

(3) All entities and individuals providing designated instruction and services shall be qualified.

(4) All entities and individuals providing designated instruction and services shall be:

(A) Employees of the school district or county office, or

(B) Employed under contract pursuant to Section 56365 of the Education Code.   Such persons shall be certified by the Department pursuant to Section 3064 of this Title, or

(C) Employees, vendors or contractors of the State Departments of Health Services or Mental Health, or any designated local public health or mental health agency.

[Authority cited: Section 56100(a) and (i), Education Code] [Reference: Section 56363, Education Code; and 34 CFR 300.12]

3051.1. (a) An individual holding an appropriate credential with specialization in language, speech, and hearing may provide services which include:

- Language, Speech, and
  Hearing Development and
  Remediation Appropriate
  Credential

(1) Referral and assessment of individuals suspected of having a disorder of language, speech, or hearing. Such individuals are not considered as part of the caseload pursuant to Section 56363.3 of the Education Code unless an individualized education

program is developed and services are provided pursuant to Section 3051.1(a)(2) and (3).

(2) Specialized instruction and services for individuals with disorders of language, speech, and hearing, including monitoring of pupil progress on a regular basis, providing information for the review, and when necessary participating in the review and revision of individualized educational programs of pupils.

(3) Consultative services to pupils, parents, teachers, or other school personnel.

(4) Coordination of speech and language services with an individual's regular and special education program.

(b) Caseloads of full-time equivalent language, speech, and hearing specialists providing instruction and services within the district, special education local plan area, or county office shall not exceed a district-wide, special education local plan area-wide, or county-wide average of fifty-five (55) individuals unless prior written approval has been granted by the State Superintendent of Public Instruction. — Caseloads

(c) Services may be provided by an aide working under the direct supervision of a credentialed language, speech, and hearing specialist if specified in the individualized education program. No more than two aides may be supervised by one credentialed language, speech, and hearing specialist. The caseloads of persons in subsection (b) shall not be increased by the use of noncertificated personnel. — Services by an Aide

[Authority cited: Section 56100(a) and (i), Education Code] [Reference: Section 56363(b)(1), 56363.3, Education Code; and 34 CFR 300.13(b)(12)]

3051.2. (a) In addition to provisions of Title 34, Code of Federal Regulations, Section 300.13(b)(1), designated audiological instruction and services may include: — Audiological Services

(1) Aural rehabilitation (auditory training, speech reading, language habilitation, and speech conservation) and habilitation with individual pupils or groups and support for the hearing-impaired pupils in the regular classroom.

(2) Monitoring hearing levels, auditory behavior, and amplification for all pupils requiring personal or group amplification in the instructional setting.

(3) Planning, organizing, and implementing an audiology program for individuals with auditory dysfunctions, as specified in the individualized education program.

(4) Consultative services regarding test findings, amplification needs and equipment, otological referrals, home training programs, acoustic treatment of rooms, and coordination of

educational services to hearing-impaired individuals.

(b) The person providing audiological services shall hold a valid credential with a specialization in clinical or rehabilitative services in audiology.

— Valid Credential

[Authority cited: Section 56100(a) and (i), Education Code; 20 USC 1414(c)(2)(B); and 34 CFR 300.600] [Reference: Section 56363(b)(2), Education Code; and 34 CFR 300.13(b)(1)]

3051.3. (a) Mobility instruction may include:

— Mobility Instruction

(1) Specialized instruction for individuals in orientation and mobility techniques.

(2) Consultative services to other educators and parents regarding instructional planning and implementation of the individualized education program relative to the development of orientation and mobility skills and independent living skills.

(b) The person providing mobility instruction and services shall hold a credential as an orientation and mobility specialist.

— Credential Requirement

[Authority cited: Section 56100(a) and (i), Education Code; 20 USC 1414(c)(2)(B); and 34 CFR 300.600] [Reference: Section 56363, Education Code]

3051.4. (a) Special education and related services provided in the home or hospital for school age pupils is limited to those pupils who have been identified as individuals with exceptional needs in accordance with Section 3030 and for whom the individualized education program team recommends such instruction or services.

—Instruction in the Home or Hospital

(b) Instruction may be delivered individually, in small groups or by teleclass.

— Instruction Options

(c) For those individuals with exceptional needs with a medical condition such as those related to surgery, accidents, short-term illness or medical treatment for a chronic illness, the individualized education program team shall review, and revise, if appropriate, the individualized education program whenever there is a significant change in the pupil's current medical condition.

— Change in Medical Condition

(d) When recommending placement for home instruction, the individualized education program team shall have in the assessment information a medical report from the attending physician and surgeon or the report of the psychologist, as appropriate, stating the diagnosed condition and certifying that the severity of the condition prevents the pupil from attending a less restrictive placement. The report shall include a projected calendar date for the pupil's return to school. The individualized

— Medical Report

education program team shall meet to reconsider the individualized education program prior to the projected calendar date for the pupil's return to school.

(e) Instruction in the home or hospital shall be provided by a regular class teacher, the special class teacher or the resource specialist teacher, if the teacher or specialist is competent to provide such instruction and services and if the provision of such instruction and services by the teacher or specialist is feasible. If not, the appropriate designated instruction and services specialist shall provide such instruction.

– Provision of Instruction

(f) The teacher providing the home instruction shall contact the pupil's previous school and teacher to determine:

– Contact Previous School

(1) The course work to be covered;

(2) The books and materials to be used;

(3) Who is responsible for issuing grades and promoting the pupil when appropriate;

(4) For pupils in grades 7 to 12, the teacher shall confer with the school guidance counselor to determine:

(A) The hours the pupil has earned toward semester course credit in each subject included in the individualized education program and the grade as of the last day of attendance;

(B) Who is responsible for issuing credits when the course work is completed;

(C) Who will issue the diploma if the pupil is to graduate.

[Authority cited: Section 56100(a) and (i), Education Code]
[Reference: Section 56001, 56363(b)(4), Education Code]

3051.5. (a) Adapted physical education is for individuals with exceptional needs who require developmental or corrective instruction and who are precluded from participation in the activities of the general physical education program, modified general physical education program, or in a specially designed physical education program in a special class. Consultative services may be provided to pupils, parents, teachers, or other school personnel for the purpose of identifying supplementary aids and services or modifications necessary for successful participation in the regular physical education program or specially designed physical education programs.

– Adapted Physical Education for Individuals with Exceptional Needs

(b) The person providing instruction and services shall have a credential authorizing the teaching of adapted physical education as established by the Commission on Teacher Credentialing.

– Credential Requirement

[Authority cited: Section 56100(a) and (i), Education Code]
[Reference: 34 CFR 300.307]

3051.6. (a) When the district, special education local plan area, or county office contracts for the services of a physical therapist or an occupational therapist, the following standards shall apply:

(1) Occupational or physical therapists shall provide services based upon recommendation of the individual education program team. Physical therapy and occupational therapy services for infants are limited by Education Code 56426.6. Physical therapy services may not exceed the services specified in the Business and Professions Code at Section 2620.

(2) The district, special education services region, or county office shall assure that the therapist has available safe and appropriate equipment.

(b) Qualifications of therapists:

(1) The therapists shall have graduated from an accredited school.

(2) A physical therapist shall be currently licensed by the Board of Medical Quality Assurance of the State of California and meet the educational standards of the Physical Therapy Examining Committee.

(3) An occupational therapist shall be currently registered with the American Occupational Therapy Association.

[Authority cited: Section 56100(a) and (i), Education Code]
[Reference: Section 56363(b)(6), Education Code; and 34 CFR 300.13(b)(5) and (7), 300.600]

3051.7. (a) Vision services shall be provided by a credentialed teacher of the visually handicapped and may include:

(1) Adaptations in curriculum, media, and the environment, as well as instruction in special skills.

(2) Consultative services to pupils, parents, teachers, and other school personnel.

(b) An assessment of and provision for services to visually impaired pupils may be conducted by an eye specialist who has training and expertise in low vision disabilities and has available the appropriate low vision aids for the purposes of assessment. The eye specialist may provide consultation to the pupil, parents, teacher and other school personnel as may be requested by the individualized education program team.

(c) Procedures which may be utilized by qualified personnel are those procedures authorized by federal and state laws and regulations and performed in accordance with these laws and regulations and standards of the profession.

(d) For the purposes of this section, an eye specialist shall mean a licensed optometrist, ophthalmologist, or other licensed

- Physical and Occupational Therapy

- Qualifications of Therapists

- Vision Services

- Assessment of and Provision for Services

- Procedures Utilized by Qualified Personnel

- Eye Specialist

A-22

physician and surgeon who has training and expertise in low vision disabilities.

[Authority cited: Section 56100(a) and (i), Education Code]
[Reference: Sections 44265.5 and 56363(b)(7), Education Code]

3051.75. (a) Vision therapy may include: Remedial and/or developmental instruction provided directly by or in consultation with the optometrist, ophthalmologist, or other qualified licensed physician and surgeon providing ongoing care to the individual.

(b) Vision therapy shall be provided by an optometrist, ophthalmologist, or by appropriate qualified school personnel when prescribed by a licensed optometrist, ophthalmologist, or other qualified licensed physician and surgeon.

(c) Procedures which may be utilized by qualified personnel are those procedures authorized by federal and state laws and regulations and performed in accordance with these laws and regulations and standards of the profession.

[Authority cited: Section 56100(a) and (i), Education Code; 20 USC 1414 (c) (2) (B); and 34 CFR 300.600] [Reference: Section 56363(b)(7), Education Code]

3051.8. (a) Specialized driver training instruction may include instruction to an individual with exceptional needs to supplement the regular driver training program. The individualized education program shall determine the need for supplementary specialized driver training team instruction. The need to supplement the regular program shall be based on an assessment of the pupil's health, physical, and/or educational needs which require modifications which cannot be met through a regular driver training program.

(b) Driver training for individuals herein described must be provided by qualified teachers, as defined by Education Code Sections 41906 and 41907.

[Authority cited: Section 56100(a) and (i), Education Code; 20 USC 1414(c)(2)(B); and 34 CFR 300.600] [Reference: Sections 41305-41306;, 41906-41907 and 56363(b)(8), Education Code]

3051.9. (a) Counseling and guidance services may be provided to an individual with exceptional needs who requires additional counseling and guidance services to supplement the regular guidance and counseling program. The individualized education program team shall determine the need for additional guidance and counseling services.

- Vision Therapy

- Providers of Vision Therapy

- Procedures Utilized by Qualified Personnel

- Specialized Driver Training Instruction

- Provided by Qualified Teachers

- Counseling and Guidance Services

(b) Counseling and guidance services necessary to implement the individualized education program may include:

— Types of Services

(1) Educational counseling in which the pupil is assisted in planning and implementing his or her immediate and long-range educational program.

(2) Career counseling in which the pupil is assisted in assessing his or her aptitudes, abilities, and interests in order to make realistic career decisions.

(3) Personal counseling in which the pupil is helped to develop his or her ability to function with social and personal responsibility.

(4) Counseling and consultation with parents and staff members on learning problems and guidance programs for pupils.

(c) The individual performing counseling services to pupils shall be qualified.

— Qualified Individual

[Authority cited: Section 56100(a) and (i), Education Code; 20 USC 1414(c)(2)(B); and 34 CFR 300.600] [Reference: Sections 35300 and 56363(b)(11), Education Code, and 34 CFR 300.13(b)(2), (b)(6), and (b)(8)]

3051.10. Psychological services may include:

(a) Counseling provided to an individual with exceptional needs by a credentialed or licensed psychologist or other qualified personnel.

(b) Consultative services to parents, pupils, teachers, and other school personnel.

(c) Planning and implementing a program of psychological counseling for individuals with exceptional needs and parents.

— Psychological Services Other Than Assessment and Development of the Individualized Education Program

[Authority cited: Section 56100(a) and (i), Education Code; 20 USC 1414(c)(2)(B); and 34 CFR 300.600] [Reference: Section 56363(b)(10), Education Code; and 34 CFR 300.13(b)(8)]

3051.11. Parent counseling and training may include:

(a) Assisting parents in understanding the special needs of their child, and

(b) Providing parents with information about child development.

— Parent Counseling and Training

[Authority cited: Education Code Section 56100(a) and (i); 20 USC 1414(c)(2)(B); and 34 CFR 300.600] [Reference: Section 56363(b)(11), Education Code; and 34 CFR 300.13(b)(6)]

3051.12. (a) Health and nursing services may include:

(1) Providing services by qualified personnel.

(2) Managing the individual's health problems on the school site.

(3) Consulting with pupils, parents, teachers, and other personnel.

(4) Group and individual counseling with parents and pupils regarding health problems.

(5) Maintaining communication with health agencies providing care to individuals.

(b) Specialized physical health care may be provided as described in Education Code Section 49423.5.

(1) Definitions.

(A) "Specialized physical health care services" means those health services prescribed by the child's licensed physician and surgeon requiring medically related training for the individual who performs the services and which are necessary during the school day to enable the child to attend school.

(B) "Standardized procedures" means protocols and procedures developed through collaboration among school or hospital administrators and health professionals, including licensed physicians and surgeons and nurses, to be utilized in the provision of the specialized physical health care services.

(C) "Qualified" means ability to demonstrate competence in Cardio-Pulmonary Resuscitation, current knowledge of community emergency medical resources, and skill in the use of equipment and performance of techniques necessary to provide specialized physical health care services for individuals with exceptional needs. In addition:

1. "Qualified" for the professional school or public health nurse or licensed physician and surgeon shall mean trained in the procedures to a level of competence and safety which meets the objectives of the training.

2. "Qualified" for the designated school personnel shall mean trained in the procedures to a level of competence and safety which meets the objectives of the training as provided by the school nurse, public health nurse, licensed physician and surgeon, or other programs which provide the training.

(D) "Supervision" means review, observation, and/or instruction of a designated school person's performance and of physical health care services, but does not necessarily require the immediate presence of the supervisor at all times.

1. "Immediate supervision" means that the supervisor shall be physically present while a procedure is being administered.

2. "Direct supervision" means that the supervisor shall be present in the same building as the person being supervised and

- Health and Nursing Services

- Provided as Described in EC Section 49423.5
- Definitions
- Specialized Physical Health Care Services

- Standardized Procedures

- Qualified

- Supervision

available for consultation and/or assistance.

3. "Indirect supervision" means that the supervisor shall be available to the qualified designated school person either in person or through electronic means to provide necessary instruction, consultation, and referral to appropriate care and services as needed. Supervision of designated school persons shall include review on-site by a qualified school nurse, qualified public health nurse, or qualified licensed physician and surgeon. Supervision shall also include review of the competence of that individual in performing the specialized health care service, maintenance of appropriate records, physical environment, and equipment.

(E) "Training" means preparation in the appropriate delivery and skillful performance of specialized physical health care services. In addition: — Training

1. Medically related training of credentialed school nurses or public health nurses shall be that training in an approved program which may be necessary to update or make current the nurse's professional skills and knowledge related to meeting pupils' needs for specialized physical health care services.

2. Medically related training of employed designated school personnel is that training in an approved program in standardized procedures provided by a qualified school nurse, qualified public health nurse, qualified licensed physician and surgeon, or other approved programs to enable the person to provide the specialized physical health care services necessary to enable the child to attend school.

(F) "Competence in Cardio-Pulmonary Resuscitation" means possession of a current valid certificate from an approved program. — CPR Competence

(2) Standards and Staffing. — Standards and Staffing

(A) Allocation of qualified designated school personnel shall be determined by the amount and type of supervision necessary to this regulation, and also the type and frequency of services needed by students in special classes and centers, and regular instructional settings. — Allocation of Personnel

(B) Approved training for qualified personnel shall be provided in one or more of the following ways: — Approved Training

1. By a qualified school nurse, qualified public health nurse, or qualified licensed physician and surgeon, as defined in these regulations.

2. By career and continuing education programs, approved by the appropriate licensing board.

3. By training programs through public or private medical institutions, i.e., hospitals, public health agencies, Visiting Nurses Associations, and Red Cross.

(3) Organization and Administration.

(A) Specific continuing specialized physical health care services required in order for the individual to benefit from special education will be included in the individualized education program. If the parent elects to perform the service during the school day, a waiver shall be signed relieving the school of the responsibility.

(B) Appropriate accommodations for safety and necessary physical care services for the individual with exceptional needs in the school setting shall be provided by the school. Personal privacy and dignity of an individual with exceptional needs shall be assured.

(C) The school district shall not be required to purchase medical equipment for an individual pupil. However, the school district, special education local plan area, or county office is responsible for providing other specialized equipment for use at school that is needed to implement the individualized education program.

(D) In accordance with Education Code Section 49423.5(a)(2), a qualified school nurse, qualified public health nurse, or qualified licensed physician and surgeon responsible for supervising the physical health care of an individual with exceptional needs in the school setting shall:

1. Coordinate the health care services to the individuals with exceptional needs on the school site.

2. Consult with appropriate personnel regarding management of health care services for individuals with exceptional needs.

3. Make appropriate referrals and maintain communication with health agencies providing care to individuals with exceptional needs.

4. Maintain or review licensed physician and surgeon and parent requests and daily documentation records.

(E) Written licensed physician and surgeon and parent requests, as well as the specific standardized procedures to be used if physical health care services are provided, shall be maintained for each individual with exceptional needs. Daily documentation of specific services which are provided shall be maintained on a district-approved form which shall include the signatures of the qualified designated school person(s) who performs the procedure.

1. Any pupil who is required to have specialized physical health care services during the school day, prescribed for him or her by a licensed physician and surgeon, may be assisted by a qualified school nurse, qualified public health nurse, or other qualified school personnel, if the school district receives:

a. A written statement from the licensed physician and

- Organization and Administration
- Continuing Services

- Appropriate Accommodations

- Medical Equipment

- Duties of Medical Professional

- Written Procedures and Documentation

surgeon stating the procedure and time schedules by which such procedures are to be given; and

b. A written statement from the parent or guardian of the pupil, indicating the desire that the school district assist the pupil in the matters set forth in the licensed physician and surgeon's statement, and granting consent for the delivery of such services.

2. This written statement of a licensed physician and surgeon and parent requests and daily documentation shall be maintained in accordance with the requirements of confidentiality of pupil records, and are considered mandatory interim pupil records.

[Authority cited: Sections 49423.5(c) and 56100(a) and (i), Education Code; 20 USC 1414(c)(2)(B); and 34 CFR 300.600] [Reference: Sections 49423.5 and 56363(b)(12), Education Code; and 34 CFR 300.13(b)(10)]

3051.13. (a) Personnel providing social worker services shall be qualified.

(b) Social work services may include:

(1) Individual and group counseling with the individual and his or her immediate family.

(2) Consultation with pupils, parents, teachers, and other personnel regarding the effects of family and other social factors on the learning and developmental requirements of individual pupils with exceptional needs.

(3) Developing a network of community resources, making appropriate referral and maintaining liaison relationships among the school, the pupil with exceptional needs, the family, and the various agencies providing social, income maintenance, employment development, mental health, or other developmental services.

– Social Worker Services

[Authority cited: Section 56100(a) and (i), Education Code; 20 USC 1414(c)(2)(B); and 34 CFR 300.600] [References: Section 56363(b)(13), Education Code; and 34 CFR 300.13(b)(11)]

3051.14. Specially designed vocational education and career development for individuals with exceptional needs regardless of severity of disability may include:

(a) Providing prevocational programs and assessing work-related skills, interests, aptitudes, and attitudes.

(b) Coordinating and modifying the regular vocational education program.

(c) Assisting individuals in developing attitudes, self-confidence, and vocational competencies to locate, secure, and retain employment in the community or sheltered

– Specially Designed Vocational Education and Career Development

environment, and to enable such individuals to become participating members of the community.

(d) Establishing work training programs within the school and community.

(e) Assisting in job placement.

(f) Instructing job trainers and employers as to the unique needs of the individuals.

(g) Maintaining regularly scheduled contact with all work stations and job-site trainers.

(h) Coordinating services with the Department of Rehabilitation, the Department of Employment Development and other agencies as designated in the individualized education program.

[Authority cited: Section 56100(a) and (i), Education Code]
[Reference: Section 56363(b)(14), Education Code; 34 CFR 300.14 (b)(3)]

3051.15. Recreation services include but are not limited to:

(a) Therapeutic recreation services which are those specialized instructional programs designed to assist pupils in becoming as independent as possible in leisure activities, and when possible and appropriate, facilitate the pupil's integration into regular recreation programs.

(b) Recreation programs in schools and the community which are those programs that emphasize the use of leisure activity in the teaching of academic, social, and daily living skills; and, the provision of nonacademic and extracurricular leisure activities and the utilization of community recreation programs and facilities.

(c) Leisure education programs which are those specific programs designed to prepare the pupil for optimum independent participation in appropriate leisure activities, including teaching social skills necessary to engage in leisure activities, and developing awareness of personal and community leisure resources.

[Authority cited: Section 56100(a) and (l), Education Code]
[Reference: Section 56363(b)(15), Education Code; 34 CFR 300.13 (b)(9)]

3051.16. Specialized Services for low-incidence disabilities may include:

(a) Specially designed instruction related to the unique needs of pupils with low-incidence disabilities provided by teachers credentialed pursuant to Education Code 44265;

- Recreation Services

- Specialized Services for Low-Incidence Disabilities

(b) Specialized services related to the unique needs of pupils with low-incidence disabilities provided by qualified individuals such as interpreters, notetakers, readers, transcribers, and other individuals who provide specialized materials and equipment.

[Authority cited: Section 56100(a) and (i), Education Code]
[Reference: Section 56363(b)(16), Education Code]

3051.17. (a) Specialized services may be provided to pupils determined eligible pursuant to Section 3030(f). Such services include but are not limited to:

- Services for Pupils with Chronic Illnesses or Acute Health Problems

(1) Individual consultation;
(2) Home or hospital instruction; and
(3) Other instructional methods using advanced communication technology.

(b) For pupils whose medical condition is in remission or in a passive state, the individualized education program team shall specify the frequency for monitoring the pupil's educational progress to assure that the illness does not interfere with the pupil's educational progress.

- Monitoring Educational Progress

(c) When a pupil identified pursuant to Section 3030(f) experiences an acute health problem which results in his or her non-attendance at school for more than five consecutive days, upon notification of the classroom teacher or the parent, the school principal or designee shall assure that an individualized education program team is convened to determine the appropriate educational services.

- Acute Health Problem

(d) If there is a pattern of sporadic illnesses, the individualized education program team shall convene to consider alternative means for the pupil to demonstrate competencies in the required course of study so that the cumulative number of absences do not prevent educational progress.

- Alternative Means to Demonstrate Competencies

[Authority cited: Section 56100(a), (i), Education Code]
[Reference: Section 56363(a), Education Code; 34 CFR 300.14(a) (1)]

3051.18. (a) Instruction and services for deaf and hard of hearing pupils shall be provided by an individual holding an appropriate credential, who has competencies to provide services to the hearing impaired and who has training, experience and proficient communication skills for educating pupils with hearing impairments. Such services may include but need not be limited to:

- Designated Instruction and Services for the Deaf and Hard of Hearing

(1) Speech, speech reading and auditory training.
(2) Instruction in oral, sign, and written language

development.

(3) Rehabilitative and educational services for hearing impaired individuals to include monitoring amplification, coordinating information for the annual review, and recommending additional services.

(4) Adapting curricula, methods, media, and the environment to facilitate the learning process.

(5) Consultation to pupils, parents, teachers, and other school personnel as necessary to maximize the pupil's experiences in the regular education program.

(b) A specially trained instructional aide, working with and under the direct supervision of the credentialed teacher of the deaf and hard-of-hearing, may assist in the implementation of the pupil's educational program.

[Authority cited: Section 56100(a) and (i), Education Code]
[Reference: Section 56363(b)(16), Education Code; and 34 CFR 300.13(a)]

3052. (a) General Provisions.

(1) An IEP team shall facilitate and supervise all assessment, intervention, and evaluation activities related to a individual's behavioral intervention plan. When the behavioral intervention plan is being developed, the IEP team shall be expanded to include the behavioral intervention case manager with documented training in behavior analysis including positive behavioral intervention(s), qualified personnel knowledgeable of the student's health needs, and others as described in Education Code Section 56341(c)(2). The behavioral intervention case manager is not intended to be a new staff person and may be an existing staff member trained in behavior analysis with an emphasis on positive behavioral interventions.

– Behavioral Intervention Plans

(2) Behavioral intervention plans shall only be implemented by, or be under the supervision of, staff with documented training in behavior analysis, including the use of positive behavioral interventions. Such interventions shall only be used to replace specified maladaptive behavior(s) with alternative acceptable behavior(s) and shall never be used solely to eliminate maladaptive behavior(s).

(3) Behavioral intervention plans shall be based upon a functional analysis assessment, shall be specified in the individualized education program, and shall be used only in a systematic manner in accordance with the provisions of this section.

(4) Behavioral emergency interventions shall not be used as a substitute for behavioral intervention plans.

(5) The elimination of any maladaptive behavior does not require the use of intrusive behavioral interventions that cause pain or trauma.

(6) To the extent possible, behavioral intervention plans shall be developed and implemented in a consistent manner appropriate to each of the individual's life settings.

(b) Functional Analysis Assessments. Whenever the systematic use of behavioral interventions in response to a serious behavior problem is proposed, a functional analysis assessment must be conducted by, or be under the supervision of a person who has documented training in behavior analysis with an emphasis on positive behavioral interventions.

– Functional Analysis Assessments

Functional analysis assessment personnel shall gather information from three sources: direct observation, interviews with significant others, and review of available data such as assessment reports prepared by other professionals and other individual records. Prior to conducting the assessment, parent notice and consent shall be given and obtained pursuant to Education Code Section 56321.

(1) A functional analysis assessment procedure shall include all of the following:

(A) Systematic observation of the occurrence of the targeted behavior for an accurate definition and description of the frequency, duration, and intensity;

(B) Systematic observation of the immediate antecedent events associated with each instance of the display of the targeted inappropriate behavior;

(C) Systematic observation and analysis of the consequences following the display of the behavior to determine the function the behavior serves for the individual, i.e., to identify the specific environmental or physiological outcomes produced by the behavior. The communicative intent of the behavior is identified in terms of what the individual is either requesting or protesting through the display of the behavior;

(D) Ecological analysis of the settings in which the behavior occurs most frequently. Factors to consider should include the physical setting, the social setting, the activities and the nature of instruction, scheduling, the quality of communication between the individual and staff and other students, the degree of independence, the degree of participation, the amount and quality of social interaction, the degree of choice, and the variety of activities;

(E) Review of records for health and medical factors which may influence behaviors (e.g. medication levels, sleep cycles, health, diet); and

(F) Review of the history of the behavior to include the

effectiveness of previously used behavioral interventions.

(2) Functional Analysis Assessment Reports. Following the assessment, a written report of the assessment results shall be prepared and a copy shall be provided to the parent. The report shall include all of the following:

(A) A description of the nature and severity of the targeted behavior(s) in objective and measurable terms;

(B) A description of the targeted behavior(s) that includes baseline data and an analysis of the antecedents and consequences that maintain the targeted behavior, and a functional analysis of the behavior across all appropriate settings in which it occurs;

(C) A description of the rate of alternative behaviors, their antecedents and consequences; and

(D) A proposed behavioral intervention plan, which shall include all of the components specified in Article 1, Section 3001(f), for consideration by the IEP team.

(c) IEP Team Meeting. Upon completion of the functional analysis assessment, an IEP team meeting shall be held to develop a behavioral intervention plan, as defined in Article 1, Section 3001(f) of these regulations. The IEP team shall include the behavioral intervention case manager. The behavioral intervention plan shall become a part of the IEP and shall be written with sufficient detail so as to direct the implementation of the plan.

 – IEP Team Meeting to Develop a Behavioral Intervention Plan

(d) Intervention. Based upon the results of the functional analysis assessment, positive programming for behavioral intervention may include the following:

 – Intervention

(1) Altering the identified antecedent event to prevent the occurrence of the behavior (e.g., providing choice, changing the setting, offering variety and a meaningful curriculum, removing environmental pollutants such as excessive noise or crowding, establishing a predictable routine for the individual);

(2) Teaching the individual alternative behaviors that produce the same consequences as the inappropriate behavior (e.g., teaching the individual to make requests or protests using socially acceptable behaviors, teaching the individual to participate with alternative communication modes as a substitute for socially unacceptable attention-getting behaviors, providing the individual with activities that are physically stimulating as alternatives for stereotypic, self-stimulatory behaviors);

(3) Teaching the individual adaptive behaviors (e.g., choice-making, self-management, relaxation techniques, and general skill development) which ameliorate negative conditions that promote the display of inappropriate behaviors; and

(4) Manipulating the consequences for the display of targeted inappropriate behaviors and alternative, acceptable behaviors so

that it is the alternative behaviors that more effectively produce desired outcomes (i.e., positively reinforcing alternative and other acceptable behaviors and ignoring or redirecting unacceptable behaviors).

(e) Acceptable Responses. When the targeted behavior(s) occurs, positive response options shall include, but are not limited to one or more of the following:

 (1) the behavior is ignored, but not the individual;

 (2) the individual is verbally or verbally and physically redirected to an activity;

 (3) the individual is provided with feedback (e.g., "You are talking too loudly");

 (4) the message of the behavior is acknowledged (e.g., "You are having a hard time with your work"); or

 (5) a brief, physical prompt is provided to interrupt or prevent aggression, self-abuse, or property destruction.

(f) Evaluation of the Behavioral Intervention Plan Effectiveness. Evaluation of the effectiveness of the behavioral intervention plan shall be determined through the following procedures:

 (1) Baseline measure of the frequency, duration, and intensity of the targeted behavior, taken during the functional analysis assessment. Baseline data shall be taken across activities, settings, people, and times of the day. The baseline data shall be used as a standard against which to evaluate intervention effectiveness;

 (2) Measures of the frequency, duration, and intensity of the targeted behavior shall be taken after the behavioral intervention plan is implemented at scheduled intervals determined by the IEP team. These measures shall also be taken across activities, settings, people, and times of the day, and may record the data in terms of time spent acting appropriately rather than time spent engaging in the inappropriate behavior;

 (3) Documentation of program implementation as specified in the behavioral intervention plan (e.g., written instructional programs and data, descriptions of environmental changes); and

 (4) Measures of program effectiveness will be reviewed by the teacher, the behavioral intervention case manager, parent or care provider, and others as appropriate at scheduled intervals determined by the IEP team. This review may be conducted in meetings, by telephone conference, or by other means, as agreed upon by the IEP team.

 (5) If the IEP team determines that changes are necessary to increase program effectiveness, the teacher and behavioral intervention case manager shall conduct additional functional analysis assessments and, based on the outcomes, shall propose

changes to the behavioral intervention plan.

(g) Modifications Without IEP Team Meeting. Minor modifications to the behavioral intervention plan can be made by the behavioral intervention case manager and the parent or parent representative. If the case manager is unavailable, a qualified designee who meets the training requirements of subsection (a)(1) shall participate in such modifications. Each modification or change shall be addressed in the behavioral intervention plan provided that the parent, or parent representative, is notified of the need and is able to review the existing program evaluation data prior to implementing the modification or change. Parents shall be informed of their right to question any modification to the plan through the IEP procedures.

– Modifications to Plan
    Without IEP Team Meeting

(h) Contingency Behavioral Intervention Plans. Nothing in this section is intended to preclude the IEP team from initially developing the behavioral intervention plan in sufficient detail to include schedules for altering specified procedures, or the frequency or duration of the procedures, without the necessity for reconvening the IEP team. Where the intervention is to be used in multiple settings, such as the classroom, home and job sites, those personnel responsible for implementation in the other sites must also be notified and consulted prior to the change.

– Contingency Plans

(i) Emergency Interventions. Emergency interventions may only be used to control unpredictable, spontaneous behavior which poses clear and present danger of serious physical harm to the individual or others or serious property damage and which cannot be immediately prevented by a response less restrictive than the temporary application of a technique used to contain the behavior.

– Emergency Interventions

(1) Emergency interventions shall not be used as a substitute for the systematic behavioral intervention plan that is designed to change, replace, modify, or eliminate a targeted behavior.

(2) Whenever a behavioral emergency occurs, only behavioral emergency interventions approved by the special education local planning area (SELPA) may be used.

(3) No emergency intervention shall be employed for longer than is necessary to contain the behavior. Any situation which requires prolonged use of an emergency intervention shall require staff to seek assistance of the school site administrator or law enforcement agency, as applicable to the situation.

(4) Emergency interventions may not include:

(A) Locked seclusion, unless it is in a facility otherwise licensed or permitted by state law to use a locked room;

(B) Employment of a device or material or objects which simultaneously immobilize all four extremities, except that techniques such as prone containment may be used as an emergency intervention by staff trained in such procedures; and

(C) An amount of force that exceeds that which is reasonable and necessary under the circumstances.

(5) To prevent emergency interventions from being used in lieu of planned, systematic behavioral interventions, the parent and residential care provider, if appropriate, shall be notified within one school day whenever an emergency intervention is used. A "Behavioral Emergency Report" shall immediately be completed and maintained in the individual's file. The report shall include all of the following:

(A) The name and age of the individual;

(B) The setting and location of the incident;

(C) The name of the staff or other persons involved;

(D) A description of the incident and the emergency intervention used, and whether the individual is currently engaged in any systematic behavioral intervention plan; and

(E) Details of any injuries sustained by the individual or others, including staff, as a result of the incident.

(6) All "Behavioral Emergency Reports" shall immediately be forwarded to, and reviewed by, a designated responsible administrator.

(7) Anytime a "Behavioral Emergency Report" is written regarding an individual who does not have a behavioral intervention plan, the designated responsible administrator shall, within two days, schedule a functional analysis assessment of that emergency behavior for the purpose of conducting an IEP review and schedule a meeting to develop an interim behavioral intervention plan with the parent/care provider.

(8) Anytime a "Behavioral Emergency Report" is written regarding an individual who has a behavioral intervention plan, any incident involving a previously unseen serious behavior problem or where a previously designed intervention is not effective should be referred to the IEP team to review and determine if the incident constitutes a need to modify the plan.

(9) "Behavioral Emergency Report" data shall be collected by SELPAs which shall report annually the number of Behavioral Emergency Reports to the California Department of Education and the Advisory Commission on Special Education.

(j) SELPA Plan. The local plan of each SELPA shall include — SELPA Plan procedures governing the systematic use of behavioral interventions and emergency interventions. These procedures shall be part of the SELPA local plan.

(1) Upon adoption, these procedures shall be available to all staff members and parents whenever a behavioral intervention plan is proposed.

(2) At a minimum, the plan shall include:

(A) The qualifications and training of personnel to be designated as behavioral intervention case managers, which shall include training in behavior analysis with an emphasis on positive behavioral interventions, who will coordinate and assist in conducting the functional analysis assessments and the development of the behavioral intervention plans;

(B) The qualifications and training required of personnel who will participate in the implementation of the behavioral intervention plans; which shall include training in positive behavioral interventions;

(C) Special training that will be required for the use of emergency behavioral interventions and the types of interventions requiring such training; and

(D) Approved behavioral emergency procedures.

(k) Nonpublic School Policy. Nonpublic schools and agencies, serving individuals pursuant to Education Code Section 56365 et seq., shall develop policies consistent with those specified in subsection (i) of this section. — Nonpublic School Policy

(l) Prohibitions. No public education agency, or nonpublic school or agency serving individuals pursuant to Education Code Section 56365 et seq., may authorize, order, consent to, or pay for any of the following interventions, or any other interventions similar to or like the following: — Prohibitions

(1) Any intervention that is designed to, or likely to, cause physical pain;

(2) Releasing noxious, toxic or otherwise unpleasant sprays, mists, or substances in proximity to the individual's face;

(3) Any intervention which denies adequate sleep, food, water, shelter, bedding, physical comfort, or access to bathroom facilities;

(4) Any intervention which is designed to subject, used to subject, or likely to subject the individual to verbal abuse, ridicule or humiliation, or which can be expected to cause excessive emotional trauma;

(5) Restrictive interventions which employ a device or material or objects that simultaneously immobilize all four extremities, including the procedure known as prone containment, except that prone containment or similar techniques may be used by trained personnel as a limited emergency intervention pursuant to subsection (i);

(6) Locked seclusion, except pursuant to subsection (i)(4)(A);

(7) Any intervention that precludes adequate supervision of the individual; and

(8) Any intervention which deprives the individual of one or more of his or her senses.

(m) Due Process Hearings. The provisions of this chapter — Due Process Hearings related to functional analysis assessments and the development and implementation of behavioral intervention plans are subject to the due process hearing procedures specified in Education Code Section 56501 et seq. No hearing officer may order the implementation of a behavioral intervention that is otherwise prohibited by this section, by SELPA policy, or by any other applicable statute or regulation.

[NOTE: Authority: Section 56523(a), Education Code. Reference: Sections 56520 and 56523, Education Code.]

3053. (a) Placement in a special day class shall not limit or restrict the consideration of other options, including services provided in a vocational education program or any combination of programs and placements as may be required to provide the services specified in a pupil's individualized education program.

 – Special Classes

 (b) The following standards for special classes shall be met:

 – Standards

 (1) A special class shall be composed of individuals whose needs as specified in the individualized education programs can be appropriately met within the class.

 (2) Pupils in a special class shall be provided with an educational program in accordance with their individualized education programs for at least the same length of time as the regular school day for that chronological peer group:

 (A) When an individual can benefit by attending a regular program for part of the day, the amount of time shall be written in the individualized education program.

 (B) When the individualized education program team determines that an individual cannot function for the period of time of a regular school day, and when it is so specified in the individualized education program, an individual may be permitted to attend a special class for less time than the regular school day for that chronological peer group.

 (3) The procedure for allocation of aides for special classes shall be specified in the local plan. Additional aide time may be provided when the severity of the handicapping conditions of the pupils or the age of the pupils justifies it, based on the individualized education programs.

 (4) Special class(es) shall be located to promote maximum appropriate interaction with regular educational programs.

 (c) The special class shall be taught by a full-time-equivalent teacher whose responsibility is the instruction, supervision, and coordination of the educational program for those individuals enrolled in the special class.

 – Special Class Teacher

The special class shall be taught by a teacher who holds an appropriate special education credential authorized by the

Commission on Teacher Credentialing and who possesses the necessary competencies to teach individuals assigned to the class. Special class teachers with a Special Education Credential employed as of September 1, 1975, as teachers in special classes for pupils in severe language disorder aphasia programs and who possess the necessary competencies to teach individuals assigned to the class, shall be authorized to continue to teach.

[Authority cited: Section 56100(a), (i), Education Code] [Reference: Sections 56001 and 56364, Education Code; and 34 CFR 300.550-554]

3054. (a) Standards. Special centers operating under this section shall:

- Special Centers

(1) Provide pupils in a special center with an educational program in accordance with their individualized education programs for at least the same length of time as the regular school day for that chronological peer group:

(A) When an individual can benefit by attending a regular class(es) or other program part of the day, the amount of time shall be written in the individualized education program.

(B) When the individualized education program team determines that an individual cannot function for the period of time of a regular school day, and when it is so specified in the individualized education program, an individual may be permitted to attend a special center for less time than the regular school day for that chronological peer group.

(2) Be staffed by qualified personnel at a pupil/adult ratio to enable implementation of the pupils' individualized education programs.

(3) Provide an emergency communication system for the health and safety of individuals with exceptional needs, such as fire, earthquake, and smog alerts.

(4) Have specialized equipment and facilities to meet the needs of individuals served in the special centers.

(b) Special centers should be located to promote maximum, appropriate interaction with regular educational programs.

- Interaction with Regular Educational Programs

[Authority cited: Section 56100(a) and (i), Education Code; 20 USC 1414(c)(2)(B); and 34 CFR 300.600]   [References: Sections 56001 and 56364, Education Code; and 34 CFR 300.550-554]

Article 6. Nonpublic, Nonsectarian School and Agency Services

[NOTE: In Section 11 of Assembly Bill 1250, (Chapter 921, Statutes of 1994), the Legislature declared that Sections 3061 to 3067, inclusive, of Title 5 of the California Code of Regulations are void and without effect on or after January 1, 1995.]

3068. Review of the pupil's individualized education program shall be conducted at least annually by the public education agency. The public education agency shall ensure that review schedules are specified in the individualized education program and contract for the pupil.

— Annual Review of Individualized Education Program

An elementary school district shall notify a high school district of all pupils placed in nonpublic school or agency programs prior to the annual review of the individualized education program for each pupil who may transfer to the high school district.

[Authority cited: Sections 56100(a), (i), (j), Education Code; 20 USC 1414(c)(2)(B); and 34 CFR 300.600] [Reference: Sections 56345, 56365-56366.5, Education Code and 34 CFR 300.4, 300.302, 300.317, 300.343-348 and 300.400-403]

3069. When an individual with exceptional needs meets public education agency requirements for completion of prescribed course of study and adopted differential proficiency standards as designated in the pupil's individualized education program, the public education agency which developed the individualized education program shall award the diploma.

— Diploma

[Authority cited: Sections 56100(a), (i), (j), Education Code; 20 USC 1414(c)(2)(B); and 34 CFR 300.600] [Reference: Sections 56345, 56365-56366.5, Education Code; and 34 CFR 300.4, 300.302, 300.317, 300.343-348 and 300.400-403]

Article 7. Procedural Safeguards

— PROCEDURAL SAFEGUARDS

3080. General Provisions.

(a) Sections 4600 through 4671 apply to the filing of a complaint, in accordance with provisions of Title 34, Code of Federal Regulations, Section 76.780-783, regarding a public agency's alleged violation of federal or state law or regulation relating to the provision of a free appropriate public education.

— General Provisions

(b) Section 3082 applies to due process hearing procedures which the resolution of disagreements between a parent and a public agency regarding the proposal, or refusal of a public agency to initiate or change the identification, assessment, or educational placement of the pupil or the provision of a free appropriate public education to the pupil.

[Authority cited: Section 56100(a) and (j), Education Code]
[Reference: Sections 56500.1 and 56500.2, Education Code; and 34 CFR 76.780-783]

3082. (a) A parent or public education agency may initiate a hearing pursuant to Education Code Sections 56500 through 56507 and Title 34, Code of Federal Regulations, Sections 300.506 through 300.514 on any of the matters described in Education Code Section 56501. The hearing shall be conducted by a hearing officer knowledgeable in administrative hearings and under contract with the State Department of Education.

- Due Process Hearing
  Procedures

(b) The hearings conducted pursuant to this section shall not be conducted according to the technical rules of evidence and those related to witnesses. Any relevant evidence shall be admitted if it is the sort of evidence on which responsible persons are accustomed to rely in the conduct of serious affairs, regardless of the existence of any common law or statutory rule which might make improper the admission of such evidence over objection in civil actions. Hearsay evidence may be used for the purpose of supplementing or explaining other evidence but shall not be sufficient in itself to support a finding unless it would be admissible over objection in civil actions. All testimony shall be under oath or affirmation which the hearing officer is empowered to administer.

- Evidence

(c) In addition to the rights afforded both parties to the hearing pursuant to Education Code Sections 56500-56507 and Title 34, Code of Federal Regulations, Section 300.514, the parties shall also have the following rights:

- Additional Rights

(1) To call witnesses, including adverse witnesses, and to cross examine witnesses for the other party.

(2) To compel the attendance of witnesses. The hearing officer shall have the right to issue Subpoenas (order to appear and give testimony) and Subpoenas Duces Tecum (order to produce document(s) or paper(s) upon a showing of reasonable necessity by a party).

(3) Absent compelling circumstances to the contrary, and upon motion to the hearing officer to have witnesses excluded from the hearing.

(d) Hearings shall be conducted in the English language; when the primary language of a party to a hearing is other than English, or other mode of communication, an interpreter shall be

- Hearings Conducted in
  English; Provision for
  Interpreter

provided who is competent as determined by the hearing officer. Cost for an interpreter shall be borne by the State Department of Education.

(e) If either the school district or the parents have an attorney present as an observer, the attorney may watch the proceedings to advise his party at a later date, but the attorney may not present oral argument, written argument or evidence, or consult in any manner in or out of the room, during the due process hearing.

— Attorney as an Observer

[Authority cited: Sections 56100(a) and (j). Education Code] [Reference: Sections 56500-56507, Education Code; and 34 CFR 300.506- 514]

CALIFORNIA CODE OF REGULATIONS - TITLE 5
DIVISION 1
CHAPTER 5.1. UNIFORM COMPLAINT PROCEDURES

SUBCHAPTER 1. COMPLAINT PROCEDURES

Article 1. Definitions

4600. General Definitions.

(a) "Appeal" means a request made in writing to a level higher than the original reviewing level by an aggrieved party requesting reconsideration or a reinvestigation of the lower adjudicating body's decision.

(b) "Complainant" means any individual, including a person's duly authorized representative or an interested third party, public agency, or organization who files a written complaint alleging violation of federal or state laws or regulations, including allegations of unlawful discrimination in programs and activities funded directly by the state or receiving any financial assistance from the state.

(c) "Complaint" means a written and signed statement alleging a violation of a federal or state law or regulation, which may include an allegation of unlawful discrimination. If the complainant is unable to put the complaint in writing, due to conditions such as illiteracy or other handicaps, the public agency shall assist the complainant in the filing of the complaint.

(d) "Complaint Investigation" means an administrative process used by the Department or local agency for the purpose of gathering data regarding the complaint.

(e) "Complaint Procedure" means an internal process used by the Department or local agency to process and resolve complaints.

(f) "Compliance Agreement" means an agreement between the Department and a local agency, following a finding of noncompliance by the Department, developed by the local agency and approved by Department to resolve the noncompliance.

(g) "Days" means calendar days unless designated otherwise.

(h) "Department" means the California Department of Education.

(i) "Direct State Intervention" means the steps taken by the Department to initially investigate complaints or effect compliance.

(j) "Local Agency" means a school district governing board or a local public or private agency which receives direct or indirect funding or any other financial assistance from the state to provide any school programs or activities or special education or related services. "Local educational agency" includes any public school district and county office of education.

– Definitions
– Appeal

– Complainant

– Complaint

– Complaint Investigation

– Complaint Procedure

– Compliance Agreement

– Days
– Department

– Direct State Intervention

– Local Agency

(k)   "Mediation" means a problem-solving activity whereby a third party assists the parties to a dispute in resolving the problem.

- Mediation

(l)   "State Mediation Agreement" means a written, voluntary agreement, approved by the Department, which is developed by the local agency and complainant with assistance from the Department to resolve an allegation of noncompliance.

- State Mediation Agreement

(m) "State Agency" means the State Departments of Mental Health or Health Services or any other state administrative unit that is or may be required to provide special education or related services to handicapped pupils pursuant to Government Code Section 7570 et seq.

- State Agency

(n)   "Superintendent" means the Superintendent of Public Instruction or his or her designee.

- Superintendent

[Authority cited: Sections 232 and 33031, Education Code; Section 11138, Government Code] [Reference: Sections 210, 220, and 260, Education Code; Sections 11135 and 11138, Government Code]

Article 2. Purpose and Scope

- PURPOSE AND SCOPE

4610. Purpose and Scope.

(a)   This Chapter applies to the filing, investigation and resolution of a complaint regarding an alleged violation by a local agency of federal or state law or regulations governing educational programs, including allegations of unlawful discrimination, in accordance with the provisions of Title 34, CFR, Sections 76.780-783 and 106.8; Title 22, CCR, Sections 98300-98382; and California Education Code Sections 49556 and 8257. The purpose of this Chapter is to establish a uniform system of complaint processing for specified programs or activities which receive state or federal funding.

(b)   This Chapter applies to the following programs administered by the Department:

(i)   Adult Basic Education established pursuant to Education Code Sections 8500 through 8538 and 52500 through 52616.5;

(ii)   Consolidated Categorical Aid Programs as listed in Education Code Section 64000(a);

(iii)   Migrant Education established pursuant to Education Code Sections 54440 through 54445;

(iv)   Vocational Education established pursuant to Education Code Sections 52300 through 52480;

(v)   Child Care and Development programs established pursuant to Education Code Sections 8200 through 8493;

(vi)   Child Nutrition programs established pursuant to

Education Code Sections 49490 through 49560; and

(vii) Special Education programs established pursuant to Education Code Sections 56000 through 56885 and 59000 through 59300.

(c) This Chapter also applies to the filing of complaints which allege unlawful discrimination on the basis of ethnic group identification, religion, age, sex, color, or physical or mental disability, in any program or activity conducted by a local agency, which is funded directly by, or that receives or benefits from any state financial assistance.

[Authority cited: Sections 232, 8261, 33031, 49531, 49551, 54445, 52355, 52451, and 56100(a) and (j), Education Code; Section 11138 Government Code] [Reference: Sections 210, 220, 260, and 49556, Education Code; Sections 11135 and 11138, Government Code]

4611. Referring Complaint Issues to Other Appropriate State or Federal Agencies.

– Referring Complaint Issues to Other Appropriate State or Federal Agencies

The following complaints shall be referred to the specified agencies for appropriate resolution and are not subject to the local and Department complaint procedures set forth in this Chapter unless these procedures are made applicable by separate interagency agreements:

(a) Allegations of child abuse shall be referred to the applicable County Department of Social Services (DSS), Protective Services Division or appropriate law enforcement agency. However, nothing in this section relieves the Department from investigating complaints pursuant to section 4650(a) (viii) (C).

(b) Health and safety complaints regarding a Child Development Program shall be referred to Department of Social Services for licensed facilities, and to the appropriate Child Development regional administrator for licensing-exempt facilities.

(c) Discrimination issues involving Child Nutrition Programs or Title IX of the Educational Amendments of 1972 shall be referred to the U.S. Office for Civil Rights (OCR). Title IX complainants will only be referred to the OCR if there is no state discrimination law or regulation at issue. Unless otherwise negotiated through a memorandum of understanding/agreement, a preliminary inquiry and/or investigation concerning these complaints will be conducted by OCR. The complainant shall be notified by certified mail if his or her complaint is transferred to OCR by the Superintendent.

(d) Employment discrimination complaints shall be sent to the

State Department of Fair Employment and Housing (DFEH) pursuant to Title 22, CCR, Section 98410. The complainant shall be notified by certified mail of any DFEH transferral.

(e) Allegations of fraud shall be referred to the responsible Department Division Director and the Department's Legal Office.

[Authority cited: Sections 33031, 71020 and 71025, Education Code; Section 11138, Government Code. [Reference: Sections 11135, 11136, and 11138, Government Code; 34 CFR 76.780-76.783.]

Article 3. Local Agency Compliance

4620. Local Educational Agency Responsibilities.

Each local education agency shall have the primary responsibility to insure compliance with applicable state and federal laws and regulations. Each local educational agency shall investigate complaints alleging failure to comply, and seek to resolve those complaints in accordance with the procedures set out in this Chapter.

[Authority cited: Sections 232 and 33031, Education Code; Section 11138, Government Code] [Reference: Section 260, Education Code; Sections 11135, Government Code; and 34 CFR 76.780 - 76.783 and 106.8]

4621. District Policies and Procedures.

(a) Each local educational agency shall adopt policies and procedures consistent with this Chapter for the investigation and resolution of complaints. Local policies shall ensure that complainants are protected from retaliation and that the identity of the complainant alleging discrimination remain confidential as appropriate. School Districts and County Offices of Education shall submit their policies and procedures to the local governing board for adoption within one year from the effective date of this chapter. Upon adoption, the district may forward a copy to the Superintendent.

(b) Each local educational agency shall include in its policies and procedures the person(s), employee(s) or agency position(s) or unit(s) responsible for receiving complaints, investigating complaints and ensuring local educational agency compliance. The local educational agency's policies shall ensure that the person(s), employee(s), position(s) or unit(s) responsible for compliance and/or investigations shall be knowledgeable about the laws/programs that he/she is assigned to investigate.

[Authority cited: Sections 232 and 33031, Education Code; Section 11138, Government Code] [Reference: Section 260, Education Code; Sections 11135, Government Code; and 34 CFR 76.780 - 76.783 and 106.8]

4622. Notice; Notice Recipients; Notice Requirements.

– Notice

Each local educational agency shall annually notify in writing, as applicable, its students, employees, parents or guardians of its students, the district advisory committee, school advisory committees, and other interested parties of their local educational agency complaint procedures, including the opportunity to appeal to the Department and the provisions of this Chapter. The notice shall include the identity (identities) of the person(s) responsible for processing complaints. The notice shall also advise the recipient of the notice of any civil law remedies that may be available, and of the appeal and review procedures contained in Sections 4650, 4652, and 4671 of this Chapter. This notice shall be in English, and when necessary, in the primary language, pursuant to Section 48985 of the Education Code, or mode of communication of the recipient of the notice.

[Authority cited: Sections 232 and 33031, Education Code; Section 11138, Government Code] [Reference: Sections 11135 and 11138, Government Code; 34 CFR 76.780-76.783 and 106.8]

Article 4. Local Complaint Procedures

– LOCAL COMPLAINT PROCEDURES

4630. Filing A Local Complaint; Procedures; Time Lines.

– Filing a Local Complaint

(a) For other than discrimination complaints, any individual, public agency or organization may file a written complaint with the administrator/superintendent of the local educational agency, alleging a matter which, if true, would constitute a violation by that local educational agency of federal or state law or regulation governing the programs listed in Section 4610(b of this Chapter.

(b) An investigation of alleged unlawful discrimination shall be initiated by filing a complaint not later than six months from the date the alleged discrimination occurred, or the date the complainant first obtained knowledge of the facts of the alleged discrimination unless the time for filing is extended by the Superintendent, upon written request by the complainant setting forth the reasons for the extension. Such extension by the Superintendent shall be made in writing. The period for filing may be extended by the Superintendent for good cause for a period not to exceed 90 days following the expiration of the time allowed. The Superintendent shall respond immediately upon receipt of requests for extensions.

(1) The complaint shall be filed by one who alleges that he or she has personally suffered unlawful discrimination, or by one who believes an individual or any specific class of individuals has been subjected to discrimination prohibited by this part.

(2) The complaint shall be filed with the local educational agency director/district superintendent or his or her designee, unless the complainant requests direct intervention by the Department pursuant to Article 6 of this Chapter.

(3) An investigation of a discrimination complaint shall be conducted in a manner that protects confidentiality of the parties and the facts.

[Authority cited: Sections 232 and 33031, Education Code; Section 11138, Government Code] [Reference: Sections 11135, 11136, and 11138, Government Code; 34 CFR 76.780-76.783 and 106.8]

4631. Responsibilities of the Local Agency.

(a) Within 60 days from receipt of the complaint, the local educational agency superintendent or his or her designee shall complete the investigation of the complaint in accordance with the local procedures developed pursuant to Section 4621 and prepare a written Local Educational Agency Decision. This time period may be extended by written agreement of the complainant.

(b) The investigation shall provide an opportunity for the complainant, or the complainant's representative, or both, and local educational agency representatives to present information relevant to the complaint. The investigation may include an opportunity for the parties to the dispute to meet to discuss the complaint or to question each other or each other's witnesses.

(c) The Local Educational Agency Decision (the Decision), shall be in writing and sent to the complainant within sixty (60) days from receipt of the complaint by the local agency. The Decision shall contain the findings and disposition of the complaint, including corrective actions if any, the rationale for such disposition, notice of the complainant's right to appeal the local educational agency decision to the Department, and the procedures to be followed for initiating an appeal to the Department.

(d) Local Educational Agencies may establish procedures for attempting to resolve complaints through mediation prior to the initiation of a formal compliance investigation. Conducting local mediation shall not extend the local time lines for investigating and resolving complaints at the local level unless the complainant agrees, in writing, to the extension of the time line. In no event shall mediation be mandatory in resolving complaints.

[Authority cited: Sections 232 and 33031, Education Code; Section 11138, Government Code] [Reference: Sections 11135, 11136, and 11138, Government Code; 34 CFR 76.780-76.783 and 106.8]

4632. Forward to Superintendent.

Upon notification by the Superintendent that the Local Educational Agency Decision has been appealed to the state level pursuant to Section 4652, the local educational agency shall forward the following to the Superintendent:

(a)   The original complaint;

(b)   A copy of the Local Educational Agency Decision;

(c)   A summary of the nature and extent of the investigation conducted by the local agency, if not covered in the Local Educational Agency Decision;

(d)   A report of any action taken to resolve the complaint;

(e)   A copy of the local educational agency complaint procedures; and

(f)   Such other relevant information as the Superintendent may require.

[Authority cited: Section 232 and 33031, Education Code; Section 11138, Government Code] [Reference: Sections 11135, 11136, and 11138, Government Code; 34 CFR 76.780-76.783 and 106.8]

Article 5.   State Complaint Procedures

4640.   Filing a State Complaint That Has Not First Been Filed at the Local Agency; Time Lines, Notice, Appeal Rights.

(a)   Referral to the Local Educational Agency for Local Resolution.

(1)   If a complaint is erroneously first sent to the Superintendent without local educational agency investigation, the Superintendent shall immediately forward the complaint to the local educational agency for processing in accordance with Article 4 of this Chapter, unless circumstances necessitating Department intervention as described at Section 4650 exist.

(2)   The complainant(s) shall be sent a letter to notify him, her, or them of 1) the transferred complaint, 2) the State request for local educational agency resolution, and 3) to advise of Department appeal procedures.

[Authority cited: Sections 232 and 33031, Education Code; Section 11138, Government Code] [Reference: Sections 11135, 11136, and 11138, Government Code; 34 CFR 76.780-76.783 and 106.8]

Article 6. Direct State Intervention

4650. Basis of Direct State Intervention.

(a) The Superintendent shall directly intervene without waiting for local agency action if one or more of the following conditions exists.

(i) The complaint includes an allegation, and the Department verifies, that a local educational agency failed to comply with the complaint procedures required by this Chapter;

(ii) Discrimination is alleged by the complainant and the facts alleged indicate that the complainant will suffer an immediate loss of some benefit such as employment or education if the Department does not intervene. However, nothing in this section gives the Department jurisdiction over employment discrimination claims.

(iii) The complaint relates to agencies other than local educational agencies funded through the Child Development and Child Nutrition Programs;

(iv) The complaint requests anonymity and presents clear and convincing evidence and the Department verifies that he or she would be in danger of retaliation if a complaint were filed locally, or has been retaliated against because of past or present complaints;

(v) The complainant alleges that the local educational agency failed or refused to implement the final decision resulting from its local investigation or local Mediation Agreement;

(vi) The local agency refuses to respond to the Superintendent's request for information regarding a complaint;

(vii) The complainant alleges and the Department verifies, or the Department has information that no action has been taken by the local educational agency within 60 calendar days of the date the complaint was filed locally.

(viii) For complaints relating to special education the following shall also be conditions for direct state intervention:

(A) The complainant alleges that a public agency, other than a local educational agency, as specified in Government Code Section 7570 et seq., fails or refuses to comply with an applicable law or regulation relating to the provision of free appropriate public education to handicapped individuals;

(B) The complainant alleges that the local educational agency or public agency fails or refuses to comply with the due process

B-8

procedures established pursuant to federal and state law and regulation; or has failed or refused to implement a due process hearing order;

(C) The complainant alleges facts that indicate that the child or group of children may be in immediate physical danger or that the health, safety or welfare of a child or group of children is threatened;

(D) The complainant alleges that a handicapped pupil is not receiving the special education or related services specified in his or her Individualized Education Program (IEP);

(E) The complaint involves a violation of federal law governing special education, 20 U.S.C. Section 1400 et seq., or its implementing regulations.

(b) The complaint shall identify upon which basis, as described in paragraph (a) of this section, that direct filing to the State is being made.

[Authority cited: Section 232 and 33031, Education Code; Section 11138, Government Code] [Reference: Sections 11135, 11136, and 11138, Government Code; 34 CFR 76.780-76.783 and 106.8]

4651. Direct State Intervention Time Line.　　　　　　　　　　　– State Intervention Time Line

When the Superintendent receives a complaint requesting direct State intervention, the Superintendent shall determine whether the complaint meets one or more of the criterion specified in Section 4650 for direct State intervention and shall immediately notify the complainant by mail of his or her determination. If the complaint is not accepted, it shall be referred for local investigation pursuant to Section 4631, or referred to another agency pursuant to Section 4611.

[Authority cited: Sections 232 and 33031, Education Code; Section 11138, Government Code] [Reference: Sections 11135, 11136, and 11138, Government Code; 34 CFR 76.780-76.783 and 106.8]

4652. Appealing Local Agency Decisions.　　　　　　　　　　　– Appealing Local Decisions

(a) Any complainant(s) may appeal a Local Educational Agency Decision to the Superintendent by filing a written appeal with the Superintendent within (15) days of receiving the Local Educational Agency Decision. Extensions for filing appeals may be granted, in writing, for good cause.

(b) The complainant shall specify the reason(s) for appealing the local educational agency decision.

(c) The appeal shall include:

(1)   a copy of the locally filed complaint; and

(2)   a copy of the Local Educational Agency Decision.

[Authority cited: Sections 232 and 33031, Education Code; Section 11138, Government Code] [Reference: Sections 11135, 11136, and 11138, Government Code; 34 CFR 76.780-76.783 and 106.8]

Article 7. State Resolution Procedures

- STATE RESOLUTION PROCEDURES

4660. Department Resolution Procedures.

- Department Procedures

(a)   When direct State intervention is warranted pursuant to any provision of Section 4650, or when an appeal has been filed of a local agency decision pursuant to Section 4652, the following procedures shall be used to resolve the issues of the complaint:

(1)   The Department shall offer to mediate the dispute which may lead to a state mediation agreement; and

(2)   The Department shall conduct an on-site investigation if either the district or the complainant waives the mediation process or the mediation fails to resolve the issues.

(b)   If the complaint involves several issues, nothing shall prohibit the parties from agreeing to mediate some of the issues while submitting the remainder for Department investigation. Mediation shall be conducted within the 60 day time line specified in Section 4662(d), and

(c)   Mediation shall not exceed thirty (30) days unless the local or public agency and the complainant agree to an extension.

[Authority cited: Sections 232 and 33031, Education Code; Section 11138, Government Code] [Reference: Sections 11135, 11136, and 11138, Government Code; 34 CFR 76.780-76.783 and 106.8]

4661. Mediation Procedures; State Mediation Agreements; Notice.

- Mediation Procedures

(a)   Initial process.

(1)   Agency and Complainant(s) Notification. Each party in the dispute shall be contacted by the Department and offered the mediation process as a possible means of resolving the complaint. Should the parties agree to enter into mediation, written confirmation shall be sent indicating the time and place of the mediation conference, and the allegations to be addressed.

(2)   Upon local agency and complainant acceptance of the Department's offer to mediate, the allegations to be addressed shall be sent by certified mail to each party.

(3) The Superintendent shall appoint a trained mediator or mediation team to assist the parties in reaching a voluntary agreement.

(b) Mediation Results - State Mediation Agreement.

(1) The mediation results will be documented in a state mediation agreement and signed by the involved parties to the dispute using the following forms as appropriate (Stipulation to Initiate Mediation, Form CS-19; Signed Mediation Agreement Letter to District, Form CS-24; and Mediation Process Agreement, Form CS-25).

(2) The mediator or mediation team shall confirm that the agreement is consistent with all applicable state and federal laws and regulations.

(3) A copy of the written state mediation agreement shall be sent to each party.

(4) The compliance status of a local agency will revert to noncompliance if the local agency does not perform the provisions of the mediation agreement within the time specified in the mediation agreement.

[Authority cited: Section 232 and 33031, Education Code; Section 11138, Government Code] [Reference: Sections 11135, 11136, and 11138, Government Code; 34 CFR 76.780-76.783 and 106.8]

4662. On-Site Investigation Process; Appointment, Notification, Time Line; Extending Investigation Time Lines.

    – On-Site Investigation Process

(a) If either party waives mediation or the mediation fails, in part or in whole, those remaining unresolved issues shall be addressed through the investigation process.

(b) Appointment.

If an on-site investigation is necessary, an investigator(s) shall be appointed by the Superintendent.

(c) Agency and Complainant(s) Notification.

At least two weeks prior to the date of an investigation, each party in the dispute shall be sent written notification by the Department of the name(s) of the investigation(s) and the investigation date(s). The notice shall explain the investigation process.

(d) Time line.

An investigation shall be completed within sixty (60) days after receiving a request for direct intervention or an appeal request, unless the parties have agreed to mediate and agree to extend the time lines. The Superintendent or his or her designee may grant extensions for the investigation only if exceptional circumstances exist with respect to the particular complaint, and provided that the complainant is informed of the extension and the reasons therefore and provided that the facts supporting the extension are documented and maintained in the complaint file.

[Authority cited: Sections 232 and 33031, Education Code; Section 11138, Government Code] [Reference: Sections 11135, 11136, and 11138, Government Code; 34 CFR 76.780-76.783 and 106.8]

4663. Department Investigation Procedures.   - Department Investigation Procedures

(a) The investigator(s) shall request all documentation regarding the allegations. The investigator(s) shall interview the complainant(s), agency administrators, staff, related committees/groups, and any other involved persons, as appropriate, to determine the facts in the case. An opportunity shall be provided for the complainant(s), or the complainant's(s') representative, or both, and the agency involved to present information.

(b) Refusal by the local agency or complainant to provide the investigator with access to records and other information relating to the complaint which the investigator is privileged to review, or any other obstruction of the investigative process shall result in either a dismissal of the complaint or imposition of official applicable sanctions against the local agency.

[Authority cited: Sections 232 and 33031, Education Code; Section 11138, Government Code] [Reference: Sections 11135, 11136, and 11138, Government Code; 34 CFR 76.780-76.783 and 106.8]

4664. Department Investigation Report.   - Department Investigation Report

An investigation report shall be submitted to the Superintendent for review and approval. The investigation report shall include the following information:

(1) A transmittal letter that includes information about how the agency or the complainants may appeal the decision to the Office of the State Superintendent;

(2) General procedures of the investigation;

(3) Citations of applicable law and regulations;

(4) Department findings of facts;

(5) Department conclusions;

(6) Department required actions, if applicable;

(7) Department recommended actions, if applicable; and

(8) Time line for corrective actions, if applicable.

(c) Report time line.

An investigation report shall be mailed to the parties within sixty (60) days from the date of receipt of the request for direct state intervention or an appeal, unless the parties have participated in mediation and agreed to an extension of the mediation time lines or the Superintendent has granted an extension pursuant to Section 4662(d).

[Authority cited: Sections 232 and 33031, Education Code; Section 11138, Government Code] [Reference: Sections 11135, 11136, and 11138, Government Code; 34 CFR 76.780-76.783 and 106.8]

4665. Discretionary Reconsideration Or Appeal Of CDE Investigation Report.

– Reconsideration or Appeal of Department Investigation Report

(a) Within 35 days of receipt of the Department investigation report, either party may request reconsideration by the Superintendent. The Superintendent may, within fifteen (15) days of receipt of the request, respond in writing to the parties either modifying the conclusions or required corrective actions of the Department report or denying the request outright. During the pending of the Superintendent's reconsideration, the Department report remains in effect and enforceable.

(b) Appeals by private agencies regarding Child Care Food Programs shall be made to the State Office of Administrative Hearings in accordance with applicable laws rather than the Superintendent. Appeals from investigations of complaints involving Child Development contractors, whether public or private, shall be made to the Superintendent of Public Instruction as provided in subsection (a) except as otherwise provided in Division 19 of Title 5 of the Code of California Regulations.

(c) For those programs governed by Part 76 of Title 34 of the Code of Federal Regulations, the parties shall be notified of the right to appeal to the United States Secretary of Education.

[Authority cited: Sections 232 and 33031, Education Code; Section 11138, Government Code] [Reference: Sections 11135, 11136, and 11138, Government Code; 34 CFR 76.1 and 76.780-76.783 and 106.8]

Article 8. Enforcement - State Procedures to Effect Compliance

– ENFORCEMENT – STATE PROCEDURES TO EFFECT COMPLIANCE

4670. Enforcement.

(a) Upon determination that a local agency violated the provisions of this chapter, the Superintendent shall notify the local agency of the action he or she will take to effect compliance. The Superintendent may use any means authorized by law to effect compliance, including:

(1)   The withholding of all or part of the local agency's relevant state or federal fiscal support;

(2)   Probationary eligibility for future state or federal support, conditional or compliance with specified conditions;

(3)   Proceeding in a court of competent jurisdiction for an appropriate order compelling compliance.

(b)   No decision to curtail state or federal funding to a local agency under this chapter shall be made until the Superintendent has determined that compliance cannot be secured by voluntary means.

(c)   If the Superintendent determines that a Child Development Contractor's Agreement shall be terminated, the procedures set forth in Sections 8257(d) or 8400 et seq. of the Education Code and the regulations promulgated pursuant thereto (Chapter 19 of Title 5, CCR, commencing with Section 17906), shall be followed.

(d)   If the Superintendent determines that a school district or county office has failed to comply with any provision of Sections 49550 through 49554 of the Education Code, the Superintendent shall certify such noncompliance to the Attorney General for investigation pursuant to Section 49556 of the Education Code.

[Authority cited: Sections 232 and 33031, Education Code; Section 11138, Government Code] [Reference: Sections 11135, 11136, and 11138, Government Code; 34 CFR 76.780-76.783 and 106.8]

4671.   Federal Review Rights.

– Federal Review Rights

If the Superintendent elects to withhold funds from a local agency that refuses or fails to comply in a program governed by 34 CFR Part 76, the Superintendent shall notify the local agency of the decision to withhold funding and of the local agency's rights of appeal pursuant to 34 CFR Section 76.401.

[Authority cited: Sections 232 and 33031, Education Code; Section 11138, Government Code] [Reference: 34 CFR 76.780-76.783]

NEW BUILDING AREA ALLOWANCES FOR SPECIAL EDUCATION PROGRAMS

(Education Code - Part 10)

(As Amended by AB 1248, Chapter 759, Statutes of 1992)

17747. (a) The allowable new building area for the purpose of providing special day class and Resource Specialist Program Facilities for special education pupils shall be negotiated and approved by the State Allocation Board, with any necessary assistance to be provided by the Special Education Division of the State Department of Education. The square footage allowances shall be computed within the maximum square footage set forth in the following schedule:

— Allowable New Building Area for Special Education Programs

— Maximum Square Footage Schedule

Special Day Class Basic Need	Grade Levels	Load-ing*	Square Footage
Nonsevere Disability			
—Specific Learning Disability	All	12	1080
—Mildly Mentally Retarded	All	12	1080
—Severe Disorder of Language	All	10	1080
Severe Disability			
—Deaf and Hard of Hearing	All	10	1080
—Visually Impaired	All	10	1330 (1080 + 250 storage)
—Orthopedically and Other Health Impaired	All	12	2000 (1080 + 400 toilets + 250 storage + 270 daily living skills + 3000 therapy + 75 therapy per additional classroom)
—Autistic	All	6	1160 (1080 + 80 toilets)
—Severely Emotionally Disturbed	All	6	1160 (1080 + 80 toilets)

—Severely Mentally Retarded	Elem.	12	1750
			(1080 + 400 toilets + 270 daily living skills)
	Secon.		2150
			(1080 + 400 toilets + 270 daily living skills + 400 vocational)
—Developmentally Disabled	All	10	2000
			(1080 + 400 toilets + 250 storage + 270 daily living skills + 3000 therapy** + 750 therapy per additional CR)
—Deaf-Blind/Multi	All	5	1400
			(1080 + 200 storage + 150 toilets)

			Pupils	Square Feet
Resource Specialist Program for those pupils with disabling conditions whose needs have been identified by the Individualized Education Program (IEP) Team, who require special education for a portion of the day, and who are assigned to a regular classroom for a majority of the schoolday.***	All	Maximum case-load for RS is 28, not all served at same time.	1–8	240
			9–28	480
			29–37	720
			38–56	960
			57–65	1200
			66–85	1440
			86–94	1680
			95–112	1920

* Special pupils may usually be grouped without accordance to type, especially in smaller districts or where attendance zones may indicate, to maximize loadings per classroom where there are children with similar educational need (Sec. 56364).

** Therapy add-ons not to be provided if on same site as orthopedically impaired.

*** To a maximum of 4 percent of the unhoused average daily attendance of the district, per new school or addition, to a maximum of 1920 square feet.

(b) The allowable new building area shall be computed by dividing the number of eligible pupils by the minimum required loading per classroom for special day classes for the type of pupils to be enrolled. No new or additional facility shall be provided for special day classes unless the number of additional eligible pupils equals one-third or more of the minimum required loading.

— Building Area Computation

NEW SCHOOL FACILITIES - MAXIMIZING INTERACTION

(Education Code - Part 10)

(AB 3359 - Chapter 1050, Statutes of 1986)

17747.5. (a) All school facilities purchased or newly constructed pursuant to this chapter for use, in whole or in part, by pupils who are individuals with exceptional needs, as defined in Section 56026, shall be designed and located on the school site so as to maximize interaction between those individuals with exceptional needs and other pupils as appropriate to the needs of both.

— Maximize Interaction

(b) School district governing boards and county offices of education shall ensure that school facilities for pupils who are individuals with exceptional needs are integrated with other school facilities in applying for the purchase or new construction of school facilities pursuant to this chapter.

— District and County Responsibilities

(c) The State Allocation Board, after consultation with the State Department of Education and representatives from county offices of education, special education services regions, and school districts, shall develop and adopt any regulations necessary to implement this section.

— Regulations

(d) Notwithstanding any other provision of law, the requirement set forth in subdivision (a) may be waived, by the Superintendent of Public Instruction, only upon compliance with the following procedure:

— Superintendent's Waiver Procedure

(1) The applicant school district or county superintendent of schools shall file a written request for waiver that documents the reasons for its inability to comply with the requirement.

(2) The State Department of Education shall verify the reasons set forth pursuant to paragraph (1), including the documentation submitted, which verification shall be completed no later than 30 days after the filing of the request for waiver with the Superintendent of Public Instruction.

(3) The Advisory Commission on Special Education, as established under Section 33590, at its first scheduled meeting

following the verification conducted pursuant to paragraph (2), shall review the request for waiver, accompanying documentation, and the verification findings of the State Department of Education. No later than 15 days following the date of that meeting, the commission shall submit its written comments and recommendations regarding the request for waiver to the Superintendent of Public Instruction.

(4) The Superintendent of Public Instruction shall review the comments and recommendations submitted by the Advisory Commission on Special Education prior to approving or rejecting the request for waiver.

(5) Any request for waiver, submitted in accordance with this section, that is not rejected within 60 days of its receipt by the State Department of Education, shall be deemed approved.

(e) This section does not apply to any application for project funding under this chapter that meets one of the following conditions:

— Section Exceptions

(1) The application was submitted to the board prior to January 1, 1987, and all of the facilities under the project for use, in whole or in part, by pupils who are individuals with exceptional needs are located on a school site on which facilities for use by other pupils are also located.

(2) The application is for any other project, for which, prior to January 1, 1987, the board approved the drawing of final plans and the preparation of final specifications.

PORTABLE CLASSROOMS FOR INFANT - PRESCHOOL CHILDREN

(Education Code - Part 10)

(AB 3421 - Chapter 576, Statutes of 1986)

17789.5. The board may lease portable classrooms to any school district or county superintendent of schools which serves infant or preschool individuals with exceptional needs, as defined in Section 56026, and which operates programs pursuant to Part 30 (commencing with Section 56000). These portable classrooms shall be adequately equipped to meet the educational needs of these students, including, but not limited to, sinks and restroom facilities.

— Portable Classrooms for Infant and Preschool Programs

COMMISSION ON SPECIAL EDUCATION

(Education Code - Part 20)

(As Amended by AB 3562, Chapter 840, Statutes of 1994)

ARTICLE 6. ADVISORY COMMISSION ON SPECIAL EDUCATION

33590. (a) There is in the state government the Advisory Commission on Special Education consisting of: — Creation and Membership

(1) A Member of the Assembly appointed by the Speaker of the Assembly.

(2) A Member of the Senate appointed by the Senate Committee on Rules.

(3) Three public members appointed by the Speaker of the Assembly, one of whom shall be a parent of a pupil in either a public or private school who has received or is currently receiving special education services due to a disabling condition.

(4) Three public members appointed by the Senate Committee on Rules, one of whom shall be a parent of a pupil in either a public or private school who has received or is currently receiving special education services due to a disabling condition.

(5) Four public members appointed by the Governor, one of whom shall be a parent of a pupil in either a public or private school who has received or is currently receiving special education services due to a disabling condition.

(6) Five public members appointed by the State Board of Education, upon the recommendation of the Superintendent of Public Instruction or the members of the State Board of Education, one of whom shall be a parent of a pupil in either a public or private school who has received or is currently receiving special education services due to a disabling condition.

(b) The commission membership shall be selected to ensure a representative group knowledgeable about the wide variety of disabling conditions that require special programs in order to achieve the goal of providing an appropriate education to all eligible pupils. — Representative Group

(c) On January 1, 1984, the appointing powers listed in subdivision (a) shall terminate the appointment of the public members appointed before that date and shall make appointments pursuant to subdivisions (a), (b), and (d).

(d) The term of each public member shall be for four years. However, the members appointed on January 1, 1984, shall be appointed on the following basis: — Four-Year Term

(1) Of the public members appointed by the Speaker of the Assembly, two shall hold office for four years, one shall hold office for two years.

(2) Of the public members appointed by the Senate Committee on Rules, two shall hold office for four years, one shall hold office for two years.

(3) Of the public members appointed by the Governor, two shall hold office for four years, two shall hold office for two years.

(4) Of the public members appointed by the State Board of Education, three shall hold office for four years, two shall hold office for two years.

(e) In no event shall any public member serve more than two terms.   — Term Limits

33591. The Members of the Legislature appointed to the   — Members of Legislature commission pursuant to Section 33590 shall have the powers and duties of a joint legislative committee on the subject of special education and shall meet with, and participate in, the work of the commission to the extent that such participation is not incompatible with their positions as Members of the Legislature.

The Members of the Legislature appointed to the commission shall serve at the pleasure of the appointing power.

33592. The members of the commission shall serve without   — Compensation compensation, except they shall receive their actual and necessary expenses incurred in the performance of their duties and responsibilities, including traveling expenses.

Reimbursement of other expenses, which are determined to be necessary for the commission to function, but do not exceed the commission's budget, may be approved by the commission and the executive secretary to the commission.

33593. The Superintendent of Public Instruction or his   — Executive Secretary representative shall serve as executive secretary to the commission.

33594. The commission shall select one of its members to be   — Chair chairman of the commission.

33595. (a) The commission shall study and provide assistance   — Study, Assist, and* and advice to the State Board of Education, the Superintendent of   Advise Public Instruction, the Legislature, and the Governor in new or continuing areas of research, program development, and evaluation in special education.

(b) Commission requests shall be transmitted by letter from   — Requests the commission chairperson to the president of the State Board of Education. Each communication shall be placed on the agenda of the next forthcoming state board meeting in accordance with the announced annual state board agenda cutoff dates. Following the state board meeting, the commission shall be notified by the

*(Section 33595 Amended in 1994)

state board as to what action has been taken on each request. Commission requests shall also be transmitted by letter from the commission chairperson to the Superintendent of Public Instruction, the Governor, and to appropriate Members of the Legislature.

33596. As used in this article, "commission" means the Advisory Commission on Special Education.

- Definition of Commission

TRANSPORTATION FEES

(Education Code - Part 23)

(Added by Chapter 1192, Statutes of 1982)

39807.5. When the governing board of any school district provides for the transportation of pupils to and from schools in accordance with the provisions of Section 39800, or between the regular full-time occupational training classes attended by them as provided by a regional occupation center or program, the governing board of the district may require the parents and guardians of all or some of the pupils transported, to pay a portion of the cost of such transportation in an amount determined by the governing board.

- Payment of Transportation Cost

The amount determined by the board shall be no greater than the statewide average nonsubsidized cost of providing such transportation to a pupil on a publicly owned or operated transit system as determined by the Superintendent of Public Instruction, in cooperation with the Department of Transportation.

For the purposes of this section, "nonsubsidized cost" means actual operating costs less federal subventions.

The governing board shall exempt from these charges pupils of parents and guardians who are indigent as set forth in rules and regulations adopted by the board.

No charge under this section shall be made for the transportation of handicapped children.

- No Charge for Handicapped Children

Nothing in this section shall be construed to sanction, perpetuate, or promote the racial or ethnic segregation of pupils in the schools.

TRANSPORTATION ALLOWANCES

(Education Code - Part 24)

(As Amended by AB 2587, Chapter 922, Statutes of 1994)

Article 10. Allowances for Transportation

41850. (a) Apportionments made pursuant to this article shall only be made for home-to-school transportation and special education transportation, as defined in this section.

— Apportionments

(b) As used in this article, "home-to-school transportation" includes all of the following:

— Home-to-School Transportation Definition

(1) The transportation of pupils between their homes and the regular full-time day school they attend, as provided by a school district or county superintendent of schools.

(2) The payment of moneys by a school district or county superintendent of schools to parents or guardians of pupils made in lieu of providing for the transportation of pupils between their homes and the regular full-time day schools they attend.

(3) Providing board and lodging to pupils by a school district or county superintendent of schools made in lieu of providing for the transportation of pupils between their homes and the regular full-time day schools they attend.

(4) The transportation of pupils between the regular full-time day schools they would attend and the regular full-time occupational training classes they attend, as provided by a regional occupational center or program.

(5) The transportation of individuals with exceptional needs as specified in their individualized education programs, who do not receive special education transportation as defined in subdivision (d).

— Individuals with Exceptional Needs

(6) The payment of moneys by a school district or county superintendent of schools for the replacement or acquisition of schoolbuses.

(c) For purposes of this article, the computation of the allowances provided to a regional occupational center or program shall be subject to all of the following:

— ROC/P Computation

(1) A regional occupational center or program shall receive no allowance for 50 percent of the total transportation costs.

(2) A regional occupational center or program shall be eligible for a transportation allowance only if the total transportation costs exceed 10 percent of the total operational budget of the regional occupational center or program.

(3) A regional occupational center or program eligible for a transportation allowance pursuant to paragraph (2) shall receive an amount equal to one-third of the transportation costs subject to reimbursement.

(d) As used in this article, "special education transportation" means either of the following:

– Special Education Transportation Definition

(1) The transportation of severely disabled special day class pupils, and orthopedically impaired pupils who require a vehicle with a wheelchair lift, who received transportation in the prior fiscal year, as specified in their individualized education program.

(2) A vehicle that was used to transport special education pupils.

41851. (a) For the 1992-93 fiscal year, from Section A of the State School Fund, the Superintendent of Public Instruction shall apportion to each school district or county superintendent of schools, as appropriate, an amount computed pursuant to this section. School districts and county superintendents of schools that provide transportation services by means of a joint powers agreement, a cooperative pupil transportation program, or a consortium shall receive transportation allowances pursuant to this section.

– Apportionment Computation for Regular Education Transportation

(b) For the 1992-93 fiscal year, each school district or county office of education shall receive a home-to-school transportation apportionment equal to the transportation allowance received in the prior fiscal year reduced by the amount of the special education transportation allowance identified pursuant to Section 41851.5.

(c) For the 1993-94 fiscal year and each fiscal year thereafter, each school district or county office of education shall receive a home-to-school transportation allowance received in the prior fiscal year, but in no event shall that home-to-school transportation allowance exceed the prior year's approved home-to-school transportation costs, increased by the amount provided in the Budget Act.

(d) For the 1993-94 and 1994-95 fiscal years, each county unified school district for which the county board of education serves as the governing board that meets all of the following criteria shall receive an additional apportionment of three hundred fifty thousand dollars ($350,000):

(1) Over 50 percent of the pupils enrolled in the school district require home-to-school transportation services.

(2) Total enrollment of the school district is less than 3,500.

(3) Total miles driven each fiscal year for home-to-school transportation exceeds 500,000.

(e) Each county unified school district that receives an additional apportionment pursuant to subdivision (d) shall report, by September 1, 1995, on the amount of revenues received and the funds expended for the home-to-school transportation program in the 1992-93, 1993-94, and 1994-95 fiscal years. The report shall be submitted to the fiscal committees and education policy committees of the Legislature and to the Legislative Analyst.

41851.1. (a) For the 1989-90 fiscal year, from Section A of the State School Fund, the Superintendent of Public Instruction shall apportion to each school district or county superintendent of schools, as appropriate, an amount computed pursuant to this section. School districts and county superintendents of schools that provide transportation services by means of a joint powers agreement, a cooperative pupil transportation program, or a consortium shall receive transportation allowances pursuant to this section.

– Fiscal Year 1989-90 Transportation Apportionment – Joint Powers, Cooperative Program, Consortium

(b) For the 1989-90 fiscal year, each school district, joint powers agency, cooperative pupil transportation program, or consortium shall receive a transportation apportionment equal to the greater of the following:

(1) Sixty-five percent of the prior year's approved transportation costs.

(2) The prior year's transportation allowance.

(c) For the 1989-90 fiscal year, each county office of education shall receive a transportation apportionment equal to the greater of the following:

(1) Eighty percent of the prior year's approved transportation costs.

(2) The prior year's transportation allowance.

(d) In the event that funds appropriated for the purposes of this section are not sufficient to fully fund the formula established by that section, the amounts apportioned shall be reduced on a proportionate basis.

41851.2. No later than December 31, 1992, the Superintendent of Public Instruction shall develop guidelines for use by individualized education program teams during their annual reviews pursuant to Section 56343. The guidelines shall clarify when special education transportation services, as defined in Section 41850, are required. The guidelines shall be developed in accordance with Section 33308.5 and shall be exemplary in nature.

– Guidelines for Use by IEP Teams

41851.5. (a) For the 1992-93 fiscal year and each fiscal year thereafter, from Section A of the State School Fund, the Superintendent of Public Instruction shall apportion to each school district or county superintendent of schools, as

– Apportionment Computation for Special Education Transportation – Joint Powers – Cooperative – Consortium appropriate, an amount computed pursuant to this section. School districts and county superintendents of schools that provide special education transportation services by means of a joint powers agreement, a cooperative pupil transportation program, or a consortium shall receive special education transportation allowances pursuant to this section.

(b) For the 1992-93 fiscal year, each school district or county office of education shall receive a special education transportation allowance equal to the lesser of the following:

– School District/County Office of Education Special Education Transportation Allowance – 1992-93

(1) The prior year's approved special education transportation costs identified pursuant to Section 41850.

(2) That portion of the prior year's transportation allowance that the school district or county superintendent of schools designates as a special education transportation allowance.

(c) For the 1993-94 fiscal year and each fiscal year thereafter, each school district or county office of education shall receive a special education transportation allowance received in the prior fiscal year, but in no event shall that special education transportation allowance exceed the prior year's approved special education transportation costs, increased by the amount provided in the annual Budget Act.

– School District/County Office of Education Special Education Transportation Allowance

41851.7. For the purpose of receiving an allowance pursuant to this section, a school district, county superintendent, or joint powers agency which transfers any part of its pupil transportation service to another entity shall report to the Superintendent of Public Instruction the proportion of the costs in the fiscal year prior to the transfer that are attributable to the part of the service transferred. In determining the allowance for the fiscal years subsequent to the transfer, the Superintendent of Public Instruction, prior to the application of any cost-of-living adjustment, shall reduce the allowance of the entity transferring the service in proportion to the costs reported, and, if appropriate, increase or establish the allowance of the entity assuming the transferred service by that amount.

– Transfer of Transportation Services

41852. (a) Any school district or county superintendent of schools that receives a transportation apportionment in the 1984-85 fiscal year, or any fiscal year thereafter, shall establish a restricted home-to-school transportation account within its general fund. The district or county superintendent shall deposit in the restricted home-to-school transportation account all transportation apportionments received pursuant to this article in any fiscal year and any other funds at the option of the district or county superintendent. Any funds remaining in the restricted home-to-school transportation account at the end of the fiscal year may remain in the restricted home-to-school transportation account for

– Restricted Home-to-School Transportation Account

expenditure in subsequent fiscal years or may be transferred to the pupil transportation equipment fund.

(b) Any school district or county superintendent of schools may establish a pupil transportation equipment fund. The fund shall receive all state and local funds designated for acquisition, rehabilitation, or replacement of pupil transportation equipment. Funds deposited in the pupil transportation equipment fund shall be used exclusively for acquisition, rehabilitation and replacement of pupil transportation equipment, except as provided in Section 41853.

— Equipment Fund

41853. If a school district or county superintendent of schools decides to discontinue its transportation services, any unencumbered funds remaining in the restricted home-to-school transportation account after transportation services are discontinued shall be transferred to the general fund of the district or county superintendent.

— Discontinuing Transportation Services

In the fiscal year in which the funds are transferred, the Superintendent of Public Instruction shall reduce the state apportionment pursuant to Section 2558 or 42238 to the district or county superintendent by the amount of the funds transferred from the restricted home-to-school transportation account to the general fund of the district or county superintendent, exclusive of reimbursements for prior year expenditures to Section 41851.5.

41854. This article shall become operative July 1, 1984.

— Operative Date

REVENUE LIMITS FOR PUPILS IN SPECIAL CLASSES AND CENTERS

(Education Code - Part 24)

(As Amended by AB 2587, Chapter 922, Statutes of 1994)

42238.9. The amount per unit of average daily attendance subtracted pursuant to Section 56712 for revenue limits for pupils in special classes and centers shall be the district's total revenue limit for the current fiscal year computed pursuant to Section 42238, including funds received pursuant to Article 4 (commencing with Section 42280), but excluding funds received pursuant to Section 42238.8, divided by the district's current year average daily attendance pursuant to Section 42238.5.

— Revenue Limits*

*(Section 42238.9 Amended in 1994)

C-12

REAPPROPRIATION OF FEDERAL FUNDS

(Education Code - Part 24)

(AB 369 - Chapter 1296, Statutes of 1993)

42242. The Superintendent of Public Instruction shall determine at the time of each apportionment the proposed receipts and expenditures of funds under the provisions of the Individuals with Disabilities Education Act (20 U.S.C. Sec. 1400 et seq.). In the event that the proposed distribution of funds results in funds not being expended, those funds are hereby reappropriated for reallocation for local entitlements for special education.
This section shall become operative July 1, 1984.

— Unexpended Federal Funds

RECOGNIZING LEARNING DISABILITIES

(Education Code - Part 25)

(AB 3040 - Chapter 1501, Statutes of 1990)

44227.7. The Legislature encourages institutions of higher education to provide, in teacher training programs, increased emphasis on the recognition of, and teaching strategies for, specific learning disabilities, including dyslexia and related disorders. Experts in the field of these disabilities should be utilized for that purpose.

— Teacher Training Programs

TEACHER QUALIFICATIONS - PUPILS WITH LOW INCIDENCE DISABILITIES

(Education Code - Part 25)

(AB 3235 - Chapter 1288, Statutes of 1994)

44265.5. (a) Pupils who are visually impaired shall be taught by teachers whose professional preparation and credential authorization are specific to that impairment.

— Visually Impaired

(b) Pupils who are deaf or hard of hearing shall be taught by teachers whose professional preparation and credential authorization are specific to that impairment.

— Deaf or Hard of Hearing

(c) Pupils who are orthopedically impaired shall be taught by teachers whose professional preparation and credential authorization are specific to that impairment.

— Orthopedically Impaired

CERTIFICATED EMPLOYEE EMPLOYMENT RIGHTS

(Education Code - Part 25)

(As Amended by SB 998 - Chapter 1452, Statutes of 1987)

44903.7. When a local plan for the education of individuals with exceptional needs is developed pursuant to Article 6 (commencing with Section 56170) of Chapter 2 of Part 30, the following provisions shall apply:

(a) Whenever any certificated employee, who is performing service for one employer, is terminated, reassigned, or transferred, or becomes an employee of another employer because of the reorganization of special education programs pursuant to Chapter 797 of the Statutes of 1980, the employee shall be entitled to the following:

— Employee Entitlements

(1) The employee shall retain the seniority date of his or her employment with the district or county office from which he or she was terminated, reassigned, or transferred, in accordance with Section 44847. In the case of termination, permanent employees shall retain the rights specified in Section 44956 or, in the case of probationary employees, Section 44957 and 44958, with the district or county office initiating the termination pursuant to Section 44955.

— Retain Seniority Rights

(2) The reassignment, transfer, or new employment caused by the reorganization of special education programs pursuant to Chapter 797 of the Statutes of 1980, shall not affect the seniority or classification of certificated employees already attained in any school district that undergoes the reorganization. These employees shall have the same status with respect to their seniority or classification, with the new employer, including time served as probationary employees. The total number of years served as a certificated employee with the former district or county office shall be credited, year for year, for placement on the salary schedule of the new district or county office.

— Seniority of Classification Not Affected

(b) All certificated employees providing service to individuals with exceptional needs shall be employed by a county office of education or an individual school district. Special education local plan areas or responsible local agencies resulting from local plans for the education of individuals with exceptional needs formulated in accordance with Part 30 (commencing with Section 56000) shall not be considered employers of certificated personnel for purposes of this section.

— Employers

(c) Subsequent to the reassignment or transfer of any certificated employee as a result of the reorganization of special education programs, pursuant to Chapter 797 of the Statutes of 1980, that employee shall have priority, except as provided in subdivision (d), in being informed of and in filling certificated positions in special education in the areas in which the employee is certificated within the district or county office by which the certificated employee is then currently employed. This priority shall expire 24 months after the date of reassignment or transfer, and may be waived by the employee during that time period.

— Priority on Being Informed/ Filling Positions

(d) A certificated employee who has served as a special education teacher in a district or county office and has been terminated from his or her employment by that district or county office pursuant to Section 44955, shall have first priority in being informed of and in filling vacant certificated positions in special education, for which the employee is certificated and was employed, in any other county office or school district that provides the same type of special education programs and services for the pupils previously served by the terminated employee. For a period of 39 months for permanent employees and 24 months for probationary employees from the date of termination, the employee shall have the first priority right to reappointment as provided in this section, if the employee has not attained the age of 65 years before reappointment.

— Other County Office/ School District

LONGER DAY - YEAR FOR COUNTY-OPERATED SPECIAL EDUCATION PROGRAMS

(Education Code - Part 26)

(As Added by AB 2557 - Chapter 115, Statutes of 1985, As Amended by SB 1264, Chapter 1603, Statutes of 1985)

46200.5. (a) In the 1985-86 fiscal year, for each county office of education that certifies to the Superintendent of Public Instruction that it offers 180 days or more of instruction per school year of special day classes pursuant to Section 56364, the Superintendent of Public Instruction shall determine an amount equal to seventy dollars ($70) per unit of current year second principal apportionment average daily attendance for special day classes. This computation shall be included in computations made by the superintendent pursuant to Article 2 (commencing with Section 56710) of Chapter 7 of Part 30.

— 180 Days or More

(b) For any county office of education that received an apportionment pursuant to subdivision (a), that offers less than

— Less Than 180 Days

180 days of instruction in the 1986-87 year or any fiscal year thereafter, and that does not provide the minimum number of instructional minutes specified in subdivision (a) of Section 46201.5 for that fiscal year, the Superintendent of Public Instruction shall reduce the special education apportionment per unit of average daily attendance for that fiscal year by an amount attributable to the increase received pursuant to subdivision (a), as adjusted in fiscal years subsequent to the 1985-86 fiscal year.

46201.5. (a) In each of the 1985-86 and 1986-87 fiscal years, for each county office of education that certifies to the Superintendent of Public Instruction that, for special day classes pursuant to Section 56364, it offers at least the amount of instructional time specified in this subdivision, the Superintendent of Public Instruction shall determine an amount equal to eighty dollars ($80) in the 1985-86 fiscal year and forty dollars ($40) in the 1986-87 fiscal year per unit of current year second principal apportionment average daily attendance for special day classes in kindergarten and grades 1 to 8 inclusive, and one hundred sixty dollars ($160) in the 1985-86 fiscal year and eighty dollars ($80) in the 1986-87 fiscal year per unit of current year second principal apportionment average daily attendance for special day classes in grades 9 to 12, inclusive.

— Computation for Special Classes

This computation shall be included in computations made by the superintendent pursuant to Article 2 (commencing with Section 56710) of Chapter 7 of Part 30.

(1) In the 1985-86 fiscal year:

(A) 34,500 minutes in kindergarten.

(B) 47,016 minutes in grades 1 to 3, inclusive.

(C) 50,000 minutes in grades 4 to 8, inclusive.

(D) 57,200 minutes in grades 9 to 12, inclusive.

(2) In the 1986-87 fiscal year:

(A) 36,000 minutes in kindergarten.

(B) 50,400 minutes in grades 1 to 3, inclusive.

(C) 54,000 minutes in grades 4 to 8, inclusive.

(D) 64,800 minutes in grades 9 to 12, inclusive.

(b) Each county office of education that receives an apportionment pursuant to subdivision (a) in a fiscal year shall, in the subsequent year, add the amount received per pupil to the county office's base special education apportionment.

— Add to Base Apportionment

(c) For each county office of education that receives an apportionment pursuant to subdivision (a) in the 1985-86 fiscal year, and that reduces the amount of instructional time offered below the minimum amounts specified in paragraph (1) of subdivision (a) in the 1986-87 fiscal year, or any fiscal year thereafter, the Superintendent of Public Instruction shall reduce the special education apportionment for the fiscal year in which

— Reduction of Apportionment When Instructional Time Is Reduced the reduction occurs by an amount attributable to the increase in the 1986-87 fiscal year special education apportionment pursuant to subdivision (b), as adjusted in the 1986-87 fiscal year and fiscal years thereafter. For each county office of education that receives an apportionment pursuant to subdivision (a) in the 1986-87 fiscal year, and that reduces the amount of instructional time offered below the minimum amounts specified in paragraph (2) of subdivision (a) in the 1987-88 fiscal year, or any fiscal year thereafter, the superintendent shall reduce the special education apportionment for the fiscal year in which the reduction occurs by an amount attributable to the increase in the 1987-88 fiscal year special education apportionment pursuant to subdivision (b), as adjusted in the 1987-88 fiscal year and fiscal years thereafter.

DAY OF ATTENDANCE

(Education Code - Part 26)

46307. Attendance of individuals with exceptional needs, identified pursuant to Chapter 4 (commencing with Section 56300) of Part 30, enrolled in a special day class or given instruction individually or in a home, hospital, or licensed children's institution who attend school for either the same number of minutes that constitutes a minimum schoolday pursuant to Chapter 2 (commencing with Section 46100), or for the number of minutes of attendance specified in that pupil's individualized education program developed pursuant to Article 3 (commencing with Section 56340) of Chapter 4 of Part 30, whichever is less, shall constitute a day of attendance. The average daily attendance of all individuals with exceptional needs shall be computed by dividing the total number of days of attendance of the pupils by the number of days on which the instruction was given by the district or county office of education.

– Day of Attendance

SUSPENSION OR EXPULSION OF PUPILS

(Education Code - Part 27)

(As Amended by AB 2543, Chapter 1198; AB 2728, Chapter 1016; AB 2752, Chapter 1017; AB 3601, Chapter 146; and AB 3816, Chapter 1287; Statutes of 1994)

48900. A pupil shall not be suspended from school or recommended for expulsion unless the superintendent or the principal of the school in which the pupil is enrolled determines that the pupil has:

  (a) Caused, attempted to cause, or threatened to cause physical injury to another person.

  (b) Possessed, sold, or otherwise furnished any firearm, knife, explosive, or other dangerous object unless, in the case of possession of any object of this type, the pupil had obtained written permission to possess the item from a certificated school employee, which is concurred in by the principal or the designee of the principal.

  (c) Unlawfully possessed, used, sold, or otherwise furnished, or been under the influence of, any controlled substance listed in Chapter 2 (commencing with Section 11053) of Division 10 of the Health and Safety Code, an alcoholic beverage, or an intoxicant of any kin.

  (d) Unlawfully offered, arranged, or negotiated to sell any controlled substance listed in Chapter 2 (commencing with Section 11053) of Division 10 of the Health and Safety Code, an alcoholic beverage, or an intoxicant of any kind, and then either sold, delivered, or otherwise furnished to any person another liquid, substance, or material and represented the liquid, substance, or material as controlled substance, alcoholic beverage, or intoxicant.

  (e) Committed or attempted to commit robbery or extortion.

  (f) Caused or attempted to cause damage to school property or private property.

  (g) Stolen or attempted to steal school property or private property.

  (h) Possessed or used tobacco, or any products containing tobacco or nicotine products, including, but not limited to, cigarettes, cigars, miniature cigars, clove cigarettes, smokeless tobacco, snuff, chew packets, and betel. However, this section does not prohibit use or possession by a pupil of his or her own prescription products.

  (i) Committed an obscene act or engaged in habitual profanity or vulgarity.

- Grounds for Suspension* or Expulsion

*(Section 48900 Amended in 1994

(j) Had unlawful possession of, or unlawfully offered, arranged, or negotiated to sell any drug paraphernalia, as defined in Section 11014.5 of the Health and Safety Code.

(k) Disrupted school activities or otherwise willfully defied the valid authority of supervisors, teachers, administrators, school officials, or other school personnel engaged in the performance of their duties.

(l) Knowingly received stolen school property or private property.

No pupil shall be suspended or expelled for any of the acts enumerated unless that act is related to school activity or school attendance occurring within a school under the jurisdiction of the superintendent or principal or occurring within any other school district. A pupil may be suspended or expelled for acts that are enumerated in this section and related to school activity or attendance that occur at any time, including, but not limited to, any of the following:

(1) While on school grounds.

(2) While going to or coming from school.

(3) During the lunch period whether on or off the campus.

(4) During, or while going to or coming from, a school sponsored activity.

It is the intent of the Legislature that alternatives to suspensions or expulsion be imposed against any pupil who is truant, tardy, or otherwise absent from school activities.

48900.1. (a) The governing board of each school district shall adopt a policy authorizing teachers to provide that the parent or guardian of a pupil who has been suspended by a teacher pursuant to Section 48910 for reasons specified in subdivision (i) or (k) of Section 48900, attend a portion of a schoolday in his or her child's or ward's classroom. The policy shall take into account reasonable factors that may prevent compliance with a notice to attend. The attendance of the parent or guardian shall be limited to the class from which the pupil was suspended.

– Attendance of Suspended Child's Parent or Guardian for Portion of Schoolday

(b) The policy shall be adopted pursuant to the procedures set forth in Sections 35291 and 35291.5. Parents and guardians shall be notified of this policy prior to its implementation. A teacher shall apply any policy adopted pursuant to this section uniformly to all pupils within the classroom.

The adopted policy shall include the procedures that the district will follow to accomplish the following:

(1) Ensure that parents or guardians who attend school for the purposes of this section meet with the school administrator or his or her designee after completing the classroom visitation and before leaving the schoolsite.

(2) Contact parents or guardians who do not respond to the request to attend school pursuant to this section.

(c) If a teacher imposes the procedure pursuant to subdivision (a), the principal shall send a written notice to the parent or guardian stating that attendance by the parent or guardian is pursuant to law. This section shall apply only to a parent or guardian who is actually living with the pupil.

(d) A parent or guardian who has received a written notice pursuant to subdivision (c) shall attend class as specified in the written notice. The notice may specify that the parent's or guardian's attendance be on the day in which the pupil is scheduled to return to class, or within a reasonable period of time thereafter, as established by the policy of the board adopted pursuant to subdivision (a).

48900.2. In addition to the reasons specified in Section 48900, a pupil may be suspended from school or recommended for expulsion if the superintendent or the principal of the school in which the pupil is enrolled determines that the pupil has committed sexual harassment as defined in Section 212.5.

— Sexual Harassment

For the purposes of this chapter, the conduct described in Section 212.5 must be considered by a reasonable person of the same gender as the victim to be sufficiently severe or pervasive to have a negative impact upon the individual's academic performance or to create an intimidating, hostile, or offensive educational environment. This section shall not apply to pupils enrolled in kindergarten and grades 1 to 3, inclusive.

48900.3. In addition to the reasons specified in Sections 48900 and 48900.2, a pupil in any of grades 4 to 12, inclusive, may be suspended from school or recommended for expulsion if the superintendent or the principal of the school in which the pupil is enrolled determines that the pupil has caused, attempted to cause, threatened to cause, or participated in an act of, hate violence, as defined in subdivision (e) of Section 33032.5.

— Hate Violence*

48900.4. In addition to the grounds specified in Sections 48900 and 48900.2, a pupil enrolled in any of grades 4 to 12, inclusive, may be suspended from school or recommended for expulsion if the superintendent or the principal of the school in which the pupil is enrolled determines that the pupil has intentionally engaged in harassment, threats, or intimidation, directed against a pupil or group of pupils, that is sufficiently severe or pervasive to have the actual and reasonably expected effect of materially disrupting classwork, creating substantial disorder, and invading the rights of that pupil or group of pupils by creating an intimidating or hostile educational environment.

— Additional Grounds*

48900.5. Suspension shall be imposed only when other means of correction fail to bring about proper conduct. However, a

— Suspension: Equal Treatment of Disabled and Nondisabled Pupils

*(Sections 48900.3 and 4890014 Added in 1994)

pupil, including an individual with exceptional needs, as defined in Section 56026, may be suspended for any of the reasons enumerated in Section 48900 upon a first offense, if the principal or superintendent of schools determines that the pupil violated subdivision (a), (b), (c), (d), or (e) of Section 48900 or that the pupil's presence causes a danger to persons or property or threatens to disrupt the instructional process.

48900.6. Instead of disciplinary action prescribed by this article, the principal of a school, the principal's designee, or the superintendent of schools, at his or her discretion, may require a pupil to perform community service on school grounds during nonschool hours. For the purposes of this section "community service" may include, but is not limited to, work performed on school grounds in the areas of outdoor beautification, campus betterment, and the teacher or peer assistance programs. This section shall not apply to instances where suspension or expulsion is required by this article.

— Community Service on School Grounds

48901. (a) No school shall permit the smoking or use of tobacco, or any product containing tobacco or nicotine products, by pupils of the school while the pupils are on campus, or while attending school-sponsored activities or while under the supervision and control of school district employees.

— Prohibition on Smoking or Use of Tobacco Products

(b) The governing board of any school district maintaining a high school shall take all steps it deems practical to discourage high school students from smoking.

48901.5. (a) No school shall permit the possession or use of any electronic signaling device that operates through the transmission or receipt of radio waves, including, but not limited to, paging and signaling equipment, by pupils of the school while the pupils are on campus, while attending school-sponsored activities, or while under the supervision and control of school district employees, without the prior consent of the principal or his or her designee. No pupil shall be prohibited from possessing or using an electronic signaling device that is determined by a licensed physician and surgeon to be essential for the health of a pupil and use of which is limited for purposes related to the health of the pupil.

— Prohibition on Use of Electronic Signaling Device

(b) The governing board of each school district shall take all steps it deems practical within existing resources to discourage pupils from possessing or using electronic signaling devices, except where the use of an electronic signaling device is essential for the health of a pupil.

48902. (a) The principal of a school or the principal's designee shall, prior to the suspension or expulsion of any pupil, notify the appropriate law enforcement authorities of the county

— Notification of Law Enforcement Authorities

or city in which the school is situated, of any acts of the student which may violate Section 245 of the Penal Code.

(b) The principal of a school or the principal's designee shall, within one schoolday after suspension or expulsion of any pupil, notify, by telephone or any other appropriate method chosen by the school, the appropriate law enforcement authority of the county or the school district in which the school is situated of any acts of the students which may violate subdivision (c) or (d) of Section 48900 of the Education Code.

(c) Notwithstanding subdivision (b), the principal of school or the principal's designee shall notify the appropriate law enforcement authorities of the county or city in which the school is located of any acts of a student that may involve the possession or sale of narcotics or of a controlled substance or a violation of Section 626.9 or 626.10 of the Penal Code.

(d) A principal, the principal's designee, or any other person reporting a known or suspected act described in subdivision (a) or (b) is not civilly or criminally liable as a result of any report authorized by this article unless it can be proven that a false report was made and that the person knew the report was false or the report was made with reckless disregard for the truth or falsity of the report.

48903. Except as provided in subdivision (g) of Section 48911 and in Section 48912, the total number of days for which a pupil may be suspended from school shall not exceed 20 school days in any school year, unless for purposes of adjustment, a pupil enrolls in or is transferred to another regular school, an opportunity school or class, or a continuation education school or class, in which case the total number of school days for which the pupil may be suspended shall not exceed 30 days in any school year.

– Restrictions on Days of Suspension

48904. (a) (1) Notwithstanding Section 1714.1 of the Civil Code, the parent or guardian of any minor whose willful misconduct results in injury or death to any pupil or any person employed by, or performing volunteer services for, a school district or private school or who willfully cuts, defaces, or otherwise injures in any way any property, real or personal, belonging to a school district or private school, or personal property of any school employee, shall be liable for all damages so caused by the minor. The liability of the parent or guardian shall not exceed ten thousand dollars ($10,000). The parent or guardian shall also be liable for the amount of any reward not exceeding ten thousand dollars ($10,000) paid pursuant to Section 53069.5 of the Government Code. The parent or guardian of a minor shall be liable to a school district or private school loaned

– Liability of Parent or Guardian for Willful Pupil Misconduct

to the minor and not returned upon demand of an employee of the district or private school authorized to make the demand.

(2) The Superintendent of Public Instruction shall compute an adjustment of the liability limits prescribed by this subdivision at a rate equivalent to the percentage change in the Implicit Price Deflator for State and Local Government Purchases of Goods and Services for the United States, as published by the United States Department of Commerce for the 12-month period ending in the third quarter of the prior fiscal year.

(b) (1) Any school district or private school whose real or personal property has been willfully cut, defaced, or otherwise injured, or whose property is loaned to a pupil and willfully not returned upon demand of an employee of the district or private school authorized to make the demand may, after affording the pupil his or her due process rights, withhold the grades, diploma, and transcripts of the pupil responsible for the damage until the pupil or the pupil's parent or guardian has paid for the damages thereto, as provided in subdivision (a).

(2) The school district or private school shall notify the parent or guardian of the pupil in writing of the pupil's alleged misconduct before withholding the pupil's grades, diploma, or transcripts pursuant to this subdivision. When the minor and parent are unable to pay for the damages, or to return the property, the school district or private school shall provide a program of voluntary work for the minor in lieu of the payment of monetary damages. Upon completion of the voluntary work, the grades, diploma, and transcripts of the pupil shall be released.

(3) The governing board of each school district or governing body of each private school shall establish rules and regulations governing procedures for the implementation of this subdivision. The procedures shall conform to, but are not necessarily limited to, those procedures established in this code for the expulsion of pupils.

48904.3. (a) Upon receiving notice that a school district has withheld the grades, diploma, or transcripts of any pupil pursuant to Section 48904, any school district to which the pupil has transferred shall likewise withhold the grades, diploma, or transcripts of the pupil as authorized by that section, until such time as it receives notice, from the district that initiated the decision to withhold, that the decision has been rescinded under the terms of that section.

(b) Any school district that has decided to withhold a pupil's grades, diploma, or transcripts pursuant to Section 48904 shall, upon receiving notice that the pupil has transferred to any school district in this state, notify the parent or guardian of pupil in

– Withholding Grades, Diplomas, or Transcripts of Pupils Causing Property Damage or Injury

writing that the decision to withhold will be enforced as specified in subdivision (a)

(c) For purposes of this section and Section 48904, "school district" is defined to include any county superintendent

48905. An employee of a school district whose person or property is injured or damaged by the willful misconduct of a pupil who attends school in such district, when the employee or the employee's property is (1) located on property owned by the district, (2) being transported to or from an activity sponsored by the district or a school within the district, (3) present at an activity sponsored by such district or school, or (4) otherwise injured or damaged in retaliation for acts lawfully undertaken by the employee in execution of the employee's duties, may request the school district to pursue legal action against the pupil who caused the injury or damage, or the pupil's parent or guardian pursuant to Section 48904.

– Injury or Damage to Person or Property of School District Employee

48906. When a principal or other school official releases a minor pupil to a peace officer for the purpose of removing the minor from the school premises, the school official shall take immediate steps to notify the parent, guardian, or responsible relative of the minor regarding the release of the minor to the officer, and regarding the place to which the minor is reportedly being taken, except when a minor has been taken into custody as a victim of suspected child abuse, as defined in Section 11165 of the Penal Code, or pursuant to Section 305 of the Welfare and Institutions Code. In those cases, the school official shall provide the peace officer with the address and telephone number of the minor's parent or guardian. The peace officer shall take immediate steps to notify the parent, guardian, or responsible relative of the minor that the minor is in custody and the place where he or she is being held. If the officer has a reasonable belief that the minor would be endangered by a disclosure of the place where the minor is being held, or that the disclosure would cause the custody of the minor to be disturbed, the officer may refuse to disclose the place where the minor is being held for a period not to exceed 24 hours. The officer shall, however, inform the parent, guardian, or responsible relative whether the child requires and is receiving medical or other treatment. The juvenile court shall review any decision not to disclose the place where the minor is being held at a subsequent detention hearing.

– Notification of Parent, Guardian or Relative of Release of Pupil to Peace Officer

48907. Students of the public schools shall have the right to exercise freedom of speech and the press including, but not limited to, the use of bulletin boards, the distribution of printed materials or petitions, the wearing of buttons, badges, and other insignia, and the right of expression in official publications, whether or not such publications or other means of expression

– Student Exercise of Free Expression

are supported financially by the school or by use of school facilities, except that expression shall be prohibited which is obscene, libelous, or slanderous. Also prohibited shall be material which so incites students as to create a clear and present danger of the commission of unlawful acts on school premises or the violation of lawful school regulations, or the substantial disruption of orderly operation of the school.

Each governing board of a school district and each county board of education shall adopt rules and regulations in the form of a written publications code, which shall include reasonable provisions for the time, place, and manner of conducting such activities within its respective jurisdiction.

Student editors of official school publications shall be responsible for assigning and editing the news, editorial, and feature content of their publications subject to the limitations of this section. However, it shall be the responsibility of a journalism adviser or advisers of student publications within each school to supervise the production of the student staff, to maintain professional standards of English and journalism, and to maintain the provisions of this section.

There shall be no prior restraint of material prepared for official school publications except insofar as it violates this section. School officials shall have the burden of showing justification without undue delay prior to any limitation of student expression under this section.

"Official school publications" refers to material produced by students in the journalism, newspaper, yearbook, or writing class and distributed to the student body either free or for a fee.

Nothing in this section shall prohibit or prevent any governing board of a school district from adopting otherwise valid rules and regulations relating to oral communication by students upon the premises of each school.

48908. All pupils shall comply with the regulations, pursue the required course of study, and submit to the authority of the teachers of the schools.

— Duties of Pupils

48909. When a petition is requested in juvenile court or a complaint is filed in any court alleging that a minor of compulsory school attendance age or any pupil currently enrolled in a public school in a grade to and including grade 12 is a person who (a) has used, sold, or possessed narcotics or other hallucinogenic drugs or substances; (b) has inhaled or breathed the fumes of, or ingested any poison classified as such in Section 4160 of the Business and Professions Code; or (c) has committed felonious assault, homicide, or rape the district attorney may, within 48 hours, provide written notice to the superintendent of the school district of attendance, notwithstanding the provisions

— Drug or Poison Use; Assault, Homicide, or Rape

of Section 827 of the Welfare and Institutions Code, and to the pupil's parent or guardian.

48910. (a) A teacher may suspend any pupil from the teacher's class, for any of the acts enumerated in Section 48900, for the day of the suspension and the day following. The teacher shall immediately report the suspension to the principal of the school and send the pupil to the principal or the principal's designee for appropriate action. If that action requires the continued presence of the pupil at the school site, the pupil shall be under appropriate supervision, as defined in policies and related regulations adopted by the governing board of the school district. As soon as possible, the teacher shall ask the parent or guardian of the pupil to attend a parent-teacher conference regarding the suspension. Whenever practicable, a school counselor or a school psychologist shall attend the conference. A school administrator shall attend the conference if the teacher or the parent or guardian so requests. The pupil shall not be returned to the class from which he or she was suspended, during the period of the suspension, without the concurrence of the teacher of the class and the principal.

    – Suspension by Teacher

(b) A pupil suspended from a class shall not be place in another regular class during the period of suspension. However, if the pupil is assigned to more than one class per day this subdivision shall apply only to other regular classes scheduled at the same time as the class from which the pupil was suspended.

(c) A teacher may also refer a pupil, for any of the acts enumerated in Section 48900, to the principal or the principal's designee for consideration of a suspension from the school.

48911. (a) The principal of the school, the principal's designee, or the superintendent of schools may suspend a pupil from the school for any of the reasons enumerated in Section 48900, and pursuant to Section 48900.5, for no more than five consecutive schooldays.

    – Suspension by Principal, Principal's Designee, or Superintendent

(b) Suspension by the principal, the principal's designee, or the superintendent shall be preceded by an informal conference conducted by the principal or the principal's designee, or the superintendent of schools between the pupil and, whenever practicable, the teacher or supervisor or school employee who referred the pupil to the principal or the principal's designee or the superintendent of schools. At the conference, the pupil shall be informed of the reason for the disciplinary action and the evidence against him or her and shall be given the opportunity to present his or her version and evidence in his or her defense.

(c) A principal or the principal's designee or the superintendent of schools may suspend a pupil without affording the pupil an opportunity for a conference only if the principal or the principal's designee or the superintendent of schools determines that an emergency situation exists. "Emergency situation," as used in this article, means a situation determined by the principal, the principal's designee, or the superintendent to constitute a clear and present danger to the lives, safety, or health of pupils or school personnel. If a pupil is suspended without a conference prior to suspension, both the parent and the pupil shall be notified of the pupil's right to a conference, and the pupil's right to return to school for the purpose of a conference. The conference shall be held within two schooldays, unless the pupil waives this right or is physically unable to attend for any reason, including, but not limited to, incarceration or hospitalization. The conference shall then be held as soon as the pupil is physically able to return to school for the conference.

(d) At the time of suspension, a school employee shall make reasonable effort to contact the pupil's parent or guardian in person or by telephone. Whenever a pupil is suspended from school, the parent or guardian shall be notified in writing of the suspension.

(e) A school employee shall report the suspension of the pupil, including the cause therefor, to the governing board of the school district or to the district superintendent in accordance with the regulations of the governing board.

(f) The parent or guardian of any pupil shall respond without delay to any request from school officials to attend a conference regarding his or her child's behavior.

No penalties may be imposed on a pupil for failure of the pupil's parent or guardian to attend a conference with school officials. Reinstatement of the suspended pupil shall not be contingent upon attendance by the pupil's parent or guardian at the conference.

(g) In a case where expulsion from any school or suspension for the balance of the semester from continuation school is being processed by the governing board, the school district superintendent or other person designated by the superintendent in writing may extend the suspension until such time as the governing board has rendered a decision in the action. However, an extension may be granted only if the superintendent or the superintendent's designee has determined, following a meeting in which the pupil and the pupil's parent or guardian are invited to participate, that the presence of the pupil at the school or in an alternative school placement would cause a danger to persons or property or a threat of disrupting the instructional process. If the pupil or the pupil's parent or guardian has requested a meeting to challenge the original suspension pursuant to Section 48914, the purpose of the meeting shall be to decide upon the extension of the suspension order under this section and may be held in conjunction with the initial meeting on the merits of the suspension.

(h) Notwithstanding subdivisions (a) and (g), an individual with exceptional needs may be suspended for up to, but not more than, 10 consecutive schooldays if he or she poses an immediate threat to the safety of others. In the case of a truly dangerous child, a suspension may exceed 10 consecutive schooldays, or the pupil's placement may be changed, or both, if either of the following occurs:

– Suspension For Up to 10 Consecutive Schooldays

(1) The pupil's parent or guardian agrees.

(2) A court order so provides.

(i) For the purposes of this section, a "principal's designee" is any one or more administrators at the schoolsite specifically designated by the principal, in writing, to assist with disciplinary procedures.

In the event that there is not an administrator in addition to the principal at the schoolsite, a certificated person at the schoolsite may be specifically designated by the principal, in writing, as a "principal's designee," to assist with disciplinary procedures. The principal may designate only one such person at a time as the principal's primary designee for the school year.

An additional person meeting the requirements of this subdivision may be designated by the principal, in writing, to act for the purposes of this article when both the principal and the principal's primary designee are absent from the schoolsite. The name of the person, and the names of any person or persons designated as "principal's designee," shall be on file in the principal's office.

This section is not an exception to, nor does it place any limitation on, Section 48903.

48911.1. (a) A pupil suspended from a school for any of the reasons enumerated in Sections 48900 and 48900.2 may be assigned, by the principal or the principle's designee, to a supervised suspension classroom for the entire period of suspension if the pupil poses no imminent danger or threat to the campus, pupils, or staff, or if an action to expel the pupil has not been initiated.

– Supervised Suspension* Classroom

(b) Pupils assigned to a supervised suspension classroom shall be separated from other pupils at the schoolsite for the period of suspension in a separate classroom, building, or site for pupils under suspension.

(c) School districts may continue to claim apportionments for each pupil assigned to and attending a supervised suspension classroom provided as follows:

*(Section 48911.1 Added in 1994)

(1) The supervised suspension classroom is staffed as otherwise provided by law.

(2) Each pupil has access to appropriate counseling services.

(3) The supervised suspension classroom promotes completion of schoolwork and tests missed by the pupil during the suspension.

(4) Each pupil is responsible for contracting his or her teacher or teachers to receive assignments to be completed while the pupil is assigned to the supervised suspension classroom. The teacher shall provide all assignments and tests that the pupil will miss while suspended. If no classroom work is assigned, the person supervising the suspension classroom shall assign schoolwork.

(d) At the time a pupil is assigned to a supervised suspension classroom, a school employee shall notify, in person or by telephone, the pupil's parent or guardian. Whenever a pupil is assigned to a supervised suspension classroom for longer than one class period, a school employee shall notify, in writing, the pupil's parent or guardian.

(e) This section does not place any limitation on a school district's ability to transfer a pupil to an opportunity school or class or a continuation education school or class.

(f) Apportionments claimed by a school district for pupils assigned to supervised suspension shall be used specifically to mitigate the cost of implementing this section.

48911.2. (a) If the number of pupils suspended from school during the prior school year exceeded 30 percent of the school's enrollment, the school should consider doing at least one of the following:

– Considerations by School*
When Suspensions Exceed
30 Percent of School's
Enrollment

(1) Implement the supervised suspension program described in Section 48911.1.

(2) Implement an alternative to the school's off-campus suspension program, which involves a progressive discipline approach that occurs during the schoolday on campus, using any of the following activities:

(A) Conferences between the school staff, parents, and pupils.

(B) Referral to the school counselor, psychologist, child welfare attendance personnel, or other school support service staff.

(C) Detention.

(D) Study teams, guidance teams, resource panel teams, or other assessment-related teams.

(b) At the end of the academic year, the school may report to the district superintendent in charge of school support services, or other comparable administrator if that position does not exist,

*(Section 48911.2 Added in 1994)

on the rate of reduction in the school's off-campus suspensions and the plan or activities used to comply with subdivision (a).

(c) It is the intent of the Legislature to encourage schools that choose to implement this section to examine alternatives to off-campus suspensions that lead to resolution of pupil misconduct without sending pupils off campus. Schools that use this section should not be precluded from suspending pupils to an off-campus site.

48911.5. The site principal of a contracting nonpublic, nonsectarian school providing services to individuals with exceptional needs under Section 56365 and 56366, shall have the same duties and responsibilities with respect to the suspension of pupils with previously identified exceptional needs prescribed for the suspension of pupils under Section 48911.
    – Nonpublic School Principal

48912. (a) The governing board may suspend a pupil from school for any of the acts enumerated in Section 48900 for any number of schooldays within the limits prescribed by Section 48903.
    – Governing Board Consideration of Suspension or Other Disciplinary Action

(b) Notwithstanding the provisions of Section 35145 of this code and Section 54950 of the Government Code, the governing board of a school district shall, unless a request has been made to the contrary, hold closed sessions if the board is considering the suspension of, disciplinary action against, or any other action against, except expulsion, any pupil, if a public hearing upon that question would lead to the giving out of information concerning a school pupil which would be in violation of Article 5 (commencing with Section 49073) of Chapter 6.5.

(c) Before calling a closed session to consider these matters, the governing board shall, in writing, by registered or certified mail or by personal service, notify the pupil and the pupil's parent or guardian, or the pupil if the pupil is an adult, of the intent of the governing board to call and hold a closed session. Unless the pupil or the pupil's parent or guardian shall, in writing, within 48 hours after receipt of the written notice of the board's intention, request that the hearing be held as a public meeting, the hearing to consider these matters shall be conducted by the governing board in closed session. In the event that a written request is served upon the clerk or secretary of the governing board, the meeting shall be public, except that any discussion at that meeting which may be in conflict with the right to privacy of any pupil other than the pupil requesting the public meeting, shall be in closed session.

48912.5. The governing board of a school district may suspend a pupil enrolled in a continuation school or class for a period not longer than the remainder of the semester if any of the
    – Continuation School Suspension

acts enumerated in Section 48900 occurred. The suspension shall meet the requirements of Section 48915.

48913. The teacher of any class from which a pupil is suspended may require the suspended pupil to complete any assignments and tests missed during the suspension.

- Completion of Work Missed by Suspended Pupil

48914. Each school district is authorized to establish a policy that permits school officials to conduct a meeting with the parent or guardian of a suspended pupil to discuss the causes, the duration, the school policy involved, and other matters pertinent to the suspension.

- Policy on Meeting with Parent or Guardian

48915. (a) The principal or the superintendent of schools shall recommend a pupil's expulsion for any of the following acts, unless the principal or superintendent finds, and so reports in writing to the governing board, that expulsion is inappropriate, due to the particular circumstance, which shall be set out in the report of the incident:

- Expulsion; Particular* Circumstances

(1) Causing serious physical injury to another person, except in self-defense.

(2) Possession of any knife, explosive, or other dangerous object of no reasonable use to the pupil at school or at a school activity off school grounds.

(3) Unlawful sale of any controlled substance listed in Chapter 2 (commencing with Section 11053) of Division 10 of the Health and Safety Code, except for the first offense for the sale of not more than one avoirdupois ounce of marijuana, other than concentrated cannabis.

(4) Robbery or extortion.

(b) The principal or the superintendent of schools shall immediately suspend, pursuant to Section 48911, any pupil found to be in possession of a firearm at school or at a school activity off school grounds and shall recommend expulsion of that pupil to the governing board. The governing board shall expel that pupil or refer that pupil to a program of study that is appropriately prepared to accommodate students who exhibit discipline problems and is not provided at a comprehensive middle, junior, or senior high school or housed at the schoolsite attended by the pupil at the time the expulsion was recommended to the school board, whenever the principal or superintendent of schools and the governing board confirm the following:

(1) The pupil was in knowing possession of the firearm.

(2) An employee of the school district verifies the pupil's possession of the firearm.

(c) Upon recommendation by the principal, superintendent of schools, or by a hearing officer or administrative panel appointed pursuant to subdivision (d) of Section 48918, the governing board may order a pupil expelled upon finding that the pupil violated

*(Section 48915 Amended in 1994)

subdivision (a), (b), (c), (d), or (e) of Section 48900, except that a pupil found in possession of a firearm shall be expelled or referred to another school as specified in subdivision (b).

(d) Upon recommendation by the principal, superintendent of schools, or by a hearing officer or administrative panel appointed pursuant to subdivision (d) of Section 48918, the governing board may order a pupil expelled upon finding that the pupil violated subdivision (f), (g), (h), (i), (j), (k), or (l) of Section 48900, or Section 48900.2 or 48900.3, and either of the following:

(1) That other means of correction are not feasible or have repeatedly failed to bring about proper conduct.

(2) That due to the nature of the violation, the presence of the pupil causes a continuing danger to the physical safety of the pupil or others.

(e) Any pupil who is authorized to be in possession of a firearm by a teacher, schoolsite administrator, or principal is exempted from the requirements of this section.

48915.1. (a) If the governing board of a school district receives a request from an individual who has been expelled from another school district for an act other than those described in subdivision (a) of Section 48915, for enrollment in a school maintained by the school district, the board shall hold a hearing to determine whether that individual poses a continuing danger either to the pupils or employees of the school district. The hearing and notice shall be conducted in accordance with the rules and regulations governing procedures for the expulsion of pupils as described in Section 48918. A school district may request information from another school district regarding a recommendation for expulsion or the expulsion of an applicant from another school district regarding a recommendation for expulsion or the expulsion of an applicant for enrollment. The school district receiving the request shall respond to the request with all deliberate speed but shall respond no later than five working days from the date of the receipt of the request.

(b) If a pupil has been expelled from his or her previous school for offenses other than those listed in subdivision (a) of Section 48915, the parent, guardian, or pupil, if the pupil is emancipated or otherwise legally of age, shall upon enrollment, inform the receiving school district of his or her status with the previous school district. If this information is not provided to the school district and the school district later determines the pupil was expelled from the previous school, the lack of compliance shall be recorded and discussed in the hearing required pursuant to subdivision (a).

(c) The governing board of a school district may make a determination to deny enrollment to an individual who has been

– Expelled Individuals;
  Enrollment in Another
  School

expelled from another school district for an act other than those described in subdivision (a) of Section 48915, for the remainder of the expulsion period after a determination has been made, pursuant to a hearing, that the individual poses a potential danger to either the pupils or employees of the school district.

(d) The governing board of a school district, when making its determination whether to enroll an individual who has been expelled from another school district for these acts, may consider the following options:

(1) Deny enrollment.

(2) Permit enrollment.

(3) Permit conditional enrollment in a regular school program or another educational program.

(e) Notwithstanding any other provision of law, the governing board of a school district, after a determination has been made, pursuant to a hearing, that an individual expelled from another school district for an act other than those described in subdivision (a) of Section 48915 does not pose a danger to either the pupils or employees of the school district, shall permit the individual to enroll in a school in the school district during the term of the expulsion, provided that he or she, subsequent to the expulsion, either has established legal residence in the school district, pursuant to Section 48200, or has enrolled in the school pursuant to an interdistrict agreement executed between the affected school districts pursuant to Chapter 5 (commencing with Section 46600).

48915.2. (a) A pupil expelled from school for any of the offenses listed in subdivision (a) of Section 48915, shall not be permitted to enroll in any other school or school district during the period of expulsion unless it is a county community school pursuant to subdivision (b) of Section 1981, or a juvenile court school, as described in Section 48645.1.

(b) After a determination has been made, pursuant to a hearing under Section 48918, that an individual expelled from another school district for any act described in subdivision (a) of Section 48915 does not pose a danger to either the pupils or employees of the school district, the governing board of a school district may permit the individual to enroll in the school district after the term of expulsion, subject to one of the following conditions:

(1) He or she has established legal residence in the school district, pursuant to Section 48200.

(2) He or she is enrolled in the school pursuant to an interdistrict agreement executed between the affected school districts pursuant to Chapter 5 (commencing with Section 46600) of Part 26.

– Enrollment During and After Period of Expulsion

48915.5. (a) In a matter involving a pupil with previously identified exceptional needs who is currently enrolled in a special education program, the governing board may order the pupil expelled pursuant to subdivisions (b) and (c) of Section 48915 only if all of the following conditions are met:

— Expulsion Conditions for Disabled Pupils Enrolled in a Special Education Program

(1) An individualized education program team meeting is held and conducted pursuant to Article 3 (commencing with Section 56340) of Chapter 2 of Part 30.

(2) The team determines that the misconduct was not caused by, or was not a direct manifestation of, the pupil's identified disability.

(3) The team determines that the pupil had been appropriately placed at the time the misconduct occurred.

The term "pupil with previously identified exceptional needs," as used in this section, means a pupil who meets the requirements of Section 56026 and who, at the time the alleged misconduct occurred, was enrolled in a special education program, including enrollment in nonpublic schools pursuant to Section 56365 and state special schools.

(b) For purposes of this section, all applicable procedural safeguards prescribed by federal and state law and regulations apply to proceedings to expel pupils with previously identified exceptional needs, except that, notwithstanding Section 56321, subdivision (e) of Section 56506, or any other provision of law, parental consent is not required prior to conducting a preexpulsion educational assessment pursuant to subdivision (e), or as a condition of the final decision of the local board to expel.

— Procedural Safeguards

(c) Each local education agency, pursuant to the requirements of Section 56221, shall develop procedures and time lines governing expulsion procedures for individuals with exceptional needs.

— Expulsion Procedures and Time Lines

(d) The parent of each pupil with previously identified exceptional needs has the right to participate in the individualized education program team meeting conducted pursuant to subdivision (a) preceding the commencement of expulsion proceedings, following the completion of a preexpulsion assessment pursuant to subdivision (e), through actual participation, representation, or a telephone conference call. The meeting shall be held at a time and place mutually convenient to the parent and local educational agency within the period, if any, of the pupil's preexpulsion suspension. A telephone conference call may be substituted for the meeting. Each parent shall be notified of his or her right to participate in the meeting at least 48 hours prior to the meeting. Unless a parent has requested a postponement, the meeting may be conducted without the parent's participation, if the notice required by this subdivision has been

— Parent Rights

provided. The notice shall specify that the meeting may be held without the parent's participation, unless the parent requests a postponement for up to three additional schooldays pursuant to this subdivision. Each parent may request that the meeting be postponed for up to three additional schooldays. In the event that a postponement has been granted, the local educational agency may extend any suspension of a pupil for the period of postponement if the pupil continues to pose an immediate threat to the safety of himself, herself, or others and the local educational agency notifies the parent that the suspension will be continued during the postponement. However, the suspension shall not be extended beyond 10 consecutive schooldays unless agreed to by the parent, or by a court order. If a parent who has received proper notice of the meeting refuses to consent to an extension beyond 10 consecutive schooldays and chooses not to participate, the meeting may be conducted without the parent's participation.

(e) In determining whether a pupil should be expelled, the individualized education program team shall base its decision on the results of a preexpulsion educational assessment conducted in accordance with the guidelines of Section 104.35 of Title 34 of the Code of Federal Regulations, which shall include a review of the appropriateness of the pupil's placement at the time of the alleged misconduct, and a determination of the relationship, if any, between the pupil's behavior and his or her disability.

− Expulsion Decision Based on Results of Preexpulsion Educational Assessment

In addition to the preexpulsion educational assessment results, the individualized education program team shall also review and consider the pupil's health records and school discipline records. The parent, pursuant to Section 300.504 of Title 34 of the Code of Federal Regulations, is entitled to written notice of the local educational agency's intent to conduct a preexpulsion assessment. The parent shall make the pupil available for the assessment at a site designated by the local educational agency without delay. The parent's right to an independent assessment under Section 56329 applies despite the fact that the pupil has been referred for expulsion.

(f) If the individualized education program team determines that the alleged misconduct was not caused by, or a direct manifestation of, the pupil's disability, and if it is determined that the pupil was appropriately placed, the pupil shall be subject to the applicable disciplinary actions and procedures prescribed under this article.

− Alleged Misconduct Not Caused by, or Manifested by, Disability

(g) The parent of each pupil with previously identified exceptional needs has the right to a due process hearing conducted pursuant to Section 1415 of Title 20 of the United States Code if the parent disagrees with the decision of the

− Parent's Right to Due Process Hearing

individualized education program team made pursuant to subdivision (f), or if the parent disagrees with the decision to rely upon information obtained, or proposed to be obtained, pursuant to subdivision (e).

(h) No expulsion hearing shall be conducted for an individual with exceptional needs until all of the following have occurred:

(1) A preexpulsion assessment is conducted.

(2) The individualized education program team meets pursuant to subdivision (a).

(3) Due process hearings and appeals, if initiated pursuant to Section 1415 of Title 20 of the United States Code, are completed.

(i) Pursuant to subdivision (a) of Section 48918, the statutory times prescribed for expulsion proceedings for individuals with exceptional needs shall commence after the completion of paragraphs (1), (2), and (3) in subdivision (h).

(j) If an individual with exceptional needs is excluded from schoolbus transportation, the pupil is entitled to be provided with an alternative form of transportation at no cost to the pupil or parent.

48915.6. The restrictions and special procedures provided in Section 48915.5 for the expulsion of a pupil with exceptional needs because of the pupil's possession of a firearm, knife, explosive, or other dangerous object of no reasonable use for the pupil, at school or at a school activity off school grounds, shall apply only if mandated under federal law, including Section 1415 of Title 20 of the United States Code.

48915.7. It is the intent of the Legislature that where community school opportunities exist, the principal shall recommend for expulsion, and the governing board shall expel, any pupil who is found to be in possession of a firearm at school or at a school activity off school grounds and that the governing board shall request the county board of education to enroll the pupil in a community school.

48916. An expulsion order shall remain in effect until the governing board may, in the manner prescribed in this article, order the readmission of a pupil. At the time an expulsion of a pupil is ordered, the governing board shall set a date, not later than the last day of the semester following the semester in which the expulsion occurred, when the pupil may apply for readmission to a school maintained by the district.

The governing board may recommend a plan of rehabilitation for the pupil, which may include, but not be limited to, periodic review as well as assessment at the time of application for readmission. The plan may also include recommendations for

*(Section 48915.6 Added in 1994

counseling, employment, community service, or other rehabilitative programs.

The governing board of each school district shall adopt rules and regulations establishing a procedure for the filing and processing of requests for readmission. Upon completion of the readmission process, the governing board shall not be required to readmit the pupil. A description of the procedure shall be made available to the pupil and the pupil's parent or guardian at the time the expulsion order is entered.

48916.5. The governing board may require a pupil who is expelled from school for reasons relating to controlled substances, as defined in Sections 11054 to 11058, inclusive, of the Health and Safety Code, or alcohol, prior to returning to school to enroll in a county-supported drug rehabilitation program. No pupil shall be required to enroll in a rehabilitation program pursuant to this section without the consent of his or her parent or guardian.

– Expulsion Relating to Controlled Substances or Alcohol

48917. The governing board, upon voting to expel a pupil, may suspend the enforcement of the expulsion order for a period of not more than one calendar year and may, as a condition of the suspension of enforcement, assign the pupil to a school, class, or program which is deemed appropriate for the rehabilitation of the pupil. The governing board's criteria for suspending the enforcement of the expulsion order shall be applied equally to all pupils, including individuals with exceptional needs as defined in Section 56026. During the period of the suspension of the expulsion order, the pupil shall be deemed to be on probationary status. The suspension of an expulsion order under this section may be revoked by the governing board upon the pupil's commission of any of the acts enumerated in Section 48900 or for any violation of the district's rules and regulations governing pupil conduct. Upon revocation of the suspension of an expulsion order, a pupil may be expelled under the terms of the original expulsion order.

– Suspension of Order to Expel

Upon satisfactory completion of the rehabilitation assignment of a pupil, the pupil shall be reinstated by the governing board in a school of the district. Upon reinstatement, the governing board may also order the expungement of any or all records of the expulsion proceedings.

A decision of the governing board to suspend an expulsion order shall not affect the time period and requirements for the filing of an appeal of the expulsion order with the county board of education required under Section 48919. Any appeal shall be filed within 30 days of the original vote of the governing board.

48918. The governing board of each school district shall establish rules and regulations governing procedures for the expulsion of pupils. These procedures shall include, but are not necessarily limited to, all the following:

(a) The pupil shall be entitled to a hearing to determine whether the pupil should be expelled. An expulsion hearing shall be held within 30 schooldays after the date the principal or the superintendent of schools determines that the pupil has committed any of the acts enumerated in Section 48900, unless the pupil requests, in writing, that the hearing be postponed. The adopted rules and regulations shall specify that the pupil is entitled to at least one postponement of an expulsion hearing, for a period of not more than 30 calendar days. Any additional postponement may be granted at the discretion of the governing board.

The decision of the governing board as to whether to expel a pupil shall be made within 10 schooldays after the conclusion of the hearing, unless the pupil requests in writing that the decision be postponed. If the hearing is held by a hearing officer or an administrative panel, or if the district governing board does not meet on a weekly basis, the governing board shall make its decision about a pupil's expulsion within 40 schooldays after the date of the pupil's removal from his or her school of attendance for the incident for which the recommendation for expulsion is made by the principal or the superintendent, unless the pupil requests in writing that the decision be postponed.

In the event that compliance by the governing board with the time requirement for the conducting of an expulsion hearing under this subdivision is impracticable, the superintendent of schools or the superintendent's designee may, for good cause, extend the time period for the holding of the expulsion hearing for an additional five schooldays. Reasons for the extension of the time for the hearing shall be included as a part of the record at the time the expulsion hearing is conducted. Upon the commencement of the hearing, all matters shall be pursued and conducted with reasonable diligence and shall be concluded without any unnecessary delay.

(b) Written notice of the hearing shall be forwarded to the pupil at least 10 calendar days prior to the date of the hearing. The notice shall include: the date and place of the hearing; a statement of the specific facts and charges upon which the proposed expulsion is based; a copy of the disciplinary rules of the district that relate to the alleged violation; a notice of the parent, guardian, or pupil's obligation pursuant to subdivision (b) of Section 48915.1; and notice of the opportunity for the pupil or the pupil's parent or guardian to appear in person or employ and be represented by counsel, to inspect and obtain copies of all documents to be used at the hearing, to confront and question all witnesses who testify at the hearing, to question all other evidence presented, and to present oral and documentary evidence on the pupil's behalf, including witnesses.

(c) Notwithstanding Section 54593 of the Government Code and Section 35145 of this code, the governing board shall conduct a hearing to consider the expulsion of a pupil in a session closed to the public, unless the pupil requests, in writing, at least five days prior to the date of the hearing, that the hearing be conducted at a public meeting. Regardless of whether the expulsion hearing is conducted in a closed or public session, the governing board may meet in closed session for the purpose of deliberating and determining whether the pupil should be expelled.

If the governing board or the hearing officer or administrative panel appointed under subdivision (d) to conduct the hearing admits any other person to a closed deliberation session, the parent or guardian of the pupil, the pupil, and the counsel of the pupil also shall be allowed to attend the closed deliberations.

(d) In lieu of conducting an expulsion hearing itself, the governing board may contract with the county hearing officer, or with the Office of Administrative Hearings of the State of California pursuant to Chapter 14 (commencing with Section 27720) of Part 3 of Division 2 of Title 3 of the Government Code and Section 35207 of this code, for a hearing officer to conduct the hearing. The governing board also may appoint an impartial administrative panel of three or more certificated persons, none of whom are members of the board or employed on the staff of the school in which the pupil is enrolled. The hearing shall be conducted in accordance with all of the procedures established under this section.

(e) Within three schooldays after the hearing, the hearing officer or administrative panel shall determine whether to recommend the expulsion of the pupil to the governing board. If the hearing officer or administrative panel decides not to recommend expulsion, the expulsion proceedings shall be terminated and the pupil immediately shall be reinstated and permitted to return to a classroom instructional program, any other instructional program, a rehabilitation program, or any combination of these programs. Placement in one or more of these programs shall be made by the superintendent of schools or the superintendent's designee after consultation with school district personnel, including the pupil's teachers, and the pupil's parent or guardian. The decision not to recommend expulsion shall be final.

(f) If the hearing officer or administrative panel recommends expulsion, findings of fact in support of the recommendation shall be prepared and submitted to the governing board. All findings of fact and recommendations shall be based solely on the evidence adduced at the hearing. If the governing board accepts the recommendation calling for expulsion, acceptance shall be based either upon a review of the findings of fact and recommendations submitted by the hearing officer or panel or upon the results of any supplementary hearing conducted pursuant to this section that the governing board may order.

The decision of the governing board to expel a pupil shall be based upon substantial evidence relevant to the charges adduced at the expulsion hearing or hearings. Except as provided in this section, no evidence to expel shall be based solely upon hearsay evidence. The governing board or the hearing officer or administrative panel may, upon a finding that good cause exists, determine that the disclosure of the identity of a witness and the testimony of that witness at the hearing would subject the witness to an unreasonable risk of harm. Upon this determination, the testimony of the witness may be presented at the hearing in the form of sworn declarations which shall be examined only the governing board or the hearing officer or administrative panel. Copies of these sworn declarations, edited to delete the name and identity of the witness, shall be made available to the pupil.

(g) A record of the hearing shall be made. The record may be maintained by any means, including electronic recording, so long a reasonably accurate and complete written transcription of the proceedings can be made.

(h) Technical rules of evidence shall not apply to the hearing, except that relevant evidence may be admitted and given probative effect only if it is the kind of evidence upon which reasonable persons are accustomed to rely in the conduct of serious affairs. A decision of the governing board to expel shall be supported by substantial evidence showing that the pupil committed any of the acts enumerated in Section 48900.

(i) Whether an expulsion hearing is conducted by the governing board or before a hearing officer or administrative panel, final action to expel a pupil shall be taken only by the governing board in a public session. Written notice of any decision to expel or to suspend the enforcement of an expulsion order during a period of probation shall be sent by the superintendent of schools or his or her designee to the pupil or the pupil's parent or guardian, and shall be accompanied by notice of the right to appeal the expulsion to the county board of education and of the obligation of the parent, guardian, or pupil under subdivision (b) of Section 48915.1, upon the pupil's enrollment in a new school district, to inform that district of the expulsion.

(j) The governing board shall maintain a record of each expulsion, including the cause therefor. Records of expulsions shall be a nonprivileged, disclosable public record.

The expulsion order and the causes therefor shall be recorded in the pupil's mandatory interim record and shall be forwarded to any school in which the pupil subsequently enrolls upon receipt of a request from the admitting school for the pupil's school records.

48919. If a pupil is expelled from school, the pupil or the pupil's parent or guardian may, within 30 days following the decision of the governing board to expel, file an appeal to the county board of education which shall hold a hearing thereon and render its decision.

– Expulsion Appeals to County Board of Education

The county board of education shall hold the hearing within 20 schooldays following the filing of a formal request under this section and shall render a decision within three schooldays of the hearing, unless the pupil requests a postponement.

The period within which an appeal is to be filed shall be determined from the date a governing board votes to expel even if enforcement of the expulsion action is suspended and the pupil is placed on probation pursuant to Section 48917. A pupil who fails to appeal the original action of the board within the prescribed time may not subsequently appeal a decision of the board to revoke probation and impose the original order of expulsion.

The county board of education shall adopt rules and regulations establishing procedures for expulsion appeals conducted under this section. The adopted rules and regulations shall include, but need not be limited to, the requirements for filing a notice of appeal, the setting of a hearing date, the furnishing of notice to the pupil and the governing board regarding the appeal, the furnishing of a copy of the expulsion hearing record to the county board of education, procedures for the conduct of the hearing, and the preservation of the record of the appeal.

The pupil shall submit a request for a copy of the written transcripts and supporting documents from the district simultaneously with the filing of the notice of appeal with the county board of education. The school district shall provide the pupil with the transcriptions, supporting documents, and records within five schooldays following the pupil's request. The pupil shall be immediately file suitable copies of these records with the county board of education.

48920. Notwithstanding the provisions of Section 54950 of the Government Code and Section 35145 of this code, the county

– County Board; Hearing Expulsion Appeal

board of education shall hear an appeal of an expulsion order in closed session, unless the pupil requests, in writing, at least five days prior to the date of the hearing, that the hearing be conducted in a public meeting. Upon the timely submission of a request for a public meeting, the county board of education shall be required to honor the request. Whether the hearing is conducted in closed or public session, the county board may meet in closed session for the purpose of deliberations. If the county board admits any representative of the pupil or the school district, the board shall, at the same time, admit representatives from the opposing party.

48921. The county board of education shall determine the appeal from a pupil expulsion upon the record of the hearing before the district governing board, together with such applicable documentation or regulations as may be ordered. No evidence other than that contained in the record of the proceedings of the school board may be heard unless a de novo proceeding is granted as provided in Section 48923.

    – Expulsion Appeals to County Board; Transcripts

It shall be the responsibility of the pupil to submit a written transcription for review by the county board. The cost of the transcript shall be borne by the pupil except in either of the following situations:

(1) Where the pupil's parent or guardian certifies to the school district that he or she cannot reasonably afford the cost of the transcript because of limited income or exceptional necessary expenses, or both.

(2) In a case in which the county board reverses the decision of the local governing board, the county board shall require the local board reimburse the pupil for the cost of such transcription.

48922. (a) The review by the county board of education of the decision of the governing board shall be limited to the following questions:

    – County Board; Scope of Review

(1) Whether the governing board acted without or in excess of it jurisdiction.

(2) Whether there was a fair hearing before the governing board.

(3) Whether there was a prejudicial abuse of discretion in the hearing.

(4) Whether there is relevant and material evidence which, in the exercise of reasonable diligence, could not have been produced or which was improperly excluded at the hearing before the governing board.

(b) As used in this section, a proceeding without or in excess of jurisdiction includes, but is not limited to, a situation where an expulsion hearing is not commenced within the time periods prescribed by this article, a situation where an expulsion order is not based upon the acts enumerated in Section 48900, or a situation involving acts not related to school activity or attendance.

(c) For purposes of this section, an abuse of discretion is established in any of the following situations:

(1) If school officials have not met the procedural requirements of this article.

(2) If the decision to expel a pupil is not supported by the findings prescribed by Section 48915.

(3) If the findings are not supported by the evidence.

A county board of education may not reverse the decision of a governing board to expel a pupil based upon a finding of an abuse of discretion unless the county board of education also determines that the abuse of discretion was prejudicial.

48923. The decision of the county board shall be limited as follows: — Decision of County Board

(a) Where the county board finds that relevant and material evidence exists which, in the exercise of reasonable diligence, could not have been produced or which was improperly excluded at the hearing before the governing board, it may do either of the following:

(1) Remand the matter to the governing board for reconsideration and may in addition order the pupil reinstated pending such reconsideration.

(2) Grant a hearing de novo upon reasonable notice thereof to the pupil and to the governing board. The hearing shall be conducted in conformance with the rules and regulations adopted by the county board under Section 48919.

(b) In all other cases, the county board shall enter an order either affirming or reversing the decision of the governing board. In any case in which the county board enters a decision reversing the local board, the county board may direct the local board to expunge the record of the pupil and the records of the district of any references to the expulsion action and such expulsion shall be deemed not to have occurred.

48924. The decision of the county board of education shall be final and binding upon the pupil and upon the governing board of the school district. The pupil and the governing board shall be notified of the final order of the county board, in writing, either by personal service or by certified mail. The order shall become final when rendered. — Finality of County Board Decision

48925. As used in this article: — Definitions

(a) "Day" means a calendar day unless otherwise specifically provided. — Day

(b) "Expulsion" means a removal of a pupil from (1) the immediate supervision and control, or (2) the general — Expulsion supervision, of school personnel, as those terms are used in Section 46300.

(c) "Schoolday" means a day upon which the schools of the district are in session or weekdays during the summer recess.

(d) "Suspension" means removal of a pupil from ongoing instruction for adjustment purposes. However, "suspension" does not mean any of the following:

(1) Reassignment to another education program or class at the same school where the pupil will receive continuing instruction for the length of the day prescribed by the governing board for pupils of the same grade level.

(2) Referral to a certificated employee designated by the principal to advise pupils.

(3) Removal from the class, but without reassignment to another class or program, for the remainder of the class period without sending the pupil to the principal or the principal's designee as provided in Section 48910. Removal from a particular class shall not occur more than once every five schooldays.

(e) "Pupil" includes a pupil's parent or guardian or legal counsel.

(Although Assembly Bill 1045 was signed into law in 1994 and amended various Education Code sections including 48915, 48915.2, 48915.5, 48916, and 48918, added 48926, and repealed 48915.7, Sec. 15 of the bill said: "This act shall not become operative unless Senate Bill 1645 of the 1993-94 Regular Session is enacted and becomes operative, in which case this act shall become operative on August 1, 1995." SB 1645 was vetoed so none of the changes included in AB 1045 are reflected in this composite of laws.)

CORPORAL PUNISHMENT PROHIBITION

(Education Code - Part 27)

49000. The Legislature finds and declares that the protection against corporal punishment, which extends to other citizens in other walks of like, should include children while they are under the control of the public schools. Children of school age are at the most vulnerable and impressionable period of their lives and it is wholly reasonable that the safeguards to the integrity and sanctity of their bodies should be, at this tender age, at least equal to that afforded to other citizens.

49001. (a) For the purposes of this section "corporal punishment" means the willful infliction of, or willfully causing the infliction of, physical pain on a pupil. An amount of force that is reasonable and necessary for a person employed by or engaged in a public school to quell a disturbance threatening physical injury to persons or damage to property, for purposes of self-defense, or to obtain possession of weapons or other dangerous objects within the control of the pupil, is not and shall not be construed to be corporal punishment within the meaning and intent of this section. Physical pain or discomfort caused by athletic competition or other such recreational activity, voluntarily engaged in by the pupil, is not and shall not be construed to be corporal punishment within the meaning and intent of this section.

(b) No person employed by or engaged in a public school shall inflict, or cause to be inflicted corporal punishment upon a pupil. Every resolution, bylaw, rule, ordinance, or other act or authority permitting or authorizing the infliction of corporal punishment upon a pupil attending a public school is void and unenforceable.

– Definition of Corporal Punishment

PUPIL RECORDS - PARENTAL ACCESS

(Education Code - Part 27)

(AB 3235 - Chapter 1288, Statutes of 1994)

49060. It is the intent of the Legislature to resolve potential conflicts between California law and the provisions of Public Law 93-380 regarding parental access to, and the confidentiality of, pupil records in order to insure the continuance of federal education funds to public educational institutions within the state, and to revise generally and update the law relating to such records.

This chapter applies to public agencies that provide educationally related services to pupils with disabilities pursuant to Chapter 26,5 (commencing with Section 7570) of Division 7 of Title 1 of the Government Code and to public agencies that educate pupils with disabilities in state hospitals or developmental centers and in youth and adult facilities.

This chapter shall have no effect regarding public community colleges, other public or private institutions of higher education, other governmental or private agencies which receive federal education funds unless described herein, or, except for Sections

– Legislative Intent;* Effect of Law

*(Section 49060 Amended in 1994)

49068 and 49069 and subdivision (b)(5) of Section 49076, private schools.

The provisions of this chapter shall prevail over the provisions of Section 12400 of this code and Chapter 3.5 (commencing with Section 6250) of Division 7 of Title 1 of the Government Code to the extent that they may pertain to access to pupil records.

CHALLENGING CONTENT OF RECORDS
(Education Code - Part 27)

(AB 3235 - Chapter 1288, Statutes of 1994)

49070. Following an inspection and review of a pupil's records, the parent of a pupil or former pupil of a school district may challenge the content of any pupil record.

- Procedures for Correcting*
  or Removing Information

(a) The parent of a pupil may file a written request with the superintendent of the district to correct or remove any information recorded in the written records concerning his or her child which the parent alleges to be any of the following:

(1) Inaccurate.

(2) An unsubstantiated personal conclusion or inference.

(3) A conclusion or inference outside of the observer's area of competence.

(4) Not based on the personal observation of a named person with the time and place of the observation noted.

(5) Misleading.

(6) In violation of the privacy or other rights of the pupil.

(b) Within 30 days of receipt of a request pursuant to subdivision (a), the superintendent or the superintendent's designee shall meet with the parent and the certificated employee who recorded the information in question, if any, and if the employee is presently employed by the school district. The superintendent shall then sustain or deny the allegations.

If the superintendent sustains any or all of the allegations, he or she shall order the correction or the removal and destruction of the information. However, in accordance with Section 49066, the superintendent shall not order a pupil's grade to be changed unless the teacher who determined the grade is, to the extent practicable, given an opportunity to state orally, in writing, or both, the reasons for which the grade was given and is, to the extent practicable, included in all discussions relating to the changing of the grade.

If the superintendent denies any or all of the allegations and refuses to order the correction or the removal of the information,

*(Section 49070 Amended in 1994)

the parent may, within 30 days of the refusal, appeal the decision in writing to the governing board of the school district.

(c) Within 30 days of receipt of an appeal pursuant to subdivision (b), the governing board shall, in closed session with the parent and the certified employee who recorded the information in question, if any, and if the employee is presently employed by the school district, determine whether or not to sustain or deny the allegations.

If the governing board sustains any or all of the allegations, it shall order the superintendent to immediately correct or remove and destroy the information from the written records of the pupil. However, in accordance with Section 49066, the governing board shall not order a pupil's grade to be changed unless the teacher who determined the grade is, to the extent practicable, included in all discussions relating to the changing of the grade.

The decision of the governing board shall be final.

Records of these administrative proceedings shall be maintained in a confidential manner and shall be destroyed one year after the decision of the governing board, unless the parent initiates legal proceedings relative to the disputed information within the prescribed period.

(d) If the final decision of the governing board is unfavorable to the parent, or if the parent accepts an unfavorable decision by the district superintendent, the parent shall have the right to submit a written statement of his or her objections to the information. This statement shall become a part of the pupil's school record until the information objected to is corrected or removed.

SPECIALIZED PHYSICAL HEALTH CARE SERVICES

(Education Code - Part 27)

(AB 3477 - Chapter 1220, Statutes of 1978)

49423.5. (a) Notwithstanding the provisions of Section 49422, any individual with exceptional needs who requires specialized physical health care services, during the regular school day, may be assisted by the following individuals:

— Qualifications of Service Providers

(1) Qualified persons who possess an appropriate credential issued pursuant to Section 44267, or hold a valid certificate of public health nursing issued by the State Department of Health Services; or

(2) Qualified designated school personnel trained in the administration of specialized physical health care provided they

perform such services under the supervision of a school nurse, public health nurse, or licensed physician and surgeon.

(b) Specialized health care or other services that require medically related training shall be provided pursuant to the procedures prescribed by Section 49423.

— Medically Related Training

(c) Persons providing specialized physical health care services shall also demonstrate competence in basic cardiopulmonary resuscitation and shall be knowledgeable of the emergency medical resources available in the community in which the services are performed.

— Providers Must Demonstrate CPR Competence

(d) "Specialized physical health care services" as used in this section include catheterization, gavage feeding, suctioning, or other services that require medically related training.

— Definitions of Services

(e) Regulations necessary to implement the provisions of this section shall be developed jointly by the State Department of Education and the State Department of Health Services, and adopted by the State Board of Education.

— Regulations

EARLY DIAGNOSIS OF LEARNING DISABILITIES

(Education Code - Part 27)

(As Amended by AB 2587, Chapter 922, Statutes of 1994)

Article 13. Early Diagnosis of Learning Disabilities

49580. The State Department of Education shall develop a testing program to be utilized at the kindergarten grade level to determine which pupils have a potential for developing learning disability problems. The testing procedure shall include an overall screening test for learning disabilities and testing for dyslexia. To the extent feasible, the department shall use existing tests and screening instruments in developing the early diagnosis of the learning disabilities testing program. In developing the program, the department shall consult with experts in the areas of learning and reading difficulties, including, but not limited to, neurologists, psychologists, persons working in these areas in postsecondary educational institutions, teachers, school nurses, education consultants, school psychologists, and other persons with appropriate knowledge and experience in the detection and treatment of learning problems and reading difficulties in early grades.

— Testing Programs for Learning Disability Problems

49581. The State Department of Education shall develop and implement a pilot project to determine the effectiveness and feasibility of implementing the early diagnosis of learning disabilities testing program developed pursuant to Section 49580. The pilot project shall administer the early diagnosis testing program to kindergarten aged pupils in order to identify pupils with the potential to develop learning disability problems. Pupils who are identified as having potential learning disability problems shall be referred to existing programs and services which are available to provide assistance.

– Pilot Project

49582. The State Department of Education shall prescribe guidelines for the early diagnosis of the learning disabilities testing program and pilot project. The guidelines shall include but need not be limited to, all of the following:

– Guidelines for Early*
Diagnosis

(a) A definition of "pupils with the potential to develop learning disability problems," as used in this article.

(b) The methods and criteria for selecting one or more sites for the establishment of the pilot project.

(c) The number of sites to be selected for purposes of establishing the pilot project.

(d) Criteria for judging the results and effectiveness of the early diagnosis testing program, as well as criteria for determining the feasibility for implementing the program at the conclusion of the pilot project.

DIFFERENTIAL PROFICIENCY STANDARDS

(Education Code - Part 28)

(As Amended By AB 2587, Chapter 922, Statutes of 1994)

51215. (a) The governing board of each school district maintaining a junior or senior high school shall adopt standards of proficiency in basic skills for pupils attending school within its school district.

– Adoption of Standards of*
Proficiency in Basic
Skills

(b) The governing board of each school district maintaining grade 6 or 8, or the equivalent, shall adopt standards of proficiency in basic skills for pupils attending these grades.

(c) These standards shall include, but need not be limited to, reading comprehension, writing, and computation skills, in the English language, necessary to success in school and life experiences, and shall be such as will enable individual achievement to be ascertained and evaluated.

– Standards Include

*(Sections 49582 and 51215
Amended in 1994)

The standards shall be directly related to the district's instructional program.

(d) Differential standards and assessment procedures which shall include, but need not be limited to, reading comprehension, writing, and computation skills, shall be adopted pursuant to this subdivision.

- Differential Standards and Assessment Procedures

(1) Differential standards and assessment procedures shall be adopted for pupils who meet all of the following conditions:

(A) Are enrolled in special education programs pursuant to Part 30 (commencing with Section 56000); or for whom individualized education programs have been developed, and for whom the regular instructional program has been modified, as necessary, under the supervision of a person who holds an appropriate credential in special education.

- For Special Education Pupils

(B) Have diagnosed learning handicaps or disabilities such that the individualized education program team determines they have not demonstrated evidence of the ability to attain the district's regular proficiency standards with appropriate educational services and support.

- Diagnosed Learning Disabilities

(2) If the team determines that these pupils have not demonstrated evidence of the ability to attain the district's regular proficiency standards with appropriate educational services and support, the team shall develop differential proficiency standards, or modify general differential standards adopted by the governing board, appropriate to the needs and potential of the pupil.

- IEP Determination

(3) Any differential standards shall be included in the individualized education program developed for the pupil pursuant to Part 30 (commencing with Section 56000).

- Differential Standards

(4) The determination and the development of differential proficiency standards shall be part of the process of developing, reviewing, and revising a pupil's individualized education program.

- Part of Ongoing Process

(5) In the case where one or more differential standards are developed for a pupil enrolled in special education, the standards may be maintained throughout the pupil's school experience, irrespective of whether the pupil continues to be enrolled in special education.

- May Be Maintained Throughout School Experience

(6) Nothing in this subdivision shall be construed to require differential proficiency standards for a pupil who a team determines can attain the district's regular proficiency standards with appropriate educational services and support.

- Not Required for Pupil Who Can Attain Regular Proficiency

(7) This subdivision shall apply prospectively and retroactively to pupils enrolled in the 9th grade, or the equivalent thereof, during the school year.

- Application of Provisions

(8) Differential standards and assessment procedures adopted pursuant to this subdivision shall permit the pupil for whom they

- Attain Standards Within Reasonable Amount of Time

are adopted to attain the standards within a reasonable amount of time but not after the state is no longer required by state or federal law to provide an education to the pupil.

(9) It is the intent of the Legislature that the attainment of a standard of proficiency by a pupil shall also reflect the attainment of a reasonable level of competence. The Legislature, therefore, recognizes that there may be some pupils who cannot meet regular or differential standards of proficiency, in reading, writing, and mathematics skills, and others who will need to remain in school beyond grade 12 or the equivalent in order to meet a standard which reflects their maximum potential.

– Reflect Reasonable Level of Competence

(10) For pupils with diagnosed learning disabilities, as well as for pupils participating in the regular school program, proficiency assessments may be part of the classroom experience, and teaching materials may be used as assessment materials.

– May Be Part of Classroom Experience

(e) Governing boards maintaining elementary or junior high schools located within a school district maintaining a high school shall adopt standards of proficiency in basic skills which are articulated with those standards adopted by the school district maintaining the high school.

– Articulation of Standards

(f) Designated employees of all school districts located within a high school district and one or more designees of the high school district shall meet as necessary to review the effectiveness of articulation procedures.

– Plan for Articulation of Standards

(g) Standards of proficiency shall be adopted by the governing board with the active involvement of parents broadly reflective of the socioeconomic composition of the district, administrators, teachers, counselors, and, with respect to standards in secondary schools, pupils.

– Active Involvement of Parents, Professionals, Pupils

WITHHOLDING OF DIPLOMA OF GRADUATION

(Education Code - Part 28)

(AB 3369 - Chapter 1333, Statutes of 1980)

51412. No diploma, certificate or other document, except transcripts and letters of recommendation, shall be conferred on a pupil as evidence of completion of a prescribed course of study or training, or of satisfactory attendance, unless such pupil has met the standards of proficiency in basic skills prescribed by the governing board of the high school district, or equivalent thereof, pursuant to Article 2.5 (commencing with Section 51215) of Chapter 2.

– Standards of Proficiency in Basic Skills

WAGES TO INDIVIDUALS WITH EXCEPTIONAL NEEDS

(Education Code - Part 28)

(AB 369 - Chapter 1296, Statutes of 1993)

51768. The governing board of any school district providing work experience and work study education may provide for employment under the program of pupils in part-time jobs located in areas outside the district, either within this state or in a contiguous state, and the employment may be by any public or private employer. The districts may pay wages to persons receiving the training whether assigned within or without the district and may provide workers' compensation insurance as may be necessary, but no payments may be made to or for private employers. However, wages to individuals with exceptional needs, as defined in Section 56026, may be paid to or for private employers as part of work experience programs funded through the annual Budget Act for these individuals.

- Wages to Individuals with Exceptional Needs

LOW INCIDENCE DISABILITIES AND VOCATIONAL ED OPPORTUNITIES

(Education Code - Part 28)

(As Amended by AB 3235, Chapter 1288, Statutes of 1994)

52315. Any visually impaired, orthopedically impaired, or deaf person who is not enrolled in a regular high school or community college program may attend a regional occupational center or regional occupational program on the same basis as a high school pupil. Additional special instruction and support services shall be provided to these persons.

- Not Enrolled in Regular* High School or Community College Program

If the Superintendent of Public Instruction determines that there would be a duplication of effort to these impaired persons if a regional occupational center or regional occupational program provided services to them, in that other programs exist that are available to them, the superintendent may disapprove of the curriculum to provide programs to these impaired persons pursuant to Section 52309 and of any state funding made available pursuant to Section 41897 for these purposes.

*(Section 52315 Amended in 1994

SCHOOL-BASED PROGRAMS COORDINATION

(Education Code - Part 28)

(As Amended by AB 3235, Chapter 1288, Statutes of 1994)

52860. If a school district and school choose to include within the provisions of this article funds allocated pursuant to Part 30 (commencing with Section 56000), the school district shall comply with all requirements of that part, with the following exceptions:

- Inclusion of Funds Allocated*
  Pursuant to Special Education Programs

(a) Resource specialist program services, designated instruction and services, and team teaching for special day classes, except special day classes operating pursuant to Section 56364.1, may be provided to pupils who have not been identified as individuals with exceptional needs, provided that all identified individuals with exceptional needs are appropriately served and a description of the services is included in the schoolsite plan.

(b) Programs for individuals with exceptional needs shall be under the direction of credentialed special education personnel, but services may be provided entirely by personnel not funded by special education moneys, provided that all services specified in the individualized education program are received by the pupil.

52863. Any governing board, on behalf of a school site council, may request the State Board of Education to grant a waiver of this article. The State Board of Education may grant a request when it finds that the failure to do so would hinder the implementation or maintenance of a successful school-based coordinated program.

- Waiver of Provisions

If the State Board of Education approves a waiver request, the waiver shall apply only to the school or schools which requested the waiver and shall be effective for no more than two years. The State Board of Education may renew a waiver request.

[Persons interested in the School-Based Programs Coordination Act should review all of Chapter 12 of Part 28 of the Education Code (commencing with Section 52800).]

*(Section 52860 Amended in 1994)

EDUCATION CODE - PART 32 - STATE SPECIAL SCHOOLS AND CENTERS

CHAPTER 1. CALIFORNIA SCHOOLS FOR THE DEAF

Article 1. Administration

— ADMINISTRATION

59000. There are two state schools for the deaf, known and designated as the California School for the Deaf, Northern California, and the California School for the Deaf, Southern California. The term "California School for the Deaf" shall refer to both schools unless the context otherwise requires.

— Location and Designation of Schools

59001. The California School for the Deaf is part of the public school system of the state except that it derives no revenue from the State School Fund, and has for its object the education of the deaf who, because of their severe hearing loss and educational needs, cannot be provided an appropriate educational program and related services in the regular public schools.

— Purpose

59002. The California Schools for the Deaf are under the administration of the State Department of Education.

The Superintendent of Public Instruction, in connection with the California Schools for the Deaf, shall do all of the following:

(a) Provide educational assessments and individual educational recommendations for individuals who are referred for those services pursuant to Section 56326.

(b) Maintain a comprehensive elementary educational program, including related services, for deaf individuals.

(c) Serve as a regional secondary educational program providing a comprehensive secondary education, including a full-range academic curriculum, appropriate prevocational and vocational preparation opportunities, and nonacademic and extracurricular activities.

— Administration

59002.5. The Superintendent of Public Instruction, in connection with the California Schools for the Deaf and in cooperation with public and private agencies, may do one or more of the following:

(a) Serve as a demonstration school to promote personnel development through student teaching, in-service education, internships, professional observations for special education and related services personnel in cooperation with institutions of higher education and local education agencies.

— Duties of Superintendent of Public Instruction

(b) Serve as a resource center to develop and disseminate special curriculum, media teaching methods, and instructional materials adapted for deaf individuals, achievement tests and other assessment methods useful to the instruction of deaf individuals.

(c) Provide counseling and information services for parents, guardians, and families of deaf individuals, and public information about deafness to community groups and other agencies.

(d) Conduct experimental programs and projects to promote improvement in special education for deaf individuals.

(e) Promote and coordinate community and continuing education opportunities for deaf individuals utilizing existing community resources.

59003. The State Department of Education in relation to the California Schools for the Deaf shall:

— Duties of Department of Education

(a) Prescribe rules for the government of the schools.

(b) Appoint the superintendents and other officers and employees.

(c) Remove for cause any officer, teacher, or employee.

(d) Fix the compensation of officers, teachers, and employees.

59004. The superintendent of the school shall have had not less than three years' experience in the art of teaching the deaf and shall hold a credential issued by the State Board of Education authorizing him to teach in secondary schools of this state.

— Qualifications of Schools Superintendent

59005. The powers and duties of the superintendents of the schools are such as are assigned by the Superintendent of Public Instruction.

— Powers and Duties

59006. The Superintendent of Public Instruction may authorize the California Schools for the Deaf to establish and maintain teacher training courses designed to prepare teachers of the public schools and such other persons holding a credential issued by the State Board of Education as are recommended by the president of a campus of the California State University, to give instruction to the deaf and the hard of hearing. The Superintendent of Public Instruction shall prescribe standards for the admission of persons to the courses, and for the content of the courses.

— Teacher Training Courses

The California Schools for the Deaf may enter into agreements with the Trustees of the California State University, the University of California, or any other university or college accredited by the State Board of Education as a teacher training educational institution, to provide practice teaching required for issuance of the credential authorizing the holder to teach the deaf and severely hard of hearing. The agreement may provide a reasonable payment, for services rendered, to teachers of the California Schools for the Deaf who have practice teachers under their direction.

59007. The State Department of Education may employ any person, otherwise qualified, who has retired for service under either the Public Employees' Retirement System or the State Teachers' Retirement System as a substitute in a position requiring certification qualifications at the California Schools for the Deaf, except that the total of that service and any service rendered pursuant to Section 23919 shall not exceed 90 teaching days in any one fiscal year.

– Employment of Retired Teacher as Substitute

Article 2. Pupils

– PUPILS

59020. Every deaf person between the ages of 3 and 21 years, who is a resident of the state and who meets the criteria set forth in this section, is entitled to an education in the California School for the Deaf free of charge.

– Eligibility and Priority for Admission

Priority in admission to the California School for the Deaf shall be given to elementary age deaf minors residing in sparsely populated regions and to secondary age deaf minors in need of a high school program, for whom appropriate comprehensive educational facilities and services are not available or cannot be reasonably provided by their local school districts or county educational agencies.

The criteria of admission to California Schools for the Deaf and Blind shall be administratively determined by the Superintendent of Public Instruction.

59023. If the parent or guardian of any pupil in the school is unable either himself or from the estate of the child to clothe the child, or pay for its transportation to and from school, or for necessary dental work, eye care, operations, and hospitalization of the child while at the school, or is unable either himself or from the estate of the child to reimburse the Department of Education for expenses incurred by it inn providing dental work, eye care, operations, or hospitalization for the child in an emergency, the parent or guardian may apply for a certificate to that effect to the superior court of the county of which the parent or guardian of the child is a resident. If the court is satisfied that the parent or guardian either himself or from the estate of the child is unable to pay for any such service, it shall issue a certificate to that effect. The application for the certificate may also be made to the court by the superintendent of the school.

– Inability to Pay Expenses

59024. If it appears to the satisfaction of the court that the parent or guardian has sufficient pecuniary ability or that there are sufficient funds in the estate of the child to provide the

– Court Action Regarding Funds to Support the Child

service for the child or to reimburse the Department of Education for expenses incurred by it in providing the service for the child in an emergency, the court shall not issue the certificate, but shall, according to the nature of the application before it, either order the superintendent to provide the child with the service or order the parent or guardian either himself or from the estate of the child, as the court determines, to reimburse the Department of Education for expenses incurred by it in providing the service for the child in an emergency.

59025. If the Department of Education is not reimbursed by the parent or guardian personally or from the estate of the child for expenditures made by the superintendent under the order of the court or if the parent or guardian does not comply with an order of the court to reimburse the Department of Education either personally or from the estate of the child for expenses incurred by it in providing the service for the child in an emergency, the superintendent may sue the parent or guardian, in the name of the state, to recover any money paid out by order of the court or due the Department of Education as reimbursement under an order of the court.

– Suit for Recovery

59026. All money expended under the authority of any such certificate for clothing and transportation, necessary dental work, eye care, operations, and hospitalization, and all money expended by the Department of Education for expenses incurred by it in providing dental work, eye care, operations, or hospitalization for the child in an emergency for which the Department of Education cannot be reimbursed by the parent or guardian of the child as shown by the certificate, constitutes a legal charge against the county from which the certificate is issued. Expenditures for clothing and transportation shall not exceed the sum of three hundred eight-five ($385) for the 1974-75 school year, and an amount thereafter which shall be adjusted annually in conformance with the Consumer Price Index, all items, of the Bureau of Labor Statistics of the United States Department of Labor, measured for the calendar year next preceding the fiscal year to which it applies. The State Controller shall determine the amount authorized pursuant to this section for the 1975-76 school year and thereafter.

– County Responsibility for Nonreimbursed Expenditures

59027. The certificate shall be presented to the superintendent of the school. When the certificate shows that the parent or guardian of the child is unable either himself or from the estate of the child to clothe the child, or pay for his transportation to and from school, or for necessary dental work, eye care, operations, and hospitalization of the child while in school, the superintendent shall clothe the child and provide the transportation, necessary dental work, eye care, operations, and

– Payment of Expenses

hospitalization. The expense of the services, or any of them, shall be advanced by the Department of Education out of money appropriated for the support of the school.

59028. Upon presentation to the county in which the certificate is issued, of an itemized claim, duly sworn to by the superintendent of the school before an officer authorized to administer oaths, for the expense for clothing, transportation, and other items provided and furnished under the authority of the certificate, or for the reimbursement of the Department of Education, the claim shall be processed and paid pursuant to the provisions of Chapter 4 (commencing with Section 29700) of Division 3 of Title 3 of the Government Code. The amount paid and all reimbursements of the Department of Education under this section shall be credited to the current appropriation for the support and maintenance of the schools.

– Audit, Approval, and Credit of the Claim

59029. All pupils in the school shall be maintained at the expense of the state, except as provided in Sections 59021, 59023 to 59028, inclusive, 59030, and 59031.

– Maintenance of Pupils

59030. The governing board of each school district of residence shall, from the general fund of the school district, pay for the transportation cost of each pupil of the district in attendance at the California School for the Deaf as a day-class pupil.

For determining the school district responsible under the provisions of this section for making the payment when the pupils reside in other than unified school district, pupils 15 years of age or older as of September 1 of each fiscal year shall be considered residents of the high school district, and pupils 14 years of age or under as of September 1 shall be considered residents of the elementary district.

– Payment of Transportation Cost for Day-Class Pupils By District of Residence

59030.5. The Superintendent of Public Instruction shall allow to the California Schools for the Deaf, an amount not to exceed three hundred eighty-nine dollars ($389) per fiscal year per unit of average daily attendance of each deaf pupil attending one of the schools as a five-day residential pupil for the purpose of providing transportation to and from the pupil's home on weekends and school holiday periods. In no case shall the total apportionment made to the schools exceed the actual total transportation expenditures of the schools.

The administrators of such schools shall arrange for transportation of such pupils utilizing the most practical means including but not be limited to, commercial bus, rail, or air, charter bus or private passenger vehicle.

– Transportation of Pupils to and from Home on Weekends and School Holiday Periods

59031. Deaf persons not residents of this state may be admitted to the benefits of the school upon paying to the Department of Education the school year cost for the

– Payment Required of Nonresidents

maintenance, care, and instruction of persons at the school, payable quarterly in advance. The cost of the care, maintenance, and instruction shall be determined by the Department of Education with the approval of the Department of Finance.

Article 3. Services

59040. The Department of Education, in connection with the California School for the Deaf, may establish and maintain a preschool and kindergarten service for the care and teaching of children under school age. The department shall prescribe the rules and regulations which shall govern the conduct of the preschool and kindergarten service, appoint such teachers as it determines necessary, and fix their salaries.

59041. The Department of Education, in connection with the California School for the Deaf, may offer courses of instruction to parents of a deaf child to assist and instruct the parents in the early care and training of such child, to train the child in play, and to do everything which will assure the child's physical, mental and social adjustment to its environment.

59042. The Superintendent of Public Instruction may authorize the California School for the Deaf to establish and maintain a testing center for deaf and hard-of-hearing minors. It shall be the purpose of this center to test hearing acuity and to give such other tests as may be necessary for advising parents and school authorities concerning an appropriate educational program for the child.

59043. Nothing in this article and no rule or regulation established thereunder shall authorize the compulsory physical examination or medical treatment of any child or minor if the parent or guardian objects on the ground that such examination or treatment is contrary to the religious beliefs of such parent or guardian.

59044. The Department of Education, in connection with the California School for the Deaf which maintains automobile driver training courses, may purchase from available funds public liability, property damage, collision, fire, theft, and comprehensive automobile insurance for motor vehicles, whether owned by private parties or such school for the deaf, used in connection with such courses.

59045. The Superintendent of Public Instruction, in conjunction with the California Schools for the Deaf, shall provide assessment and instructional planning services for individuals who are referred for those services pursuant to Section 56326.

- SERVICES
- Authority to Establish Preschool and Kindergarten Service

- Courses of Instruction For Parents

- Testing Center

- Prohibition of Compulsory Medical Treatment Over Objection of Parents

- Insurance for Automobile Driver Training Courses

- Educational Assessment Service

CHAPTER 2. CALIFORNIA SCHOOL FOR THE BLIND

Article 1. Administration

59100. There is one state school for the blind, known and designated as the California School for the Blind.

59101. The California School for the Blind is a part of the public school system of the state except that it derives no revenue from the State School Fund, and has for its object the education of visually impaired, blind, and deaf-blind pupils who, because of their severe sensory loss and educational needs, cannot be provided an appropriate educational needs, cannot be provided an appropriate educational program and related services in the regular public schools.

59102. The California School for the Blind is under the administration of the State Department of Education.

The Superintendent of Public Instruction, in connection with the California School for the Blind, shall do all of the following:

(a) Provide educational assessments and individual educational recommendations for individuals referred for those services pursuant to Section 56326.

(b) Maintain a comprehensive elementary and secondary educational program, including related services and nonacademic and extracurricular activities for visually impaired, blind, and deaf-blind individuals.

59102.5. The Superintendent of Public Instruction, in connection with the California School for the Blind and in cooperation with public and private agencies, may:

(a) Serve as a demonstration school to promote personnel development through student teaching, in-service education, internships, and professional observations for special education and related services personnel, in cooperation with institutions of higher education and local education agencies.

(b) Serve as a resource center to develop and disseminate special curriculum, media, teaching methods and instructional materials adapted for visually impaired, blind, and deaf-blind individuals, and public information about sensory losses to community groups and other agencies.

(c) Provide counseling and information services to parents, guardians, and families of visually impaired, blind, or deaf-blind individuals, and public information about sensory losses to community groups and other agencies.

(d) Conduct experimental programs and projects to promote improvement in special education for visually impaired, blind, and deaf-blind individuals.

(e) Promote community and continuing education opportunities for visually impaired, blind, and deaf-blind individuals utilizing existing community resources.

59103. The Department of Education in relation to the California School for the Blind shall:

– Duties of Department of Education

(a) Prescribe rules for the government of the school.

(b) Appoint the superintendent and other officers and employees.

(c) Remove for cause any officer, teacher, or employee.

(d) Fix the compensation of officers, teachers, and employees.

Article 2. Teaching Force

– TEACHING FORCE

59110. The superintendent of the school shall have had not less than three years' experience in the art of teaching the blind and shall hold a credential issued by the State Board of Education authorizing him to teach in secondary schools of this state.

– Qualifications of Superintendent

59111. The powers and duties of the superintendent of the school are such as are assigned by the Superintendent of Public Instruction.

– Powers and Duties

59112. There is hereby created at the California School for the Blind the position of fieldworker to be appointed by the superintendent of the school with the approval of the Superintendent of Public Instruction. The fieldworker shall be a member of the teaching staff of the California School for the Blind and shall receive a salary fixed and payable in accordance with law.

– Qualifications of Fieldworker

The fieldworker shall visit graduates and former pupils of the school in their homes to advise them regarding the extension and continuance of their education, to assist them in securing remunerative employment, to improve their economic condition in all possible ways, and to provide them with preparatory instruction found necessary for a selected occupation. The fieldworker shall be a person who has had special training for such work. Blindness shall not be grounds to disqualify a person for this position.

59113. The Department of Education may employ any person, otherwise qualified, who has retired for service under either the Public Employees' Retirement System or the State Teachers' Retirement System as a substitute in a position requiring certification qualifications at the California School for the Blind; provided, that the total of such service and any service rendered pursuant to Section 23919 shall not exceed 90 teaching days in any one fiscal year.

– Employment of Retired Teacher As Substitute

Article 3. Pupils

59120. Every blind person resident of this state, of suitable age and capacity, is entitled to an education in the California School for the Blind free of charge.

59123. All pupils in the school shall be maintained at the expense of the state, except as provided in Sections 59121, 59124 to 59128, inclusive, and 59131.

59124. The governing board of each school district of residence shall, from the general fund of the school district, pay for the transportation cost of each pupil of the district in attendance at the California School for the Blind as a day-class pupil.

For determining the school district responsible under the provisions of this section for making the payment when the pupils reside in other than a unified school district, pupils 15 years of age or older as of September 1 of each fiscal year shall be considered residents of the high school district, and pupils 14 years of age or under as of September 1 shall be considered residents of the elementary district.

59124.5. The Superintendent of Public Instruction shall allow to the California School for the Blind, an amount not to exceed three hundred eighty-nine dollars ($389) per fiscal year per unit of average daily attendance of each blind pupil attending the school as a five-day residential pupil for the purpose of providing transportation to and from the pupil's home on weekends and school holiday periods. In no case shall the total apportionment made to the school exceed the actual total transportation expenditures of the school.

The administrators of such schools shall arrange for transportation of such pupils utilizing the most practical means including, but not limited to, commercial bus, rail, or air, charter bus or private passenger vehicle.

59125. If the parent or guardian of any pupil in the school is unable either himself or from the estate of the child to clothe the child, or pay for its transportation to and from school, or for necessary dental work, eye care, operations, and hospitalization of the child while at the school, or is unable either himself or from the estate of the child to reimburse the Department of Education for expenses incurred by it in providing dental work, eye care, operations, or hospitalization for the child in an emergency, the parent or guardian may apply for a certificate to that effect to the superior court of the county of which the parent or guardian of the child is resident. If the court is satisfied that the parent or guardian either himself or from the estate of the child is unable to pay for any such service, it shall issue a certificate to that effect. The application for the certificate may also be made to the court by the superintendent of the school.

59126. The certificate shall be presented to the superintendent of the school and the superintendent when the certificate shows the parent or guardian of the child is unable either himself or from the estate of the child to clothe the child, or pay for his transportation to and from school, or for necessary dental work, eye care, operations, and hospitalization of the child while in school, shall clothe the child and provide the transportation, dental work, eye care, operations, and hospitalization. The expense of the services, or any of them, shall be advanced by the Department of Education out of money appropriated for the support of the school.

– Payment of Expenses

59127. All money expended under the authority of any such certificate for clothing and transportation, necessary dental work, eye care, operations and hospitalization, and all money expended by the Department of Education for expenses incurred by it in providing dental work, eye care, operations, or hospitalization for the child in an emergency for which the Department of Education cannot be reimbursed by the parent or guardian of the child as shown by the certificate, constitutes a legal charge against the county from which the certificate is issued. Expenditures for clothing and transportation shall not exceed the sum of three hundred eighty-five dollars ($385) for the 1974-75 school year, and an amount thereafter which shall be adjusted annually in conformance with the Consumer Price Index, all items, of the Bureau of Labor Statistics of the United States Department of Labor, measured for the calendar year next preceding the fiscal year to which it applies. The State Controller shall determine the amount authorized pursuant to this section for the 1975-76 school year and thereafter.

– County Responsibility for Nonreimbursed Expenditures

59128. Upon presentation to the county in which the certificate is issued, of an itemized claim, duly sworn to by the superintendent of the school before an officer authorized to administer oaths, for the expense for clothing, transportation, and other items provided and furnished under the authority of the certificate, or for the reimbursement of the Department of Education, the claim shall be processed and paid pursuant to the provisions of Chapter 4 (commencing with Section 29700) of Division 3 of Title 3 of the Government Code. The amount paid and all reimbursements of the Department of Education under this section shall be credited to the current appropriation for the support and maintenance of the school.

– Presentation, Audit, Approval of Claim Against County

59129. If it appears to the satisfaction of the court that the parent or guardian has sufficient pecuniary ability or that there are sufficient funds in the estate of the child to provide the

– Court Powers

service for the child or to reimburse the Department of Education for expenses incurred by it on providing the service for the child in an emergency, the court shall not issue the certification, but shall according to the nature of the application before it, either order the superintendent to provide the child with the service, or order the parent or guardian either himself or from the estate of the child, as the court determines, to reimburse the Department of Education for expenses incurred by it in providing the service for the child in an emergency.

59130. If the Department of Education is not reimbursed by the parent or guardian personally or from the estate of the child for expenditures made by the superintendent under the order of the court or if the parent or guardian does not comply with an order of the court to reimburse the Department of Education either personally or from the estate of the child for expenses incurred by it in providing the service for the child in an emergency the superintendent may sue the parent or guardian, in the name of the state, to recover any money paid out by order of the court or due the Department of Education as reimbursement under an order of the court.

– Suit by Department to Recover Money Paid Out or Due as Reimbursement

59131. Blind persons not residents of this state may be admitted to the benefits of the school upon paying the Department of Education the sum of the school year for the maintenance, care, and instruction of persons at the school, payable in quarterly in advance. The cost of the care, maintenance, and instruction shall be determined by the Department of Education with the approval of the Department of Finance.

– Payment Required of Nonresidents

Article 4. Services and Courses

– SERVICES AND COURSES

59140. The Department of Education, in connection with the California School for the Blind, shall establish and maintain a kindergarten service for the care and teaching of children under school age. The department shall prescribe the rules and regulations which shall govern the conduct of the kindergarten service, appoint such teachers as it determines necessary, and fix their salaries.

– Kindergarten

59141. The Department of Education shall create the position of visiting teacher to blind children of preschool age. With the consent of the parents of any blind child of preschool age it shall be the duties of such visiting teacher to assist and instruct the parents in the early care and training of said child, to train the child in play, and to do everything which will assure the child's physical, mental and social adjustment to its environment. The Department of Education shall maintain a sufficient number of

– Visiting Teachers

visiting teachers to adequately serve the need of parents of preschool blind children in accordance with the known number of such children. In any event the caseload of each visiting teacher shall not exceed a number of clients that can be adequately and fully served.

59142. The Department of Education, in addition to the teaching and education of the blind of suitable age, shall adopt measures and prescribe rules for the giving of vocational training to the pupils at the school, in order that they may be equipped upon their graduation to engage in occupations or industries by which they may become self-supporting. The board shall determine the nature and scope of the vocational training, with the view of best adapting the blind to follow useful and productive pursuits, after the completion of their education.

    — Vocational Training

59143. The Superintendent of Public Instruction may authorize the California School for the Blind to establish and maintain, either independently or in cooperation with the University of California or Trustees of the California State University, teacher training courses for teachers of the blind. The Superintendent of Public Instruction shall establish standards for the admission of persons to the courses, and for the content of the courses.

    — Teacher Training

The California School for the Blind may enter into one or more agreements with the Trustees of the California State University, the University of California, or any other university or college accredited by the State Board of Education as a teacher training educational institution, to provide practice teaching required for issuance of the credentials authorizing the holder to teach visually impaired, blind, or deaf-blind individuals, or provide orientation and mobility instruction. The agreement or agreements may provide for a reasonable payment, for services rendered, to teachers of the California School for the Blind who have practice teachers under their direction.

59144. The Superintendent of Public Instruction, in conjunction with the California School for the Blind, shall provide assessment and instructional planning services for individuals who are referred for those services pursuant to Section 56326.

    — Instructional Planning Service for the Blind

CHAPTER 3. DIAGNOSTIC CENTERS

Article 1. Administration

    — ADMINISTRATION

59200. There are three diagnostic centers, to be known and designated as Diagnostic Center, Northern California, Diagnostic

    — Designation of Centers

Center, Central California, and Diagnostic Center, Southern California.

59201. The diagnostic centers are a part of the public school system of the state, except that they derive no revenue from the State School Fund, and have for their object the diagnosis of disabled children, and the determination of the treatment and educational program for those children. These centers provide temporary residence for children, who, by reason of their disabilities, need educational diagnostic services not available in regular public school classes.

— Status and Purpose

59202. The centers are under the administration of the Superintendent of Public Instruction.

— Administration

59203. The Superintendent of Public Instruction, in relation to the diagnostic centers, shall do all of the following:

— Duties of Superintendent of Public Instruction

(a) Prescribe rules for the government of the centers.

(b) Appoint the superintendents of the centers and other officers and employees.

(c) Remove for cause any officer, teacher, or employee.

(d) Fix the compensation of teachers.

(e) Determine the length of, and the time for, vacations of teachers.

(f) Contract with the University of California, or with other public or private hospitals or schools of medicine, for the establishment and maintenance of diagnostic service and treatment centers for disabled children.

59204. The Superintendent of Public Instruction, in connection with the diagnostic centers, also shall do all of the following:

— Special Services and Assessments

(a) Make comprehensive diagnostic assessments of individuals referred for that service pursuant to Section 56326.

(b) Provide instructional planning services for individuals assessed under subdivision (a).

(c) Provide counseling services for parents, guardians, and families of disabled children.

(d) Maintain a model assessment service and demonstration classrooms to develop appropriate individual educational programs for pupils and to assist local school districts in providing appropriate programs and services for disabled children.

59204.5. The Superintendent of Public Instruction, in connection with the diagnostic centers and in cooperation with public and private agencies, may:

— Experimental Assessment Projects; Demonstration School

(a) Conduct experimental assessment projects designed to meet needs of those categories of disabled children selected by the Superintendent of Public Instruction.

(b) Serve as a demonstration program to promote personnel development through student teaching, in-service education, internships, and professional observations for special education and related services personnel, in cooperation with institutions of higher education and local education agencies.

Article 2. Teaching Force

59210. The powers and duties of the superintendents of the diagnostic centers are such as are assigned by the Superintendent of Public Instruction.

59211. The Superintendent of Public Instruction may, in cooperation with an accredited college or university, authorize the diagnostic centers to establish and maintain teacher training courses designed to prepare teachers to teacher training courses designed to prepare teachers to instruct disabled children in special classes in the public school system. The Superintendent of Public Instruction, in cooperation with an accredited college or university, shall prescribe standards for the admission of persons to the courses, and for the contents of the courses. Courses conducted in the diagnostic centers shall be counted toward requirements of a credential in the area of the educationally handicapped upon the establishment of the credential.

The diagnostic centers may enter into one or more agreements with Trustees of the California State University, the University of California, or any other university or college accredited by the State Board of Education as a teacher training educational institution, to provide practice teaching required for issuance of the credential authorizing the holder to teach the educationally handicapped. The agreement or agreements may provide for a reasonable payment, for services rendered, to teachers of the diagnostic centers who have practice teachers under their direction.

Article 3. Pupils

59220. Every resident of California less than 21 years of age, of suitable age and capacity, as determined by means of diagnosis at the diagnostic centers, is entitled to services, free of charge.

Disabled children who are not residents of California may be admitted to a diagnostic center upon paying to the State Department of Education, quarterly in advance, the actual support cost at the average cost of maintaining pupils in the center for the period in question. This cost shall be determined by the State Department of Education with the approval of the Department of Finance.

59223. The Superintendent of Public Instruction shall allow to the diagnostic centers an amount not to exceed three hundred eighty-nine dollars ($389) per fiscal year per unit of average daily attendance of each pupil attending one of the diagnostic centers as a five-day residential pupil for the purpose of providing transportation to and from the pupil's home on weekends and school holiday periods. In no case shall the total apportionment made to the centers exceed the actual total transportation expenditures of the centers.

The administrators of the centers shall arrange for transportation of the pupils, utilizing the most practical means, including, but not limited to, commercial bus, rail, or air, charter bus, or private passenger vehicle.

– Transportation of Pupils
 to and from Home on
 Weekends and School Holiday
 Periods

CHAPTER 4. FINANCE

Article 1. Local Contribution

– LOCAL CONTRIBUTION

59300. Notwithstanding any provision of this part to the contrary, the district of residence of the parent or guardian of any pupil attending a state-operated school pursuant to this part, excluding day pupils, shall pay the school of attendance for each pupil an amount equal to 10 percent of the excess annual cost of education of pupils attending a state-operated school pursuant to this part.

– Ten Percent Excess Cost

SPECIAL EDUCATION PROGRAM SUNSET DATE

(Education Code - Part 34)

(AB 2298 - Chapter 528, Statutes of 1992)

62000.8. The special education program shall sunset on June 30, 1998.

— Sunset Date of June 30, 1998

NONCODIFIED SECTIONS

[Noncodified sections of statutes have the same force of law as codified sections but they do not appear in a specific code (e.g. Education Code or Government Code). If a noncodified section becomes law, it appears in the chaptered version of the legislative bill.]

REVIEW OF FUNDING FORMULAS FOR INFANT AND PRESCHOOL PROGRAMS

(Noncodified Section)

(AB 369 - Chapter 1296, Statutes of 1993)

SECTION 36.3.   During the 1993-94 fiscal year, the superintendent shall review the current funding formulas for special education and related services provided to individuals with exceptional needs between the ages of birth and five years of age, pursuant to Chapter 4.4 (commencing with Section 56425) and Chapter 4.45 (commencing with Section 56440) to determine if the funding is distributed on an equitable basis and in a manner that does not provide an incentive to categorize children under any one particular disability label.   Upon completion of the review, the superintendent shall make recommendations for any revisions to the funding formulas to the Legislature.

— Review Current Funding Formulas for Infant/Preschool

VOIDED TITLE 5 REGULATIONS

(Noncodified Section)

(AB 1250 - Chapter 921, Statutes of 1994)

Section 11. The Legislature hereby declares that Sections 3061 to 3067, inclusive, of Title 5 of the California Code of Regulations are void and without effect on or after January 1, 1995.

— Sections 3061-3067 of Title 5 Regulations Voided

SPECIAL EDUCATION PROGRAMS FOR HARD-OF-HEARING OR DEAF PUPILS

(Noncodified Sections)

(AB 1836 - Chapter 1126, Statutes of 1994)

Section 5. By amending Sections 56000.5, 56001, and 56345 of the Education Code by Sections 1, 2, 2.5, and 4 of this act, and by adding Section 56026.2 to the Education Code by Section 3, it is the intent of the Legislature to ensure that state law complies with the requirements of federal law under the Individuals with Disabilities Education Act (20 U.S.C. Sec. 1400 et seq.)

– Legislative Intent

Section 6. The changes made to Section 56000.5, 56001, and 56345 of the Education Code by Sections 1, 2, 2.5, and 4 and the provisions of Section 56026.2, as added to the Education Code by Section 3, shall be implemented only to the extent that funds are specifically appropriated for that purpose in the annual Budget Act. Notwithstanding Section 17610 of the Government Code, if the Commission on State Mandates determines that this act contains costs mandated by the state, reimbursement to local agencies and school districts for those costs shall be made pursuant to Part 7 (commencing with Section 17500) of Division 4 of Title 2 of the Government Code. If the statewide cost of the claim for reimbursement does not exceed one million dollars ($1,000,000), reimbursement shall be made from the State Mandates Claims Fund. Notwithstanding Section 17580 of the Government Code, unless otherwise specified in this act, the provisions of this act shall become operative on the same date that the act takes effect pursuant to the California Constitution.

– Implemented to Extent Funds are Appropriated

INDIVIDUALIZED EDUCATION PROGRAM FOR VISUALLY IMPAIRED PUPILS

(Noncodified Sections)

(AB 2445 - Chapter 998, Statutes of 1994)

Section 1. The Legislature hereby finds and declares the following:

(a) Functionally blind pupils and some pupils with other severe visual impairments who have the ability to read require instruction in braille if they are to maximize their academic potential and have the greatest chances for success throughout their lives. There are pupils in California who are visually

– Legislative Findings and Declarations

impaired for whom braille is the appropriate reading method but who are not receiving instruction in braille. In the development of the individualized education programs for pupils who are visually impaired, there is a presumption that proficiency in braille reading and writing is essential for the pupils' satisfactory education progress and independent functioning.

Section 4. It is the intent of the Legislature in enacting this act not to exceed any requirements mandated by federal law or its implementing regulations.

– Not to Exceed Federal Mandates

RESTRAINING DEVICES IN SCHOOLBUSES

(Noncodified Section)

(AB 2798 - Chapter 513, Statutes of 1994)

Section 1. The Legislature recognizes that disabled pupils are entitled to safe and secure transportation. It is the intent of the Legislature, therefore, that schoolbuses be properly equipped with restraining devices to safely transport pupils who are confined to wheelchairs. It is also the intent of the Legislature that no school district deny transportation to any pupil due to the incompatibility of a wheelchair and bus securement systems.

– Transporting Pupils Confined to Wheelchairs

FEDERAL FUNDING OF SPECIAL EDUCATION UNDER PART B OF THE IDEA

ASSEMBLY JOINT RESOLUTION 87

RESOLUTION CHAPTER 73, STATUTES OF 1994

WHEREAS, The Congress of the United States enacted the Education for All Handicapped Children Act of 1975 (Public Law 94-142), now known as the Individuals with Disabilities Education Act (IDEA), to assure that all children with disabilities in the United States have available to them a free appropriate public education which emphasizes special education and related services designed to meet their unique needs, to assure that the rights of children with disabilities and their parents or guardians are protected, to assist states and localities to provide for the education of all children with disabilities, and to assess and assure the effectiveness of efforts to educate children with disabilities; and

WHEREAS, The Congress of the United States developed a formula in 1975 to determine the maximum amount of funding to which states are entitled for purposes of implementing the federal mandates to provide special education and related services. That entitlement amounts to "40 per centum, for the fiscal year ending September 30, 1982, and for each fiscal year thereafter, of the average per pupil expenditure in public elementary and secondary schools in the United States," multiplied by the number of children receiving special education and related services; and

WHEREAS, 1995 budget appropriations measures currently pending before Congress only propose to fund special education programs in the states, under Part B of IDEA, at approximately 7 percent. That amount is 3 percent less than Section 1411 of Title 20 of the United States Code authorized for the fiscal year ending September 30, 1979; and

WHEREAS, The California Master Plan for Special Education was approved for statewide implementation in 1980 on the basis of the anticipated federal commitment to fund special education programs at the federally authorized level; and

WHEREAS, The Governor's Budget for the 1994-95 fiscal year includes $1.6 billion in General Fund support for special education programs; and

WHEREAS, The State of California anticipates receiving approximately $220 million in federal special education funds under Part B of IDEA for the 1994-95 school year, even though the federally authorized level of funding would provide over $900 million annually to California; and

WHEREAS, In addition to the $168 million local general fund contribution required by state law, local educational agencies in California have to pay for the underfunded federal mandates for special education programs, at the cost of approximately $600 million annually, from regular education program money, thereby reducing funding that is available for other education programs; and

WHEREAS, Whether or not California participates in the IDEA grant program, the state has to meet the requirements of Section 504 of the federal Rehabilitation Act of 1973 (29 U.S.C. Sec. 701) and its implementing regulations (34 C.F.R. 104), which prohibit recipients of federal financial assistance, including educational institutions, from discriminating on the basis of disability, yet not federal funds are available under that act for state grants; and

WHEREAS, California is committed to providing a free and appropriate public education to children and youth with disabilities, in order to meet their unique needs; and

WHEREAS, The California Legislature is extremely concerned that, since 1978, Congress has not given states the full amount of financial assistance necessary to achieve its goal of ensuring children and youth with disabilities equal protection of the laws; now, therefore, be it

Resolved by the Assembly and Senate of the State of California, jointly, That the Legislature respectfully memorializes the President and Congress of the United States to provide the full 40 percent federal share of funding for special education programs by the year 2000, so that California and other states participating in these critical programs will not have to take funding from other vital state and local programs to fund underfunded federal mandates; and be it further

Resolved, That the Chief Clerk of the Assembly transmit copies of this resolution to the President and Vice President of the United States, to the Speaker of the House of Representatives, to the Majority Leader of the Senate, to the Chair of the Senate Committee on the Budget and the Chair of the House Committee on the Budget, to the Senate Committee on Appropriations and the Chair of the House Committee on Appropriations, to each Senator and Representative from California in the Congress of the United States, and to the United States Secretary of Education.

NEW FUNDING MECHANISM FOR SPECIAL EDUCATION

ASSEMBLY CONCURRENT RESOLUTION 151

RESOLUTION CHAPTER 118, STATUTES OF 1994

(Supplemental Report on the 1994 Budget Bill)

Report on New Funding Model for the Master Plan for Special Education

It is the intent of the Legislature that the Superintendent of Public Instruction (SPI), the Director of Finance, and the Legislative Analyst, or a designee of each of these persons, shall develop a new funding mechanism for special education programs and services offered in this state. The new funding mechanism shall include, but not be limited to, the following:

a. A method to ensure equity in funding between school districts and county offices of education that provides services to pupils with exceptional needs.

b. An elimination of financial incentives to place pupils in special education programs.

c. A system that recognizes the interaction between funding for special education programs and services, revenue limits for school districts, and funding for categorical programs.

d. A proposal to phase in the newly developed funding formula on a gradual basis over two to five years, so as not to disrupt educational services to students enrolled in regular and special education programs.

In developing the funding mechanism, the SPI, the Director of Finance, and the Legislative Analyst, or designee of each of these persons, shall consult teachers, parents, and administrators of both regular and special education pupils, members of the Advisory Commission on Special Education, and other interested parties.

The three agencies shall reach an overall consensus on a new funding model, but not necessarily consensus on each of its components, and shall submit the new funding model to the appropriate chairs of the committees that consider appropriations, the appropriate policy committee chairs, and the Chair of the Joint Legislative Budget Committee on or before May 31, 1995.

INTERAGENCY RESPONSIBILITIES FOR RELATED SERVICES

(Government Code)

(AB 3632 - Chapter 1747, Statutes of 1984, As Amended by
AB 882 - Chapter 1274, Statutes of 1985, As Amended by
AB 3012 - Chapter 1133, Statutes of 1986, As Amended by
AB 1744 - Chapter 677, Statutes of 1989, As Amended by
AB 1528 - Chapter 182, Statutes of 1990, As Amended by
AB 1060 - Chapter 223, Statutes of 1991, As Amended by
AB 1248 - Chapter 759, Statutes of 1992, As Amended by
AB 1399 - Chapter 489, Statutes of 1993, As Amended by
AB 1892 - Chapter 1128, Statutes of 1994)

SECTION 1. The Legislature hereby finds and declares that a number of state and federal programs make funds available for the provision of education and related services to children with handicaps who are of school age. The Legislature further finds and declares that California has not maximized, or sufficiently coordinated existing state programs, in providing supportive services which are necessary to assist a handicapped child to benefit from special education. — Legislative Findings and Intent

It is the intent of the Legislature that existing services rendered by state and local government agencies serving handicapped children be maximized and coordinated. It is the further intent of the Legislature that specific state and local interagency responsibilities be clarified by this act in order to better serve the educational needs of the state's handicapped children.

CHAPTER 26.5. INTERAGENCY RESPONSIBILITIES FOR PROVIDING SERVICES TO HANDICAPPED CHILDREN

7570. Ensuring maximum utilization of all state and federal resources available to provide children and youth with disabilities, as defined in subsection (1) of Section 1401 of Title 20 of the United States Code, with a free appropriate public education, the provision of related services, as defined in subsection (17) of Section 1401 of Title 20 of the United States Code, and designated instruction and services, as defined in Section 56363 of the Education Code, to children and youth with disabilities, shall be the joint responsibility of the Superintendent of Public Instruction and the Secretary of Health and Welfare. The Superintendent of Public Instruction shall ensure that this chapter is carried out through monitoring and supervision. — Joint Responsibility

7571. The Secretary of Health and Welfare may designate a department of state government to assume he responsibilities described in Section 7570. The secretary, or his or her designee, shall also designate a single agency in each county to coordinate the service responsibilities described in Section 7572.

– Secretary May Designate Department to Assume Responsibilities

7572. (a) A child shall be assessed in all areas related to the suspected disability by those qualified to make a determination of the child's need for the service before any action is taken with respect to the provision of related services or designated instruction and services to a child, including, but not limited to, services in the areas of, occupational therapy, physical therapy, psychotherapy, and other mental health assessments. All assessments required or conducted pursuant to this section shall be governed by the assessment procedures contained in Article 2 (commencing with Section 56320) of Chapter 4 of Part 30 of the Education Code.

– Child Assessed in All Areas Related to Suspected Disability

(b) Occupational therapy and physical therapy assessments shall be conducted by qualified medical personnel as specified in regulations developed by the State Department of Health Services in consultation with the State Department of Education.

– OT/PT Assessments

(c) Psychotherapy and other mental health assessments shall be conducted by qualified mental health professionals as specified in regulations developed by the State Department of Mental Health, in consultation with the State Department of Education, pursuant to this chapter.

– Psychotherapy Assessment

(d) A related service or designated instruction and service shall only be added to the child's individualized education program by the individualized education program team, as described in Part 30 (commencing with Section 56000) of the Education Code, if a formal assessment has been conducted pursuant to this section, and a qualified person conducting the assessment recommended the service in order for the child to benefit from special education. In no case shall the inclusion of necessary related services in a pupil's individualized education plan be contingent upon identifying the funding source. Nothing in this section shall prevent a parent from obtaining an independent assessment in accordance with subdivision (b) of Section 56329 of the Education Code, which shall be considered by the individualized education program team.

– Adding to IEP

(1) Whenever an assessment has been conducted pursuant to subdivision (b) or (c), the recommendation of the person who conducted the assessment shall be reviewed and discussed with the parent and with appropriate members of the individualized education program team prior to the meeting of the individualized education program team. When the proposed recommendation of the person has been discussed with the parent and there is

– Related Service Recommendation

disagreement on the recommendation pertaining to the related service, the parent shall be notified in writing and may require the person who conducted the assessment to attend the individualized education program team meeting to discuss the recommendation. The person who conducted the assessment shall attend the individualized education program team meeting if requested. Following this discussion and review, the recommendation of the person who conducted the assessment shall be the recommendation of the individualized education program team members who are attending on behalf of the local educational agency.

(2) If an independent assessment for the provision of related services or designated instruction and services is submitted to the individualized education program team, review of that assessment shall be conducted by the person specified in subdivisions (b) and (c). The recommendation of the person who reviewed the independent assessment shall be reviewed and discussed with the parent and with appropriate members of the individualized education program team prior to the meeting of the individualized education program team. The parent shall be notified in writing and may request the person who reviewed the independent assessment to attend the individualized education program team meeting to discuss the recommendation. The person who reviewed the independent assessment shall attend the individualized education program team meeting if requested. Following this review and discussion, the recommendation of the person who reviewed the independent assessment shall be the recommendation of the individualized education program team members who are attending on behalf of the local agency.

— Independent Assessment

(3) Any disputes between the parent and team members representing the public agencies regarding a recommendation made in accordance with paragraphs (1) and (2) shall be resolved pursuant to Chapter 5 (commencing with Section 56500) of Part 30 of the Education Code.

— Resolving Recommendation Disputes

(e) Whenever a related service or designated instruction and service specified in subdivision (b) or (c) is to be considered for inclusion in the child's individualized educational program, the local education agency shall invite the responsible public agency representative to meet with the individualized education program team to determine the need for the service and participate in developing the individualized education program. If the responsible public agency representative cannot meet with the individualized education program team, then the representative shall provide written information concerning the need for the service pursuant to subdivision (d). Conference calls, together with written recommendations, are acceptable forms of

— Participation in Developing IEP

participation. If the responsible public agency representative will not be available to participate in the individualized education program meeting, the local educational agency shall ensure that a qualified substitute is available to explain and interpret the evaluation pursuant to subdivision (d) of Section 56341 of the Education Code. A copy of the information shall be provided by the responsible public agency to the parents or any adult pupil for whom no guardian or conservator has been appointed.

7572.5. (a) When an assessment is conducted pursuant to Article 2 (commencing with Section 56320) of Chapter 4 of Part 30 of Division 4 of the Education Code, which determines that a child is seriously emotionally disturbed, as defined in Section 300.5 of Title 34 of the Code of Federal Regulations, and any member of the individualized education program team recommends residential placement based on relevant assessment information, the individualized education program team shall be expanded to include a representative of the county mental health department.

- Expanded IEP Team and Residential Recommendations

(b) The expanded individualized education program team shall review the assessment and determine whether:

- Review Assessment

(1) The child's needs can reasonably be met through any combination of nonresidential services, preventing the need for out-of-home care.

(2) Residential care is necessary for the child to benefit from educational services.

(3) Residential services are available which address the needs identified in the assessment and which will ameliorate the conditions leading to the seriously emotionally disturbed designation.

(c) If the review required in subdivision (b) results in an individualized education program which calls for residential placement, the individualized education program shall include all the items outlined in Section 56345 of the Education Code, and shall also include:

- IEP Content

(1) Designation of the county mental health department as lead case manager. Lead case management responsibility may be delegated to the county welfare department by agreement between the county welfare department and the designated mental health department. The mental health department shall retain financial responsibility for provision of case management services.

(2) Provision for a review of the case progress, the continuing need for out-of-home placement, the extent of compliance with the individualized education program, and progress toward alleviating the need for out-of-home care, by the full individualized education program team at least every six months.

(3) Identification of an appropriate residential facility for placement with the assistance of the county welfare department as necessary.

7572.55. (a) Residential placements for a child with a disability who is seriously emotionally disturbed may be made out-of-state only after in-state alternatives have been considered and are found not to meet the child's needs and only when the requirements of Section 7572.5, and subdivision (e) of Section 56365 of the Education Code have been met. The local education agency shall document the alternatives to out-of-state residential placement that were considered and the reasons why they were rejected.

    – Restriction on Out-of-State* Placements

(b) Out-of-state placements shall be made only in a privately operated school certified by the California Department of Education.

    – School Certified by CDE

(c) A plan shall be developed for using less restrictive alternatives and in-state alternatives as soon as they become available, unless it is in the best educational interest of the child to remain in the out-of-state school. If the child is a ward or dependent of the court, this plan shall be documented in the record.

    – Plan for In-State Alternatives

7573. The Superintendent of Public Instruction shall ensure that local education agencies provide special education and those related services and designated instruction and services contained in a child's individualized education program that are necessary for the child to benefit educationally from his or her instructional program. Local education agencies shall be responsible only for the provision of those services which are provided by qualified personnel whose employment standards are covered by the Education Code and implementing regulations.

    – LEA Responsibility

7575. (a) (1) Notwithstanding any other provision of law, the State Department of Health Services, or any designated local agency administering the California Children's Services, shall be responsible for the provision of medically necessary occupational therapy and physical therapy, as specified by Article 2 (commencing with Section 248) of Chapter 2 of Part 1 of Division 1 of the Health and Safety Code, by reason of medical diagnosis and when contained in the child's individualized education program.

    – Responsibility for Provision of OT/PT

(2) Related services or designated instruction and services not deemed to be medically necessary by the State Department of Health Services, which the individualized education program team determines are necessary in order to assist a child to benefit from special education, shall be provided by the local education agency by qualified personnel whose employment standards are covered by the Education Code and implementing regulations.

*(Section 7572.55 Added in 1994)

F-5

(b) The department shall determine whether a California Children's Services eligible pupil, or a pupil with a private medical referral needs medically necessary occupational therapy or physical therapy. A medical referral shall be based on a written report from a licensed physician and surgeon who has examined the pupil. The written report shall include the following:

   — Determination for Medically Necessary Therapy

(1) The diagnosed neuromuscular, musculoskeletal, or physical disabling condition prompting the referral.

(2) The referring physician's treatment goals and objectives.

(3) The basis for determining the recommended treatment goals and objectives, including how these will ameliorate or improve the pupil's diagnosed condition.

(4) The relationship of the medical disability to the pupil's need for special education and related services.

(5) Relevant medical records.

(c) The department shall provide the service directly or by contracting with another public agency, qualified individual, or a state-certified nonpublic nonsectarian school or agency.

   — Providing the Service

(d) Local education agencies shall provide necessary space and equipment for the provision of occupational therapy and physical therapy in the most efficient and effective manner.

   — Space and Equipment

(e) The department shall also be responsible for providing the services of a home health aide when the local education agency considers a less restrictive placement from home to school for a pupil for whom both of the following conditions exist:

   — Services of a Home Health Aide

(1) The California Medical Assistance Program provides a life-supporting medical service via a home health agency during the time in which the pupil would be in school or traveling between school and home.

(2) The medical service provided requires that the pupil receive the personal assistance or attention of a nurse, home health aide, parent or guardian, or some other specially trained adult in order to be effectively delivered.

7576. Notwithstanding any other provision of law, the State Department of Mental Health, or any community mental health service designated by the State Department of Mental Health, shall be responsible for the provision of psychotherapy or other mental health services, as defined by regulation by the State Department of Mental Health, developed in consultation with the State Department of Education, when required in the child's individualized education program. This service shall be provided directly or by contracting with another public agency, qualified individual, or a state-certified nonpublic, nonsectarian school or agency.

   — Responsibility for Provision of Psychotherapy

7577. (a) The State Department of Rehabilitation and the State Department of Education shall jointly develop assessment procedures for determining client eligibility for State Department of Rehabilitation services for disabled pupils in secondary schools to help them make the transition from high school to work. The assessment procedures shall be distributed to local education agencies.

— Assessment Procedures for Rehabilitation Services

(b) The State Department of Rehabilitation shall maintain the current level of services to secondary school pupils in project work ability and shall seek ways to augment services with funds that may become available.

— Project Workability

7578. The provision of special education programs and related services for disabled children and youth residing in state hospitals shall be ensured by the State Department of Developmental Services, the State Department of Mental Health and the Superintendent of Public Instruction in accordance with Chapter 8 (commencing with Section 56850) of Part 30 of the Education Code.

— Programs for State Hospital Children

7579. (a) Prior to placing a disabled child or a child suspected of being disabled in a residential facility, outside the child's home, a court, regional center for the developmentally disabled, or public agency other than an educational agency, shall notify the administrator of the special education local plan area in which the residential facility is located. The administrator of the special education local plan area shall provide the court or other placing agency with information about the availability of an appropriate public or nonpublic, nonsectarian special education program in a special education local plan area where the residential facility is located.

— Prior Notification on Residential Placements

(b) Notwithstanding Section 56159 of the Education Code, the involvement of the administrator of the special education local plan area in the placement discussion, pursuant to subdivision (a), shall in no way obligate a public education agency to pay for the residential costs and the cost of noneducational services for a child placed in a licensed children's institution or foster family home.

— Involvement of SELPA Administrator

(c) It is the intent of the Legislature that this section will encourage communication between the courts and other public agencies that engage in referring children to, or placing children in, residential facilities, and representatives of local education agencies. It is not the intent of this section to hinder the courts or public agencies in their responsibilities for placing disabled children in residential facilities when appropriate.

— Encourage Communication

— Do Not Hinder Placement

7579.1. (a) Prior to the discharge of any disabled child or youth who has an active individualized education program from

— Prior to Discharging Disabled Child

a public hospital, proprietary hospital, or residential medical facility pursuant to Article 5.5 (commencing with Section 56167) of Chapter 2 of Part 30 of the Education Code, a licensed children's institution or foster family home pursuant to Article 5 (commencing with Section 56155) of Chapter 2 of Part 30 of the Education Code, or a state hospital for the developmentally disabled or mentally disordered, the following shall occur:

(1) The operator of the hospital or medical facility, or the agency that placed the child in the licensed children's institution or foster family home, shall, at least 10 days prior to the discharge of a disabled child or youth, notify in writing the local educational agency in which the special education program for the child is being provided, and the receiving special education local plan area where the child is being transferred, of the impending discharge.

— Notify of Impending Discharge

(2) The operator or placing agency, as part of the written notification, shall provide the receiving special education local plan area with a copy of the child's individualized education program, the identity of the individual responsible for representing the interests of the child for educational and related services for the impending placement, and other relevant information about the child that will be useful in implementing the child's individualized education program in the receiving special education local plan area.

— Provide Receiving Special Education Local Plan Area with a Copy of Child's IEP

(b) Once the disabled child or youth has been discharged, it shall be the responsibility of the receiving local educational agency to ensure that the disabled child or youth receives an appropriate educational placement that commences without delay upon his or her discharge from the hospital, institution, facility, or foster family home in accordance with Section 56325 of the Education Code. Responsibility for the provision of special education rests with the school district of residence of the parent or guardian of the child unless the child is placed in another hospital, institution, facility, or foster family home in which case the responsibility of special education rests with the school district in which the child resides pursuant to Sections 56156.5, 56156.6, and 56167 of the Education Code.

— Ensure that the Child Receives an Appropriate Educational Placement Without Delay

(c) Special education local plan area directors shall document instances where the procedures in subdivision (a) are not being adhered to and report these instances to the Superintendent of Public Instruction.

— Document Instances Where Procedures Are Not Being Adhered To

7579.2. It is the intent of the Legislature that any disabled individual who has an active individualized education program and is being discharged from a state developmental center or state hospital be discharged to the community as close as possible to

— Discharged to the Community Close to Home

the home of the individual's parent, guardian, or conservator in keeping with the individual's right to receive special education and related services in the least restrictive environment.

7579.5. (a) A surrogate parent shall not be appointed for a child who is a dependent or ward of the court unless the court specifically limits the right of the parent or guardian to make educational decisions for the child. A surrogate parent shall not be appointed for a child who has reached the age of majority unless the child has been declared incompetent by a court of law.

— Appointment of Surrogate Parent

(b) A local educational agency shall appoint a surrogate parent for a child under one or more of the following circumstances:

— Local Educational Agency Shall Appoint the Surrogate Parent

(1) The child is adjudicated a dependent or ward of the court pursuant to Section 300, 601, or 602 of the Welfare and Institutions Code upon referral of the child to a local educational agency for special education and related services, or in cases where the child already has a valid individualized education program.

(2) No parent for the child can be identified.

(3) The local educational agency, after reasonable efforts, cannot discover the location of a parent.

(c) When appointing a surrogate parent, the local educational agency shall, as a first preference, select a relative caretaker, foster parent, or court appointed special advocate, if any of these individuals exist and is willing and able to serve. If none of these individuals is willing or able to act as a surrogate parent, the local educational agency shall select the surrogate parent of its choice. If the child is moved from the home of the relative caretaker or foster parent who has been appointed as a surrogate parent, the local educational agency shall appoint another surrogate parent.

— First Preference: Relative Caretaker, Foster Parent, Court Appointed Special Advocate

(d) For the purposes of this section, the surrogate parent shall serve as the child's parent and shall have the rights relative to the child's education that a parent has under Title 20 (commencing with Section 1400) of the United States Code and pursuant to Part 300 of Title 34 (commencing with Section 300.1) of the Code of Federal Regulations. The surrogate parent may represent the child in matters relating to identification, assessment, instructional planning and development, educational placement, reviewing and revising the individualized education program, and in all other matters relating to the provision of a free appropriate public education of the child. Notwithstanding any other provision of law, this representation shall include the provision of written consent to the individualized education program including nonemergency medical services, mental health treatment services, and occupational or physical therapy services

— Educational and Representation Responsibilities

pursuant to this chapter. The surrogate parent may sign any consent relating to individualized education program purposes.

(e) As far as practical, a surrogate parent should be culturally sensitive to his or her assigned child.

– Culturally Sensitive

(f) Individuals who would have a conflict of interest in representing the child, as specified under federal regulations, shall not be appointed as a surrogate parent. "An individual who would have a conflict of interest," for purposes of this section, means a person having any interests that might restrict or bias his or her ability to advocate for all of the services required to ensure a free appropriate public education for an individual with exceptional needs, as defined in Section 56026 of the Education Code.

– Conflict of Interest

(g) Except for individuals who have a conflict of interest in representing the child, and notwithstanding any other law or regulation, individuals who may serve as surrogate parents include, but are not limited to, foster care providers, retired teachers, social workers, and probation officers who are not employees of a public agency involved in the education or care of the child. The surrogate parent shall not be an employee of a public or private agency that is involved in the education or care of the child. If a conflict of interest arises subsequent to the appointment of the surrogate parent, the local educational agency shall terminate the appointment and appoint another surrogate parent.

– Persons Who May Serve As Surrogate Parents

(h) The surrogate parent and the local educational agency appointing the surrogate parent shall be held harmless by the State of California when acting in their official capacity except for acts or omissions that are found to have been wanton, reckless, or malicious.

– Liability Protection

(i) Nothing in this section shall be interpreted to prevent a parent or guardian of an individual with exceptional needs from designating another adult individual to represent the interests of the child for educational and related services.

– Parent or Guardian May Designate Another Adult to Represent Child's Interests

(j) If funding for implementation of this section is provided, it may only be provided from Item 6110-161-890 of the annual Budget Act.

– Funding for Implementation

7580. Prior to licensing a community care facility, as defined in Section 1502 of the Health and Safety Code, in which a disabled child or youth may be placed, or prior to a modification of a community care facility's license to permit expansion of the facility, the State Department of Social Services shall consult with the administrator of the special education local plan area in order to consider the impact of licensure upon local education agencies.

– Community Care Facility's Impact on Education

7581. The residential and noneducational costs of a child placed in a medical or residential facility by a public agency, other than a local education agency, or independently placed in a facility by the parent of the child, shall not be the responsibility of the state or local education agency, but shall be the responsibility of the placing agency or parent.

- Responsibility for Residential/Noneducational Costs

7582. Assessments and therapy treatment services provided under programs of the State Department of Health Services or the State Department of Mental Health, or their designated local agencies, rendered to a child referred by a local education agency for an assessment or a disabled child or youth with an individualized education program, shall be exempt from financial eligibility standards and family repayment requirements for these services when rendered pursuant to this chapter.

- Exemption from Financial Eligibility Standards/ Repayment

7584. As used in this chapter, "disabled youth," "child," or "pupil" means individuals with exceptional needs as defined in Section 56026 of the Education Code.

- Definition of "Disabled Youth"

7585. (a) Whenever any department or any local agency designated by that department fails to provide a related service or designated instruction and service required pursuant to Section 7575 or 7576, and specified in the child's individualized education program, the parent, adult pupil, or any local education agency referred to in this chapter, shall submit a written notification of the failure to provide the service to the Superintendent of Public Instruction or the Secretary of Health and Welfare.

- Failure to Provide a Service

(b) When either the Superintendent of Public Instruction or the Secretary of Health and Welfare receives a written notification of the failure to provide a service as specified in subdivision (a), a copy shall immediately be transmitted to the other party. The superintendent, or his or her designee, and the secretary, or his or her designee, shall meet to resolve the issue within 15 calendar days of receipt of the notification. A written copy of the meeting resolution shall be mailed to the parent, the local education agency, and affected departments, within 10 days of the meeting.

- Superintendent and Secretary of Health and Welfare Meet to Resolve Issue

(c) If the issue cannot be resolved within 15 calendar days to the satisfaction of the superintendent and the secretary, they shall jointly submit the issue in writing to the Director of the Office of Administrative Hearings, or his or her designee, in the State Department of General Services.

- Submit Unresolved Issue to Office of Administrative Hearings

(d) The Director of the Office of Administrative Hearings, or his or her designee, shall review the issue and submit his or her findings in the case to the superintendent and the secretary within 30 calendar days of receipt of the case. The decision of the Director of the Office of Administrative Hearings, or his or her

- Decision Binding

designee, shall be binding on the departments and their designated agencies who are parties to the dispute.

(e) If the meeting, conducted pursuant to subdivision (b), fails to resolve the issue to the satisfaction of the parent or local education agency, either party may appeal to the Director of the Office of Administrative Hearings, whose decision shall be the final administrative determination and binding on all parties.

– Appeal

(f) Whenever notification is filed pursuant to subdivision (a), the pupil affected by the dispute shall be provided with the appropriate related service or designated instruction and service pending resolution of the dispute, if the pupil had been receiving the service. The Superintendent of Public Instruction and the Secretary of Health and Welfare shall ensure that funds are available for provision of the service pending resolution of the issue pursuant to subdivision (e).

– Services Pending Dispute Resolution

(g) Nothing in this section prevents a parent or adult pupil from filing for a due process hearing under Section 7586.

– Due Process Hearing

(h) The Superintendent of Public Instruction and the Secretary of Health and Welfare shall submit to the Legislature on July 1 of each year a joint report on the written notifications received pursuant to subdivision (a) on the failure of departments or their designated local agencies to provide occupational therapy, physical therapy, or psychotherapy. This joint report shall include, but not be limited to, a description of the nature of these disputes, a summary of the outcomes of these disputes, and any recommendations for changes to the procedure set forth in subdivision (a) or with regard to any interagency agreement and regulations which might exist as a result of the implementation of this chapter.

– Report to Legislature

(i) The contract between the State Department of Education and the Office of Administrative Hearings for conducting due process hearings shall include payment for services rendered by the Office of Administrative Hearings which are required by this section.

– Contract for Hearings

7586. (a) All state departments, and their designated local agencies shall be governed by the procedural safeguards required in Section 1415 of Title 20 of the United States Code. A due process hearing arising over a related service or designated instruction and service shall be filed with the Superintendent of Public Instruction. Resolution of all issues shall be through the due process hearing process established in Chapter 5 (commencing with Section 56500) of Part 30 of Division 4 of the Education Code. The decision issued in the due process hearing shall be binding on the department having responsibility for the services in issue as prescribed by this chapter.

– Procedural Safeguards

(b) Upon receipt of a request for a due process hearing involving an agency other than an educational agency, the Superintendent of Public Instruction shall immediately notify the state and local agencies involved by sending a copy of the request to the agencies.

(c) All hearing requests that involve multiple services that are the responsibility of more than one state department shall give rise to one hearing with all responsible state or local agencies joined as parties.

(d) No public agency, state or local, may request a due process hearing pursuant to Section 56501 of the Education Code against another public agency.

7586.5. Not later than January 1, 1988, the Superintendent of Public Instruction and the Secretary of Health and Welfare shall jointly submit to the Legislature and the Governor a report on the implementation of this chapter. The report shall include, but not be limited to, information regarding the number of complaints and due process hearings resulting from this chapter.

7586.7. The Superintendent of Public Instruction and the Secretary of Health and Welfare shall jointly prepare and implement within existing resources a plan for in-service training of state and local personnel responsible for implementing the provisions of this chapter.

7587. By January 1, 1986, each state department named in this chapter shall develop regulations, as necessary, for the department or designated local agency to implement this act. All regulations shall be reviewed by the Superintendent of Public Instruction prior to filing with the Office of Administrative Law, in order to ensure consistency with federal and state laws and regulations governing the education of disabled children. The directors of each department shall adopt all regulations pursuant to this section as emergency regulations in accordance with Chapter 3.5 (commencing with Section 11340) of Part 1 of Division 3 of Title 2. For the purpose of the Administrative Procedure Act, the adoption of the regulations shall be deemed to be an emergency and necessary for the immediate preservation of the public peace, health and safety, or general welfare. These regulations shall not be subject to the review and approval of the Office of Administrative Law and shall not be subject to automatic repeal until the final regulations take effect on or before May 1, 1987, and the final regulations shall become effective immediately upon filing with the Secretary of State. Regulations adopted pursuant to this section shall be developed with the maximum feasible opportunity for public participation and comments.

- Notification of Hearing Request

- One Hearing

- Restriction on Public Agency Hearing Requests

- Report on Implementation of Law

- In-Service Training

- Regulations

7588. This chapter shall become operative on July 1, 1986, except Section 7583 which shall become operative on January 1, 1985.

— July 1, 1986, Operative Date

CALIFORNIA CODE OF REGULATIONS - TITLE 2
DIVISION 9
JOINT REGULATIONS FOR HANDICAPPED CHILDREN

CHAPTER 1. INTERAGENCY RESPONSIBILITIES FOR PROVIDING SERVICES TO HANDICAPPED CHILDREN

[The following emergency regulations implementing the provisions of Chapter 26.5 of the Government Code are in effect until final regulations, which have been in the development stage for over seven years, become effective.]

Article 1. General Provisions

— GENERAL PROVISIONS

60000. The provisions of this chapter shall implement Chapter 26 (sic) (commencing with Section 7570) of Division 7 of Title 1 of the Government Code relating to interagency responsibilities for providing services to handicapped children. This chapter applies to the State Departments of Education, Mental Health, Health Services, Social Services, and their designated local agencies.

— Scope

The intent of this chapter is to assure conformity with Public Law 94-142: The Education for All Handicapped Children Act of 1975, (20 U.S.C. Section 1401 et seq.) and Section 504 of Public Law 93-112: The Rehabilitation Act of 1973, (29 U.S.C. Section 794), and their implementing regulations including Sections 76.1 et seq., 104.1 et seq., and 300.1 et seq. of Title 34 of the Code of Federal Regulations. Thus, provisions of this chapter shall be construed as supplemental to, and in the context of, federal and state laws and regulations relating to individuals with exceptional needs.

(Note: Chapter 26.5 of the Government Code is the correct reference.)

60010. (a) Words shall have their usual meaning unless the context or a definition clearly indicates a different meaning. Words used in their present tense include the future tense; words in the singular form include the plural form; and use of the masculine gender include the feminine gender. Use of the word "shall" denotes mandatory conduct; "may" denotes permissive conduct.

— General Definitions

(b)   "Confidentiality" means the protection of spoken and written communications, including clinical and educational records governed by the provisions of Section 99.3 of Title 45 (sic) of the Code of Federal Regulations, Section 300.500 of Title 34 of the Code of Federal Regulations, Sections 827, 4514, 5328, and 10850 of the Welfare and Institutions Code, and Section 2890 of Title 17 of the California Administrative Code (sic).

(c)   "County superintendent of schools" means either an appointed or elected official who, within the county's jurisdiction, supervises and ensures adherence to education laws as defined in the California State Constitution, Education Code, and Title 5 of the California Administrative Code (sic).

(d)   "Designated instruction and service" and "related services" means a component of program options as described in Sections 56361(b) and 56363(b) of the Education Code, Section 1401(17) of Title 20 of the United States Code, and Section 300.13 of Title 34 of the Code of Federal Regulations.

(e)   "Individualized education program team" means a team which is constituted in accordance with Section 56341 of the Education Code, and Section 300.344 of Title 34 of the Code of Federal Regulations.

(f)   "Expanded individualized education program team" means a team which is constituted in accordance with Section 56341 of the Education Code and pursuant to Section 7572.5 of the Government Code includes a representative of the county mental health department.

(g)   "Individual with exceptional needs" means those individuals who meet the requirements of Section 56026 of the Education Code and Sections 3030 and 3031 of Title 5 of the California Administrative Code (sic).

(h)   "Interagency agreement" means a negotiated written document which defines each agency's role and responsibilities for serving individuals with exceptional needs and assist in promoting coordination of these services.

(i)   "Parent" means those persons described in Section 56028 of the Education Code.

(j)   "Special education" means specially designed instruction as described in Section 56031 of the Education Code and Section 300.14 of Title 34 of the Code of Federal Regulations.

(k)   "Responsible local education agency" means the school district or county office specified in Section 56030 of the Education Code.

(l)   "Special education services region" means the school district organized in accordance with Section 56032 of the Education Code.

(m) "Special education local plan area" means the service area covered by the local plan developed in accordance with Section 56170 of the Education Code.

Article 2. Mental Health and Related Services

60020. (a) "Psychotherapy and other mental health services" means those services defined in Sections 542 to 543, inclusive, of Title 9 of the California Administrative Code (sic), and provided by a local mental health program directly or by contract.

(b) "Mental health assessments" means assessment, as described in Section 543, subdivision (b) of Title 9 of the California Administrative Code (sic), conducted by mental health professionals and conducted in accordance with Section 56320 of the Education Code by a person employed or designated by a local mental health program.

(c) "Mental health professionals" means psychiatrists, psychologists, clinical social workers, and marriage, family and child counselors meeting the appropriate criteria specified in Sections 5600.2 and 5650 of the Welfare and Institutions Code, and Article 8 of subchapter 3 of Title 9 of the California Administrative Code (sic).

(d) "Local mental health program" means a county community mental health program established in accordance with the Short-Doyle Act (Part 2 (commencing with Section 5600) of Division 5 of the Welfare and Institutions Code) or the county welfare agency when designated pursuant to Section 7572.5 of the Government Code.

(e) "Local Mental Health Director" means the officer appointed by the county governing body to manage a local mental health program.

60030. (a) In order to facilitate the provision of services required by subdivisions (a),(c),(d), and (e) of Section 7572 and Section 7572.5 of the Government Code:

(1) The Local Mental Health Director shall appoint liaison person(s) for the local mental health program. The County Superintendent of Schools shall ensure the appointment of liaison person(s) for the special education local plan areas by the superintendent or designee of the responsible local education agency of the special education local plan area.

(2) The Local Mental Health Director and the County Superintendent of Schools shall ensure, prior to July 1, 1986, that an interagency agreement is developed. Every three years thereafter the interagency agreement shall be renewed, and revised, if necessary. This provision does not preclude the

parties from revising the interagency agreement at any time they determine a revision is necessary.

(b) The interagency agreement shall include, but not be limited to, a delineation of the process and procedure for:

(1) Interagency referrals of pupils which minimize time line delays. This may include written parental consent on the receiving agency's forms.

(2) Timely exchange of pupil information in accordance with application procedures ensuring confidentiality.

(3) Participation of mental health professionals, including those contracted to provide services, at individualized education program team meetings pursuant to subdivision (d) and (e) of Section 7572 and Section 7576 of the Government Code.

(4) Developing or amending the mental health related services goals and objectives, and the frequency and duration of such services indicated on the pupil's individualized education program.

(5) Transportation of individuals with exceptional needs to and from the mental health service site when such service is not provided at the school.

(6) Provision by the school of an assigned, appropriate space for delivery mental health services or a combination of education and mental health services to be provided at the school.

(7) Continuation of mental health services during periods of school vacation when required by the individualized education program.

(8) Identification of existing public and state-certified nonpublic educational programs, treatment modalities, and location of appropriate residential placements which may be used for placement by the expanded individualized education program team.

(9) Out-of-home placement of seriously emotionally disturbed pupils in accordance with the educational and treatment goals on the individualized education program.

60040. (a) A responsible local education agency preparing an initial assessment plan in accordance with Section 56320 et. seq. of the Education Code may, with written parental consent, refer the pupil suspected of being an individual with exceptional needs to the local mental health program to determine the need for mental health services when:

– Referral and Assessment

(1) The pupil meets the requirements of (b)(4) of this section; and,

(2) The provision of psychological and counseling services described in Sections 3051.9, 3051.10, and 3051.11 of Title 5 of the California Administrative Code (sic) is not appropriate to meet the pupil's needs.

(b)   Prior to referring an individual with exceptional needs to a local mental health program to determine the need for mental health services, the responsible local education agency shall ensure that:

(1)   Written parental consent has been obtained;

(2)   An assessment has been made by school site personnel in accordance with Sections 56001(j), 56324, and 56320(b)(3) of the Education Code;

(3)   Counseling and guidance described in Sections 3051.9, 3951.10, and 3051.11 of Title 5 of the California Administrative Code (sic) has been provided to the pupil and the individualized education program team has determined that such counseling is not meeting the pupil's needs;

(4)   A review of all assessment data, including observations of the pupil in a variety of educational and natural settings, documents that:

(A)   The behavioral characteristics of the pupil adversely affect the pupil's educational performance as measured by: standardized achievement tests reported in scores and compared to measured ability when appropriate; teacher observations; work samples; and grade reports reflecting classroom functioning; or, other measures determined to be appropriate by the individualized education program team.

(B)   The behavioral characteristics of the pupil cannot be defined solely as a behavior disorder or a temporary adjustment problem, or cannot be resolved with short-term counseling.

(C)   The age of onset was from 30 months to 21 years and has been observed for at least 6 months.

(D)   The behavioral characteristics of the pupil are present in several settings, including the school, the community, and the home.

(E)   The adverse behavioral characteristics of the pupil are severe, as indicated by their rate of occurrence and intensity.

(c)   When referring a pupil suspected of being an individual with exceptional needs or an identified individual with exceptional needs to the local mental health program, the responsible local education agency shall:

(1)   Obtain written parental consent to forward educational information to the local mental health program.   Educational information shall include:

(A)   A copy of the assessment reports completed in accordance with Section 56327 of the Education Code.

(B)   Current, relevant behavior observations of the pupil in a variety of educational and natural settings.

(C)   A report prepared by personnel who provided "specialized" counseling and guidance services to the individual with exceptional needs as described in Sections 3051.9, 3051.10, and 3051.11 of Title 5 of the California Administrative Code (sic) and, when appropriate, an explanation why such counseling and guidance will not meet the needs of the pupil suspected of being an individual with exceptional needs.

(2) Obtain written parental consent to allow the mental health professional to observe the pupil during school.

(3) Propose a date for the individualized education program team meeting.

(d) The local mental health program shall be responsible for reviewing the educational information, observing, if necessary, the pupil in the school environment, and determining if mental health assessments are needed.

(1) If mental health assessments are deemed necessary by a mental health professional, a mental health assessment plan shall be developed and the parent's written informed consent obtained pursuant to Section 300.500 of Title 34 of the Code of Federal Regulations and Section 7572 of the Government Code.

(2) When the mental health assessments cannot be completed within the required time limit specified in Section 56344 of the Education Code, the local mental health professional or designee shall, no later than 15 days prior to the scheduled meeting, notify the individualized education program team administrator or designee.

(3) The individualized education program team administrator or designee shall contact the parent to obtain permission for an extension, not to exceed 15 days, of the individualized education program team meeting to allow the mental health assessments to be completed.

(e) The local mental health program shall provide to the individualized education program team a written assessment report in accordance with Section 56327 of the Education Code.

60050. (a) When mental health services are to be provided, the following written information shall be included in the individualized education program:

— Individualized Education Program

(1) A description of the mental health services to be provided;

(2) The goals and objectives of the mental health services, with appropriate objective criteria and evaluation procedures to determine whether objectives are being achieved; and

(3) Initiation, frequency, and duration of the mental health services to be provided to the pupil.

(b) Parental approval for the provision of mental health treatment services shall be supported by a signed consent for treatment.

Article 3. 24-Hour Out-of-Home Care

60100. (a) The local mental health program and the special education local plan area liaison person(s) shall define the process and procedures for coordinating local services to promote alternatives to out-of-home care.

(b) If the individualized education program team has determined that local educational program options cannot implement the pupil's individualized education program and is considering a recommendation of residential placement for a pupil who meets the eligibility criteria specified in Section 3030(i) of Title 5 of the California Administrative Code (sic), the team meeting shall continue if a representative of the local mental health program is present.

(1) If a representative from the local mental health program is not present, the individualized education program team meeting shall be adjourned and reconvened within 15 calendar days with mental health participation.

(2) If the pupil is a dependent or ward of the court, the agency vested with care, custody, and control of the pupil shall be notified of the individualized education program meeting and shall function as a pupil's legally responsible agent for purposes of participating in the individualized education program team process.

(c) If the local mental health program determines that additional mental health assessments are needed. the mental health representative shall proceed in accordance with Section 60040.

(d) The expanded individualized education program team shall consider all possible alternatives to out-of-home placement. Such alternatives may include any combination of cooperatively developed education and mental health service options, as described in Sections 56361 and 56365 of the Education Code and mental health services, as described in Sections 542 and 543 of Title 9 of the California Administrative Code (sic).

(e) When residential placement is the final decision of the expanded individualized education program team, the team shall develop a written statement documenting the pupil's educational and mental health treatment needs that support the recommendation for this placement.

(f) The expanded individualized education program team shall identify one or more appropriate, least restrictive and least costly residential placement alternatives. The facility must have a rate set in accordance with Section 60200(d) and shall be:

(1) Located within or adjacent to the county of residence of the pupil's parents or other legacy responsible agent pursuant to

– Placement of Seriously
  Emotionally Disturbed
  Pupils

Section 300.552(a)(3) of Title 34 of the Code of Federal Regulations, except when documentation is provided that no nearby placement alternative is able to implement the individualized education program; and

(2)   A privately operated residential facility licensed by the Department of Social Services with an appropriate off-grounds public school program available to pupils; or,

(3)   A privately operated residential facility licensed by the Department of Social Services with an appropriate on-grounds public school program available to pupils; or,

(4)   A privately operated residential facility licensed by the Department of Social Services wherein a nonpublic, nonsectarian school program is certified by the State Department of Education and available to pupils.

(g)   The local mental health program representative to the expanded individualized education program team shall be responsible for notifying the Local Mental Health Director or designee of the team's decision within one working day of the individualized education program team meeting.

60110.   (a)   The Local Mental Health Director or designee shall designate a lead case manager to finalize the pupil placement plan with the approval of the parent and the individualized education program team within 15 days from the decision to place the pupil in a residential facility. Actual placement must be accomplished as soon as possible.

– Case Management

(b)   Pupils who have been adjudicated as dependents or wards of the court shall receive case management for required child welfare services and Aid to Families with Dependent Children-Foster Care services from the agency vested with the care, custody, and control of the pupil.

(c)   Case management is defined pursuant to subdivision (a) of Section 548 of Title 9 of the California Administrative Code (sic) and shall include the following responsibilities:

(1)   Convening parent(s) and representatives of public and private agencies in accordance with subsection (f) of Section 60100 in order to identify the appropriate residential placement.

(2)   Verifying with the educational administrator or designee the approval of the local governing board of the district, special education service region, or county office pursuant to Section 56342 of the Education Code.

(3)   Completing the local mental health program payment authorization in order to initiate out-of-home care payments.

(4)   Coordinating the completion of the necessary County Welfare Department, local mental health program, and responsible local education agency financial paperwork or contracts.

(5)   Coordinating the completion of the residential placement as soon as possible.

(6)   Developing the plan for and assisting the family and pupil in the pupil's social and emotional transition from home to the residential facility and the subsequent return to the home.

(7)   Facilitating the enrollment of the pupil in the residential facility.

(8)   Conducting quarterly face-to-face contacts with the pupil at the residential facility to monitor the level of care and supervision and the implementation of the treatment services and the individualized education program.

(9)   Notifying the parent or legal guardian and the local education agency administrator or designee when there is a discrepancy in the level of care, supervision, provision of treatment services, and the requirements of the individualized education program.

(10)   Coordinating the six-month expanded individualized education team meeting with the local education agency administrator or designee.

Article 4.   Financial Provision for 24-Hour Out-of-Home Placement

60200. (a) The purpose of this article is to establish conditions and limitations for reimbursement for the provision of related services and 24-hour out-of-home placement described in Articles 2 and 3. These services and placements are to be provided at no cost to the parent.

(b)   The local mental health program shall be financially responsible for:

(1)   Provision of mental health services as recommended by a local mental health program representative and included in an individualized education program.   Services shall be provided either directly or by contract.   Contract services shall be delivered in accordance with Section 523 of Title 9 of the California Administrative Code (sic). These services must be provided within the State of California.

(2)   Reimbursement to the provider for these mental health services shall be a negotiated net amount or rate approved by the Director of Mental Health as provided in Section 5705.2 of the Welfare and Institutions Code, or the providers' actual reasonable cost.

(c)   The local education agency shall be fiscally responsible for:

(1)   Transportation provided during school hours to and from a mental health treatment center as specified in the pupil's

individualized education program and in accordance with Section 300.13(b)(13) of Title 34 of the Code of Federal Regulations.

(2)   Those items agreed upon in the nonpublic school services contract pursuant to Section 3066 of Title 5 of the California Administrative Code (sic), with the exclusion of mental health services and 24-hour out-of-home care, for a seriously emotionally disturbed pupil who has been placed pursuant to Section 7572.5 of the Government Code.

(3)   Mental health services when an individual with exceptional needs is placed in a nonpublic school outside of the State of California.

(d)   The State Department of Social Services shall be responsible for determining the rate to be paid to providers for 24-hour out-of-home care for a seriously emotionally disturbed pupil in accordance with Section 18350 of the Welfare and Institutions Code.

(e)   The County Welfare Department shall be responsible for issuing payments to providers for 24-hour out-of-home care for a seriously emotionally disturbed pupil in accordance with Section 18351 of the Welfare and Institutions Code.

Article 5. Occupational Therapy and Physical Therapy

– OCCUPATIONAL THERAPY AND PHYSICAL THERAPY

60300. (a) "Medical Therapy Conference Team" means a team composed of the child, parent or guardian, Medical Therapy Unit Conference physician, occupational therapist or physical therapist or both, if appropriate. Other attendees may be invited with parental consent and team approval for the purpose of coordination of patient services.

– Definitions

(b)   "California Children Services Panel" means that group of physicians and other providers of services and equipment who have applied to and been approved by California Children Services to give services.

(c)   "Independent county agency" means a county meeting the population criteria pursuant to Section 252 of the Health and Safety Code.

(d)   "Dependent county agency" means a county meeting the population criteria pursuant to Sections 252 and 258 of the Health and Safety Code.

(e)   "Medical therapy unit" means a designated public school location where the California Children Services medical therapy services are provided.

(f)   "Occupational therapy and physical therapy "means medically necessary services provided by qualified medical personnel in accordance with Section 250 of the Health and Safety Code by reason of a medical diagnosis.

(g) "Qualified medical personnel" means occupational therapists and physical therapists licensed to practice in the State of California who are employed or designated by California Children Services.

(h) "Medically necessary therapy" means that therapy which has as its purpose the improvement or amelioration of a neuromuscular or musculoskeletal condition and shall include standard habilitation and rehabilitation procedures. This therapy shall not include interventions which can be carried out by educational personnel.

(i) "Necessary equipment" means that equipment provided by a local education agency which enables the medical therapy unit staff to provide the therapy services to individuals with exceptional needs.

(j) "Necessary space" means facilities needed by a medical therapy unit which includes one, but not necessarily both, of the following:

(1) "A primary medical therapy unit" which provides areas for conferences, office(s) private evaluation, treatment, training bathroom and kitchen, storage, and workshop. The specific requirements are dependent upon local needs as determined by joint agreement of the local California Children Services and local education agencies, and approved by both State Departments of Health Services and Education.

(2) "A satellite unit" is an adjunct to the primary medical therapy unit and is an assigned private area with necessary equipment to enable the California Children Services' staff to provide services at a site closest to the pupil's school of attendance.

60310. (a) In order to facilitate the provisions of services described in subdivisions (a), (b), (d), and (e) of Section 7527 of the Government Code, and subdivisions (a), (b) and (c) of Section 7575 of the Government Code, each independent county agency and each authorized dependent county agency of California Children Services shall appoint a liaison person for the county agency of California Children Services.

– Local Interagency Agreement

The County Superintendent of Schools shall ensure the appointment of a liaison person for the special education local plan areas by the superintendent or the designee of the responsible local education agency of the special education local plan area.

(b) Each independent county agency and each dependent county agency of California Children Services and the County Superintendent of Schools shall ensure, prior to July 6, 1986, the development and implementation of a local interagency agreement which shall include, but not be limited to a delineation of the process and procedure for:

(1) Identification of a liaison person within each local education agency in the special education local plan areas and within each California Children Services' county agency;

(2) Referral of pupils, birth to twenty-one years of age, who have or are suspected of having a neuromuscular, musculoskeletal, or other physical impairment requiring medically necessary occupational therapy or physical therapy.

(3) Timely exchange between the agencies of pertinent information concerning the individual with exception needs upon receiving parent's written, informed consent obtained in accordance with Section 300.500 of Title 34. of the Code of Federal Regulations;

(4) Giving adequate notice to the local California Children Services' agency for all individualized education program team meetings when participation by their staff is required;

(5) Participation of California Children Services' representative in the individualized education program team meetings;

(6) Developing or amending the therapy services indicated on the pupil's individualized education program in accordance with Section 56341 of the Education Code;

(7) Transportation of individuals with exceptional needs to receive California Children Services' medically necessary occupational therapy or physical therapy services at the primary medical therapy unit or satellite unit;

(8) Determining the location of California Children Services' primary medical therapy or satellite units;

(9) Provision and maintenance of necessary space and equipment, including the administrative and fiscal responsibilities;

(10) Approval of the utilization of designated therapy space when not in use by California Children Services' staff; and,

(11) Provision of medically necessary therapy services to pupils residing in State Special Schools, when appropriate.

60320. (a) The individualized education program team shall keep a record of all referrals of parents of handicapped pupils to California Children Services to determine the need for medically necessary occupational therapy or physical therapy.

– Referral and Assessment

(1) The local education agency or State Special School shall notify California Children Services of the proposed date of the individualized education program meeting.

(2) California Children Services shall develop an assessment plan and obtain the parent's written informed consent pursuant to Section 300.500 of Title 34 of the Code of Federal Regulations and Section 7572 of the Government Code.

(3)   The California Children Services shall notify the local education agency or the State Special School if the evaluations cannot be completed in time for the individualized education program team meeting. This notice shall include the date when the evaluations are expected to be completed and any request for extension of the 50-day time line in Section 56344 of the Education Code.

(4)   The individualized education program team administrator or designee shall seek the parent's written agreement to the time extension.

(b)   To qualify for the provision of medically necessary occupational therapy or physical therapy, California Children Services, the pupil must:

(1)   Meet the eligibility requirements as defined in Sections 250.5 and 253.5 of the Health and Safety Code;

(2)   Need medically necessary therapy as recommended or approved by the Medical Therapy Conference Team; and,

(3)   Be recommended to the individualized education program team by a California Children Services panel physician of the appropriate specialty for treating the condition requiring therapy.

(c)   California Children Services shall provide the individualized education program team with the necessary assessment information in accordance with Section 56327 of the Education Code. When the California Children Services' panel physician determines that a pupil does not need medically necessary therapy the individualized education program team shall be provided with a statement which delineates the bases for the determination.

(d)   For those pupils who meet eligibility requirements defined in Section 250.5 of the Health and Safety Code and whose disabilities are such that skilled services of occupational or physical therapists are not required to meet their needs, the Medical Therapy Conference Team shall identify consultation needs.

(e)   When providing medically necessary therapy, the California Children Services' treatment plan may be used as the required written information for inclusion as a related service on the individualized education program and shall be attached thereto.

(f)   For those pupils who do not need medically necessary therapy the individualized education program team will review the California Children Services' report and the independent assessment as well as assess the pupil in all areas of suspected disability to determine which activities may be required to assist the pupil to benefit from special education.

(g) When the individualized education program team determines that the activities are necessary, goals and objectives relating to the activities identified in the assessment reports shall be written and provided by qualified personnel whose employment standards are defined in Article 4 (commencing with Section 44200) of Chapter 2 of Part 25 of Division 2 of the Education Code.

60330. (a) The primary medical therapy unit and satellite units shall be for the exclusive use of the California Children Services' staff when they are on site. The special education administrator of the local education agency in which the units are located shall coordinate with the California Children Services' staff for other use of the space.

– Space and Equipment For Occupational Therapy and Physical Therapy

(b) Each special education local plan required in Section 56200 of the Education Code shall include:

(1) Which local education agency shall be responsible for the provision, maintenance, and operation of the facility housing the primary medical therapy unit and satellite units on a twelve-month basis;

(2) Which local education agency shall have the fiscal responsibility for the provision and maintenance of necessary equipment and instructional supplies; and

(3) The process for any change of responsibility or relocation of the primary medical therapy unit and any satellite units.

(c) The state Departments of Education and Health Services shall develop guidelines for local use when designing, remodeling, relocating, and equipping a medical therapy unit and any satellite unit.

(d) All construction and relocation of primary medical therapy units must be approved by the State Departments of Education and Health Services.

Article 6. Home Health Aide

– HOME HEALTH AIDE

60400. (a) Individuals with exceptional needs eligible for a home health aide in accordance with Section 7575(e) of the Government Code shall be all of the following:

– Specialized Health Needs Aide

(1) A Medi-Cal beneficiary.

(2) Receiving services from a home health agency pursuant to Section 51337 of Title 22 of the California Administrative Code (sic).

(3) Considered for an educational placement outside of the home.

(b) Individuals with exceptional needs who are not beneficiaries of Medi-Cal shall have their specialized health needs provided by the responsible educational agency, pursuant to Section 49423.5 of the Education Code.

Article 7. Licensing a Community Care Facility

60500. (a) "Shall consult" as used in Section 7580 of the Government Code, means the exchange of written information between the Community Care Licensing district of five of the Department of Social Services, the applicant facility, and the special education local plan area administrator in consultation with the local district in which the facility is to be located.

(b)   Community Care Licensing district offices and the county office of education shall annually exchange information describing how special education services are geographically organized and designate contact persons in the county of five of education and the Social Services district office.

(c)   Community Care Licensing district offices, upon receiving an application to license a new group home or small family home or to increase the capacity of an existing group home or small family home which serves or will serve pupils, birth to eighteen years of age, shall provide the county office of education with a copy of the application face sheet (LIC 200). The county office of education shall forward the face sheet to the appropriate special education local plan area administrator.

(d)   Within 15 days of the receipt of the application face sheet, the special education local plan area administrator and the administrator of the local educational agency in which the new or expanded facility is located shall provide the applicant with the following information:

(1)   The types and locations of public and state certified nonpublic special education programs available within the special education local plan area for the proposed pupil population; and

(2)   The ability of the education agencies within the special education local plan area to absorb, expand, or to open new programs to meet the needs of the proposed pupil population given the limitations of Instructional Personnel Service units, available school facilities, funds, and staff.

(e)   The Community Care Licensing District Office of the Department of Social Services shall notify the county office of education when a group home or small family home is licensed by providing a copy of the license notice (LIC 272).

(f)   The county office of education, in accordance with Section 56156(d) of the Education Code, shall provide the special education local plan area administrator with a list of the currently licensed group homes and small family homes within the county.

Article 8. Procedural Safeguards

60550. (a)   Due process hearing procedures apply to the resolution of disagreements between a parent and a public agency regarding the proposal or refusal of a public agency to initiate or change the identification, assessment, educational placement, or the provision of special education and related services to the pupil.

(b)   Upon receiving a request for a due process hearing regarding the services provided or refused by another agency, the Superintendent of Public Instruction shall send the state and local agency involved a copy of the hearing request, the name of the assigned mediator, and the date of the mediation meeting in accordance with Section 56503 of the Education Code. Nothing in this section shall preclude any party from waiving mediation.

(c)   If the mediator cannot resolve the issues, a state-level hearing shall be conducted by a hearing officer assigned by the Office of Administrative Hearings (sic) in accordance with Section 56505 of the Education Code.

(d)   The agency which provides the service in dispute is responsible for preparing documentation and providing testimony supporting its position.

(e)   The State Department of Education is fiscally responsible for services by the mediator and the Office of Administrative Hearings in response to a parent's request for a due process hearing.

Article 9. Interagency Dispute Resolution

60600. (a) The procedures of this article apply when there is a dispute between or among the State Department of Education or local education agency or both and any agency included in Sections 7575 and 7576 of the Government Code over the provision of occupational therapy. physical therapy, psychotherapy, or other mental health services, when such services are contained in a child's individualized education program.

(b)   A dispute over the provision of services means a dispute over which agency is to actually deliver the service, or to pay for the services, when the service is contained in the child's individualized education program.

(c)   These procedures apply only where the disputed service has been included in the individualized education program in accordance with Chapter 26 (commencing with Section 7570) of Division 7 of Title 1 of the Government Code. Whenever a service has been included in an individualized education program by an individualized education program team without the recommendation of the qualified professional in accordance with Section 7572 of the Government Code, the local education agency shall be solely responsible for the provision of the service. In such circumstances, the dispute, if any, is between the parent and the local educational agency and shall be resolved through the due process or complaint procedures. pursuant to Chapter 5 (commencing with Section 56500) of Part 30 of Division 4 of the Education Code, as applicable.

60610. (a) Whenever notification is filed pursuant to subdivision (a) of Section 7585 of the Government Code, the dispute procedures shall not interfere with the pupil's right to receive a free, appropriate public education.

— Resolution Procedure

(1)   If one of the agencies specified in Sections 7575, 7576, 7577, and 7578 of the Government Code has been providing the service prior to notification of the failure to provide a related service or designated instruction and service that agency shall continue to provide the service until the dispute resolution proceedings are completed.

(2)   If no agency specified in this section has provided the service prior to the notification of the dispute, the State Superintendent of Public Instruction shall ensure that the service is provided in accordance with the individualized education program, until the dispute resolution proceedings are completed.

(3)   Arrangements, other than those specified in subparagraphs (1) and (2), may be by written agreement between the involved public agencies, provided the pupil's individualized education program is not altered, except as to which agency delivers or pays for the service if such specification is included in the individualized education program.

(b)   In resolving the dispute, the Superintendent of Public Instruction and Secretary of the Health and Welfare Agency shall meet to resolve the issue within 15 days of receipt of notice.

(c)   Once the dispute resolution procedures have been completed, the agency determined responsible for the service shall pay for, or provide the service, and shall reimburse the other agency which provided the service pursuant to paragraph (a) of this section, if applicable.

(d)   A written copy of the resolution shall be mailed to affected parties pursuant to Section 7585 of the Government Code.

CALIFORNIA CHILDREN'S SERVICE MEDICAL THERAPY

(Health and Safety Code)

(AB 3012 - Chapter 1133, Statutes of 1986)

255.3. When the California Children's Service medical therapy unit conference team, based on a medical referral recommending medically necessary occupational or physical therapy in accordance with subdivision (b) of Section 7575 of the Government Code, finds that a handicapped child, as defined in Section 250.5, needs medically necessary occupational or physical therapy, that child shall be determined to be eligible for therapy services. If the California Children's Services medical consultant disagrees with such a determination of eligibility by the California Children's Services medical therapy unit conference team, the medical consultant shall communicate with the conference team to ask for further justification of its determination, and shall weigh the conference team's arguments in support of its decision in reaching his or her own determination.

    – Medically Necessary OT/PT

This section shall not change eligibility criteria for the California Children's Services programs as described in Sections 250.5 and 253.5. This section shall not apply to children diagnosed as specific learning disabled, unless they otherwise meet the eligibility criteria of the California Children's Services.

DEPENDENT CHILD OF THE COURT AND EDUCATIONAL DECISIONS

(Welfare and Institutions Code)

(SB 1646, Chapter 383, Statutes of 1992)

361. (a) In all cases in which a minor is adjudged a dependent child of the court on the ground that the minor is a person described by Section 300, the court may limit the control to be exercised over the dependent child by any parent or guardian and shall by its order clearly and specifically set forth all such limitations. Any limitation on the right of the parent or guardian to make educational decisions for the child shall be specifically addressed in the court order. The limitations shall not exceed those necessary to protect the child.

    – Dependent Child of the Court; Educational Decisions

    (b) No dependent child shall be taken from the physical custody of his or her parents or guardian or guardians with whom the child resides at the time the petition was initiated unless the

    – Physical Custody

juvenile court finds clear and convincing evidence of any of the following:

(1) There is a substantial danger to the physical health of the minor or would be if the minor was returned home, and there are no reasonable means by which the minor's physical health can be protected without removing the minor from the minor's parents' or guardians' physical custody. The fact that a minor has been adjudicated a dependent child of the court pursuant to subdivision (e) of Section 300 shall constitute prima facie evidence that the minor cannot be safely left in the custody of the parent or guardian with whom the minor resided at the time of injury.

(2) The parent or guardian of the minor is unwilling to have physical custody of the minor, and the parent or guardian has been notified that if the minor remains out of their physical custody for the period specified in Section 366.25 or 366.26, the minor may be declared permanently free from their custody and control.

(3) The minor is suffering severe emotional damage, as indicated by extreme anxiety, depression, withdrawal, or untoward aggressive behavior toward self or others, and there are no reasonable means by which the minor's emotional health may be protected without removing the minor from the physical custody of his or her parent or guardian.

(4) The minor or sibling of the minor has been sexually abused, or is deemed to be at substantial risk of being sexually abused, by a parent, guardian, or member of his or her household, or other person known to his or her parent, and there are no reasonable means by which the minor can be protected from further sexual abuse or substantial risk of sexual abuse without removing the minor from his or her parent or guardian, or the minor does not wish to return to his or her parent or guardian.

(5) The minor has been left without any provision for his or her support, or a parent who has been incarcerated or institutionalized cannot arrange for the care of the minor, or a relative or other adult custodian with whom the child has been left by the parent is unwilling or unable to provide care or support for the child and the whereabouts of the parent is unknown and reasonable efforts to located him or her have been unsuccessful.

(c) The court shall make a determination as to whether   — Court Determination
reasonable efforts were made to prevent or to eliminate the need for removal of the minor from his or her home or, if the minor is removed for one of the reasons stated in paragraph (5) of subdivision (b), whether it was reasonable under the

circumstances not to make any such efforts. The court shall state the facts on which the decision to remove the minor is based.

(d) The court shall make all of the findings required by subdivision (a) of Section 366 in either of the following circumstances:

 — Court Findings

(1) The minor has been taken from the custody of his or her parents or guardians and has been living in an out-of-home placement pursuant to Section 319.

(2) The minor has been living in a voluntary out-of-home placement pursuant to Section 16507.4.

PLACEMENT OUT-OF-HOME TO BE AS NEAR THE CHILD'S HOME AS POSSIBLE

(Welfare and Institutions Code)

(AB 1892 - Chapter 1128, Statutes of 1994)

362.2. It is the intent of the Legislature that if a placement out-of-home is necessary pursuant to an individualized education program, that this placement be as near the child's home as possible, unless it is not in the best interest of the child. When the court determines that it is the best interest of the child to be placed out-of-state, the court shall read into the record that in-state alternatives have been explored and that they cannot meet the needs of the child, and the court shall state on the record the reasons for the out-of-state placement.

 — Legislative Intent*

INDIVIDUALS WITH EXCEPTIONAL NEEDS COMMITTED TO YOUTH AUTHORITY

(Welfare and Institutions Code)

(AB 820 - Chapter 175, Statutes of 1993)

1742. When the juvenile court commits to the Youth Authority a person identified as an individual with exceptional needs, as defined by Section 56026 of the Education Code, the juvenile court, subject to the requirements of subdivision (a) of Section 727 and subdivision (b) of Section 737, shall not order the juvenile conveyed to the physical custody of the Youth Authority until the juvenile's individualized education program previously developed pursuant to Article 3 (commencing with Section 56340) of Chapter 4 of Part 30 of Division 4 of Title 2

 — IEP of Individual
  Committed to Youth
  Authority

*(Section 362.2 Added in 1994)

of the Education Code for the individual with exceptional needs, has been furnished to the Department of the Youth Authority.

To facilitate this process the juvenile court shall assure that the probation officer communicates with appropriate staff at the juvenile court school, county office of education, or special education local planning area.

LOCKED OR SECURED COMMUNITY TREATMENT FACILITY PROGRAMS

(Welfare and Institutions Code)

(SB 282 - Chapter 1245, Statutes of 1993)

4094. (a) The State Department of Mental Health shall establish, by regulations adopted at the earliest possible date, but no later than December 31, 1994, program standards for any facility licensed as a community treatment facility. This section shall apply only to community treatment facilities described in this subdivision.

– Regulations for Community Treatment Facility Program Standards

(b) A certification of compliance issued by the State Department of Mental Health shall be a condition of licensure for the community treatment facility by the State Department of Social Services. The department may, upon the request of a county, delegate the certification and supervision of a community treatment facility to the county department of mental health.

– Certification of Compliance

(c) The State Department of Mental Health shall adopt regulations to include, but not be limited to, the following:

– Department of Mental Health Regulations

(1) Procedures by which the Director of Mental Health shall certify that a facility requesting licensure as a community treatment facility pursuant to Section 1502 of the Health and Safety Code is in compliance with program standards established pursuant to this section.

(2) Procedures by which the Director of Mental Health shall deny a certification to a facility or decertify a facility licensed as a community treatment facility pursuant to Section 1502 of the Health and Safety Code, but no longer complying with program standards established pursuant to this section, in accordance with Chapter 5 (commencing with Section 11500) of Part 1 of Division 3 of Title 2 of the Government Code.

(3) Provisions for site visits by the State Department of Mental Health for the purpose of reviewing a facility's compliance with program standards established pursuant to this section.

(4) Provisions for the community care licensing staff of the State Department of Social Services to report to the State Department of Mental Health when there is reasonable cause to

believe that a community treatment facility is not in compliance with program standards established pursuant to this section.

(5) Provisions for the State Department of Mental Health to provide consultation and documentation to the State Department of Social Services in any administrative proceeding regarding denial, suspension, or revocation of a community treatment facility license.

(d) The standards adopted by regulations pursuant to subdivision (a) shall include, but not be limited to, standards for treatment staffing and for the use of psychotropic medication, discipline, and restraint in the facilities. The standards shall also meet the requirements of Section 4094.5. — Standards

(e) During the initial public comment period for the adoption of the regulations required by this section, the community care facility licensing regulations proposed by the State Department of Social Services and the program standards proposed by the State Department of Mental Health shall be presented simultaneously. — Public Comment Period for Adoption of Regulations

(f) A minor shall be admitted to a community treatment facility only if the requirements of Section 4094.5 and either of the following conditions is met: — Admittance to Community Treatment Facility

(1) The minor is within the jurisdiction of the juvenile court, and has made voluntary application for mental health services pursuant to Section 6552.

(2) Informed consent is given by a parent, guardian, conservator, or other person having custody of the minor.

(g) Any minor admitted to a community treatment facility shall have the same due process rights afforded to a minor who may be admitted to a state hospital, pursuant to the holding in In re Roger S. (1977) 19 Cal. 3d 921. Minors who are wards or dependents of the court and to whom this subdivision applies shall be afforded due process in accordance with Section 6552 and related case law, including In re Michael E. (1975) 15 Cal. 3d 183. Regulations adopted pursuant to Section 4094 shall specify the procedures for ensuring these rights, including provisions for notification of rights and the time and place of hearings. — Due Process Rights

(h) Notwithstanding Section 13340 of the Government Code, the sum of forty-five thousand dollars ($45,000) is hereby appropriated annually from the General Fund to the State Department of Mental Health for one personnel year to carry out the provisions of this section. — Personnel Funding to Carry Out Provisions

4094.5. Regulations for community treatment facilities adopted pursuant to Section 4094 shall include, but not be limited to, the following: — Scope of Regulations

(a) Only seriously emotionally disturbed children, as defined in Section 5699.2, for whom other less restrictive mental health — Seriously Emotionally Disturbed Children interventions have been tried, as documented in the case plan, or who are currently placed in an acute psychiatric hospital or state hospital or in a facility outside the state for mental health treatment, and who may require periods of containment to participate in, and benefit from, mental health treatment, shall be placed in a community treatment facility. For purposes of this subdivision, lesser restrictive interventions shall include, but are not limited to, outpatient therapy, family counseling, case management, family preservation efforts, special education classes, or nonpublic schooling.

(b) A facility shall have the capacity to provide secure   – Secure Containment
containment. For purposes of this section, a facility or an area of a facility shall be defined as secure if residents are not permitted to leave the premises of their own volition. All or part of a facility, including its perimeter, but not a room alone, may be locked or secure. If a facility uses perimeter fencing, all beds within the perimeter shall be considered secure beds. All beds outside of a locked or secure wing or facility shall be considered nonsecure beds.

(c) A locked or secure program in a facility shall not be used   – Locked or Secure Program
for disciplinary purposes, but shall be used for the protection of   Used for Protection of
the minor. It may be used as a treatment modality for a child   Minor
needing that level of care. The use of the secure facility program shall be for as short a period as possible, consistent with the child's case plan and safety. The department shall develop regulations governing the oversight, review, and duration of the use of secure beds.

(d) Fire clearance approval shall be obtained pursuant to   – Fire Clearance
Section 1531.2 of the Health and Safety Code.

(e) (1) Prior to admission, any child admitted to a community treatment facility shall have been certified as seriously emotionally disturbed, as defined in Section 5699.2, by a licensed mental health professional. The child shall, prior to admission, have been determined to be in need of the level of care provided by a community treatment facility, by a county interagency placement committee, as prescribed by Section 4096.

(2) Any county cost associated with the certification and the   – County Cost
determination provided for in paragraph (1) may be billed as a utilization review expense.

4094.6. The patients' rights provisions contained in Sections   – Patients' Rights
5325, 5325.1, 5325.2, and 5326 shall be available to any child admitted to, or eligible for admission to, a community treatment facility. Every child placed in a community treatment facility shall have a right to a hearing by writ of habeas corpus, within two judicial days of the filing of a petition for the writ of habeas corpus with the superior court of the county in which the facility

is located, for his or her release. Regulations adopted pursuant to Section 4094 shall specify the procedures by which this right shall be ensured. These regulations shall generally be consistent with the procedures contained in Section 5275 et seq., concerning habeas corpus for individuals, including children, subject to various involuntary holds.

4094.7. (a) A community treatment facility may have both secure and nonsecure beds. However, the State Department of Mental Health shall limit the total number of beds in community treatment facilities to not more than 400 statewide. The State Department of Mental Health shall certify community treatment facilities in such a manner as to ensure an adequate dispersal of these facilities within the state. The State Department of Mental Health shall ensure that there is at least one facility in each of the State Department of Social Services' four regional licensing divisions.

– Secure and Nonsecure Beds

– Not More Than 400 Beds Statewide

(b) The State Department of Mental Health shall notify the State Department of Social Services when a facility has been certified and has met the program standards pursuant to Section 4094. The State Department of Social Services shall license a community treatment facility for a specified number of secure beds and a specified number of nonsecure beds.

– Certification Notification

The number of secure and nonsecure beds in a facility shall be modified only with the approval of both the State Department of Social Services and the State Department of Mental Health.

(c) The State Department of Mental Health shall develop, with the advice of the State Department of Social Services, county representatives, providers, and interested parties, the criteria to be used to determine which programs among applicant providers shall be licensed. The State Department of Mental Health shall determine which agencies best meet the criteria, certify them in accordance with Section 4094, and refer them to the State Department of Social Services for licensure.

– Criteria for Determining Program Licensing

(d) Any community treatment facility proposing to serve seriously emotionally disturbed foster children shall be incorporated as a nonprofit organization.

– Nonprofit Organization

(e) No later than January 1, 1996, the State Department of Mental Health shall submit its recommendation to the appropriate policy committees of the Legislature relative to the limitation on the number of beds set forth in this section.

– Recommendation to Legislature

[For related provisions pertaining to community treatment facilities, see Sections 1502 and 1530.9 of the Health and Safety Code and Sections 5585.58 and 5600.4 of the Welfare and Institutions Code.]

MEDI-CAL COVERED SERVICES

(Welfare and Institutions Code)

(SB 256 - Chapter 654, Statutes of 1993)

14132.06. (a) Services specified in this section that are provided by a local educational agency are covered Medi-Cal benefits, to the extent federal financial participation is available, and subject to utilization controls and standards adopted by the department, and consistent with Medi-Cal requirements for physician prescription, order, and supervision.

– Services Provided by a Local Educational Agency

(b) Any provider enrolled on or after January 1, 1993, to provide services pursuant to this section may bill for those services provided on or after January 1, 1993.

(c) Nothing is this section is intended to increase the scope of practice of any health professional health care practitioners permitted to directly bill the Medi-Cal program.

(d) Nothing in this section is intended to increase the scope of practice of any health professional providing services under this section or Medi-Cal requirements for physician prescription, order, and supervision.

(e) (1) For purposes of this section, the local educational agency shall, as a condition of enrollment to provide services under this section, be considered the provider of services. A local educational agency provider shall, as a condition of enrollment to provide services under section, enter into, and maintain, a contract with the department in accordance with guidelines contained in regulations adopted by the director and published in Title 22 of the California Code of Regulations.

(2) Notwithstanding paragraph (1), a local educational agency providing services pursuant to this section shall utilize current safety net and traditional health care providers, when those providers are accessible to participate in this program, rather than adding duplicate capacity.

(f) For purposes of this section, covered services may include all of the following local educational agency services:

– Included Services

(1) Health and mental health evaluations and health and mental health education.

(2) Medical transportation.

(3) Nursing services.

(4) Occupational therapy.

(5) Physical therapy.

(6) Physician services.

(7) Psychology and counseling services.

(8) School health aide services.

(9) Speech pathology services and audiology services.

(g) Local educational agencies may, but need not, provide any or all of the services specified in subdivision (f).

(h) For purposes of this section, "local educational agency" means the same as defined by subdivision (e) of Section 33509 of the Education Code.

SERIOUSLY EMOTIONALLY DISTURBED OUT-OF-HOME CARE

(Welfare and Institutions Code)

(AB 882 - Chapter 1274, Statutes of 1985; As Amended by SB 370 - Chapter 1294, Statutes of 1989; As Amended by SB 1176 - Chapter 46, Statutes of 1990 and AB 3596 - Chapter 737, Statutes of 1990)

CHAPTER 6. SERIOUSLY EMOTIONALLY DISTURBED CHILDREN: 24-HOUR OUT-OF-HOME CARE

— 24-HOUR OUT-OF-HOME CARE

18350. (a) Payments for 24-hour out-of-home care shall be provided under this chapter on behalf of any seriously emotionally disturbed child who has been placed out-of-home pursuant to an individualized education program developed under Section 7572.5 of the Government Code. These payments shall not constitute an aid payment or aid program.

— Payments

(b) Payments shall only be made to children placed in privately operated residential facilities licensed in accordance with the Community Care Facilities Act.

(c) Payments for care and supervision shall be based on rates established in accordance with Sections 11460 to 11467, inclusive.

(d) Payments for 24-hour out-of-home care under this section shall not result in any cost to the seriously emotionally disturbed child or his or her parent or parents.

18351. (a) Payments shall be issued by the county welfare department to residential care providers upon receipt of authorization documents from the State Department of Mental Health or a designated county mental health agency. The county welfare department located in the same county as the county mental health agency designated to provide case management services shall be responsible for payment under this section. Authorization documents shall be submitted directly to the county welfare department clerical unit responsible for issuance of warrants and shall include information sufficient to demonstrate

— Issued by County Welfare Department

that the child meets all eligibility criteria established in regulations by the State Department of Mental Health, developed in consultation with the State Department of Education.

(b) The county welfare department shall submit reports to the State Department of Social Services for reimbursement of payments issued to seriously emotionally disturbed children for 24-hour out-of-home care.

18352. County welfare departments may, at their option and with approval of the State Department of Social Services and other appropriate agencies, enter into agreements with other local agencies for the delivery of a single payment for all related services for a seriously emotionally disturbed child to a residential care provider.

– Agreements for Single Payment

18353. When an individualized education program calls for 24-hour out-of-home care, the county welfare department shall provide assistance, as necessary, in identifying a facility suited to the child's needs and in placing the child in the facility.

– Provide Assistance in Identifying Facility

18354. (a) If a provider of 24-hour out-of-home care to a child who has been placed pursuant to Section 7572.5 of the Government Code in a 24-hour out-of-home placement disputes an action of the designated county mental health agency regarding the providers eligibility for payment, the provider may request a review of the issue by the designated county mental health agency. Designated county mental health agencies may establish policies and procedures, as may be necessary, to implement this subdivision.

– Disputes Regarding the Provider's Eligibility for Payment

(b) If the issue remains unresolved after the review by the designated county mental health agency, then the provider may request a review of the issue by the State Department of Mental Health. The Director of Mental Health may establish policies and procedures, as may be necessary, to implement this subdivision. The review under this subdivision shall be limited to the issue of whether the eligibility for payment criteria established by the State Department of Mental Health was correctly applied.

18355. Notwithstanding any other provision of the law, 24-hour out-of-home care for seriously emotionally disturbed children who are placed in accordance with Section 7572.5 of the Government Code shall be funded from a separate appropriation in the budget of the State Department of Social Services in order to fund both 24-hour out-of-home care payment and local administrative costs. Reimbursement for 24-hour out-of-home care payment costs shall be from that appropriation, subject to the same sharing ratio as prescribed in subdivision (c) of Section 15200, and available funds. Reimbursements for local administrative costs shall also be from that appropriation, subject

– Separate Appropriation

to the same sharing ratio as prescribed in Section 15204.2 for the Aid to Families with Dependent Children program, and available funds.

18356. (a) When a local mental health department places a client out-of-state pursuant to Chapter 26.5 (commencing with Section 7570) of Division 7 of Title 1 of the Government Code, it shall prepare a report for the Director of Mental Health. The report shall be sent to the State Department of Mental Health within 15 days after the actual placement.

– Report on Out-of-State Placements

(b) The report shall summarize the local mental health department's efforts to locate, develop, or adapt an appropriate program for the client within the state. The report shall also identify the circumstances which led to the out-of-state placement, including the child's experience with California placements, distance from the child's family, child treatment needs which cannot be met in California placement, and any other factors leading to the placement.

(c) The report shall identify any special circumstances, such as legal interventions, including mediation hearings, fair hearings, compliance complaints, or any other legal procedure resulting in an order which mandates the child's placement out of state.

(d) The report shall identify provisions for case management, case supervision, and family visitation in the case of out-of-state placements.

CALIFORNIA EARLY INTERVENTION SERVICES ACT

(Government Code)

(SB 1085 - Chapter 945, Statutes of 1993)

TITLE 14. CALIFORNIA EARLY INTERVENTION SERVICES ACT

CHAPTER 1. GENERAL PROVISIONS

– GENERAL PROVISIONS

95000. This title may be cited as the California Early Intervention Services Act.

– Title

95001. (a) The Legislature hereby finds and declares all of the following:

– Legislative Findings

(1) There is a need to provide appropriate early intervention services individually designed for infants and toddlers from birth through two years of age, who have disabilities or are at risk of having disabilities, to enhance their development and to minimize the potential for developmental delays.

(2) Early intervention services for infants and toddlers with disabilities or at risk represent an investment of resources, in that these services reduce the ultimate costs to our society, by minimizing the need for special education and related services in later school years and by minimizing the likelihood of institutionalization. These services also maximize the ability of families to better provide for the special needs of their child. Early intervention services for infants and toddlers with disabilities maximize the potential to be effective in the context of daily life and activities, including the potential to live independently, and exercise the full rights of citizenship. The earlier intervention is started, the greater is the ultimate cost-effectiveness and the higher is the educational attainment and quality of life achieved by children with disabilities.

(3) The family is the constant in the child's life, while the service system and personnel within those systems fluctuate. Because the primary responsibility of an infant or toddler's well-being rests with the family, services should
support and enhance the family's capability to meet the special developmental needs of their infant or toddler with disabilities.

(4) Family to family support strengthens families' ability to fully participate in services planning and their capacity to care for their infant or toddler with disabilities.

(5) Meeting the complex needs of infants with disabilities and their families requires active state and local coordinated,

collaborative and accessible service delivery systems that are flexible, culturally competent and responsive to family identified needs. When health, developmental, educational and social programs are coordinated, they are proven to be cost-effective, not only for systems, but for families as well.

(6) Family-professional collaboration contributes to changing the ways that early intervention services are provided and to enhancing their effectiveness.

(7) Infants and toddlers with disabilities are a part of their communities, and as citizens make valuable contributions to society as a whole.

(b) Therefore, it is the intent of the Legislature that: – Legislative Intent

(1) Funding provided under Part H of the Individuals with Disabilities Education Act (20 U.S.C. Sec. 1471 et seq.), be used to improve and enhance early intervention services as defined in this title by developing innovative ways of providing family focused, coordinated services, which are built upon existing systems.

(2) The State Department of Developmental Services, the California Department of Education, the State Department of Health Services, the State Department of Mental Health, the State Department of Social Services, and the State Department of Alcohol and Drug Programs coordinate services to infants and toddlers with disabilities and their families. These agencies need to collaborate with families and communities to provide family centered, comprehensive, multidisciplinary, interagency community-based, early intervention services for infants and toddlers with disabilities.

(3) Families be well informed, supported, and respected as capable and collaborative decisionmakers regarding services for their child.

(4) Professionals be supported to enhance their training and maintain a high level of expertise in their field, as well as knowledge of what constitutes most effective early intervention practices.

(5) Families and professionals join in collaborative partnerships to develop early intervention services which meet the needs of infants and toddlers with disabilities, and that such partnerships be the basis for the development of services which meet the needs of the culturally and linguistically diverse population of California.

(6) To the maximum extent possible, infants and toddlers with disabilities and their families be provided services in the most natural environment, and include the use of natural supports and existing community resources.

(7) The services delivery system be responsive to the families and children it serves within the context of cooperation and coordination among the various agencies.

(8) Early intervention program quality be assured and maintained through established early intervention program and personnel standards.

(9) The early intervention system be responsive to public input and participation in the development of implementation policies and procedures for early intervention services through the forum of an interagency coordinating council established pursuant to federal regulations under Part H of the Individuals with Disabilities Education Act.

(c) It is not the intent of the Legislature to require the State Department of Education to implement this title unless adequate reimbursement, as specified and agreed to by the department, is provided to the department from federal funds from Part H of the Individuals with Disabilities Education Act.

95002. The purpose of this title is to provide a statewide system of coordinated, comprehensive, family-centered, multidisciplinary, interagency programs, responsible for providing appropriate early intervention services and support to all eligible infants and toddlers and their families.

– Purpose

95003. (a) The state's participation in Part H of the Individuals with Disabilities Education Act (20 U.S.C. Sec. 1471 et seq.) shall be contingent on the receipt of federal funds to cover the costs of complying with the federal statutes and regulations that impose new requirements on the state. The State Department of Developmental Services and the State Department of Education shall annually report to the Department of Finance during preparation of the Governor's Budget, and the May revision, the budget year costs and federal funds projected to be available.

– State's Participation Contingent on Receipt of Federal Funds

(b) If the amount of funding provided by the federal government pursuant to Part H of the Individuals with Disabilities Education Act for the 1993-94 fiscal year, or any fiscal year thereafter, is not sufficient to fund the full increased costs of participation in this federal program by the local education agencies, as required pursuant to this title, for infants and toddlers from birth through two years of age identified pursuant to Section 95014, and that lack of federal funding would require an increased contribution from the General Fund or a contribution from a local educational agency in order to fund those required and supplemental costs, the state shall terminate its participation in the program. Termination of the program shall occur on July 1 if local education agencies have been notified of the termination prior to March 10 of that calendar

– Termination Provision

year. If this notification is provided after March 10 of a calendar year, then termination shall not occur earlier than July 1 of the subsequent calendar year. The voluntary contribution by a state or local agency of funding for any of the programs or services required pursuant to this title shall not constitute grounds for terminating the state's participation in that federal program. It is the intent of the Legislature that if the program terminates, the termination shall be carried out in an orderly manner with notification of parents and certificated personnel.

(c) This title shall remain in effect only until the state terminates its participation in Part H of the Individuals with Disabilities Education Act (20 U.S.C. Sec. 1471 et seq.) for individuals from birth through two years of age and notifies the Secretary of the Senate of the termination, and as of that later date is repealed. As the lead agency, the State Department of Developmental Services shall, upon notification by the Department of Finance or the State Department of Education as to the insufficiency of federal funds and the termination of this program, be responsible for the payment of services pursuant to this title when no other agency or department is required to make these payments.

95004. The early intervention services specified in this title shall be provided as follows:

(a) Direct services for eligible infants and toddlers and their families shall be provided pursuant to the existing regional center system under the Lanterman Developmental Disabilities Services Act (Division 4.5 (commencing with Section 4500) of the Welfare and Institutions Code) and the existing local education agency system under appropriate sections of Part 30 (commencing with Section 56000) of the Education Code and regulations adopted pursuant thereto, and Part H of the Individuals with Disabilities Education Act (20 U.S.C. Sec. 1471 et seq.).

(b) Existing obligations of the state to provide these services at state expense shall not be expanded.

(c) It is the intent of the Legislature that services be provided in accordance with Sections 303.124, 303.126, and 303.527 of Title 34 of the Code of Federal Regulations.

CHAPTER 2. ADMINISTRATION

95006. This title shall be administered under the shared direction of the Secretary of the Health and Welfare Agency and the Superintendent of Public Instruction. The planning, development, implementation, and monitoring of the statewide system of early intervention services shall be conducted by the

- Title Remains in Effect Only Until State Terminates Participation in Part H (IDEA)

- Responsibility of DDS if Termination of Program Occurs

- Provision of Direct Services

- State Expense Shall Not Be Expanded

- Services Provided in Accordance with Federal Regulations

- ADMINISTRATION

- Administered Under Shared Direction of Secretary of Health and Welfare and Superintendent of Public Instruction

State Department of Developmental Services in collaboration with the State Department of Education with the advice and assistance of an interagency coordinating council established pursuant to federal regulations.

95007. The State Department of Developmental Services shall serve as the lead agency responsible for administration and coordination of the statewide system. The specific duties and responsibilities of the State Department of Developmental Services shall include, but are not limited to, all of the following:

— DDS Serves as Lead Agency; Duties and Responsibilities

(a) Establishing a single point of contact with the federal Office of Special Education Programs for the administration of Part H of the Individuals with Disabilities Education Act.

— Single Point of Contact

(b) Administering the state early intervention system in accordance with Part H of the Individuals with Disabilities Education Act (20 U.S.C. Sec. 1471 et seq.), and applicable regulations and approved state application.

— Administer System

(c) Administering mandatory and discretionary components as specified in Sections 95022 and 95024.

— Administer Components

(d) Administering fiscal arrangements and interagency agreements with participating agencies and community-based organizations to implement this title.

— Administer Fiscal Arrangements/Interagency Agreements

(e) Establishing interagency procedures, including the designation of local coordinating structures, as are necessary to share agency information and to coordinate policymaking activities.

— Establish Interagency Procedures

(f) Adopting written procedures for receiving and resolving complaints regarding violations of Part H of the Individuals with Disabilities Education Act by public agencies covered under this title, as specified in Section 1476(b)(9) of Title 20 of the United States Code and appropriate federal regulations.

— Adopt Procedures for Receiving and Resolving Complaints

(g) Establishing, adopting, and implementing procedural safeguards that comply with the requirements of Part H of the Individuals with Disabilities Education Act, as specified in Section 1480 of Title 20 of the United States Code and appropriate federal regulations.

— Procedural Safeguards

(h) Monitoring of agencies, institutions, and organizations receiving assistance under this title.

— Monitor Entities Receiving Assistance

(i) Establishing innovative approaches to information distribution, family support services, and interagency coordination at the local level.

— Establish Innovative Approaches

(j) Ensuring the provision of appropriate early intervention services to all infants eligible under Part H of the Individuals with Disabilities Education Act (20 U.S.C. Sec. 1471 et seq.) and under Section 95014, except for those infants who have solely a low incidence disability as defined in Section 56026.5 of the Education Code and who are not eligible for services under

— Ensure Provision of Appropriate Services – Except for Infants Who Have Solely a Low Incidence Disability

the Lanterman Development Disabilities Services Act (Division 4.5 (commencing with Section 4500) of the Welfare and Institutions Code).

The development and implementation of subdivisions (e) to (h), inclusive, shall be a collaborative effort between the State Department of Developmental Services and the State Department of Education. In establishing the written procedures for receiving and resolving complaints as specified in subdivision (f) and in establishing and implementing procedural safeguards as specified in subdivision (g), it is the intent of the Legislature that these procedures be identical for all infants served under this act and shall be in accordance with Section 303.400 and subdivision (b) of Section 303.420 of Title 34 of the Code of Federal Regulations. The procedural safeguards and due process requirements established under this title shall replace and be used in lieu of due process procedures contained in Chapter 1 (commencing with Section 4500) of Division 4.5 of the Welfare and Institutions Code and Part 30 (commencing with Section 56500) of the Education Code for infants and their families eligible under this title.

— Collaborative Effort

— Procedural Safeguards be Identical for All Infants

95008. The State Department of Education shall be responsible for administering services and programs for infants with solely visual, hearing, and severe orthopedic impairments, and any combination thereof, who meet the criteria in Sections 56026 and 56026.5 of the Education Code, and in subdivisions (a), (b), (d), or (e) of Section 3030 of, and Section 3031 of, Title 5 of the California Code of Regulations and Part H of the Individuals with Disabilities Education Act (20 U.S.C. Section 1471 et seq.) and who are not eligible for services under the Lanterman Developmental Disabilities Services Act (Division 4.5 (commencing with Section 4500) of the Welfare and Institutions Code).

— Education Responsible for Administering Programs for Infants with Solely Visual, Hearing, and Severe Orthopedic Impairments

95009. The development of joint regulations for meeting the requirements of this title shall be the shared responsibility of the State Department of Developmental Services on behalf of the Secretary of the Health and Welfare Agency, and the State Department of Education on behalf of the Superintendent of Public Instruction. The joint regulations shall be agreed upon by both departments. These regulations shall be developed and approved by October 1, 1995. The Department of Finance shall review and comment upon the joint regulations prior to any public hearing on them.

— Development of Joint Regulations

CHAPTER 3. STATE INTERAGENCY COORDINATION

95012. (a) The following departments shall cooperate and coordinate their early intervention services for eligible infants and their families under this title:

(1) State Department of Developmental Services.
(2) State Department of Education.
(3) State Department of Health Services.
(4) State Department of Social Services.
(5) State Department of Mental Health.
(6) State Department of Alcohol and Drug Programs.

(b) Each participating department shall enter into an interagency agreement with the State Department of Developmental Services. Each interagency agreement shall specify, at a minimum, the agency's current and continuing level of financial participation in providing services to infants and toddlers with disabilities and their families. Each interagency agreement shall also specify procedures for resolving disputes in a timely manner. Interagency agreements shall also contain provisions for ensuring effective cooperation and coordination among agencies concerning policymaking activities associated with the implementation of this title, including legislative proposals, regulation development, and fiscal planning. All interagency agreements shall be reviewed annually and revised as necessary.

CHAPTER 4. ELIGIBILITY

95014. (a) The term "eligible infant or toddler" for the purposes of this title means infants and toddlers from birth through two years of age, for whom a need for early intervention services, as specified in the Individuals with Disabilities Education Act (20 U.S.C. Sec. 1471 et seq.) and applicable regulations, is documented by means of assessment and evaluation as required in Sections 95016 and 95018 and who meet one of the following criteria:

(1) Infants and toddlers with a developmental delay in one or more of the following five areas: cognitive development; physical and motor development, including vision and hearing; communication development; social or emotional development; or adaptive development. Developmentally delayed infants and toddlers are those who are determined to have a significant difference between the expected level of development for their age and their current level of functioning. This determination shall be made by qualified personnel who are recognized by, or part of, a multidisciplinary team, including the parents.

(2) Infants and toddlers with established risk conditions, who are infants and toddlers with conditions of known etiology or conditions with established harmful developmental consequences. The conditions shall be diagnosed by a qualified personnel recognized by, or part of, a multidisciplinary team, including the parents. The condition shall be certified as having a high probability of leading to developmental delay if the delay is not evident at the time of diagnosis.

(3) Infants and toddlers who are at high risk of having substantial developmental disability due to a combination of biomedical risk factors, the presence of which is diagnosed by qualified clinicians recognized by, or part of, a multidisciplinary team, including the parents.

(b) Regional centers and local education agencies shall be responsible for ensuring that eligible infants and toddlers are served as follows:

- Regional Centers and Local Education Agencies

(1) The State Department of Developmental Services and regional centers shall be responsible for the provision of appropriate early intervention services in accordance with Part H of the Individuals with Disabilities Education Act (20 U.S.C. Sec. 1471 et seq.) for all infants eligible under Section 95014, except for those infants with solely a visual, hearing, or severe orthopedic impairment, or any combination thereof, who meet the criteria in Sections 56026 and 56026.5 of the Education Code, and in subdivisions (a), (b), (d), or (e) of Section 3030 of, and Section 3031 of, Title 5 of the California Code of Regulations.

- Services Provided by DDS and Regional Centers

(2) The State Department of Education and local education agencies shall be responsible for the provision of appropriate early intervention services in accordance with Part H of the Individuals with Disabilities Education Act (20 U.S.C. Sec. 1471 et seq.) for infants with solely a visual, hearing, or severe orthopedic impairment, or any combination thereof who meet the criteria in Sections 56026 and 56026.5 of the Education Code, and in subdivisions (a), (b), (d), or (e) of Section 3030 of, and Section 3031 of, Title 5 of the California Code of Regulations, and who are not eligible for services under the Lanterman Developmental Services Disabilities Act (Division 4.5 (commencing with Section 4500) of the Welfare and Institutions Code).

- Services Provided by Education

(c) For infants and toddlers and their families who are eligible to receive services from both a regional center and a local education agency, the regional center shall be the agency responsible for providing or purchasing appropriate early intervention services that are beyond the mandated responsibilities of local education agencies. The local education agency shall provide special education services up to its funded program

- Infants/Toddlers Eligible to Receive Services from Both a Regional Center and a Local Education Agency capacity as established annually by the State Department of Education in consultation with the State Department of Developmental Services and the Department of Finance.

(d) No agency or multidisciplinary team, including any agency listed in Section 95012, shall presume or determine eligibility, including eligibility for medical services, for any other agency. However, regional centers and local education agencies shall coordinate intake, evaluation, assessment, and individualized family service plans for infants and toddlers and their families who are served by an agency.

— Shall Not Determine Eligibility for Any Other Agency

(e) Upon termination of the program pursuant to Section 95003, the State Department of Developmental Services shall be responsible for the payment of services pursuant to this title.

— DDS Responsible for Payment of Services Upon Termination

CHAPTER 5. SERVICES

— SERVICES

95016. (a) Each infant or toddler referred for evaluation for early intervention services shall have a timely, comprehensive, multidisciplinary evaluation of his or her needs and level of functioning in order to determine eligibility. If the infant or toddler is determined eligible, an assessment shall be conducted to identify the child's unique strengths and needs and the services appropriate to meet those needs; and the resources, priorities and concerns of the family and the supports and services necessary to enhance the family's capacity to meet the developmental needs of their infant or toddler. Family assessments shall be family directed and voluntary on the part of the family.

— Timely, Comprehensive, Multidisciplinary Evaluation

(b) Regional centers and local education agencies or their designees shall be responsible for ensuring that the requirements of this section are implemented. The procedures, requirements, and timelines for evaluation and assessment shall be consistent with the statutes and regulations under Part H of the Individuals with Disabilities Education Act (20 U.S.C. 1471 et seq.), applicable regulations, and this title, and shall be specified in regulations adopted pursuant to Section 95028.

— Responsibility for Ensuring Requirements are Implemented

95018. Each eligible infant or toddler and family shall be provided a service coordinator who will be responsible for facilitating the implementation of the individualized family service plan and for coordinating with other agencies and persons providing services to the family. The qualifications, responsibilities, and functions of service coordinators shall be consistent with the statutes and regulations under Part H and this title, and shall be specified in regulations adopted pursuant to Section 95028. Pursuant to Section 303.521 of Title 34 of the Code of Federal Regulations, service coordination is not subject

— Service Coordinator

to any fees that might be established for any other federal or state program.

95020. (a) Each eligible infant or toddler shall have an individualized family service plan. The individualized family service plan shall be used in place of an individualized program plan required pursuant to Sections 4646 and 4646.5 of the Welfare and Institutions Code, the individual education plan required pursuant to Section 56340 of the Education Code, or any other applicable service plan.

- Individualized Family Service Plan (IFSP)

(b) For an infant or toddler who has been evaluated for the first time, a meeting to determine eligibility and to develop the initial individualized family service plan shall be conducted within 45 calendar days of receipt of the written referral. Written parent consent to evaluate and assess shall be obtained within the 45-day timeline. A regional center, local education agency, or their designees shall initiate and conduct this meeting.

- Meeting to Determine Eligibility and Develop Initial IFSP Conducted Within 45 Days of Receipt of Written Referral

(c) The individualized family service plan shall be in writing and shall address all of the following:

- Content of IFSP

(1) A statement of the infant or toddler's present levels of physical development including vision, hearing, and health status, cognitive development, communication development, social and emotional development, and adaptive developments.

(2) With the concurrence of the family, a statement of the family's concerns, priorities, and resources related to meeting the special developmental needs of the eligible infant or toddler.

(3) A statement of the major outcomes expected to be achieved for the infant or toddler and family where services for the family are related to meeting the special developmental needs of the eligible infant or toddler.

(4) The criteria, procedures, and timelines used to determine the degree to which progress toward achieving the outcomes is being made and whether modifications or revisions are necessary.

(5) A statement of the specific early intervention services necessary to meet the unique needs of the infant or toddler as identified in paragraph (3), including, but not limited to, the frequency, intensity, location, duration, and method of delivering the services, and ways of providing services in natural environments.

(6) A statement of the agency responsible for providing the identified services.

(7) The name of the service coordinator who shall be responsible for facilitating implementation of the plan and coordinating with other agencies and persons.

(8) The steps to be taken to ensure transition of the infant or toddler upon reaching three years of age to other appropriate services. These may include, as appropriate, special education

or other services offered in natural environments.

(9) The projected dates for the initiation of services in paragraph (5) and the anticipated duration of those services.

(d) Each service identified on the individualized family service plan shall be designated as one of three types:

– Types of Services
   Identified in IFSP

(1) An early intervention service, as defined in Part H (20 U.S.C. Section 1472 (2)), and applicable regulations, that is provided or purchased through the regional center, local education agency, or other participating agency. The State Department of Health Services, State Department of Social Services, State Department of Mental Health, and State Department of Alcohol and Drug Programs shall provide services in accordance with state and federal law and applicable regulations, and up to the level of funding as appropriated by the Legislature. Early intervention services identified on an individualized family service plan that exceed the funding, statutory, and regulatory requirements of these departments shall be provided or purchased by regional centers or local education agencies under subdivisions (b) and (c) of Section 95014. The State Department of Health Services, State Department of Social Services, State Department of Mental Health, and State Department of Alcohol and Drug Programs shall not be required to provide early intervention services over their existing funding, statutory, and regulatory requirements.

(2) Any other service, other than those specified in paragraph (1), which the eligible infant or toddler or his or her family may receive from other state programs, subject to the eligibility standards of those programs.

(3) A referral to a nonrequired service that may be provided to an eligible infant or toddler or his or her family. Nonrequired services are those services that are not defined as early intervention services or do not relate to meeting the special developmental needs of an eligible infant or toddler related to the disability, but which may be helpful to the family. The granting or denial of nonrequired services by any public or private agency is not subject to appeal under this title.

(e) An annual review, and other periodic reviews of the individualized family service plan for an infant's or toddler and the infant or toddler's family shall be conducted to determine the degree of progress that is being made in achieving the outcomes specified in the plan and whether modification or revision of the outcomes or services is necessary. The frequency, participants, purpose, and required processes for annual and periodic reviews shall be consistent with the statutes and regulations under Part H and this title, and shall be specified in regulations adopted pursuant to Section 95028.

– Annual and Periodic
   Reviews

95022. The statewide system of early intervention shall be administered by the State Department of Developmental Services in collaboration with the State Department of Education and with the advice and assistance of an interagency coordinating council established pursuant to federal regulations and shall include all of the following mandatory components:

- Components of Statewide System of Early Intervention

(a) A central directory that includes information about early intervention services, resources, and experts available in the state, professionals and other groups providing services to eligible infants and toddlers, and research and demonstration projects being conducted in the state. The central directory shall specify the nature and scope of the services available and the telephone number and address for each of the sources listed in the directory.

- Central Directory

(b) A public awareness program focusing on early identification of eligible infants and toddlers and the dissemination of information about the purpose and scope of the system of early intervention services and how to access evaluation and other early intervention services.

- Public Awareness Program

(c) Personnel standards that ensure that personnel are appropriately and adequately prepared and trained.

- Personnel Standards

(d) A comprehensive system of personnel development that provides training for personnel including, but not limited to, public and private providers, primary referral sources, paraprofessionals, and persons who will serve as service coordinators. The training shall specifically address at least all of the following:

- Comprehensive System of Personnel Development – Training

(1) Understanding the early intervention services system, including the family service plan process.

(2) Meeting the interrelated social, emotional, and health needs of eligible infants and toddlers.

(3) Assisting families in meeting the special developmental needs of the infant or toddler, assisting professionals to utilize best practices in family focused early intervention services and promoting family professional collaboration.

(4) Reflecting the unique needs of local communities and promoting culturally competent service delivery.

(e) A comprehensive child-find system, including policies and procedures that ensure that all infants and toddlers who may be eligible for services under this title are identified, located, and evaluated, that services are coordinated between participating agencies, and that infants and toddlers are referred to the appropriate agency.

- Child-Find System

(f) A surrogate parent program established pursuant to Section 303.405 of Title 34 of the Code of Federal Regulations to be used by regional centers and local education agencies.

- Surrogate Parent Program

CHAPTER 6. FUNDING

95024. (a) Any increased cost to local educational agencies due to the implementation of this title shall be funded from the Part H federal funds provided for the purposes of this title.

(b) Any increased costs to regional centers due to the implementation of this title shall be funded from the Part H federal funds provided for the purposes of this title.

(c) The annual Budget Act shall specify the amount of federal Part H funds allocated for local assistance and for state operations individually, for the State Department of Developmental Services, and for the State Department of Education.

(d) If federal funds are available after mandatory components and increased costs in subdivisions (a) and (b), if any, are funded, the lead agency, in consultation with the State Department of Education, may do the following:

(1) Designate local interagency coordination areas throughout the state and allocate available Part H funds to fund interagency coordination activities, including, but not limited to, outreach and public awareness, and interagency approaches to service planning and delivery. If the lead agency chooses to designate and fund local interagency coordination areas, the lead agency shall first offer to enter into a contract with the regional center or a local education agency. If the regional center or any of the local education agencies do not accept the offer, the lead agency, in consultation with the State Department of Education and the approval of the regional center and local education agencies in the area, may directly enter into a contract with a private, nonprofit organization. Nothing in this section shall preclude a regional center or local education agency that enters into a contract with the lead agency from subcontracting with a private, nonprofit organization.

(2) Allocate funds to support family resource services, including, but not limited to, parent-to-parent support, information dissemination and referral, public awareness, family-professional collaboration activities, and transition assistance for families.

(e) If an expenditure plan is developed under subdivision (d), the lead agency, in consultation with the State Department of Education, shall give high priority to funding family resource services.

(f) Nothing in this section shall be construed to limit the lead agency's authority, in consultation with the State Department of Education, to allocate discretionary Part H funds for any legitimate purpose consistent with the statutes and regulations under Part H (20 U.S.C. Secs. 1471 to 1485, inclusive) and this title.

CHAPTER 7. DATA COLLECTION

– DATA COLLECTION

95026. The lead agency shall maintain a system for compiling data required by the federal Office of Special Education Programs, through Part H of the Individuals with Disabilities Education Act, including the number of eligible infants and toddlers and their families in need of appropriate early intervention services, the number of eligible infants and toddlers and their families served, the types of services provided, and other information required by the federal Office of Special Education Programs. All participating agencies listed in Section 95012 shall assist in the development of the system and shall cooperate with the lead agency in meeting federal data requirements. The feasibility of using existing systems and including social security numbers shall be explored to facilitate data collection.

– DDS Shall Maintain System
  For Compiling Data

CHAPTER 8. REGULATIONS

– REGULATIONS

95028. (a) On or before October 1, 1995, the State Department of Developmental Services, on behalf of the Secretary of the Health and Welfare Agency, and the State Department of Education, on behalf of the Superintendent of Public Instruction, shall jointly develop, approve, and implement regulations, as necessary, to comply with the requirements of this title and Part H, as specified in federal statutes and regulations.

– Timeline for Regulations

(b) The regulations developed pursuant to this section shall include, but are not limited to, the following requirements:

– Scope of Regulations

(1) The administrative structure for planning and implementation of the requirements of this title and Part H.

(2) Eligibility for Part H services.

(3) Evaluation and assessment.

(4) Individualized family service plans.

(5) Service coordination.

(6) The program and service components of the statewide system for early intervention services.

(7) The duties and responsibilities of the lead agency as specified in Section 95006, including procedural safeguards and the process for resolving complaints against a public agency for violation of the requirements of Part H.

(c) The State Department of Developmental Services shall adopt regulations to implement this title in accordance with Chapter 3.5 (commencing with Section 11340) of Part 1 of

– DDS Shall Adopt Regulations

Division 3 of Title 2. Initial regulations to implement this title shall be adopted as emergency regulations. The adoption of these initial emergency regulations shall be considered by the Office of Administrative Law to be an emergency and necessary for the immediate preservation of the public peace, health and safety, or general welfare. The initial emergency regulations shall remain in effect for no more than 180 days. These regulations shall be jointly developed by the State Department of Developmental Services and the State Department of Education by July 1, 1994. The Department of Finance shall review and comment upon the emergency regulations prior to their adoption.

— Emergency Regulations

CHAPTER 9. EVALUATION

— EVALUATION

95029. The State Department of Developmental Services and the State Department of Education shall ensure that an independent evaluation of the program and its structure is completed by October 1, 1996. The evaluation shall address the following issues:

— Scope of Evaluation

(a) The efficiency and cost-effectiveness of the state administrative structure, the local interagency coordinating structure, and the mandatory program components.

(b) The degree to which programs and services provided through regional centers and local education agencies fulfill the purpose of Part H of the Individuals with Disabilities Education Act.

(c) The extent to which implementation of the program has resulted in improved services for infants and their families, and greater satisfaction with service delivery by families.

(d) The outcomes and effectiveness of family resource centers.

(e) The adequacy of the Part H funding models. The evaluation shall be funded with federal funds.

CHAPTER 10. TERMINATION

— TERMINATION

95030. Unless repealed earlier pursuant to subdivision (c) of Section 95003, this division shall remain in effect only until January 1, 1998, and as of that date is repealed, unless a later enacted statute, which is chaptered before January 1, 1998, deletes or extends that date.

— January 1, 1998 Sunset Date

LIST OF SPECIAL EDUCATION CODE SECTIONS - LEGISLATIVE BILLS
EDUCATION CODE - PART 30. SPECIAL EDUCATION PROGRAMS

The following is a list of special education code sections and the most recent legislative bills which affected them. See Page I-3 for year bills were enacted.

EDUCATION CODE SECTION	LEGISLATIVE BILL NUMBER	EDUCATION CODE SECTION	LEGISLATIVE BILL NUMBER	EDUCATION CODE SECTION	LEGISLATIVE BILL NUMBER
56000	AB 369	56156	AB 1528	56323	SB 1870
56000.5	AB 1836	56156.5	SB 998	56324	AB 3075
56001	AB 1836	56156.6	AB 817	56325	AB 3880
56020	SB 1870	56157	SB 998	56326	AB 1248
56021	SB 1870	56159	SB 998	56327	AB 2652
56022	SB 1870	56160	AB 2355	56328	SB 998
56023	SB 1870	56161	AB 1537	56329	SB 1345
56024	SB 1870	56162	SB 1345	56333	AB 3075
56025	SB 1870	56163	AB 817	56337	SB 1870
56026	AB 369	56164	AB 817	56337.5	AB 2773
56026.2	AB 1836	56165	AB 817	56338	AB 3075
56026.5	AB 1248	56166	AB 817	56339	AB 2773
56027	SB 998	56166.5	AB 817	56340	SB 998
56028	AB 1528	56167	AB 1155	56340.1	AB 369
56029	SB 1870	56167.5	AB 3246	56341	AB 369
56030	SB 1870	56168	AB 2355	56342	SB 998
56030.5	AB 1248	56169	AB 3246	56343	AB 1845
56031	AB 1248	56169.5	AB 3246	56343.5	AB 456
56032	AB 369	56169.7	AB 3246	56344	AB 2773
56033	SB 1870	56170	AB 1891	56345	AB 1836
56034	AB 3601	56171	AB 2773	56345.1	AB 2773
56035	AB 2355	56172	SB 998	56345.5	SB 998
56040	AB 3075	56190	SB 1870	56346	AB 3235
56041	AB 2773	56191	AB 1055	56347	SB 2403
56042	AB 2355	56192	AB 1248	56350	AB 2445
56050	AB 369	56193	SB 1870	56351	AB 2445
56060	SB 1870	56194	SB 998	56352	AB 2445
56061	SB 1870	56200	AB 369	56360	SB 998
56062	SB 1870	56201	SB 2059	56361	AB 675
56063	SB 1870	56210	SB 823	56361.2	AB 3246
56100	AB 3235	56211	SB 823	56361.5	SB 998
56101	AB 369	56212	SB 823	56362	AB 456
56120	SB 1870	56213	SB 823	56362.1	AB 1055
56121	SB 1870	56214	SB 823	56362.5	SB 1634
56122	SB 1870	56214.5	SB 823	56362.7	SB 386
56123	SB 1870	56217	SB 823	56363	AB 1892
56124	SB 1870	56218	SB 823	56363.1	AB 3235
56125	SB 1870	56220	SB 998	56363.3	SB 998
56126	SB 1870	56221	AB 2798	56363.5	SB 998
56127	SB 1870	56222	AB 817	56364	AB 369
56128	SB 1870	56240	SB 998	56364.1	AB 2652
56129	SB 998	56241	SB 1870	56364.5	SB 998
56130	SB 1870	56242	AB 3513	56365	AB 2971
56131	SB 1870	56243	SB 2403	56365.5	AB 2925
56132	SB 1870	56244	SB 2194	56366	AB 2971
56133	AB 3075	56245	AB 1487	56366.1	AB 3793
56134	AB 369	56300	SB 998	56366.2	AB 2971
56135	AB 369	56301	SB 998	56366.3	AB 3793
56136	AB 2652	56302	AB 1060	56366.4	AB 2355
56137	AB 1892	56303	SB 1870	56366.5	SB 998
56138	AB 2773	56320	AB 2652	56366.6	AB 2355
56140	SB 585	56320.1	AB 369	56366.7	AB 3793
56150	AB 456	56321	AB 2773	56367	AB 369
56155	AB 817	56321.5	AB 2267	56368	AB 1248
56155.5	AB 3601	56322	SB 998	56369	SB 998

EDUCATION CODE SECTION	LEGISLATIVE BILL NUMBER	EDUCATION CODE SECTION	LEGISLATIVE BILL NUMBER	EDUCATION CODE SECTION	LEGISLATIVE BILL NUMBER
56370	SB 896	56500.1	AB 2773	56740	AB 2971
56380	SB 998	56500.2	AB 2773	56741	AB 1250
56381	AB 3075	56500.3	AB 2773	56742	SB 769
56382	AB 369	56501	AB 2773	56743	AB 1250
56400	AB 456	56502	AB 369	56750	SB 1870
56425	AB 3246	56503	AB 2773	56751	SB 769
56425.5	AB 1248	56504	SB 1345	56752	AB 3075
56426	AB 369	56504.5	AB 2773	56753	AB 3075
56426.1	AB 369	56505	AB 3235	56754	AB 3075
56426.2	AB 369	56505.1	AB 2773	56760	SB 998
56426.25	AB 369	56505.2	AB 2355	56761	SB 998
56426.3	AB 3246	56506	AB 3075	56762	SB 1870
56426.4	AB 3246	56507	AB 2773	56771	SB 1264
56426.5	AB 369	56508	AB 2773	56775	AB 1250
56426.6	AB 369	56520	AB 1248	56775.5	AB 1537
56426.7	AB 3235	56521	AB 1248	56776	AB 1537
56426.8	AB 3235	56523	AB 2586	56777	AB 1537
56426.9	AB 3235	56524	AB 2586	56780	AB 456
56427	AB 369	56600	SB 2059	56781	AB 456
56428	SB 1264	56600.5	SB 2059	56782	AB 456
56429	AB 3235	56601	AB 2773	56783	AB 456
56430	AB 675	56602	AB 1250	56790	SB 1870
56431	AB 3246	56603	SB 1870	56791	SB 1870
56440	AB 3235	56604	SB 2059	56792	SB 1870
56441	AB 369	56605	SB 2059	56820	SB 1870
56441.1	AB 2666	56606	SB 998	56821	SB 1870
56441.2	AB 2666	56700	SB 998	56822	AB 3235
56441.3	AB 2666	56701	SB 1870	56823	SB 998
56441.4	AB 1248	56702	SB 1870	56824	SB 998
56441.5	AB 1248	56710	SB 1870	56825	SB 998
56441.6	AB 2666	56711	AB 1250	56826	SB 998
56441.7	AB 2666	56712	SB 732	56827	AB 2875
56441.8	AB 675	56713	SB 1345	56828	AB 1891
56441.9	AB 2666	56714	SB 1870	56829	SB 769
56441.10	SB 2059	56720	SB 1870	56830	AB 2587
56441.11	AB 3235	56721	SB 3075	56831	AB 369
56441.13	AB 2666	56722	AB 369	56840	AB 1242
56441.14	AB 2666	56723	AB 813	56840.1	AB 1242
56442	AB 2666	56724	AB 3075	56841	AB 1242
56443	AB 2666	56725	AB 1248	56842	AB 1242
56445	AB 2666	56726	SB 769	56843	AB 1242
56446	AB 2587	56727	AB 456	56844	AB 1242
56447	AB 2666	56728	AB 1248	56845.1	AB 1242
56447.1	AB 2666	56728.5	AB 1537	56845.2	AB 1242
56448	AB 3783	56728.6	AB 1248	56845.5	AB 1242
56449	AB 2666	56728.7	AB 1250	56848	AB 1242
56452	AB 2386	56728.8	AB 1248	56848.5	AB 1242
56453	AB 3075	56728.9	SB 1347	56849	AB 1242
56454	AB 2386	56730	SB 1870	56850	AB 369
56456	AB 2386	56730.5	SB 1264	56851	AB 369
56460	AB 2386	56730.6	SB 769	56852	AB 369
56461	AB 2386	56730.7	AB 1446	56852.5	SB 1345
56462	AB 3562	56731	AB 2973	56853	AB 369
56463	AB 2386	56732	AB 1250	56854	SB 1345
56470	AB 2386	56733	SB 1870	56855	AB 1202
56471	SB 2059	56734	AB 3057	56856	AB 1345
56472	AB 2386	56735	SB 769	56857	SB 679
56473	AB 2386	56736	SB 1345	56857.5	SB 1345
56474	AB 2386	56737	AB 1248	56858	AB 982
56475	AB 369	56738	AB 675	56858.5	SB 1345
56500	SB 998	56739	AB 1892	56858.7	SB 1345

EDUCATION CODE - PART 30. SPECIAL EDUCATION PROGRAMS

Bills Enacted in 1980: SB 1870, AB 1202, AB 3075
Bills Enacted in 1981: SB 769, AB 817, AB 1055
Bills Enacted in 1982: SB 386, SB 1345, AB 2652
Bills Enacted in 1983: SB 679, SB 813, AB 1892
Bills Enacted in 1984: SB 1634
Bills Enacted in 1985: SB 1264, AB 456, AB 982, AB 1537
Bills Enacted in 1986: SB 2403, AB 3246
Bills Enacted in 1987: SB 998, AB 1155, AB 2386, AB 2666
Bills Enacted in 1988: SB 2059, AB 3513
Bills Enacted in 1990: SB 823, SB 2194, AB 1528, AB 2586, AB 2875,
                        AB 3057, AB 3880
Bills Enacted in 1991: AB 675, AB 1060, AB 1487, AB 1845
Bills Enacted in 1992: AB 1248, AB 1446, AB 2267, AB 2773, AB 2925, AB 3783
Bills Enacted in 1993: SB 896, AB 369, AB 1242, AB 1891, AB 2355
Bills Enacted in 1994: SB 732, SB 1347, AB 1250, AB 1836, AB 2445, AB 2587,
                        AB 2798, AB 2971, AB 3235, AB 3562, AB 3601, AB 3793

THE FOLLOWING STATUTES HAVE MODIFIED SPECIAL EDUCATION CODE SECTIONS IN PART 30 OF THE EDUCATION CODE SINCE 1980:

BILL/AUTHOR	CHAPTER NUMBER/EFFECTIVE DATE
1980	
Senate Bill 1870 (Rodda)	- Chapter 797 - Statutes of 1980 July 28, 1980
Assembly Bill 3075 (Papan)	- Chapter 1353 - Statutes of 1980 September 30, 1980
Assembly Bill 507 (Chacon)	- Chapter 1339 - Statutes of 1980 January 1, 1981
Assembly Bill 1202 (Hart)	- Chapter 1191 - Statutes of 1980 September 29, 1980
Assembly Bill 2286 (Kapiloff)	- Chapter 1325 - Statutes of 1980 January 1, 1981
Assembly Bill 2394 (Egeland)	- Chapter 1276 - Statutes of 1980 January 1, 1981
Assembly Bill 3043 (Vasconcellos)	- Chapter 1373 - Statutes of 1980 January 1, 1981
Assembly Bill 3269 (Hart)	- Chapter 1329 - Statutes of 1980 January 1, 1981
Senate Bill 1616 (Watson)	- Chapter 1218 - Statutes of 1980 January 1, 1981
1981	
Senate Bill 769 (Sieroty)	- Chapter 1094 - Statutes of 1981 January 1, 1982, With Computation or Recomputations of Allowances Deemed Operative for Entire 1981-82 Fiscal Year
Senate Bill 1192 (Rains)	- Chapter 714 - Statutes of 1981 January 1, 1982
Assembly Bill 61 (L. Greene)	- Chapter 1093 - Statutes of 1981 January 1, 1982
Assembly Bill 92 (Lehman)	- Chapter 1176 - Statutes of 1981 January 1, 1982
Assembly Bill 159 (Kapiloff)	- Chapter 149 - Statutes of 1981 January 1, 1982

BILL/AUTHOR	CHAPTER NUMBER/EFFECTIVE DATE
Assembly Bill 817 (Papan)	- Chapter 1044 - Statutes of 1981 January 1, 1982/July 1, 1982
Assembly Bill 933 (Kapiloff)	- Chapter 893 - Statutes of 1981 January 1, 1982
Assembly Bill 1055 (Farr)	- Chapter 972 - Statutes of 1981 January 1, 1982

1982

Senate Bill 386 (Stiern)	- Chapter 866 - Statutes of 1982 September 9, 1982
Senate Bill 1345 (Sieroty)	- Chapter 1201 - Statutes of 1982 September 22, 1982
Senate Bill 2058 (Rains)	- Chapter 466 - Statutes of 1982 January 1, 1983
Assembly Bill 1124 (Hughes)	- Chapter 11 - Statutes of 1982 January 27, 1983
Assembly Bill 1253 (Vasconcellos)	- Chapter 115 - Statutes of 1982 March 12, 1982
Assembly Bill 2652 (Moore)	- Chapter 1334 - Statutes of 1982 January 1, 1983
Assembly Bill 3049 (Kapiloff)	- Chapter 644 - Statutes of 1982 January 1, 1983

1983

Senate Bill 679 (Seymour)	- Chapter 922 - Statutes of 1983 September 20, 1983
Senate Bill 813 (Hart)	- Chapter 498 - Statutes of 1983 July 28, 1983
Assembly Bill 1063 (Hughes)	- Chapter 501 - Statutes of 1983 July 28, 1983
Assembly Bill 1892 (Felando)	- Chapter 1099 - Statutes of 1983 January 1, 1984

BILL/AUTHOR	CHAPTER NUMBER/EFFECTIVE DATE

1984

Senate Bill 585 (Seymour)	- Chapter 1668 - Statutes of 1984 January 1, 1985
Senate Bill 1379 (Alquist)	- Chapter 268 - Statutes of 1984 June 29, 1984
Senate Bill 1634 (Keene)	- Chapter 144 - Statutes of 1984 January 1, 1985
Assembly Bill 2841 (Felando)	- Chapter 1677 - Statutes of 1984 September 30, 1984
Assembly Bill 3007 (Mountjoy)	- Chapter 1717 - Statutes of 1984 September 30, 1984

1985

Senate Bill 1264 (Seymour)	- Chapter 1603 - Statutes of 1985 October 2, 1985
Assembly Bill 72 (Felando)	- Chapter 55 - Statutes of 1985 June 4, 1985
Assembly Bill 456 (Papan)	- Chapter 795 - Statutes of 1985 January 1, 1986
Assembly Bill 982 (O'Connell)	- Chapter 1546 - Statutes of 1985 January 1, 1986
Assembly Bill 1537 (Farr)	- Chapter 999 - Statutes of 1985 September 26, 1985
Assembly Bill 1807 (Harris)	- Chapter 106 - Statutes of 1985 January 1, 1986
Assembly Bill 2557 (Papan)	- Chapter 115 - Statutes of 1985 June 28, 1985

1986

Senate Bill 656 (Seymour)	- Chapter 7 - Statutes of 1986 February 18, 1986
Senate Bill 2403 (Seymour)	- Chapter 233 - Statutes of 1986 July 2, 1986
Assembly Bill 3011 (Farr)	- Chapter 374 - Statutes of 1986 July 16, 1986

BILL/AUTHOR	CHAPTER NUMBER/EFFECTIVE DATE
Assembly Bill 3246 (Papan)	- Chapter 1296 - Statutes of 1986 January 1, 1987/July 1, 1987
Assembly Bill 3263 (O'Connell)	- Chapter 1124 - Statutes of 1986 January 1, 1987
Assembly Bill 4074 (Allen)	- Chapter 703 - Statutes of 1986 January 1, 1987

1987

Senate Bill 998 (Hart)	- Chapter 1452 - Statutes of 1987 January 1, 1988
Assembly Bill 93 (O'Connell)	- Chapter 917 - Statutes of 1987 January 1, 1988
Assembly Bill 1155 (Johnston)	- Chapter 393 - Statutes of 1987 September 2, 1987
Assembly Bill 2386 (Allen)	- Chapter 1484 - Statutes of 1987 January 1, 1988
Assembly Bill 2666 (Hannigan)	- Chapter 311 - Statutes of 1987 July 30, 1987

1988

Senate Bill 2059 (Seymour)	- Chapter 1508 - Statutes of 1988 January 1, 1989
Assembly Bill 2658 (Speier)	- Chapter 35 - Statutes of 1988 March 17, 1988
Assembly Bill 3513 (N. Waters)	- Chapter 449 - Statutes of 1988 January 1, 1989

1989

(No Bills Amending Part 30 of the Education Code)

1990

Senate Bill 823 (Bergeson)	- Chapter 1135 - Statutes of 1990 January 1, 1991
Senate Bill 1320 (Seymour)	- Chapter 523 - Statutes of 1990 January 1, 1991
Senate Bill 2194 (Morgan)	- Chapter 1596 - Statutes of 1990 January 1, 1991

BILL/AUTHOR	CHAPTER NUMBER/EFFECTIVE DATE
Assembly Bill 812 (Campbell)	- Chapter 118 - Statutes of 1990 January 1, 1991
Assembly Bill 1528 (Farr)	- Chapter 182 - Statutes of 1990 January 1, 1991
Assembly Bill 2586 (Hughes)	- Chapter 959 - Statutes of 1990 January 1, 1991
Assembly Bill 2875 (O'Connell)	- Chapter 1263 - Statutes of 1990 January 1, 1991
Assembly Bill 3040 (Speier)	- Chapter 1501 - Statutes of 1990 January 1, 1991
Assembly Bill 3057 (Polanco)	- Chapter 1623 - Statutes of 1990 January 1, 1991
Assembly Bill 3451 (Hannigan)	- Chapter 184 - Statutes of 1990 June 29, 1990
Assembly Bill 3880 (Farr)	- Chapter 1234 - Statutes of 1990 January 1, 1991

1991

Assembly Bill 675 (O'Connell)	- Chapter 756 - Statutes of 1991 October 9, 1991
Assembly Bill 1060 (Farr)	- Chapter 223 - Statutes of 1991 January 1, 1992
Assembly Bill 1134 (Campbell)	- Chapter 325 - Statutes of 1991 January 1, 1992
Assembly Bill 1487 (Horcher)	- Chapter 1091 - Statutes of 1991 January 1, 1992
Assembly Bill 1845 (Gotch)	- Chapter 109 - Statutes of 1991 July 11, 1991

1992

Senate Bill 807 (McCorquodale)	- Chapter 1361 - Statutes of 1992 January 1, 1993
Assembly Bill 1248 (Alpert)	- Chapter 759 - Statutes of 1992 September 21, 1992

BILL/AUTHOR	CHAPTER NUMBER/EFFECTIVE DATE
Assembly Bill 1446 (Quackenbush)	- Chapter 90 - Statutes of 1992 January 1, 1993
Assembly Bill 2267 (Hannigan)	- Chapter 106 - Statutes of 1992 January 1, 1993
Assembly Bill 2773 (Farr)	- Chapter 1360 - Statutes of 1992 January 1, 1993
Assembly Bill 2925 (Eastin)	- Chapter 1213 - Statutes of 1992 January 1, 1993
Assembly Bill 3783 (Farr)	- Chapter 1061 - Statutes of 1992 January 1, 1993

1993

Senate Bill 896 (McCorquodale)	- Chapter 984 - Statutes of 1993 January 1, 1994
Assembly Bill 369 (O'Connell)	- Chapter 1296 - Statutes of 1993 October 11, 1993
Assembly Bill 599 (Speier)	- Chapter 1295 - Statutes of 1993 January 1, 1994
Assembly Bill 1242 (V. Brown)	- Chapter 688 - Statutes of 1993 January 1, 1994
Assembly Bill 1891 (Polanco)	- Chapter 51 - Statutes of 1993 June 30, 1993
Assembly Bill 2211 (Goldsmith)	- Chapter 589 - Statutes of 1993 January 1, 1994
Assembly Bill 2355 (Eastin)	- Chapter 939 - Statutes of 1993 October 8, 1993

1994

Senate Bill 732 (Bergeson)	- Chapter 936 - Statutes of 1994 September 28, 1994
Senate Bill 1347 (Russell)	- Chapter 333 - Statutes of 1994 January 1, 1995
Assembly Bill 1250 (Campbell)	- Chapter 921 - Statutes of 1994 January 1, 1995
Assembly Bill 1836 (Eastin)	- Chapter 1126 - Statutes of 1994 September 30, 1994

BILL/AUTHOR	CHAPTER NUMBER/EFFECTIVE DATE
Assembly Bill 2445 (Conroy)	- Chapter 998 - Statutes of 1994 January 1, 1995
Assembly Bill 2587 (Eastin)	- Chapter 922 - Statutes of 1994 January 1, 1995
Assembly Bill 2798 (Bronshvag)	- Chapter 513 - Statutes of 1994 January 1, 1995
Assembly Bill 2971 (O'Connell)	- Chapter 1172 - Statutes of 1994 January 1, 1995
Assembly Bill 3235 (Solis)	- Chapter 1288 - Statutes of 1994 January 1, 1995
Assembly Bill 3562 (Eastin)	- Chapter 840 - Statutes of 1994 January 1, 1995
Assembly Bill 3601 (Committee on Judiciary)	- Chapter 146 - Statutes of 1994 January 1, 1995
Assembly Bill 3793 (Eastin)	- Chapter 661 - Statutes of 1994 January 1, 1995

C

E

F

G

H

K-19

N

P

Q

R

U

V

X Y Z

Publications Available from the Department of Education

This publication is one of over 600 that are available from the California Department of Education. Some of the more recent publications or those most widely used are the following:

Item No.	Title (Date of publication)	Price
1151	Adoption Recommendations of the Curriculum Development and Supplemental Materials Commission, 1994: Follow-up Adoption, Science (1994)	$5.50
0883	The Ages of Infancy: Caring for Young, Mobile, and Older Infants (videocassette and guide) (1990)	65.00 *
1163	The Arts: Partnerships As a Catalyst for Educational Reform (1994)	10/10.00 †
1079	Beyond Retention: A Study of Retention Rates, Practices, and Successful Alternatives in California (1993)	4.25
1067	California Private School Directory, 1993-94 (1993)	16.00
1086	California Public Education: A Decade After *A Nation at Risk* (1993)	4.75
1091	California Public School Directory (1994)	16.00
1036	California Strategic Plan for Parental Involvement in Education (1992)	5.75
0488	Caught in the Middle: Educational Reform for Young Adolescents in California Public Schools (1987)	6.75
0874	The Changing History–Social Science Curriculum: A Booklet for Parents (1990)	12/5.00 ‡
1053	The Changing History–Social Science Curriculum: A Booklet for Parents (Spanish) (1993)	12/5.00 ‡
0867	The Changing Language Arts Curriculum: A Booklet for Parents (1990)	12/5.00 ‡
1145	The Changing Language Arts Curriculum: A Booklet for Parents (Chinese) (1994)	12/5.00 ‡
1115	The Changing Language Arts Curriculum: A Booklet for Parents (Korean) (1993)	12/5.00 ‡
0928	The Changing Language Arts Curriculum: A Booklet for Parents (Spanish) (1991)	12/5.00 ‡
0777	The Changing Mathematics Curriculum: A Booklet for Parents (1989)	12/5.00 ‡
0891	The Changing Mathematics Curriculum: A Booklet for Parents (Spanish) (1991)	12/5.00 ‡
1142	The Changing Mathematics Curriculum: A Booklet for Parents (Korean) (1994)	12/5.00 ‡
1072	Commodity Administrative Manual (1993)	13.00
0978	Course Models for the History–Social Science Framework, Grade Five—United States History and Geography: Making a New Nation (1991)	8.50
1034	Course Models for the History–Social Science Framework, Grade Six—World History and Geography: Ancient Civilizations (1993)	9.50
1132	Course Models for the History–Social Science Framework, Grade Seven—World History and Geography: Medieval and Early Modern Times (1994)	12.75
1093	Differentiating the Core Curriculum and Instruction to Provide Advanced Learning Opportunities (1994)	6.50
1045	Discoveries of Infancy: Cognitive Development and Learning (videocassette and guide) (1992)	65.00 *
1098	English as a Second Language: Implementing Effective Adult Education Programs (1993)	6.00
1046	English-as-a-Second-Language Model Standards for Adult Education Programs (1992)	7.00
0041	English–Language Arts Framework for California Public Schools (1987)	5.00
0927	English–Language Arts Model Curriculum Standards: Grades Nine Through Twelve (1991)	6.00
1056	Essential Connections: Ten Keys to Culturally Sensitive Care (videocassette and guide) (1993)	65.00 *
1124	Exemplary Program Standards for Child Development Programs Serving Preschool and School-Age Children (Spanish) (1994)	5.50
0751	First Moves: Welcoming a Child to a New Caregiving Setting (videocassette and guide) (1988)	65.00 *
0839	Flexible, Fearful, or Feisty: The Different Temperaments of Infants and Toddlers (videocassette and guide) (1990)	65.00 *
0804	Foreign Language Framework for California Public Schools (1989)	6.50
1116	The Framework in Focus: Answers to Key Questions About the English–Language Arts Framework (1993)	5.50
0809	Getting in Tune: Creating Nurturing Relationships with Infants and Toddlers (videocassette and guide) (1990)	65.00 *
1089	Greatest Hits in Environmental Education (1993)	7.00
1083	Handbook for Teaching Vietnamese-Speaking Students (1994)	5.50 §
1064	Health Framework for California Public Schools, Kindergarten Through Grade Twelve (1994)	8.50
0737	Here They Come: Ready or Not—Report of the School Readiness Task Force (summary report) (1988)	3.50
0712	History–Social Science Framework for California Public Schools (1988)	7.75
1154	Home Economics Education Career Path Guide and Model Curriculum Standards (1994)	17.00
1140	I Can Learn: A Handbook for Parents, Teachers, and Students (1994)	8.00
1114	Implementation of Middle Grade Reforms in California Public Schools (1993)	6.50
1071	Independent Study Operations Manual (1993)	30.00
0878	Infant/Toddler Caregiving: A Guide to Creating Partnerships with Parents (1990)	10.00
0880	Infant/Toddler Caregiving: A Guide to Language Development and Communication (1990)	10.00
0877	Infant/Toddler Caregiving: A Guide to Routines (1990)	10.00

*Videocassette also available in Chinese (Cantonese) and Spanish at the same price.

†Ten copies is the minimum number that can be ordered. For over 10 copies, the price is 70 cents per copy for quantities up to 99 copies; the price is 50 cents per copy for quantities over 100 copies.

‡Twelve copies is the minimum number that can be ordered. For over 12 copies, the price is 40 cents per copy for quantities up to 99 copies; the price is 30 cents per copy for quantities over 100 copies.

§Also available at the same price for students who speak Cantonese, Japanese, Korean, Pilipino, and Portuguese.

Item No.	Title (Date of publication)	Price
0879	Infant/Toddler Caregiving: A Guide to Setting Up Environments (1990)	$10.00
0876	Infant/Toddler Caregiving: A Guide to Social–Emotional Growth and Socialization (1990)	10.00
1128	Instructional Materials Approved for Legal Compliance (1994)	14.00
1024	It's Elementary! Elementary Grades Task Force Report (1992)	6.50
1147	It's Elementary! (Abridged Version) (1994)	3.50 *
0869	It's Not Just Routine: Feeding, Diapering, and Napping Infants and Toddlers (videocassette and guide) (1990)	65.00 †
1104	Just Kids: A Practical Guide for Working with Children Prenatally Substance-Exposed	8.25
1107	Literature for History–Social Science, Kindergarten Through Grade Eight (1993)	8.00
1066	Literature for Science and Mathematics (1993)	9.50
1033	Mathematics Framework for California Public Schools, 1992 Edition (1992)	6.75
1113	On Alert! Gang Prevention: School In-service Guidelines (1994)	6.50
1137	Organizing a Successful Parent Center: A Guide and Resource (1994)	4.75
1065	Physical Education Framework for California Public Schools, Kindergarten Through Grade Twelve (1994)	6.75
0845	Physical Education Model Curriculum Standards, Grades Nine Through Twelve (1991)	5.50
1119	Prelude to Performance Assessment in the Arts (1994)	8.00
1032	Program Guidelines for Individuals Who Are Severely Orthopedically Impaired (1992)	8.00
1094	Program Quality Review Training Materials for Elementary and Middle Level Schools (1994)	7.50
1048	Read to Me: Recommended Readings for Children Ages Two Through Seven (1992)	5.50
0831	Recommended Literature, Grades Nine Through Twelve (1990)	5.50
0895	Recommended Readings in Spanish Literature: Kindergarten Through Grade Eight (1991)	4.25
0753	Respectfully Yours: Magda Gerber's Approach to Professional Infant/Toddler Care (videocassette and guide) (1988)	65.00 †
1118	Roads to the Future: Final Report (1994)	10.00
1117	Roads to the Future: Summary Report (1994)	8.00
1127	Sampler of History–Social Science Assessment—Elementary, A (Preliminary edition) (1994)	8.25
1125	Sampler of Science Assessment—Elementary, A (Preliminary edition) (1994)	9.00
1088	School District Organization Handbook (1993)	16.00
1042	School Nutrition Facility Planning Guide (1992)	8.00
1038	Science Facilities Design in California Public Schools (1992)	6.25
0870	Science Framework for California Public Schools (1990)	8.00
1087	Secondary Textbook Review: Mathematical Analysis, Grades 9–12 (1993)	11.50
1040	Second to None: A Vision of the New California High School (1992)	5.75
0970	Self-assessment Guide for School District Fiscal Policy Teams: Facilities Planning and Construction (1991)	4.50
0980	Simplified Buying Guide: Child and Adult Care Food Program (1992)	8.50
0752	Space to Grow: Creating a Child Care Environment for Infants and Toddlers (videocassette and guide) (1988)	65.00 †
1043	Success for Beginning Teachers: The California New Teacher Project, 1988–1992 (1992)	5.50
1134	Teachers' Catalog of Grants, Fellowships, and Awards (1994)	5.50
1044	Together in Care: Meeting the Intimacy Needs of Infants and Toddlers in Groups (videocassette and guide) (1992)	65.00 †
0846	Toward a State of Esteem: The Final Report of the California Task Force to Promote Self-esteem and Personal and Social Responsibility (1990)	5.00
0758	Visions for Infant/Toddler Care: Guidelines for Professional Caregiving (1989)	6.50
0805	Visual and Performing Arts Framework for California Public Schools (1989)	7.25
1016	With History–Social Science for All: Access for Every Student (1992)	5.50
0989	Work Permit Handbook (1991)	7.75
1073	Writing Assessment Handbook: High School (1993)	9.25

*Single price applies to quantities up to eight copies. For 9 to 99 copies, the price is $3.00 each; for 100 to 249 copies, $2.00; for 250–499 copies, $1.50; for 500 or more copies, $1.00.

†Videocassette also available in Chinese (Cantonese) and Spanish at the same price.

Orders should be directed to:

California Department of Education
Bureau of Publications, Sales Unit
P.O. Box 271
Sacramento, CA 95812-0271

Please include the item number for each title ordered.

Mail orders must be accompanied by a check, a purchase order, or a credit card number, including expiration date (VISA or MasterCard only). Purchase orders without checks are accepted from governmental agencies only. Telephone orders will be accepted toll-free (1-800-995-4099) for credit card purchases only. Sales tax should be added to all orders from California purchasers. Stated prices, which include shipping charges to anywhere in the United States, are subject to change.

Publications Catalog: Educational Resources and its supplement contain illustrated, annotated listings of departmental publications. Free copies may be obtained by writing to the address given above or by calling (916) 445-1260.

94 75827

94-46 003-0093-94 300 1-95 20M